Toxic truths

Manchester University Press

Toxic truths

Environmental justice and citizen science in a post-truth age

EDITED BY THOM DAVIES AND ALICE MAH

Manchester University Press

Published by Manchester University Press
Altrincham Street, Manchester M1 7JA

www.manchesteruniversitypress.co.uk

British Library Cataloguing-in-Publication Data
A catalogue record for this book is available from the British Library

ISBN   978 1 5261 3702 9   hardback
ISBN   978 1 5261 3700 5   open access

First published 2020

The publisher has no responsibility for the persistence or accuracy of URLs for any external or third-party internet websites referred to in this book, and does not guarantee that any content on such websites is, or will remain, accurate or appropriate.

Typeset by
Servis Filmsetting Ltd, Stockport, Cheshire

Contents

Figures

Tables

Contributors

Barbara Allen is Professor of Science, Technology, and Society at Virginia Tech University, Washington DC Campus.

Jessica Blickley is a Biology Instructor in the Natural Sciences Division at Pasadena City College, California.

KD Brown is a PhD candidate in the Department of Geography at the University of North Carolina at Chapel Hill.

Phil Brown is University Distinguished Professor of Sociology and Health Sciences and Director of the Social Science Environmental Health Research Institute (SSEHRI) at Northeastern University, Massachusetts.

Marissa Chan is the Environmental Research and Policy Coordinator at Black Women for Wellness in Los Angeles, California.

Ashley Collier-Oxandale is Postdoctoral Researcher in Environmental Engineering at the University of Colorado, Boulder.

Larry Cooper is Administrative Director of the Rural Empowerment Association for Community Help (REACH) in Duplin County, North Carolina.

Alissa Cordner is Assistant Professor of Sociology at Whitman College, Washington.

Thom Davies is Assistant Professor in the School of Geography at the University of Nottingham, UK.

Marina Da Silva is a PhD student in Visual Sociology at Goldsmiths, University of London.

João Porto de Albuquerque is Professor and Director of the Institute of Global Sustainable Development at the University of Warwick, UK.

André Albino de Almeida is Assistant Professor at the Technical College of Limeira, State University of Campinas (Unicamp), Brazil.

Vanessa De La Rosa is Postdoctoral Researcher in the Social Science Environmental Health Research Institute (SSEHRI) at Northeastern University, Massachusetts.

Amelia Fiske is Senior Research Fellow in the Institute for History and Ethics of Medicine at the Technical University of Munich, Germany.

Devon Hall is the co-founder and program manager of the Rural Empowerment Association for Community Help (REACH) in Duplin County, North Carolina.

Michael Hannigan is Associate Professor in the Department of Mechanical Engineering, University of Colorado, Boulder.

Elizabeth Hoover is Manning Assistant Professor of American Studies at Brown University.

Ivano Iavarone is a Researcher in the Department of Environment and Health at the Italian National Institute of Health.

Anneleen Kenis is Postdoctoral Fellow of the Research Foundation – Flanders (FWO), affiliated with KU Leuven, Belgium, and Lecturer at King's College London, UK.

Peter C. Little is Assistant Professor of Anthropology at Rhode Island College.

Miguel A. López-Navarro is Associate Professor in the Business Administration and Marketing Department at Jaume I University, Spain.

Alice Mah is Professor of Sociology at the University of Warwick, UK.

Naeema Muhammad is Organizing Co-Director of the North Carolina Environmental Justice Network.

Sandy Navarro is a Community Organizer and Promotora de Salud for LA Grit Media in Los Angeles, California.

Roberto Pasetto is a Researcher in the Department of Environment and Health at the Italian National Institute of Health.

Sarah Rhodes is a Research Affiliate at the Gillings School of Global Public Health, University of North Carolina at Chapel Hill.

Jody A. Roberts is director of the Institute for Research at the Science History Institute and managing director of the West Coast Office, Berkeley.

James L. Sadd is Professor of Environmental Science at Occidental College in Los Angeles, California.

Bhavna Shamasunder is Associate Professor at the Urban and Environmental Policy Department at Occidental College in Los Angeles.

Nicholas Shapiro is Assistant Professor of Biology and Society at the University of California, Los Angeles.

Xinhong Wang is Honorary Research Fellow at the Department of Sociology at the University of Warwick, UK.

Yuanni Wang is a PhD student at the Department of Sociology at Hohai University in Nanjing China.

Nicole J. Wong is Director of Policy and Organizing at the Redeemer Community Partnership in Los Angeles, California.

Nasser Zakariya is Associate Professor in the Department of Rhetoric at University of California, Berkeley.

Acknowledgments

This book would not have been possible without the help of numerous people. We would like to thank, first, the contributors to this volume for their timely and important work. Together they demonstrate why environmental justice must remain an interdisciplinary field that draws strength from its many branches. On a personal note, we are indebted to the local residents from various toxic landscapes who have, over the years, shared their experience of living with pollution and shaped our understanding of environmental injustice. This book builds on the academic work of a great many scholars, but we would like to acknowledge the countless communities around the world who are currently fighting for environmental justice.

The idea for this book germinated in the debris of the Brexit referendum in the United Kingdom and the election of Donald Trump as President of the United States in 2016. It took form in 2017 after a Toxic Expertise workshop at the University of Warwick, titled "Pollution, Environmental Justice, and Citizen Science," and was further strengthened through a related workshop in 2018, titled "(In)visibility and Pollution: Making 'Sense' of Toxic Hazards and Environmental Justice."

We would like to thank the Toxic Expertise team for their dedication to the project and their assistance in organizing the annual workshops, including India Holme, Thomas Verbeek, Xinhong Wang, Calvin Jephcote, Loretta Lou, David Brown, and Chris Waite. Extended thanks are due to the international advisors on this project: Scott Frickel, Jennifer Gabrys, Gordon Walker, Anna Lora-Wainwright, Gwen Ottinger, Shaun Breslin, and Robert Bullard, and the support of colleagues including Hannah Jones and Goldie Osuri. We would also like to thank everyone at Manchester University Press for their support and enthusiasm for this project.

This work was supported by the European Research Council (ERC) under the European Union's Horizon 2020 research and innovation program (grant agreement no. 639583), which funded the Toxic Expertise workshops that brought the contributors together and paid to make this book Open Access. For those reading the analogue version of *Toxic Truths*, we hope you agree with us that there is nothing quite comparable to holding a real book.

Abbreviations

AFF	aqueous firefighting foam
ARARs	applicable or relevant and appropriate requirements
ATFE	Akwesasne Task Force on the Environment
ATSDR	Agency for Toxic Substances and Disease Registry
BPA	bisphenol
BTEX	benzene, toluene, ethylbenzene, and xylene
CAFOs	concentrated animal feeding operations
CARB	California Air Resources Board
CBO	community-based organizations
CBPEH	community-based participatory environmental health
CBPR	community-based participatory research
CCT	Concerned Citizens of Tillery
CDC	Centers for Disease Control and Prevention
CDPR	community-driven participatory research
CERCLA	Comprehensive Environmental Response, Compensation, and Liability Act
CHEIHO	"Community Health Effects of Industrial Hog Operations"
DoD	Department of Defense (USA)
EC	European Commission
EDCs	endocrine disrupting compounds
EEA	European Environmental Agency
EJ	environmental justice
EPA	Environmental Protection Agency (USA)
EPSEAL	Étude participative en santé environnement ancrée localement sur le front industriel de Fos-sur-Mer et Port-Saint-Louis-du-Rhône
EU	European Union
FACE	For a Clean Environment
FEMA	Federal Emergency Management Agency
FERP	First Environment Research Project
Fos	Fos-sur-Mer

GM   General Motors
HAPs   hazardous air pollutants
ICS   industrially contaminated site
IHOs   industrial hog operations
LBB   Louisiana Bucket Brigade
LGBTQIA2S+   lesbian, gay, bisexual, transgender, queer and/or questioning, intersex, asexual, two-spirit, etc.
MASH   Mohawks Agree on Safe Health
MCA   Mohawk Council of Akwesasne
NCDEQ   North Carolina Department of Environmental Quality
NCEJN   North Carolina Environmental Justice Network
NGO   nongovernmental organization
NHANES   National Health and Nutrition Examination Survey (NC: North Carolina)
NSF   National Science Foundation
NYSDEC   New York State Department of Environmental Conservation
NYSDOH   New York State Department of Health
PBDEs   polybrominated diphenyl ethers
PCBs   polychlorinated biphenyls
PFAS   per- and polyfluorinated compounds
PFOA   perfluorooctanoic acid
PFOS   perfluorooctane sulfonate
PM   particulate matter
PM10   particulate matter $\leq$ 10 μm in aerodynamic diameter
ppb   parts per billion
ppm   parts per million
ppt   parts per trillion
PSL   Port-Saint-Louis-du-Rhône
REACH   Rural Empowerment Association for Community Help
SBRP   Superfund Basic Research Program
SRMT   St Regis Mohawk Tribe
SSEHRI   Social Science Environmental Health Research Institute
STAND-LA   Stand Together Against Neighborhood Drilling) [in LA]
STEEP   Sources, Transport, Exposure and Effects of PFASs
STS   science and technology studies
TCDD   2,3,7,8-tetrachlorodibenzo-p-dioxin
TCE   trichloroethylene
UCMR   Unregulated Contaminant Monitoring Rule
UNC   University of North Carolina at Chapel Hill
WHO   World Health Organization

Introduction: Tackling environmental injustice in a post-truth age

Thom Davies and Alice Mah

It is difficult to make sense of a historical moment when you are caught in the middle of it – and difficult to tell if it even *is* a moment, or just a small part of something far bigger. Over the past few years we have witnessed rising authoritarianism, extreme weather events attributed to climate change, the fallout from political populism, and – as this book goes to print – a global pandemic. In 2016, the Oxford English Dictionary made *post-truth* its word of the year, defining it as: "denoting circumstances in which objective facts are less influential in shaping public opinion than appeals to emotion and personal belief." Two years later, the OED's word of the year was *toxic*, chosen because of the "the sheer scope of its application … in an array of contexts, both in its literal and more metaphorical senses." For all of these worrying trends, it is tempting to make proclamations about imminent global catastrophe and the novelty of our toxic, post-truth times. However, the Brave New World has been heralded for decades.

In the 1980s, the Bhopal and Chernobyl incidents sent shock waves around the world, highlighting the catastrophic consequences of industrial disaster. These followed in the wake of Rachel Carson's book *Silent Spring* (1962), a powerful indictment of the use of chemical pesticides, and coincided with the growing US anti-toxics movement. The anthropologist Kim Fortun (2012, 446–449) describes the 1984 Bhopal gas tragedy as the beginning of an era of "late industrialism" characterized by pervasive and normalized disasters: a "world noisy with media"; a "world of even more experts"; and a world where "people can't think … paralyzed by issue complexity."

And yet we *must* think. This book comes at a critical juncture for questioning claims about the environment and the nature of science and expertise. A new political climate of "alternative facts" and "fake news" has threatened to reduce science and expertise to an unaccustomed diminution. As Lockie (2017, 1) puts it: "post-truth politics could hardly stand in more direct opposition to the values most of us bring to scholarship, research, and advocacy." The election of Donald Trump in the USA and the Brexit referendum in the UK in 2016 ushered in a new era of post-truth. However, post-truth politics is hardly the preserve of the global North. Populist leaders such as Narendra Modi in India, Vladimir Putin in Russia, Recep Tayyip Erdoğan in Turkey, and Jair Bolsonaro in Brazil have all offered their own versions of post-truth. Such populism has introduced a new wave of climate change denial, and alongside this political tumult, environmental vulnerabilities are deepening at both global and local levels. As we write this book, Trump is defunding environmental protection and has pulled the USA from the Paris climate agreement; Brexit is threatening to derail environmental regulation in the UK; and Bolsonaro is opening up vast tracts of Amazonian rainforest – the world's largest carbon sink – to permanent exploitation. What does this mean for the role of science in environmental controversies?

Environmental justice is about making claims about the environment (Bullard 1990; Walker 2012; Schlosberg 2013). Around the world today, ethnic minority and low-income communities continue to be disproportionately burdened by toxic pollution (Bullard and Wright 2009; Pellow 2018). Environmental injustice appears wherever social inequality and pollution collide. For decades, environmental justice activists have campaigned against the misuses of science, while at the same time engaging in community-led citizen science. Polluted communities have faced uphill environmental justice battles against powerful corporations and state regulators to prove their cases of toxic exposure (Bullard 1990; Taylor 2014; Pellow 2018). Some communities have engaged in "popular epidemiology" (Brown 1993) by doing their own health surveys, monitoring, and research, in the absence of official information. Others have forged important "citizen–expert alliances" (Allen 2003) in their campaigns, drawing not only on work from professional scientists, but also on the skills of lawyers, economists, artists, and journalists.

In an age of post-truth politics, where science and expertise are increasingly under attack, what is the role for grassroots citizen science in environmental justice campaigns? Amid populist politicians and denigrated experts, environmental justice activists face new challenges. Yet the availability of new digital technologies, "big data," and the Internet has meant greater community involvement in pollution monitoring. Neighborhood mobilization has become an increasingly widespread phenomenon and a powerful means of making claims about environmental threats. The specter of post-truth has not only created a new set of environmental concerns (such as the shift toward even greater climate change denial in the USA), but has also undermined the very notion of what it means to be an expert. Rarely have science and expertise been so questioned, diminished, and vulnerable as they are today. These changes have surfaced at a time when more people than ever are able to produce and circulate their own forms of knowledge across various media platforms. Knowledge claims about the environment – wherever they come from – face "post-factual" ways of being dismissed (Lockie 2017). This book, which grapples with questions about the production of knowledge, and the place of science within society, is thus well timed to respond to these debates.

Toxic Truths examines the role of science, politics, and values in the global struggle against environmental injustice, from e-waste extraction in urban Ghana to "strongly participatory" citizen science in southern France; from toxic tours in Ecuador to "soft confrontation" in China. By using the phrase "toxic truths" we highlight the heterogeneity of perspectives about pollution, which are rarely fixed, certain, or uncontested. Yet we also acknowledge that not all understandings of pollution are rendered equal: some toxic truths are given elevated status, while other perceptions of pollution are sidelined. It is not just multiple truths about toxic pollution and the environment that exist, but also political ecologies in which the silencing of certain truths may have toxic consequences. Which truths count and which are ignored is a central question within environmental justice and citizen science in a post-truth age.

The contributions in this book argue for the importance of science, knowledge, and data that are produced *by* and *for* ordinary people living with environmental risks and hazards. Yet we are also attuned to the fact that data alone will never be enough to halt environmental injustice, especially as toxic pollution is so embedded within global and local structures of inequality (Boudia and Jas 2014). We highlight inspiring case studies of community-based participatory environmental health and justice research; different ways of sensing, witnessing, and interpreting environmental injustice; political strategies for seeking environmental justice; and ways of expanding the concepts and forms of engagement of citizen science around the world. We emphasize the enduring legacies of environmental justice activism and participatory citizen science, while also drawing attention to emerging struggles and strategies. Together, these interdisciplinary contributions ask critical questions about how to overcome widening environmental inequality around the world, pushing the analytical boundaries of existing concepts and practices within the environmental justice movement. By examining the enduring salience of expertise in everyday life, the contributors to this book underscore the importance of environmental justice and public engagements with science in a post-truth era.

Environmental justice: an incomplete history

Environmental justice is an affirmation of an unequal present and a yearning for a better future. In this sense, the movement and discipline are both utopian and dystopian. The terms *environmental justice* and *environmental injustice* are difficult to define, being variously descriptive, normative, hopeful, pessimistic, political, and mobilizing (Holifield et al. 2018). To paraphrase David Schlosberg (1999), there is no such *thing* as environmental justice: much like the term "environmentalism," any attempt to pin down the concept in a definitive manner necessarily excludes an array of other definitions. Arguably, the breadth and flexibility of the term explains its enduring appeal. At its core, environmental justice is based on the principle that all people have the right to be protected from environmental threats and to benefit from living in a clean and healthy environment.

Early environmental activism and research focused on the disproportionate burden of environmental hazards near to ethnic minority and low-income communities, linked to the concept of environmental racism in the United States (see Bullard 1983, 1990; Bullard and Wright 2009; Agyeman et al. 2016). The report *Toxic Wastes and Race in the United States* (1987), by the United Church of Christ Commission for Racial Justice, gained wide public attention as the first study to document national patterns of racial discrimination in the siting of hazardous waste facilities. In 1991, leading environmental activists of color gathered at the first People of Color Environmental Leadership Summit in Washington, DC and adopted 17 principles of environmental justice, which continue to inspire generations of environmental justice activists (see Pellow 2007). Since the early 1990s, the language and frame of environmental justice has expanded, spreading *horizontally* to a broader range of issues and places, *vertically* to the global scale of environmental injustices, *conceptually* to include the human relationship to the nonhuman world, and *temporally* to consider future generations and longer time scales (Almond 1995; Meyer and Roser 2010; Nixon 2011; Schlosberg 2013; Martinez-Alier et al. 2016; Davies 2019). Such is the reach of the concept that environmental justice activism and scholarship "has now expanded to encompass almost everything that is unsustainable about the world" (Holifield et al. 2018, 2).

In historical terms, the environmental justice movement is a relatively recent phenomenon – a "millennial" movement – born in the 1980s out of the civil rights, anti-toxics, and community health movements in the USA. Although the academic discipline of environmental justice is reasonably new, environmental violence and inequality are certainly not recent occurrences. Contemporary hazards such as microplastic contamination, nuclear radiation, and e-waste seem to embody our late-modern age, but the existence of waste and pollution pre-exist the dawning of the so-called Anthropocene (Alexis-Martin and Davies 2017). Despite claims that we have entered a "new age of toxicity" (Walker 2011: xi), our relationship with environmental pollution is built on centuries of unequal social relations. As Pellow (2018, 9) argues, there is a "long environmental justice movement" which predates the first well-documented grassroots toxic struggles in the USA, such as the Warren County protests in 1982, or the Love Canal disaster in 1978. The *longue durée* of the environmental justice movement can be traced back to other moments and struggles, including indigenous involvement in the Earth Day protests of 1970, or the Memphis Sanitation workers strike in 1968 (Zimring 2015). Casting our net wider still, this extended view of environmental justice presents the movement as not just a product of the 1980s or "a child of the sixties" (Guha 2014, 1), but the culmination of environmental history that stretches back much further in time and space. Just as environmental pollution can reveal its consequences slowly over time (Nixon 2011), a corollary can be found with the environmental justice movement, which emerged gradually and is still unfolding today.

Writing in the late nineteenth century, sociologist W. E. B. Du Bois published what could be considered an environmental justice study of Philadelphia (Du Bois 1899), and scholars have found documents that evoke environmental justice themes from hundreds of years prior. For instance, writings in the wake of a yellow fever epidemic in 1793 are possibly "one of the earliest environmental justice documents" (Taylor 2011, 280), and over a century before this, toxic factories were being relocated near black communities in what is now Manhattan. In England, the first extensive environmental inequalities triggered by the Industrial Revolution and the squalor of rapid urbanization were met by protest in 1831, with "cholera riots" throughout many towns and cities (Porter 2005), as well as artistic invocations of the environment through the wistful words of William Wordsworth (1770–1850) and the bucolic romanticism of William Morris (24 (1834–1896), among many others. Beyond Europe, others have argued that environmental injustice and subaltern environmentalism are as old as colonization itself, with environmental inequality being a cornerstone of settler/colonial governance since at least the seventeenth century (Whyte 2016; Murphy 2017; Pellow 2018; Pulido and De Lara 2018; Sealey-Huggins 2018). Though some have highlighted the emergence of a "green imperialism" since the early 1700s (Grove 1996; Bonyhady 2003), others have argued – more convincingly, we feel – that "a core component of European colonization was the production of many environmental injustices, as people and land were exploited for the benefit of colonizers" (Pellow 2018, 9). Toxic pollution is entrenched within the long injustices of colonialism, racism, and the patriarchy "that require land and bodies as sacrifice zones" (Liboiron et al. 2018).

Not only is the history of environmental justice temporally deep, it is also geographically diverse and still expanding. Any account of environmental justice will therefore remain incomplete, not least because it is still being written. Right now, across the world, thousands of communities are embroiled in the midst of ongoing toxic struggles. Environmental justice also belies its seemingly American past, and today it is increasingly clear that "the concept has travelled to different places" (Holifield et al. 2018, 2). Despite scholarly work on environmental justice remaining skewed toward American case studies (Reed and George 2011), many scholars have demonstrated how issues of environmental justice are truly *global* in nature (Walker 2009a; Armiero and Sedrez 2014; Guha 2014; Pellow 2018). This book adds empirical credence to this, with case studies from twelve countries spread across five continents. Through these chapters we will see how environmental justice is spatially dispersed, reaching far beyond the confines of the USA and the racialized geographies of the Deep South where the phrase "environmental justice" was first coined (Bullard 1990).

As Robert D. Bullard, who is often noted as the father of the discipline, has argued in his pathbreaking book *Dumping in Dixie* (1990), environmental pollution and toxic dumping have always followed "the path of least resistance" (Bullard 1990, 3). Environmental injustice and toxic pollution not only reflect social inequalities, they also sustain them. Some have argued that environmental justice should be viewed as "deeply intersectional" (Malin and Ryder 2018), not only because the experience of pollution rarely fits neatly into isolated silos of social injustice – along traditional lines of race, class, gender – but also because of the changing material complexities of pollution itself, where *multiple* toxicants often overlap, interconnect, and intersect in unpredictable ways. Other aspects of environmental injustice, however, have remained tragically entrenched. More than three decades after the first wave of environmental justice research, the same toxic geographies in the Deep South that inspired this movement are still being exposed to high levels of chemical pollution and the barely concealed violence of environmental racism (Davies 2018, 2019). Power and politics have always been central to the story of environmental justice. Across the world today, many years after Bullard's pioneering work, the ubiquity of pollution is only matched by its unevenness.

What do we mean by justice?

Environmental justice is an empirically grounded or "shoe-leather" discipline, emerging from the real-life problems and harsh realities of grassroots activism. As such, environmental justice scholarship has "always worn its normative heart on its sleeve" (Edwards et al. 2016, 754), less concerned perhaps than other disciplines with finer semantic points, such as the meaning of the term "justice." When scholar-activists have been confronted with the actualities of environmental violence and seen first hand the damage that toxic inequality can cause, it is little surprise that much research has focused on the resistive potential of creating "facts" about pollution, rather than the philosophies of what "justice" might actually look like. In doing so, earlier environmental justice research has "assumed that *injustice* is self-evident and unproblematic" (Walker 2009b, emphasis added).

But what does "justice" actually mean within environmental justice? Increasingly, academics have questioned the meaning of "justice" within the uniquely interdisciplinary practice of environmental justice scholarship (e.g., Ottinger 2017; Pellow 2018; Allen 2018), with some suggesting that the intricacies of actually-existing environmental justice highlight the inherent multivalence, plurality, and diversity of what "justice" can actually mean (Schlosberg 2004). When it comes to the lived experience of environmental injustice, there can in fact be "multiple, even incommensurable, variations of justice" (Lyons 2018, 421). Likewise, other scholars have highlighted the overlap between differing types of injustice, suggesting "different forms of injustice tend to maintain and reinforce each other" (Bell and Carrick 2018, 102). Broadly speaking however – and to give context to the interventions made in this book – we highlight three significant lenses through which justice has been approached within environmental discourse: distributive (geographical); procedural (participatory); and capabilities (well-being). Elements of all three versions of justice can be found throughout the case studies presented in *Toxic Truths*.

The first tranche of environmental justice scholarship, for example, highlighted *distributive* notions of justice: that is to say, they were concerned with the geographic placement of environmental hazards in relation to marginalized communities (Bullard 1990; Cutter 1995). The unbalanced geography of environmental hazards, which shifts with the contours of race and class, provided the initial motivation for environmental justice research, and pioneering studies within this interdisciplinary field found that "blacks and other economically disadvantaged groups are often concentrated in areas that expose them to high levels of toxic pollution" (Bullard 1990, 6). In this book, Roberto Pasetto and

Ivano Iavorone (Chapter 9) follow this distribution orientated form of justice, with a focus on polluted sites in Italy. Through an epidemiological analysis, they highlight how the placement of environmentally hazardous industry disproportionately impacts women, children, and ethnic minorities. Anneleen Kenis also touches on the theme of distributive justice in her chapter on air quality in Antwerp and London (Chapter 13). She highlights how the scale and geographies upon which distribution is measured are a politicized phenomenon: "there is not just one space, not just one environmental justice that can be claimed, but rather a continuous negotiation about where to draw the fault lines." Using geographic distribution as a cornerstone of environmental justice has been criticized, however. As Walker described, "without carefully reasoned accounts of the ways in which socio-environmental inequality mattered and 'injustice' was being produced, the value of revealing difference was severely diminished" (Walker 2009b, 204). The need to expand ideas of justice beyond distribution was emphasized further when environmental justice scholarship moved beyond the highly racialized geographies of the USA.

A further body of environmental justice research places justice as a *procedural* concern. This form of environmental justice was born out of participatory democracy, and places the focus of justice squarely on access to decision making and accurate information upon which to base decisions (Yenneti and Day 2015). The procedural turn within environmental justice also came from the realization that decisions about environmental burdens are often made by the people who are least likely to be directed affected by them, or who may even derive benefit (Bell and Carrick 2018). As Bullard and Johnson (2000, 7) explain, procedural justice is centered around the "meaningful involvement of all people regardless of race, colour, national origin or income with respect to the development, implementation and enforcement of environmental laws, regulations and policies." This move from a distributional to a procedural logic of justice, which involves public hearings and access to reliable information, is predicated on the redistribution of power relations (Pellow 2018).

In this book, Barbara Allen's research in southern France most closely aligns with this form of justice (Chapter 2). Allen's contribution highlights how strongly participatory science can produce more sustainable outcomes, and thus become "an incredible tool for shaping local and even national environments." Likewise, Peter Little's chapter on e-waste pollution in Ghana (Chapter 6) discusses the how grassroots (re)presentations of pollution through participatory photography can help "democratize science." As a criterion for recognizing systematic wrongdoing, procedural justice also relates to the *recognition paradigm* of environmental justice (see Whyte 2018). However, this interpretation of justice has been criticized for relying too heavily on appeals to the state for recompense, when – paradoxically – it is the state that is often the *source* of hegemonic environmental violence. As is so often the case, "the state and its related systems are part of the structure of toxicity that allows the ubiquity and tonnage of toxicants to be produced and circulate in the first place" (Liboiron et al. 2018, 336). In other words, pursuing environmental justice through a procedural lens places too much weight on the hope that the state and the legal system will ultimately – through policy change, advocacy, and the enforcement of regulations – protect those it is currently helping to injure. In this book, Xinhong Wang and Yuanni Wang address this tension through the notion of "soft confrontation" (Chapter 10), highlighting how activists in China have to confront very carefully forms of pollution that are ultimately linked to a repressive government. Yet neutralizing justice to only mean involvement in decision making can also stifle the significance of environmental justice struggles. As Ambriz and Correia (2017, 54) argue, "representation and participation, however important, are never enough."

The third major form of justice that we highlight here takes inspiration from American philosopher Martha Nussbaum (2011) and Indian economist Amartya Sen (2009) and is concentrated on *capabilities*. The capabilities approach to justice is centered around the ability of individuals to live freely and unhindered in the world, and, though linked to the location of environmental hazards, "is a thicker notion of justice than one concerned only with distribution" (Day 2018, 25). In short, a capabilities approach is about ensuring the well-being of a population, where "justice is not about achieving an appropriate distribution of things between people, but rather about people being able to live lives that they consider worthwhile" (Edwards et al. 2016, 755). In this sense, this form of justice relates more closely to the praxis of environmental justice, with its focus on the everyday abilities of people to live happy lives. In this book, elements of the capabilities approach to justice can be found in Elizabeth Hoover's fascinating account of the Akwesasne tribe's search for environmental justice (Chapter 11). Though the capabilities approach to environmental justice is, for some, a "core theoretical edifice within which to understand and theorize (environmental) justice" (Edwards et al. 2016, 758, parenthesis in original) others have criticized it for overly emphasizing *individual* experiences of environmental injustice (Dean 2009). The lack of attention to the wider community, as well as a failure to attend to the larger structural forces that sustain environmental inequality, is sometimes overlooked.

This also allies itself with Pulido's long-standing critique of environmental justice: that it has "focused largely on procedure and has not significantly tackled underlying structural inequality, regional capital investment patterns, or pollution reduction, and as such can only achieve marginal gains" (Pulido 1994).

The wider political scaffolding upon which environmental inequality is built is of key importance. As others before us have argued, environmental justice "epitomizes the tension at the heart of any radical normative project: its radical aspirations constantly come up against the constraints of what is politically possible to mainstream society" (Edwards et al. 2016, 766). The somewhat conciliatory approach of some forms of environmental justice have led other scholars to propose a more radical alternative (Pulido and De Lara 2018). For example, David Pellow proposes "critical environmental justice" (Pellow 2018) as a framework for addressing limitations and tensions within earlier generations of environmental justice research, foregrounding four pillars of critical environmental justice: (1) *intersectional* forms of inequality and oppression; (2) the role of *scale* in the production and possible resolution of environmental injustices; (3) recognition that social inequalities are deeply embedded in *state power*; and (4) *indispensability*, arguing that "excluded, marginalized, and othered populations, beings, and things … must not be viewed as expendable but rather as *indispensable* to our collective futures" (Pellow 2018, 26). Drawing on the three different meanings of justice outlined above, we now turn to the practice of seeking environmennal justice through public and participatory engagements with science.

Environmental justice and citizen science

Environmental justice activists typically adopt dual orientations toward science, of mistrust and reliance: (1) challenging the methods, questions, and uses of science, particularly in the context of vested corporate interests, while (2) relying on science itself, as a necessary tool to make investigations, provide evidence, and make arguments. Many environmental justice scholars have embraced the term "citizen science" as a way of describing community-based participatory science to tackle toxic problems (Ottinger 2017; Martinez-Alier et al. 2016; Gabrys et al. 2016). Other environmental justice researchers use different terms for similar practices, including "civic science" (Fortun and Fortun 2005; Wylie 2018), "popular epidemiology" (Brown 1993), "street science" (Corburn 2005), "community-based participatory research" (Allen; Brown et al.; Rhodes et al.; Shamasunder et al., this volume), and "participatory sensing" (Loreto et al. 2017), among others. Wylie (2018) proposes that "civic science" could help to distinguish between grassroots-led and professional science-led kinds of citizen science, and also to get away from the language of "citizens." We recognize the limitations of citizen science as a concept, but we nonetheless use this term as a shorthand description for a wide range of public engagements with science within environmental justice struggles.

Citizen science has become a popular concept within academic research, activism, and public engagement worldwide (Riesch and Potter 2014). The term "citizen science" was originally coined by the British Science and Technology Studies scholar Alan Irwin in 1995 to highlight the importance of citizen expertise and knowledge for environmental policy, particularly science produced by and for ordinary citizens. Around the same time, American ornithologist and participatory research organizer Rick Bonney (1996) used the term "citizen science" to refer to scientific projects in which the public is involved in data collection for scientific research, for example to report observations of birds, wildlife, and plants. Strasser et al. (2018) trace two distinct historical precedents for the emergence of these different types of citizen science: the radical science movements from the 1960s and 1970s, on the one hand, and amateur naturalists, on the other. Reflecting its origins, citizen science today encompasses different levels of public engagement with science, from data sensing and crowdsourcing (see de Albuquerque and de Almeida, this volume) to deeply participatory research including the design, collection, and analysis of research (see Allen, this volume).

Within the radical science movement tradition, citizen science emerged out of calls for the democratization of science and expertise to include perspectives from wider publics (Irwin 1995). For decades, scholars of science and technology studies (STS) have argued that scientific expertise is highly political and embedded in power relations (Irwin 1995; Epstein 1996; Fischer 2000; Frickel et al. 2010). With its calls for epistemic democratization, some commentators have suggested that STS is implicated in post-truth politics, an allegation that many STS scholars refute (see Collins, Evans, and Weinel 2017; Sismondo 2017). For example, Frickel (2017, 2) highlights an important difference between the early science movement and the US March for Science in 2017: "today's science movement is not contesting what shapes scientific questions, methods and uses as it did in the 1970s. Rather, this mobilization is responding to what many see as a growing threat to science itself." Reflecting on issues of trust in science, Collins et al. (2017: 582) remark that in STS debates, "understanding who can legitimately contribute to expert debate requires social scientists to use their special understanding of the formation of knowledge to reject the misuse of expertise by certain elite experts and give credit to the work of low status, experience-based experts." Similarly, Allen (in this volume) argues that "the kinds of new knowledge that residents of environmentally compromised communities produce, while different from the science they are arguing against, are substantively and categorically opposite from the popular press version of 'alt facts' in our post-truth era."

Drawing upon research projects spread across five continents, *Toxic Truths* interrogates several ways that local communities, residents, and activists engage with science. We foreground many community-based participatory research projects that align with different typologies of citizen science, across a continium of levels of participation (Haklay 2013). Yet, through attending to the power of embodied experience and witnessing pollution and the politics of science, we remain critical about the capacity of citizen science to enact environmental justice. As others have noted (see Chilvers 2008), caution is needed when viewing public participation as a panacea for solving environmental inequalities – not least, due to the ever-increasing professionalization of citizen-led processes, with participation itself "becoming a lucrative industry" (Castree 2016, 411). Consequently, this book seeks to expand concepts and methods of citizen science, unpacking assumptions and questioning conventions. The contributors interrogate the meaning of "justice" within the environmental justice movement (see Chapter 2), and question the role and interpretation of citizenship within citizen science research (see Chapter 11).

The use of citizen science in environmental justice creates a tension between, on the one hand, producing contextual, embodied knowledge rooted in subjective experience that can aid environmental justice advocacy, and, on the other hand, producing knowledge that will be regarded as rigorous, trustworthy, and suitably scientific. These tensions are all the more pertinent in a post-truth age.

Tackling environmental injustice in a post-truth age

Questions over trust in science, facts, and values have always been central to environmental justice struggles. These questions have endured and intensified in recent years. What, if anything, is different for grassroots environmental conflicts in a post-truth context? According to Mair (2017, 4), the invocation of post-truth presents a "new phase in an ongoing struggle – over theories of truth, belief and knowledge, in the context of a radically altered information environment." The post-truth age was heralded by the 2016 election of Donald Trump and the UK vote for Brexit, but the idea of post-truth has a longer history. According to the Oxford English Dictionary, "post-truth" was coined in 1992 in an article about the Persian Gulf War and Reagan in the *Nation* by Serbian-American playwright Steve Tesich (Kreitner 2016). The term gathered pace in subsequent years, reaching fever pitch in 2016.

Post-truth "emphasises the weakness of factual, science-based explanations in the face of strong narratives or a compelling story" (Berling and Bueger 2017). To put it another way, "the post-truth condition enables us to see more clearly the complementarity of politics and science as spheres of thought and action. Each in its own way is involved in a struggle for 'modal power', namely, control over what is possible" (Fuller 2018, 181). In the context of environmental justice struggles, where competing facts and values are brought to the fore, it is possible to see such questions through a post-truth lens.

While the "post-truth" label has stuck, there has been a backlash against the term for being elitist, asymmetrical, and derogatory (Collins, Evans, and Weinel 2017; Jasonoff and Simmet 2017). After all, truth has long been a contested terrain (Shapin 1994). Jasanoff and Simmet (2017, 752) argue that the idea of post-truth is ahistorical and remind us that "debates about public facts have always also been debates about social meanings, rooted in realities that are subjectively experienced as all-encompassing and complete, even when they are partial and contingent." To what extent is the terrain of struggle shifting?

Unlike other social movements, environmental justice has also become an academic field in its own right, where – in an ideal world – scholars, activists, and citizens coalesce around a shared goal. A rare blend of expertise and political mobilization is needed to achieve environmental justice, making the role of experts critically important (Ottinger and Cohen 2011). As Cole and Foster (2001, 20) suggest, the environmental justice movement can be likened to a river nourished by a series of tributaries, each one offering a different utilization of expertise. Yet we should be aware that "producing knowledge of environmental injustices has too often fallen short in helping rectify them" (Holifield et al. 2018, 9).

"Perhaps the notion that truth has been cast aside in the public sphere is itself at fault," Jasanoff and Simmet (2017: 752) argue: "The very idea of a 'post' implies a past where things were radically different, a past whose loss we should universally mourn." The authors make the provocative case to "restore truth to its rightful place in democracy" (2017, 751) and to engage "more energetically with the aims of truth-making" (2017, 766). In *Toxic Truths*, we take up this call. How can we engage critically, rigorously, and energetically with "the aims of truth-making" in the context of environmental justice?

Toxic and environmental health threats "are first and foremost political issues, involving economic and societal choices" (Boudia and Jas 2014: 23). At the same time, scientific knowledge and techniques "play a determining role in rendering the toxic world visible and in making the resulting issues public" (Boudia and Jas 2014, 2). The health risks of toxic pollution are often overlooked due to the problem of "undone science" (Frickel et al. 2010), scientific research that faces political barriers to being done, typically because it poses a threat to established authority. In a post-truth era where science itself is increasingly under threat, the problem of undone science is even greater.

However, reproducing data is not enough to create the political change necessary to prevent the circulation of toxicity. We know from climate change consensus that scientific facts – no matter how convincing – will never be enough on their own. When it comes to seeking environmental justice, however authentic, peer-reviewed, and citizen-led the toxic truths are, if political structures go unchanged, environmental injustice will persist. Shapiro, Zakariya, and Roberts argue in this book (Chapter 14) that "the most open-sourced, inexpensive, accurate, and easy-to-build sensor will not amount to an environmental justice excalibur or a toxin deterring shield." Indeed, the scholarly practice of environmental justice needs grounding in the harsh realities of persistent pollution. Too often, small-scale environmental justice victories and academic successes are positioned as panaceas for far-reaching environmental inequalities.

How can we tackle enduring and systemic environmental injustice? Despite the use of participatory citizen science in environmental justice activism, not all efforts lead to political change. Allen (this volume) addresses this challenge by posing the important question: "What kind of science can serve as 'change-agent' knowledge – what are the ingredients that can facilitate action?" Several of the chapters in *Toxic Truths* address this question. The interdisciplinary contributions negotiate local and global environmental justice challenges, including toxic exposures, air pollution, and chemical contamination, among others, in rich, empirical detail. The authors draw on a range of qualitative and quantitative social science methods, including community-based participatory research (CBPR), epidemiology, ethnography, visual methods, and other innovative methods of participatory environmental justice and citizen science research. This book therefore mirrors the "methodological pluralism" (Holifield et al. 2018, 3) that environmental justice research has been famous for, spanning quantitative and qualitative, ethnographic and activist approaches. These environmental threats are often inflicted on the world's most marginalized groups, with race, class, indigeneity, citizenship, and other social markers all shaping the topographies of environmental injustice (Pellow 2007). *Toxic Truths* offers inspiring cases of tackling environmental injustice, including the public discovery of emerging contaminants of concern; the power of embodied, contextual knowledge in different local communities with heavy toxic burdens for shaping public perceptions, policy, and activism; the use of sensing to monitor pollution in contaminated communities; and the role of political strategies alongside the use of scientific evidence in environmental justice campaigns.

Structure of the book

Toxic Truths is split into four interconnected sections, each one linking to the next. Part I, "Environmental Justice and Participatory Citizen Science," presents four empirically rich case studies of pioneering community-based participatory environmental justice research; Part II, "Sensing and Witnessing Injustice," focuses on the innovative methods and embodied senses that members of the public and academics have adopted to bear witness to, measure, and understand environmental injustice; Part III, "Political Strategies for Seeking Environmental Justice," showcases how pollution can become political, through examples of citizen science projects and environmental inequalities mobilizing and politicizing communities, leading to various acts of resistance; and finally, Part IV, "Expanding Citizen Science," explores the possibilities as well as limitations of citizen science for achieving environmental justice, in conceptual, pedagogical, and political terms.

In the first chapter, Phil Brown, Vanessa De La Rosa, and Alissa Cordner examine the impact of social movements on environmental policy and science, demonstrating how power is embedded firmly within the production of scientific knowledge. They discuss the notion of *toxic trespass* – how industrial chemicals increasingly violate the borders of our bodies and environments. They also show how the continual industrial development of new chemicals has placed citizens at the forefront of science. The authors look in detail at a significant set of hazardous chemicals that are coming to attention – per- and polyfluorinated compounds (PFAS) – and explore the important interconnections between scientific discovery, environmental justice activism, and the political, social, and economic components that reproduce and resist chemical hazards.

Continuing the theme of collaboration between civic organizations and scientific experts, Barbara Allen puts forward the notion of *strongly participatory science,* and details an exemplary community-based project in a polluted industrial zone near Marseille, France. Discussing her long-term collaborative research in the region, she demonstrates how the co-production of environmental knowledge with local communities can create better scientific results, leading to what she calls "knowledge justice." Allen demonstrates how the public can – and should – be involved at each stage of the research, from defining the environmental problem in the first place, to the data collection and analysis stages. The chapter argues that incorporating embodied public knowledge about environmental health, as well as working in deep collaboration with local communities, can strengthen science in areas of contested environmental risk.

Adding empirical weight to the notion of pollution trespassing the boundaries of human bodies and toxic geographies, Bhavna Shamasunder and her co-authors explore the environmental health impacts of neighborhood oil drilling in Los Angeles, California. Three quarters of the oil wells in Los Angeles are within 1,500 feet (457 meters) of homes, schools, hospitals, or playgrounds, and like many cases of environmental injustice, they are also unequally distributed along race and class lines. This toxic problem has created a smorgasbord of health issues, with local inhabitants complaining of nose bleeds, asthma, infertility problems, and other illnesses, all linked to the dense concentration of urban oil installations. The authors used household surveys and low-cost sensor systems for their community-based research. The monitoring equipment was positioned and maintained by community members themselves, making this an interesting example of participatory citizen science research. The authors put the health concerns of local residents at the center of their work but argue that scientific data collection is just one part of a larger strategy to improve community health. In this fascinating example of a community seeking *crude justice*, the authors conclude by arguing that "community-academic collaborations [are] of continued relevance in on-the-ground struggles for environmental justice."

While much environmental justice research has highlighted the distinctly *urban* aspects of toxicity, there are many forms of pastoral pollution that occur far beyond cities, towns, and urban spaces. Sarah Rhodes and KD Brown, along with their scholar-activist collaborators build on the theme of community-driven participatory research and explore the toxic realities of quintessentially rural issues. Moving the geographical focus to the countryside of North Carolina, they explore the environmental racism and pollution of the sprawling hog industry. The region they discuss has the highest density of pig farms in the USA, which has created a number of environmental and health problems. In the wake of Hurricane Florence in 2018, for example, satellite imagery released by NASA showed the scale of this environmental issue, with dark plumes of contaminated floodwater streaming far into the Atlantic Ocean. On the ground, however, the everyday realities of hog farm pollution are daily environmental concerns, with noxious smells, pathogenic microbes, nutrient pollution, and greenhouse gases all impacting the lives of local residents. The authors unpick the politics and environmental racism that is entrenched within the multibillion-dollar hog industry, arguing that "scientific evidence is silenced" in the post-truth era. Written by a coalition of local environmental activists and academics, this chapter draws on a wealth of grounded collaborative research experience. It sets out some key lessons, including the promotion of research equity and the importance of acknowledging the mistreatment of marginalized groups. Echoing Barbara Allen's chapter in this volume, they also advocate for the close involvement of community members throughout all stages of the research process.

All four chapters in Part I share the community-based participatory research tradition of citizen science. These perspectives strongly defend science as a "necessary tool," scientific argument as "obligatory," and participatory citizen science as a robust mode of making change. The next part of the book, "Sensing and Witnessing Injustice," takes a different approach. Here we see how scholars draw on alternative senses and ways of understanding pollution, including the importance of touch and sight. The chapters in Part II discuss how different approaches are needed to make sense of environmental pollution in contested toxic geographies. This section of the book also shifts the geographic focus away from the Global North, to sites less well covered in the annals of environmental justice research, including critical research in sub-Saharan Africa and South America.

The polluted petrochemical landscape of the Ecuadorian jungle is the focus of Amelia Fiske's contribution, which begins Part II of the book with an account of "toxic tours." In rich ethnographic detail, she looks at the role of bodily knowledge in comprehending toxicity. Specifically, she examines the act of observing contaminated soil cores using an auger as a means of sensing – or touching – injustice. She explains that the embodied act of smelling, observing, and handling the polluted sludge "makes the toxic histories of oil extraction tangible." Such toxic encounters with the sticky materiality of oil makes the presence of pollution undeniable, allowing those on the tours to better experience what it is like to live alongside petrochemical facilities. By focusing on one prosaic object – the auger – Friske brings questions of justice to the fore, suggesting that such tactile witnessing becomes part of an "evidentiary assemblage" which includes formal scientific knowledge, but also involves the human senses, memory, and narrative accounts of contested toxic geographies.

Shifting the sensorial focus from *touching* toxic pollution to rendering it *visible*, Peter C. Little draws on long-term ethnographic research in postcolonial Ghana, where he explores the role of participatory photography as a means of documenting environmental injustice in the informal e-waste industry. Focusing on Agbogbloshie – a scrapyard in the capital, Accra – Little explores the extent to which community-based photography augments contemporary environmental justice research. Resting at the intersection of environmental studies and citizen science, the chapter considers how e-waste workers photographically document the toxic risks that they are exposed to in their everyday lives, including circulating images of their own wounded bodies. Though it is profoundly challenging to visually represent structural violence, this form of participatory photography is presented as an alternative way of engaging with local knowledge and embodied experience.

Instead of visualization being used as a tool to explore environmental hazards, Marina Da Silva continues the focus on images by exploring the visual *as* a form of pollution. She discusses "visual pollution" in urban areas, specifically focusing on the Brazilian city of São Paulo. Da Silva examines the contentious "clean city law" (*Lei Cidade Limpa*) which legislates against commercial advertisements and signage as well as unsanctioned street art. In 2007 São Paulo became the first global city to ban adverts in public areas. Though much praised in the media as a radical and progressive move, this legislation took place in a context where other forms of toxicity, such as air pollution, were being sidelined. Like other forms of environmental harm, visual pollution is contested, with disputed thresholds and definitions: the boundary between street art, graffiti, and state-sanctioned advertisements is highly unstable. Drawing on her own visual methodology, Da Silva demonstrates how the contours of visual pollution are subjective, with what "counts" as pollution remaining distinctly political. As is often the case, the legal attempt to control the geographies of pollution also had social consequences. Echoing the "ugly laws" that sprang up in cities across the USA in the early twentieth century (see Schweik 2009), the populist environmental agenda that developed the "clean city law" in Brazil further marginalized the city's homeless population, who were considered antithetical to the city's desired aesthetic. This chapter comes at a critical juncture in Brazil's relationship with the environment: in 2019, Jair Bolsonaro became Brazil's first "post-truth" president, after running on a populist platform of racism, homophobia, and climate change denial. Environmental justice, beyond that of visual pollution, is an increasing concern in Brazil, with vast swathes of Amazonian rainforest at risk and the new regime threatening to open up indigenous land to exploitation and reduce environmental protections.

All three chapters in Part II of the book focus on the role of the senses, not only in exploring what can be defined as pollution, but also in extending the ways in which we can interpret and measure environmental harm. Part III, "Political Strategies for Seeking Environmental Justice," does not take science as its main theme, but instead interrogates the *uses* of science, and the political strategies enmeshed around them. The chapters in this section discuss the terms of orientation to confrontation, from subtle acts of resistance against industrial pollution in China using gradual tactics of "soft confrontation," to utilizing top-down national data in Italy to achieve environmental justice. Miguel López-Navarro starts Part III by investigating one of southern Europe's largest petrochemical complexes, in Tarragona, northeast Spain. He analyzes how a local environmental group justified and articulated a discourse of confrontation with the regional government and heavy industry. This confrontation was based around an environmental air quality study that they promoted, which was carried out by allied scientific experts. Although the dominant academic discourse of business–NGO (nongovernmental organization) relations is one of collaboration, López-Navarro argues that deliberate confrontation can lead to advances in solving environmental issues. Confrontational stances toward toxic industry do not necessarily prevent successful dialogue or participation in multi-stakeholder deliberation, but can in fact have positive environmental outcomes.

Staying with the theme of investigating large-scale industrial areas, Roberto Pasetto and Ivano Iavarone use an epidemiological surveillance approach to understand the health impacts of contaminated sites in Italy. Placing their study within the history of environmental justice from the USA in the 1980s, the authors explore how communities that have become overburdened by the accumulation of pollution are often also socially deprived. While much environmental justice research adopts community-driven ethnographic perspectives, the authors suggest a "top-down environmental approach" can also be effective in revealing the impacts of toxic pollution and use data from a national monitoring system. Though a macro data approach may overlook the local complexities and unique histories of specific locations, large-scale epidemiological approaches can complement the demands of local communities for environmental justice.

While accessing data on toxic pollution is relatively easy in liberal democracies such as Italy or the USA, researching and resisting environmental injustice in more repressive states presents different challenges. Xinhong Wang and Yuanni Wang explore how communities in China confront environmental pollution. Despite a plethora of pollution concerns in the country, the concept of environmental justice has rarely been used explicitly within environmental civil society discourses in China (see Lora-Wainwright 2017; Mah and Wang 2017). This chapter focuses on a voluntary environmental protection organization in Hunan Province and its subtle strategies for seeking environmental justice. The authors examine the careful actions taken by this organization and its efforts to combat environmental pollution, framing these tactics of resistance as a form of *soft confrontation*. As they explain, such soft confrontation allows civil society to negotiate and "push back" against pollution from state-owned industrial facilities, without falling foul of the authorities. Notwithstanding the many obstacles to a fully independent civil society in China, the chapter demonstrates how environmental organizations are successfully able to promote environmental campaigns, often by collaborating closely with government institutions. In a semi-authoritarian context, these local environmental protection organizations must walk the tightrope of depoliticizing their pollution reporting activities while also subtly demanding change. This chapter demonstrates how confronting toxic pollution takes many forms.

The three chapters in Part III of the book deal with the notions of confrontation and collaboration. The chapters in Part IV, "Expanding Citizen Science," also keep politics foregrounded, while focusing critically and reflexively on the role of citizen science in seeking environmental justice, in terms of its uses, its power, and its limitations. Elizabeth Hoover begins the last part of the book by critically interrogating what citizen science means to Indigenous communities that see themselves as citizens of their tribal nation first, and of the settler nation second. By problematizing the notion of citizenship in a settler colonial context, Hoover asks important questions about the role of expertise and science, and considers the cultural, social, and political processes that structure research in Indigenous communities. Drawing on years of grounded community research, the chapter documents the experience of the Mohawk community of Akwesasne, a Native American tribe of about 15,000 people which straddles the international border between Canada and the USA. The search for environmental justice here is complicated by a jurisdictionally challenging situation: Akwesasne land is crisscrossed by three state governments, three tribal governments, and two federal governments. She examines how the tribe set out to determine the extent to which a local contaminated site was impacting community health by cooperating with a research university. Hoover describes how the tribe eventually partnered with the academics on the first large-scale environmental health community-based participatory research project in the area. Using interviews with community fieldworkers, study participants, and scientists, the chapter examines the successes and challenges of this collaborative project. Such collaborative and participatory research can blur the binaries between scientist and citizen, and between subject and researcher.

Building on the theme of critical engagements with citizen science, João Porto de Albuquerque and André Albino de Almeida discuss the concept of citizen science from a *pedagogical* perspective. They highlight how generating data through community involvement in science is just one aspect of its role in environmental justice movements, and different modes of sensing can be used to co-learn about the environment. In conversation with critical theoretical perspectives developed by Brazilian educator and philosopher Paulo Freire (1921–1997), the authors unsettle the asymmetrical relationship that often exists between citizen and expert. For example, one can question how *participatory* citizen science projects really are, where "more often than not, a small group of people (frequently, white and male) are much more actively engaged in shaping the project and making its most critical decisions." Drawing on Freire, the authors argue that experts and citizens should "educate each other," with dialogue enabling greater participation and equity in environmental citizen science projects. This theme resonates with Steve Wing's (2005, 58) call for a "science of environmental justice." Wing argues that different values and asymmetrical relationships between experts and citizens are important to recognize and address for seeking environmental justice: "Although scientists and communities facing environmental injustices share some interests, differences in their values and social privilege present barriers to the development of a progressive science of environmental justice" (Wing 2005, 62).

Reflecting on a different challenge for citizen science, Anneleen Kenis's chapter examines the difficult work of making pollution political, as a matter of concern (Latour 2004). Citizen movements are often forced to adopt different strategies to put environmental risks on the public agenda. In a comparative study of Belgium and the UK, Kenis explores this tension, discussing the translation and politicization of air pollution. In order for an entity like air to become politically salient, citizens have no choice but to engage with science, and Kenis explores the choices and discursive strategies that citizen movements make during this process. The chapter focuses on how different pollutants and spatial interpretations of toxic air can lead to contrasting forms of political action. Something as seemingly natural and invisible as air can be mobilized in different ways, depending on how the facts about air pollution are constructed. Ultimately, translating air into a political issue is a process that not only involves scientists, but also policy makers, citizens, and other actors.

Concluding this volume, Nicholas Shapiro, Nasser Zakariya, and Jody Roberts look "beyond the data treadmill," exploring the limits of deploying civic science tools to achieve environmental justice. Framing their discussion of citizen science around their own attempts to monitor and communicate toxic formaldehyde risk, the authors reflect on the fact that even the best, most accurate, and easy-to-use pollution sensor will not deter toxins or achieve environmental justice. In other words, creating data about pollution alone will not provide the answer. The authors emphasize how projects that engage with science in order to achieve justice – including citizen science projects – cannot fully escape reproducing hierarchies of knowledge and power. The authors warn that "we should be careful not to assume that providing new data will provide new political answers" and highlight the inherent power relations incumbent to science. They argue against a "politics of enumeration" and suggest citizen scientists look beyond the creation of toxic data, numbers, and exposure information to combat pollution. Instead, "extra-numerical evidentiary projects" that are less concerned with questions of quantity and more centered on social and political change may be more successful. The contributors do not *reject* citizen science in a post-truth age, but instead ask "Yes, and?," calling for a more expansive repertoire of interventionalist practices that may help achieve environmental justice.

Overall, the chapters in this book provide rich accounts of environmental justice efforts to engage with science and other forms of expertise to tackle the toxic issues of our times. Although the contributors to *Toxic Truths* write variously from geographical, anthropological, sociological, STS, and activist perspectives, they are united in situating power, politics, and inequality as central to stories of toxic pollution and the attempts to achieve environmental justice.

The chapters capture the current contested realities of pollution in this uncertain age. Together, the contributors lay bare environmental inequalities that are in some sense a continuation of the toxic status quo, but also offer hope for a better, more equitable, and less polluted future.

References

Agyeman, J., Schlosberg, D., Craven, L., and Matthews, C. 2016. Trends and directions in environmental justice: From inequity to everyday life, community, and just sustainabilities. *Annual Review of Environment and Resources*, 41, 321–340.

Alexis-Martin, B. and Davies, T. 2017. Towards nuclear geography: Zones, bodies, and communities. *Geography Compass*, 11(9).

Allen, B. L. 2003. *Uneasy Alchemy: Citizens and Experts in Louisiana's Chemical Corridor Disputes.* Cambridge, MA: MIT Press.

Allen, B. L. 2018. Strongly participatory science and knowledge justice in an environmentally contested region. *Science, Technology, & Human Values*, 43(6), 947–971.

Almond, B. 1995. Rights and justice in the environment debate. In D. E. Cooper and J. A. Palmer (eds), *Just Environments: Intergenerational, International and Interspecies Issues.* London: Routledge, pp. 3–20.

Ambriz, N. and Correia, D. 2017. Conversations in environmental justice: An interview with Julie Sze. *Capitalism Nature Socialism*, 28(2), 54–63.

Armiero, M. and Sedrez, L. (eds) 2014. *A History of Environmentalism: Local Struggles, Global Histories.* London: Bloomsbury.

Bell, D. and Carrick, J. 2018. Procedural environmental justice. In R. Holifield, J. Chakraborty, and G. Walker (eds), *The Routledge Handbook of Environmental Justice.* London: Routledge, pp. 101–112.

Berling, T. and Bueger, C. 2017. Expertise in the age of post-factual politics: An outline of reflexive strategies. *Geoforum*, 84, 332–341.

Bonney, R. 1996. Citizen science: A lab tradition. *Living Bird*, 15, 7–15.

Bonyhady, T. 2003. *The Colonial Earth.* Melbourne: Melbourne University Press.

Boudia, S. and Jas, N. 2014. Introduction: The greatness and misery of science in a toxic world. In S. Boudia and N. Jas (eds), *Powerless Science? Science and Politics in a Toxic World.* New York: Berghahn Books, pp. 1–28.

Brown, P. 1993. When the public knows better: Popular epidemiology challenges the system. *Environment: Science and Policy for Sustainable Development*, 35(8), 16–41.

Bullard, R. 1983. Solid waste sites and the black Houston community. *Sociological Inquiry*, 53, 273–288.

Bullard, R. D. 1990. *Dumping in Dixie: Race, Class, and Environmental Quality.* Boulder, CO: Westview Press.

Bullard, R. D. and Johnson, S. G. 2000. Environmental justice: Grassroots activism and its impact on public policy decision making. *Journal of Social Issues*, 56(3), 555–578.

Bullard, R. D. and Wright, B. 2009. *Race, Place, and Environmental Justice after Hurricane Katrina*. Boulder, CO: Westview Press.

Carson, R. 1962. *Silent Spring*. Boston, MA: Houghton Mifflin Harcourt.

Castree, N. 2016. *A Companion to Environmental Geography*. London: John Wiley.

Chilvers, J. 2008. Environmental risk, uncertainty, and participation: Mapping an emergent epistemic community. *Environment and Planning A*, 40(12), 2990–3008.

Cole, L. W. and Foster, S. R. 2001. *From the Ground Up: Environmental Racism and the Rise of the Environmental Justice Movement*. New York: NYU Press.

Collins, H., Evans, R., and Weinel, M. 2017. STS as science or politics? *Social Studies of Science*, 47(4), 580–586.

Corburn, J. 2005. *Street Science: Community Knowledge and Environmental Health Justice*. Cambridge, MA: MIT Press.

Cutter, S. L. 1995. Race, class and environmental justice. *Progress in Human Geography*, 19(1), 111–122 .

Davies, T. 2018. Toxic space and time: Slow violence, necropolitics, and petrochemical pollution. *Annals of the American Association of Geographers*, 108(5), 1–17.

Davies, T. 2019. Slow violence and toxic geographies: "Out of sight" to whom? *Environment and Planning C: Politics and Space*, 1–19.

Day, R. 2018. A capabilities approach to environmental justice. In R. Holifield, J. Chakraborty, and G. Walker (eds), *The Routledge Handbook of Environmental Justice*. London: Routledge, pp. 124–135.

Dean, H. 2009. Critiquing capabilities: The distractions of a beguiling concept. *Critical Social Policy*, 29(2), 261–278.

Du Bois, W. E. B. 1899. *The Philadelphia Negro: A Social Study*. Philadelphia: Ginn.

Edwards, G. A., Reid, L., and Hunter, C. 2016. Environmental justice, capabilities, and the theorization of well-being. *Progress in Human Geography*, 40(6), 754–769.

Epstein, S. 1996. *Impure Science: AIDS, Activism, and the Politics of Knowledge* (vol. 7). London: University of California Press.

Fischer, F. 2000. *Citizens, Experts, and the Environment: The Politics of Local Knowledge*. London: Duke University Press.

Fortun, K. 2012. Ethnography and late industrialism. *Cultural Anthropology*, 27(3), 446–464.

Fortun, K. and Fortun, M. 2005. Scientific imaginaries and ethical plateaus in contemporary US toxicology. *American Anthropologist*, 107(1), 43–54.

Frickel, S. 2017. Chair's column. *Skatology: Newsletter of the ASA Section on Science, Knowledge and Technology*. Spring edition, pp. 1–3.

Frickel, S., Gibbon, S., Howard, J., Kempner, J., Ottinger, G., and Hess, D. J. 2010. Undone science: Charting social movement and civil society challenges to research agenda setting. *Science, Technology, & Human Values*, 35(4), 444–473.

Fuller, S. 2018. *Post-Truth: Knowledge as a Power Game*. London: Anthem Press.

Gabrys, J., Pritchard, H., and Barratt. 2016. Just good enough data: Figuring data citizenships through air pollution sensing and data stories. *Big Data & Society*. DOI: 10.1177/2053951716679677.

Grove, R. H. 1996. *Green Imperialism: Colonial Expansion, Tropical Island Edens and the Origins of Environmentalism, 1600–1860*. Cambridge: Cambridge University Press.

Guha, R. 2014. *Environmentalism: A Global History*. London: Penguin.

Haklay, M. 2013. Citizen science and volunteered geographic information: Overview and typology of participation. In D. Sui, S. Elwood, and M. Goodchild (eds), *Crowdsourcing Geographic Knowledge*. New York: Springer, pp. 105–122.

Holifield, R., Chakraborty, J., and Walker, G. 2018. *The Routledge Handbook of Environmental Justice*. London: Routledge.

Irwin, A. 1995. *Citizen Science: A Study of People, Expertise and Sustainable Development*. London and New York: Routledge.

Jasanoff, S. and Simmet, H. R. 2017. No funeral bells: Public reason in a "post-truth" age. *Social Studies of Science*, 47(5), 751–770.

Kreitner, R. 2016. Post-truth and its consequences: What a 25-year-old essay tells us about the current moment. *The Nation*, November 30. https://www.thenation.com/article/post-truth-and-its-consequences-what-a-25-year-old-essay-tells-us-about-the-current-moment/ (last accessed January 21, 2020).

Latour, B. 2004. *Politics of Nature*. Cambridge, MA: Harvard University Press.

Lora-Wainwright, A. 2017. *Resigned Activism: Living with Pollution in Rural China*. Cambridge, MA: MIT Press.

Loreto, V., Haklay, M., Hotho, A., Servedio, V. D., Stumme, G., Theunis, J., and Tria, F. (eds) 2017. *Participatory Sensing, Opinions and Collective Awareness*. Cham: Springer.

Liboiron, M., Tironi, M., and Calvillo, N. 2018. Toxic politics: Acting in a permanently polluted world. *Social Studies of Science*, 48(3), 331–349.

Lockie, S. 2017. Post-truth politics and the social sciences. *Environmental Sociology*, 3(1), 1–5.

Lyons, K. 2018. Chemical warfare in Colombia, evidentiary ecologies and senti-actuando practices of justice. *Social Studies of Science*, 48(3), 414–437.

Mah, A. and Wang, X. 2017. Research on environmental justice in China: Limitations and possibilities. *Chinese Journal of Environmental Law*, 1(2), 263–272.

Mair, J. 2017. Post-truth anthropology. *Anthropology Today*, 33(3), 3–4.

Malin, S. A. and Ryder, S. S. 2018. Developing deeply intersectional environmental justice scholarship. *Environmental Sociology*, 4(1), 1–7.

Martinez-Alier, J., Temper, L., Del Bene, D., and Scheidel, A. 2016. Is there a global environmental justice movement? *Journal of Peasant Studies*, 43(3), 731–755.

Meyer, L. H. and Roser, D. 2010. Climate justice and historical emissions. *Critical Review of International Social and Political Philosophy*, 13(1), 229–253.

Murphy, M. 2017. Alterlife and decolonial chemical relations. *Cultural Anthropology*, 32(4), 494–503.

Nixon, R. 2011. *Slow Violence and the Environmentalism of the Poor*. London: Harvard University Press.

Nussbaum, M. C. 2011. *Creating Capabilities: The Human Development Approach*. London: Harvard University Press.

Ottinger, G. 2017. Making sense of citizen science: Stories as a hermeneutic resource. *Energy Research & Social Science*, 31, 41–49.

Ottinger, G. and Cohen, B. R. 2011. *Technoscience and Environmental Justice: Expert Cultures in a Grassroots Movement*. Boston, MA: MIT Press.

Pellow, D. N. 2007. *Resisting Global Toxics: Transnational Movements for Environmental Justice*. New York: MIT Press.

Pellow, D. N. 2018. *What Is Critical Environmental Justice?* Cambridge: Polity.

Porter, D. 2005. *Health, Civilization and the State: A History of Public Health from Ancient to Modern Times*. London: Routledge.

Pulido, L. 1994. Restructuring and the contraction and expansion of environmental rights in the United States. *Environment and Planning A*, 26(6), 915–936.

Pulido, L. and De Lara, J. 2018. Reimagining "justice" in environmental justice: Radical ecologies, decolonial thought, and the Black Radical Tradition. *Environment and Planning E: Nature and Space*. DOI: 10.1177/2514848618770363.

Reed, M. G. and George, C. 2011. Where in the world is environmental justice? *Progress in Human Geography*, 35(6), 835–842.

Riesch, H. and Potter, C. 2014. Citizen science as seen by scientists: Methodological, epistemological and ethical dimensions. *Public Understanding of Science*, 23(1), 107–120.

Schlosberg, D. 1999. *Environmental Justice and The New Pluralism: The Challenge of Difference for Environmentalism*. Oxford: Oxford University Press.

Schlosberg, D. 2004 Reconceiving environmental justice: Global movements and political theories. *Environmental Politics*, 13(3), 517–540.

Schlosberg, D. 2013. Theorising environmental justice: The expanding sphere of a discourse. *Environmental Politics*, 22(1), 37–55.

Schweik, S. M. 2009. *The Ugly Laws: Disability in public*. New York: NYU Press.

Sealey-Huggins, L. 2018. The climate crisis is a racist crisis: Structural racism, inequality and climate change. In A. Johnson, R. Joseph-Salisbury, and B. Kamunge (eds), *The Fire Now: Anti-Racist Scholarship in Times of Explicit Racial Violence*. London: Zed Books, pp. 99–113.

Sen, A. K. 2009. *The Idea of Justice*. Cambridge, MA: Harvard University Press.

Shapin, S. 1994. *A Social History of Truth: Civility and Science in Seventeenth-Century England*. Chicago: University of Chicago Press.

Sismondo, S. 2017. Post-truth? *Social Studies of Science*, 47(1), 3–6.

Strasser, B., Baudry, J., Mahr, D., Sanchez, G., and Tancoigne, E. 2019. "Citizen science"? Rethinking science and public participation. *Science & Technology Studies*, 32, 52–76.

Taylor, D. E. 2011. Introduction: The evolution of environmental justice activism, research, and scholarship. *Environmental Practice*, 13(4), 280–301.

Taylor, D. E. 2014. *Toxic Communities: Environmental Racism, Industrial Pollution, and Residential Mobility*. New York: NYU Press.

United Church of Christ. 1987. *Toxic Wastes and Race in the United States*. New York: UC Commission for Racial Justice.

Walker B. L. 2011. *Toxic Archipelago: A History of Industrial Disease in Japan*. Seattle: University of Washington Press.

Walker, G. 2009a. Globalizing environmental justice: The geography and politics of frame contextualization and evolution. *Global Social Policy*, 9(3), 355–382.

Walker, G. 2009b. Environmental justice and normative thinking. *Antipode*, 41(1), 203–205.

Walker, G. 2012. *Environmental Justice: Concepts, Evidence and Politics*. London: Routledge.

Whyte, K. 2016. Our ancestors' dystopia now: Indigenous conservation and the Anthropocene. In U. K. Heise, J. Christensen, and M. Niemann (eds), *The Routledge Companion to the Environmental Humanities*. London: Routledge.

Whyte, K. 2018. The recognition paradigm of environmental injustice. In R. Holifield, J. Chakraborty, and G. Walker (eds), *The Routledge Handbook of Environmental Justice*. London: Routledge, pp. 113–123.

Wing, S. 2005. Environmental justice, science and public health. *Environmental Health Perspectives*, 113, 54–63.

Wylie, S. A. 2018. *Fractivism: Corporate Bodies and Chemical Bonds*. Durham, NC: Duke University Press.

Yenneti, K. and Day, R. 2015. Procedural (in)justice in the implementation of solar energy: The case of Charanaka solar park, Gujarat, India. *Energy Policy*, 86, 664–673.

Zimring, C. A. 2015. Clean and white: A history of environmental racism in the United States. New York: NYU Press.

Part I

Environmental justice and participatory citizen science

Introduction to Part I

Alice Mah

The dumping of highly toxic PCBs (polychlorinated biphenyls) in Warren County, North Carolina sparked the first national protest by African Americans against environmental racism in 1982. In a special issue entitled "Water Contamination: Citizens Respond" in *Science for the Public*, a left-wing American magazine on science and technology which ran between 1969 and 1989, Geiser and Waneck (1983) published an article on "PCBs and Warren County." The authors argued that the decision to site the PCB waste in Afton in Warren County was not only unjust; it was also unscientific. The landfill was located only 5 to 10 feet (1.5 to 3 meters) below the surface, close to drinking wells: "Only the most optimistic could believe that the Afton landfill would not leach into the groundwater. Unless a more permanent solution is found, it will only be a matter of time before the PCBs end up in these people's wells" (Geiser and Waneck 1983, 17). The special issue also featured an interview with Reverend Bruce Young, a member of the citizens group For a Clean Environment (FACE) that was fighting to address toxic contamination linked to a childhood leukemia cluster in Woburn, Massachusetts. Reverend Young and other citizen activists conducted their own community health study in Woburn in partnership with public health scientists. Woburn became a model for "popular epidemiology" in which "laypeople detect and act on environmental hazards and diseases," often with conflicts between lay and professional ways of knowing (Brown 1992, 268).

From its beginnings, the US environmental justice movement has involved community members in identifying local environmental and health problems, collaborating with scientists and other experts to find evidence of environmental racism, and using their research to advocate for community empowerment (Bullard 1990). Community-based participatory research (CBPR) has been at the forefront of research that connects environmental justice and citizen science (see Minkler and Wallerstein 2003; Corburn 2005; Israel et al. 2005; Wing 2005; Minkler et al. 2008; Wilson et al. 2018). This "collaborative approach to research equitably involves community members, organizational representatives, and researchers in all aspects of the research process" (Israel et al. 1998, 177). CBPR is used widely in public health, with roots in popular epidemiology. In the early 2000s, the "LA School" of environmental justice research embraced CBPR in a shift toward community-based and collaborative strategies (Morello-Frosch et al. 2002; Petersen et al. 2006; Cohen et al. 2012). Numerous community-based environmental justice organizations have engaged in community-driven research to address local issues of pollution, land use, and toxic exposure. Their research is based on a "framework that moves science from the realm of neutrality, seen in conventional social research, to the realm of values, which strengthens its utility" (Wilson et al. 2018, 283).

Phil Brown, Vanessa De La Rosa, and Alissa Cordner open this book with an incisive analysis of "toxic trespass" in environmental justice communities, where people are routinely exposed to contamination from industrial products and their waste streams. This builds on decades of community-engaged research from environmental sociologist Phil Brown, who coined the term "popular epidemiology" to describe residents' efforts to link illnesses and toxic pollution in Love Canal, New York and Woburn, Massachusetts (Brown 1992). In this chapter, Brown, De La Rosa, and Cordner identify the case of per- and polyfluorinated compounds (PFAS) as "perhaps the most visible class of chemicals now coming to public attention," situating their community-based participatory research within the historical context of environmental justice and citizen science. The authors highlight the combination of the scientific and social discovery of PFAS contamination through community-based research and the need to push for protective government regulation and corporate reform. They argue that this work is particularly urgent in the Trump era, when "citizen science and community-based research face increasing attacks from industry and regulatory bodies attempting to undermine the use of and invalidate results from these studies."

While community-based participatory research has been conducted in different places around the world (Mosavel et al. 2005; Conrad and Hilchey 2011), CBPR is most prevalent, particularly in an EJ (environmental justice) context, within US scholarship and activism. Moving beyond the US context, yet remaining in dialogue with it, Barbara Allen's chapter reflects on the results of her community-based participatory environmental health (CBPEH) research study conducted in the Étang de Berre industrial region in the south of France. A renowned scholar of science and technology studies (STS), Barbara Allen's earlier work focused on "citizen–expert alliances" in Cancer Alley, the infamous petrochemical corridor of environmental injustice in Louisiana (Allen 2003). Allen brings her experience in the USA of working with citizens, experts, scientists, and CBPEH methodologies (alongside epidemiologist Alison Cohen, who worked on CBPEH with environmental justice communities in California) to develop an "extreme" or "strongly participatory" form of citizen science in France. As Allen explains in her chapter: "Strongly participatory science is knowledge-making that is collaborative all the way down – from the problem definition, methodological considerations and data collection, to the final analyses." Contrasting this robust, community-led participatory science with the "deception and demagoguery of populism and post-truth politics," Allen concludes her chapter by arguing that the inclusion of embodied public knowledge about environmental health in the Étang de Berre case led to more relevant and effective science, including significant impacts for local policy.

In the next chapter, Bhavna Shamasunder and her co-authors discuss the results and implications of their community-based participatory research study of the public health and environmental justice consequences of oil development in LA. The Los Angeles basin hosts one of the highest concentrations of crude oil in the world, including more than 5,000 active oil wells situated among a dense population of more than 10 million people. Poor communities and communities of color bear the greatest burdens of this incredible concentration of oil wells; they are located in closer proximity to the wells and have outdated emissions equipment. Shamasunder and her co-authors used a community-based participatory research approach involving bilingual Spanish and English surveys of 205 residences within a 1,500-foot (457 meter) buffer of the wells, alongside low-cost sensors to measure methane emissions in the area. Their research showed spikes of methane emissions and significantly high rates of asthma in the local population, yet relatively low levels of local knowledge about the oil wells or the mechanisms for seeking environmental regulation. The research offers an important first step in efforts to examine potential health impacts on residents who live close to oil wells and to support community organizing around "crude justice." It also underscores the "epistemic injustice" (Fricker 2007, 1) that occurs "when a gap in collective interpretive resources puts someone at an unfair disadvantage when it comes to making sense of their social experiences."

In another excellent community-based study, Sarah Rhodes and KD Brown, together with their scholar-activist co-authors, build on the legacy of the "people's professor" Dr. Steve Wing, an epidemiologist who was a founding member of the North Carolina Environmental Justice Network. Throughout his life, Wing (2005, 61) was committed to the creation of a "science of environmental justice," which he defined as "a science for the people, applied research that addresses issues of concern to communities experiencing environmental injustice, poor public health conditions, and lack of political power." The authors carry forward Wing's commitment to community-based participatory research to the environmental injustices of the hog industry in North Carolina. There is a heavy concentration of industrial hog operations in North Carolina, with close to 3,000 hog farms that are disproportionately located in communities of color. Affected communities are exposed to antibiotic-resistant bacteria from industrial hog operations, which are associated with a number of health problems. Residents, activists, and researchers also face significant backlash from the powerful livestock industry and the state. Drawing on years of collective scholar-activist experience, this chapter offers reflections on historical legacies, lessons learned, and future challenges for CBPR in relation to entrenched corporate interests and environmental injustices in North Carolina.

This first part of *Toxic Truths* demonstrates the extraordinary potential of CBPR for environmental justice advocacy, from the public discovery of emerging contaminants, to the policy impacts of "strongly participatory" environmental health research in a contested French industrial region, to the enduring struggles over environmental justice near concentrated toxic industries in Los Angeles and North Carolina. In a post-truth era, these movements continue to thrive, even as they meet with resistance. All of the authors in this section share a commitment to participatory, community-based science, both as a necessary tool for advocating for environmental justice and social change, and as a form of research that is strengthened rather than undermined by local participation in the research process. As Robert Bullard (1990, 152) argued in his classic environmental justice book *Dumping in Dixie*, communities "should be prepared to remain in environmental justice struggles for years and possibly generations to come," but it is also important for grassroots groups to know that there have been citizen victories.

References

Allen, B. L. 2003. *Uneasy Alchemy: Citizens and Experts in Louisiana's Chemical Corridor Disputes.* Cambridge, MA: MIT Press.

Brown, P. 1992. Popular epidemiology and toxic waste contamination: Lay and professional ways of knowing. *Journal of Health and Social Behavior*, 33 (September), 267–281.

Bullard, R. D. 1990. *Dumping in Dixie: Race, class, and Environmental Quality*. Boulder, CO: Westview Press.

Cohen, A., Lopez, A., Malloy, N., et al. 2012. Our environment, our health: A community-based participatory environmental health survey in Richmond, California. *Health Education & Behavior*, 39(2), 198–209.

Conrad, C. C. and Hilchey, K. G. 2011. A review of citizen science and community-based environmental monitoring: Issues and opportunities. *Environmental Monitoring and Assessment*, 176, 273–291.

Corburn, J. 2005. *Street Science: Community Knowledge and Environmental Health Justice*. Cambridge, MA: MIT Press.

Fricker, M. 2007. *Epistemic Injustice: Power and the Ethics of Knowing*. Oxford: Oxford University Press.

Geiser, K. and Waneck, G. 1983. PBCs and Warren County. *Science for the Public*, July/August, 13–18.

Israel, B. A., Eng, E., Sculz, A. J., and Parker, A. E. (eds) 2005. *Methods in Community-based Participatory Research*. San Francisco, CA: Jossey-Bass.

Israel, B. A., Schulz, A. J., Parker, E. A., and Becker, A. B. 1998. Review of community-based research: Assessing partnership approaches to improve public health. *Annual Review of Public Health*, 19, 173–202.

Minkler, M., Vásquez, V. B., Tajik, M., and Petersen, D. 2008. Promoting environmental justice through community-based participatory research: The role of community and partnership capacity. *Health Education & Behavior*, 35, 119–137.

Minkler, M. and Wallerstein, N. 2003. *Community-based Participatory Research for Health*. San Francisco, CA: Jossey-Bass.

Morello-Frosch, R., Pastor, M., Porras, C., and Sadd, J. 2002. Environmental justice and regional inequality in southern California: Implications for future research. *Environmental Health Perspectives*, 110, 149–154.

Mosavel, M., Simon, C., Van Stade, D., and Buchbinder, M. 2005. Community-based participatory research (CBPR) in South Africa: Engaging multiple constituents to shape the research question. *Social Science & Medicine*, 61(12), 2577–2587.

Petersen, D., Minkler, M., Vásquez, V. B., and Baden, A. C. 2006. Community-based participatory research as a tool for policy change: A case study of the Southern California Environmental Justice Collaborative. *Review of Policy Research*, 23(2), 339–354.

Wilson, S., Aber, A., Wright, L., and Ravichandran, V. 2018. A review of community-engaged research approaches used to achieve environmental justice and eliminate disparities. In R. Holifield, J. Chakraborty, and G. Walker (eds), *The Routledge Handbook of Environmental Justice*. London: Routledge, pp. 283–296.

Wing, S. 2005. Environmental justice, science and public health. *Environmental Health Perspectives*, 113, 54–63.

1

Toxic trespass: Science, activism, and policy concerning chemicals in our bodies

Phil Brown, Vanessa De La Rosa, and Alissa Cordner

Exposure to chemical trespassers is ubiquitous for all people, with a daily onslaught of air particulates from factories and power plants, parabens in personal care products, phthalates and bisphenol (BPA) in consumer products, flame retardants in furniture, radiation from uranium mine tailings, polychlorinated biphenyls (PCBs) in fish and marine mammals, and trichloroethylene (TCE) from common industrial usage. The US Centers for Disease Control and Prevention's benchmark National Health and Nutrition Examination Survey (NHANES) shows how common it is for environmental chemicals to enter our bodies, and a large number of academic and advocacy household exposure and biomonitoring studies add to that knowledge (Centers for Disease Control and Prevention 2018). This is a *toxic trespass* of chemicals that violate our bodies and environment without permission (Redfield 1984; Malkan 2003; Schafer et al. 2004; Shamasunder and Morello-Frosch 2016). Toxic trespass has generated much conflict, affected policy making, spurred legislation, raised public awareness, attracted media coverage, and spawned social movement activity. Dealing with toxic trespass brings to light disputes between laypeople and professionals, citizens and governments, and among professionals, because the consequences of exposure are often poorly understood and because environmentally induced diseases are among the most prominent types of "contested illnesses" (Brown 2007). Toxic trespass often disproportionately impacts environmental justice (EJ) communities, because polluting facilities are concentrated in low-income communities and communities of color, and exposure to many chemicals through consumer products is also higher for marginalized populations (Helm et al. 2018; Mitro et al. 2018). Precisely because environmental diseases are so common in daily life and all aspects of the economy, these diseases have become highly politicized and have spurred much social movement activism.

In this chapter, we discuss the social and scientific discovery of environmental contaminants and the response by science, government, and social movements. We begin with a select history of how embodied contamination became an important issue, and then discuss how academics and progressive lay–professional alliances have altered traditional perspectives on science in order to place environmental health science in the service of those affected by contamination. As a case study for how these concerns are played out within a major contamination problem, we focus on per- and polyfluorinated compounds (PFAS), perhaps the most visible class of chemicals now coming to public attention. Our PFAS Project at Northeastern University's Social Science Environmental Health Research Institute (SSEHRI) has played a large role in community organizing and academic–community partnerships around PFAS, including collaborations at the transdisciplinary intersection of social and life sciences. Lessons from our case study can be applied to many other forms of toxic trespass from hazardous substances, and can demonstrate a framework of community-based participatory research and community-engaged research for social scientists and life scientists to effect change.

Theoretical understandings of science

Scientists and people impacted by environmental issues increasingly merge their efforts and expertise to use and critique existing science, while also developing and applying new research approaches. For individuals impacted by environmental health problems, whether localized sites of contamination or broader exposures through daily life and consumer products, science is a necessary tool to uncover and reduce toxic exposures, identify and alleviate associated health effects, and prevent future exposures. We use the term "science" to refer to the systematic collection of evidence and observations to describe and explain something about the world. While scientific authority rests on science being seen as "value-free and politically neutral" (Kinchy and Kleinman 2003, 380), most sociologists challenge the supposedly bright line between science and other areas of society, arguing that science is as much socially constructed as it is empirically based, since it is conducted by people with diverse social positions, and because science takes place within a social context (Gieryn 1983; Jasanoff et al. 1995).

Despite the increasing relevance of civic science (often called citizen science) and research conducted outside of traditional scientific institutions for environmental health research, scientific arguments and more formalized investigations are obligatory in fields like science policy, chemical product development, or environmental activism. The process of *scientization* refers to how scientific authority is increasingly valued and required for regulatory, legal, and social movement activities (Michaels and Monforton 2005; Morello-Frosch et al. 2006; Kinchy 2010). Participation in these scientized fields typically depends on *expertise*, or the in-depth and appropriately credentialed technical knowledge and experience that is particular to a topic, sector, or discipline. Highly scientized fields routinely exclude lay voices and the experiences of those directly impacted by risks, such as workers or residents who live near polluting facilities (Morello-Frosch et al. 2006).

Recent work in sociology and science and technology studies (STS), especially the *new political sociology of science* approach, has identified the networks, institutions, and power structures of inequality that affect the production and consumption of scientific knowledge and ignorance (Frickel and Moore 2006). In addition to power, disciplinary norms and practices contribute to socially produced gaps in scientific knowledge through both deliberate actions as well as unintentional, influential institutional logics (Hess 2009; Frickel et al. 2010; Kempler et al. 2011; Moore et al. 2011; Kleinman and Suryanarayanan 2012). Funding priorities are often set by federal agencies or the military and thus reflect elite priorities (Moore 2008), disciplines compete for intellectual territory and scarce grant dollars (Frickel and Gross 2005), and the research questions of interest to the government or industry often receive greater attention than those of interest to communities and non-elites (Hess 2009; Frickel et al. 2010).

Some uncertainty is inherent in the environmental health research process, related to choosing research questions or methods, interpreting scientific results, communicating results to multiple publics, and applying results for policy making (Cordner and Brown 2013). The length and complexity of exposure pathways, described below, make it very difficult to link exposures and disease outcomes, even if information is not intentionally concealed or strategically manipulated by responsible parties, as is often the case when industries attempt to delay recognition of their products' hazards using scientific arguments (Markowitz and Rosner 2002; Michaels 2008; Proctor and Schiebinger 2008; Oreskes and Conway 2010; Cordner 2016). All of these issues matter greatly for scholars working with impacted EJ communities, who have greater environmental hazards, combined with less resource to deal with those hazards.

As this section has shown, science is highly affected by social, political, economic, and ideological factors – all of those involving use of power by those in charge, and opposition to that power by those affected. To continue this train of thought, we now turn to the impact of social movements on environmental science and policy.

Social discovery and social movements

Rachel Carson's groundbreaking *Silent Spring* in 1962 ushered in the modern environmental movement by bringing mass public attention to environmental health effects of toxics. Carson showed how pesticides were serious hazards, causing morbidity and mortality in animals and humans (Carson 1962). Like many other pioneers in public health, Carson was sharply criticized by many for being unscientific and for attacking major economic sectors. Carson's work and the growing US environmental movement led to significant regulation of pesticides and other chemicals, and eventually to the passage of the National Environmental Protection Act and the establishment of the Environmental Protection Agency (EPA). Her work inspired a new generation of environmental activists largely concerned with ecological and animal effects. Although most readers paid less attention to human health concerns in the book, Carson made the first link to breast cancer and the role of endocrine disrupting compounds (EDCs), which would later be shown as central to many diseases and conditions.

The modern environmental movement gained additional support when hazardous waste under a school in Niagara Falls, New York in 1978 introduced human health as a central concern in an environmental crisis (Levine 1982; Gibbs 2011). Residents learned from state health officials that toxic chemicals permeated the Love Canal neighborhood because the city bought a dumpsite on which to build a school from Hooker Chemical Company for one dollar, with a clause guaranteeing no corporate liability. The revelation meshed with residents' awareness of having seen noxious substances oozing from the site and experiencing unusual health effects. As residents organized to learn more, they discovered high rates of miscarriages, birth defects, cancers, and chromosome damage (Levine 1982). Newly minted activists, with no scientific or social movement background, quickly learned the relevant science and took direct action by community organizing, demonstrating, organizing health studies, and demanding action by state and federal governments. The contamination at Love Canal prompted the creation of the Superfund Program by the US Environmental Protection Agency (EPA).

A few years later there was a similar occurrence in Woburn, Massachusetts, when TCE from W. R. Grace Chemicals and Beatrice Foods was dumped, leading to a childhood leukemia cluster. There, in addition to social discovery, residents worked with scientists to conduct a large health study that became a model for "popular epidemiology," in which laypeople, often residents in contaminated communities, link illness rates and clusters with local pollution – in this case TCE (Brown and Mikkelsen 1990). Soon it was clear that a widespread toxic crisis was stimulating a new toxic waste movement (Brown and Masterson-Allen 1993), eventually leading to countless communities around the country taking similar action when faced with toxic contamination.

Since many of the contaminated communities were in minority and low-income areas, the environmental justice movement developed, linking institutionalized racism to environmental contamination (Bullard 1990; Mohai et al. 2009; Agyeman et al. 2016). The EJ movement took things a step further by incorporating the centrality of racial and class structures. The discovery of toxic trespass in EJ communities is particularly important because these communities typically face higher burdens of exposure to pollution and negative associated health outcomes. EJ is fundamentally about the distribution of environmental hazards and the rights of all people – in particular those most affected by environmental hazards – to be recognized and participate in environmental decision-making processes (Mohai et al. 2009; Schlosberg 2009; Agyeman et al. 2016).

How, then, do affected residents uncover diseases and conditions in their midst, and link them to environmental factors? Despite the general absence of appropriate surveillance and epidemiological activity, it is striking that ordinary citizens can make the relevant connections. They, along with a growing cadre of forward-looking scientists and health professionals, have helped to bring to public attention to the many *contested illnesses* that are now prevalent (Brown, Morello-Frosch, and Zavestoski 2012). Describing an emerging public understanding of the endocrine disruptor hypothesis, which sought to explain many of the newly contested illnesses, Krimsky (2000) defined *social discovery* as the growing awareness of a previously unrecognized or poorly understood social problem, disease, environmental hazard, or social phenomenon. The production of a *public hypothesis* – the growing awareness by the lay public of a previously unrecognized or poorly understood social problem, disease, environmental hazard, or social phenomenon – is not necessarily incremental or inevitable, but rather involves struggles between countervailing forces under public scrutiny (Krimsky 2000). People may develop concerns about environmentally induced diseases when they observe illness clusters, as noted above in Woburn, especially if there is a known, nearby contamination source such as an abandoned toxic waste site, operating incinerator, or chemical factory. At other times, people learn about increased cancer rates from annual cancer registry reports, which is what led to major attention to research on environmental factors and breast cancer on Long Island, New York and Cape Cod, Massachusetts (Brown et al. 2006). Sometimes people notice health effects in animals, and become concerned that humans too will be affected. For example, the Tennant family in the Mid-Ohio Valley uncovered toxic perfluorooctanoic acid (PFOA) contamination on land used by DuPont after their entire cattle herd died (Lyons 2007). The Tennant family sued DuPont and eventually won a major class action lawsuit. One result of the case was the C8 Study, a groundbreaking 69,000-person epidemiological study that linked PFOA to six diseases and conditions and raised national attention on the entire class of per- and polyfluorinated compounds (PFAS), making it one of the most prominent group of contaminants today (Frisbee et al. 2009). We will go into detail on that case later.

Social discovery meets scientific discovery

Activist attention has combined with new scientific discovery to focus attention on contaminants that were previously understudied or emerging. As a result, rapid shifts have occurred in cases of emerging contaminants, for example PFAS, flame retardants, BPA, PFOA, and phthalates, as shown in Figure 1.1. Some scientists increasingly saw the need to put their talent to work to solve pressing problems that affected human health, while others sought to counter industry-dominated science that covered up hazards. This increased research has mobilized regulatory changes at the state and federal level, amplified community stories, and empowered the formation of community-based social movement organizations that continue to push for increased research funding, new and larger studies, transparency, and a seat at the decision-making table.

Exposure pathway

Identifying toxic trespass when it occurs requires defining and evaluating the *exposure pathway*, the link between the exposure source and how people are exposed to environmental contaminants (Maxwell 2009). The elements of the exposure pathway include the source (such as landfills, spills, or factory emission stacks), fate and transport (how contaminants travel through and act in different environmental media once released), the exposure point (household dust, contaminated drinking water), and the exposure route (inhalation, dermal, or ingestion). An important link between exposure pathways and disease outcomes

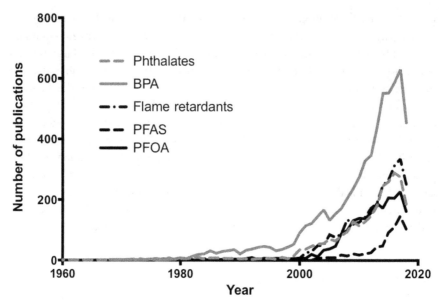

Note: Search terms used in PubMed were: *PFAS* (Title/Abstract), *PFOA* (Title/Abstract), *BPA* (Title/Abstract), *Flame retardants* (Title/Abstract), and *Phthalates* (Title/Abstract). The number of publications matching these terms were plotted by year. Publications prior to 1960 are not depicted in the graph above. This cut-off resulted in the exclusion of only four phthalate publications.

1.1 Published scientific research on various emerging contaminants. Research on emerging contaminants has increased over the last two decades.

is understanding *internal* exposures and toxicity. In addition to identifying disease endpoints in studies, toxicologists can measure adverse effects at the molecular and tissue level such as genetic mutations, altered immune responses, altered hormone responses, and changes in tissue morphology that can lead to disease. The toxicity of a chemical depends on many factors: the timing of exposure from preconception through childhood and adulthood; where the chemical is present in the body; how much is present; duration of exposure; genetic susceptibility; and interaction with social variables like stress, green space, and exposure to violence. Many chemicals are removed from the body quickly, thanks to our primary defense against foreign chemicals, the liver (Casarett et al. 2001). However, compounds that tend not to degrade, including PCBs, DDT (dichlorodiphenyltrichloroethane), PFAS, many flame retardants, and other industrial by-products, can accumulate in our bodies and the food chain because of their chemical and physical properties (Casarett et al. 2001).

Transdisciplinary social science–environmental work

To study complex environmental phenomena like the exposure pathway, sociologists and other social scientists are increasingly engaged in transdisciplinary collaborations in environmental health fields (Hoover et al. 2015; Finn and Collman 2016; Matz et al. 2016). With a strong focus on environmental inequalities, research has moved away from isolated disciplinary silos toward engaged, transdisciplinary work in partnership with impacted communities to investigate exposures and health effects, mitigate hazards, influence environmental policy, and prevent new exposures. In such collaborations, sociologists and other EJ researchers become active members of environmental health research teams rather than just observers. Hoover et al. (2015) describe this as a shift from "social science *of* environmental health," which investigates environmental health crises, exposures, contamination, and disasters, and by examining the production of scientific knowledge around environmental health issues from a political economic or EJ perspective (e.g., Edelstein 1988; Bullard 1990; Kroll-Smith and Couch 1990; Faber 2008), to "social science *with* environmental health." This work involves directly collaborating in environmental health research projects with health scientists, residents, and community-based organizations (Hoover et al. 2015).

For one example, we can look at the long-term relationship between the community-based science organization Silent Spring Institute; academic researchers at Brown University, Northeastern University, and UC-Berkeley; and the community activist group Communities for a Better Environment (in northern California). A formative element of that work stemmed from the response to participants' calls for sharing environmental health data from biomonitoring and household exposure studies. The partners developed best practices and built an ethical framework for the individual and community report-back of environmental health data, which was quite uncommon at the time (many researchers and Institutional Review Boards believed that such data would "worry" participants). In both conducting and studying the process of report-back as it took place in Cape Cod, Massachusetts and in Richmond and Bolinas, California, the team reflexively engaged with the community and research participants to (1) understand the individual and collective needs of participants related to their environmental health data; (2) understand how taking part in research and receiving data influences the creation of shared definitions of exposure; (3) investigate how personal and collective histories influence the understanding of data; and (4) understand generally how receiving environmental health data influences participants personally and politically (Adams et al. 2011; Brown et al. 2012).

These transdisciplinary collaborations are challenging for social scientists and environmental health scientists alike because of the additional layers of collaboration, risk communication, and transdisciplinary communication required. Few environmental health scientists receive formal training in the nuances of environmental communication and risk issues surrounding contaminated sites. Likewise, few social scientists studying environmental health issues receive formal training in the environmental health sciences they are studying and must learn to communicate with environmental health scientists. This cross-training is especially important when social scientists and environmental health scientists are working with EJ groups and communities. Such work should be guided by EJ principles, including deep and meaningful involvement of marginalized populations, the protection of all populations from environmental hazards, an emphasis on prevention and precautionary approaches as the best risk mitigation, and redress of disproportionate exposures (Bullard 2008).

Biomonitoring and household exposure research

Biomonitoring involves testing for the presence and accumulation of chemicals or chemical breakdown products in the human body, often using blood or urine. Such studies can provide insight on our internal exposure and the persistence of chemicals in our body. Together, biomonitoring studies and exposure measurements in various media, such as air, water, household dust, or soil, enable scientists to estimate our exposure. As noted above, the CDC's NHANES biomonitoring project has played a central role in showing exposure in a sample of the US population, expanding from 21 chemicals in 2001 to 265 chemicals in 2015 (Centers for Disease Control and Prevention 2018).

Academic researchers have also conducted extensive biomonitoring, often seeking to link exposure with health effects. Much academic research involves studies conducted by university researchers with the primary aim of peer-reviewed publications. Exposure scientists and environmental epidemiologists have increasingly found this an interesting area, and some have been outspoken about using their research for public betterment via regulation and product changes (Dodson et al. 2017; Zota et al. 2017; Helm et al. 2018).

Other academics have embraced community-based participatory research (CBPR), in which scientists and community groups co-create research questions, methods, and dissemination, and control over all aspects of the research process is shared with community partners. Goals of CBPR projects include increased community engagement in research to generate more accurate scientific knowledge, improved public trust and understanding of environmental health science, utilization of culturally and socially appropriate interventions, improved public health decisions, policy changes, and reductions in environmental injustice (O'Fallon and Dearry 2002; Wallerstein et al. 2017).

Silent Spring Institute's household exposure study on Cape Cod, mentioned above, provides an example of a CBPR study that tested for household exposure to environmental contaminants. The study focused on exposure to EDCs, including the first indoor measures for 30 compounds, and identified a wood floor finish as a widespread ongoing source of PCBs (Rudel et al. 2003, 2008). In subsequent exposure monitoring, Silent Spring expanded the household exposure study to Richmond, California to measure exposure to similar chemicals in a poor, minority community (Brody et al. 2009). What was most striking was the pronounced toxic trespass of the indoor environment with chemicals from heavy oil combustion and the disproportionate cumulative impact of pollution in the Richmond community from exposures due to both industrial and household sources (Brody et al. 2009; Rudel et al. 2010). These studies activated and expanded community engagement around EJ issues and encouraged community members to think in new ways about sources of chemicals around them. Empowered community members shared their exposure data to inform policy changes (Brown et al. 2012).

Civic science (aka "citizen science" and "community science") involves academic–community partnerships and community monitoring (Irwin 1995; Corburn 2005; Kinchy 2017). In addition to gathering and integrating more scientific observations than would be possible in traditionally funded and traditionally operated projects, citizen science has the capacity to democratize the research process. Among the many examples of how citizen science has contributed to biomonitoring and exposure research, popular epidemiology has been used by contaminated communities in the following ways: residents in Woburn, Massachusetts conducted health studies of childhood leukemia (Brown 1987); the Louisiana Bucket Brigade monitored various petroleum emissions (Allen 2003; Ottinger 2010); farmworkers have measured pesticide drift (Harrison 2011); Gulf Coast residents have used balloon mapping to monitor the BP oil spill; and residents have used inexpensive hydrogen sulfide detectors using photographic paper to see the toxic hazards from fracking (Wylie and Thomas 2014).

In addition to citizen science projects, *advocacy biomonitoring* involves measuring people's exposures with the purpose of developing knowledge to be used for activism and public outreach (Morello-Frosch et al. 2009). Pioneered by the Environmental Working Group's "Body Burden" study of 10 individuals (Houlihan et al. 2003), advocacy biomonitoring involves laypeople, working through activist organizations to produce important environmental health science. These projects are often initiated by non-scientists, who contract outside laboratories to conduct the chemical analyses. Sample sizes are small, typically ranging from three to thirty people, so results are not intended to be analyzed statistically but rather to illustrate the chemicals present in ordinary people. In many advocacy biomonitoring projects, people publicly share their chemical exposure data along with photographs and biographies. Projects typically target chemicals that are less studied and poorly regulated. In participating in these studies, people emphasize the importance of going beyond individual solutions to press for regulatory and corporate reform in order to reduce exposures (Washburn 2013; Morello-Frosch and Brown 2014; MacKendrick 2018). A new variant, conducted by Silent Spring Institute, uses crowdsourced biomonitoring gathered from individuals using the Detox Me Action Kit, in which people pay to participate in urine biomonitoring of 10 emerging contaminants (Silent Spring Institute 2018). In the current Trump era, citizen science and community-based research face increasing attacks from industry and regulatory bodies attempting to undermine the use of and invalidate results from these studies. Under the guise of science transparency, the community-based and advocacy biomonitoring studies that are integral in the scientific and social discovery of emerging contaminants are often called into question by misleading chemical regulation policies, such as the recently proposed transparency in regulatory science rule and rejection of a ban on the pesticide chlorpyrifos (Paris et al. 2017; Berg et al. 2018; Dillon et al. 2018).

The history of exposure science, environmental health activism, and biomonitoring and household exposure research discussed so far provide us with an overview of toxic trespass. With that in hand we now turn to a case study of a major new set of chemical contaminants, a case that shows the many intersections between environmental activism, scientific discovery, and the many social, political, and economic factors that are central to chemical hazards.

Case study: per- and polyfluorinated compounds

PFAS are a class of chemicals that has become a contaminant of concern for residents and activists, regulators, and many industry representatives due to its persistence, widespread exposure, and contamination. The social and scientific discovery of PFAS touches on many of the issues we have raised so far, including the scientific challenges of establishing an exposure-to-disease pathway, the need for transdisciplinary and collaborative research, and the two-way relationship between scientific research and public health advocacy. Our PFAS Project team of 10 researchers at Northeastern University's Social Science

Environmental Health Research Institute – faculty, postdocs, graduate students, and undergraduates – has been at the forefront of raising awareness of PFAS contamination and documenting the social discovery of this class of chemicals (Cordner et al. 2016, 2019). We have been working for three years to make known the extent and health effects of PFAS contamination by publicly tracking new cases of discovery in real time and making this information accessible on an interactive map; aiding community groups and local and state governments in remediation, research, and regulatory action; engaging with journalists who publicize the problem; giving presentations at conferences and webinars of environmental activists and educators; organizing national conferences; and facilitating a national coalition of PFAS activist groups. Much of this work involves efforts with Silent Spring Institute, a collaborator on this and other projects for over a decade. Especially significant is the role of doctoral students and postdocs who are supported by a joint Northeastern SSEHRI/Silent Spring training program funded by the National Institute of Environmental Health Sciences, part of the National Institutes of Health.

PFAS are an unusual chemical class because of their dual nature of contamination: the site-specific contaminated communities, and the ubiquitous low-level contamination of everyday life. This sets them apart both from other occupational/contaminated community sites where consumer exposure is rare, and from other emerging chemicals like flame retardants without identified contaminated communities. However, some aspects of the PFAS story are common among other emerging contaminants. In particular, PFAS are widely used and sometimes their use is well known (e.g., in Teflon and Scotchguard), while other times it is invisible and unknown (e.g., in dental floss and other personal care products).

PFAS are a class of nearly 5,000 human-made fluorinated chemicals containing chains of carbon and fluorine atoms widely used in industrial processes and consumer goods (Organisation for Economic Co-operation and Development 2018). The most widely known PFAS chemicals are perfluoroocatanoic acid (PFOA), which was used to manufacture Teflon coatings, and perfluorooctane sulfonate (PFOS), used in Scotchgard fabric protectors, firefighting foam, and in semiconductor devices. PFAS are also widely used in aqueous firefighting foam (AFFF) used at military sites, airports, and firefighting training facilities. PFOA was first developed by DuPont chemists in 1938 and studied by DuPont for toxicological and exposure concerns starting in the 1960s (Lyons 2007), but significant awareness of PFAS within the regulatory and academic science community did not occur until decades later. Figure 1.1 (above) shows the rapid increases in publications on PFOA and PFAS since 2000. PFAS's historical legacy and social construction is similar to flame retardants in that problems early on in the 1970s led to a small amount of action, such as regulation, yet received little attention for decades (Cordner 2016). A more recent rapid rise in both research and public interest in PFAS is likely due to a combination of factors, including increased widespread contamination in communities, national exposure studies documenting widespread water contamination, new state and federal regulations, and improvements in technologies for detecting and identifying new types of PFAS chemicals for study.

Epidemiological and toxicological research has linked PFAS exposure to multiple health conditions. Following over 50 years of toxic trespass and a $650 million legal settlement by DuPont, the C8 Study's 69,000-participant epidemiological study in the Mid-Ohio Valley linked PFOA exposure with high cholesterol, ulcerative colitis, thyroid disease, testicular and kidney cancers, and pregnancy-induced hypertension (C8 Science Panel). Research apart from the C8 Study has found other suspected health impacts that include endocrine disruption, obesity, reproductive problems, birth defects, other types of cancer, stroke, and developmental problems in children (Lau 2015).

Apart from the well-known Mid-Ohio Valley situations, numerous communities have similarly experienced widespread PFAS contamination of drinking water due to their proximity to manufacturing sites, including Decatur AL (3M and Daikin), the Cape Fear River area in North Carolina (Chemours), Hoosick Falls, New York and North Bennington, Vermont (Saint Gobain Performance Plastics), and Cottage Grove, Minnesota (3M). Learning about exposure routes and potential health effects for these and many other sites has been hampered by decades of corporate deception in hiding data on PFAS hazards. Leading PFAS manufacturer 3M learned as early as 1970 from internal studies that workers were widely exposed to PFOA (Lyons 2007). Later epidemiological studies found that PFOA exposure increased workers' mortality rates, including doubling their chance of dying from prostate cancer and stroke (Lindstrom et al. 2011).

Widespread exposure to PFAS had been long linked to industry releases at manufacturing sites, but recent years have seen discovery at military, airport, and other sites where PFAS-containing AFFFs were used in flammable liquid fuel fires or for firefighter training. The US Department of Defense (DoD) has identified 401 current or former military sites with known or suspected PFAS contamination, including 126 sites with PFOA or PFAS levels above the EPA health advisory level, mostly due to the use of AFFFs for training or fire suppression (Sullivan 2018).

In some cases of contamination on military bases, officials have been supportive of research on PFAS fate and transport, exposure assessment, and remediation, and have quickly provided clean drinking water to impacted residents when PFOA and/or PFOS are detected above the EPA's health guideline. This situation is unlike other military contamination instances, such as PCB contamination at Alaska's St Lawrence Island (Lerner 2012) or TCE contamination at Camp LeJeune (Bove et al. 2014), for two reasons. First, the activists generally have not been military service members or veterans, but affected civilians living on or near military bases, and hence their activism has been less constrained because they are not subject to the formal constraints placed on service members or to veterans' general patriotic reluctance to criticize the military. Second, in most other cases of military-site contamination, military secrecy and wartime control have clamped down on scientific and social discovery; this was the case with "atomic veterans" exposed to radiation testing (Wasserman and Solomon 1982), service members exposed to Agent Orange (Martini 2012) during the Vietnam War, and veterans who experienced Gulf War related illness (Brown et al. 2001). In those cases, organizing has been perceived as a threat to military policy and national security, and advocates have faced high levels of government silence and resistance. In contrast, PFAS are used in routine firefighting training and usage, falling into a general category of safety. Further, because AFFF foam is also used in civilian airports and in fire training sites for municipal firefighters, there is very broad general concern for safety issues with these chemicals, both in use and in storage.

As with many chemicals, scientists and the public are playing a catch-up game, as older chemicals are phased out and replaced with newer, but similar ones. While PFOA and PFOS are no longer produced by manufacturers in the USA, replacement compounds including short-chain PFAS and GenX are widely used in spite of growing concerns about widespread exposures and toxicity (Perez et al. 2013; Danish Ministry of the Environment 2015; Rae et al. 2015; Rosenmai et al. 2016; Sun et al. 2016; US EPA 2017). Corporations are protected from sharing names of chemicals in new products and mixtures, making it difficult or impossible for scientists to study the new replacements. Even the EPA, charged with evaluating new uses of chemicals, cannot gain access to chemical data (Richter et al. 2018).

There are many possible exposure pathways for PFAS, including direct exposure through occupational work, ingestion of drinking water, oral or dermal intake from consumer products containing PFAS, or ingestion of food grown on land treated with PFAS-contaminated biosolids. The EPA's Unregulated Contaminant Monitoring Rule (UCMR) found PFAS drinking water contamination affecting an estimated 15.1 million US residents in 27 states (US EPA 2018). The public is in constant contact with PFAS through everyday consumer products, such as fast food wrappers, though they are not generally aware of the extent of these exposures (Guo et al. 2009; Kotthoff et al. 2015; Liu et al. 2015;

Schaider et al. 2017). Research by the CDC's NHANES national biomonitoring program tested a nationally representative sample of US residents for 12 PFAS compounds from 1999 to 2014 and found four PFAS in the serum of nearly all the people tested (Centers for Disease Control and Prevention 2017, 2018). This is particularly concerning because these chemicals have demonstrated the potential for low-dose or hormone disrupting effects, and are persistent and bio-accumlative in the body and food chain (Post et al. 2012). These types of studies documenting widespread exposure (Environmental Working Group 2017) have brought PFAS to the attention of a new audience of environmental health scientists and involved the public, especially communities whose drinking water is contaminated with PFAS.

The combination of scientific and social discovery has had many impacts. In 2006, following pressure by regulators, scientists, and the national non-profit the Environmental Working Group, eight major PFAS manufacturers developed a voluntary PFOA Stewardship Program with the EPA to reduce long-chain PFAS emissions to all media and eliminate their use from products over the next decade (US EPA 2006). In 2009, the EPA developed Provisional Health Advisory levels for both PFOA and PFOS in drinking water (US EPA 2009). These levels were subsequently lowered in 2016 with a combined PFOA+PFOS health advisory level of 70 ppt (parts per trillion) (US EPA 2016a, 2016b). Some states have set advisory levels even lower than the EPA level, and New Jersey and Michigan even have made regulatory levels that are enforceable by law (Interstate Technology Regulatory Council 2018). States are beginning to look beyond PFOA and PFOS to other PFAS, conducting additional water testing, placing restrictions on the emissions of local industries after discoveries of local contamination, and developing drinking water guidelines for additional PFAS (New Jersey Drinking Water Quality Institute 2015; Hagerty 2018). Current and former military sites are installing carbon-activated filtration systems and/or providing alternative water sources. Following an appropriation in the omnibus 2018 Defense Authorization Bill, the Agency for Toxic Substances and Disease Registry, a part of the Centers for Disease Control and Prevention, will conduct a nationwide study of PFAS health effects.

The field of stakeholders working on PFAS is broad, and includes regulatory and academic scientists; industry advocates; regulatory agencies; military scientists and policy makers; legislators at the state and federal levels; residents of impacted communities; and community and social movement groups at the local, state, regional, national, and international levels. The PFAS movement has experienced a major shift, from targeted advocacy led by professional scientists and litigators to a grassroots effort in dozens of communities that is well networked at the national level (https://pfasproject.net/). The PFAS social movement extends from the local level, with individual activists and concerned residents advocating for biomonitoring, water testing, site clean-up, or delivery of uncontaminated water, to national non-profits that work on PFAS policy and other environmental and health-related issues. Contamination in Hoosick Falls, New York from a plastics manufacturing site is a good example of the grassroots movement happening nationwide around PFAS contamination. When PFOA municipal water contamination was discovered by a local resident in 2015, residents established a community activist group that advocated for a water testing study and ultimately led to the designation of Hoosick Falls as a state Superfund site. After learning of the contamination in Hoosick Falls, concerned residents in nearby North Bennington, Vermont began testing their drinking water for PFOA. Academics and students at Bennington College offered a course on PFAS that was open to all community members. Through these classes, citizens were educated about the health effects of PFOA and were able to amplify their local concerns and demands for safer water. A transdisciplinary team of faculty collaborated with local residents on two National Science Foundation grants to organize the class and fund the water testing.

Other community groups have also used science for their social movement activism, often working in collaboration with academics and supportive regulators. For example, Testing for Pease formed after residents learned that the drinking water supplying the Pease Tradeport, an industrial park on the site of the former Pease Air Force Base in Portsmouth, New Hampshire, was contaminated with high levels of PFAS from AFFFs. Testing for Pease is one of the best organized and most sophisticated of the community groups dealing with PFAS, and is involved with PFAS-related advocacy at the local, state, and national level. They pushed the New Hampshire Health Department for blood testing, organized residents, and helped other communities learn how to deal with PFAS contamination. In 2018, their co-leader Andrea Amico was one of only two representatives of contaminated communities invited to a national EPA summit on PFAS research and policy. Testing for Pease has written several research proposals with academics that will fund transdisciplinary CBPR projects to examine PFAS effects on children's responses to vaccines, and to test water to learn what chemicals are not being removed from common filtration systems. Extensive community organizing is occurring throughout the USA, with a national coalition of groups led by Testing for Pease and Toxics Action Center.

Conclusion

We have shown that toxic trespass is widespread, with all people subject to contamination by industrial products and their waste stream, as well as many household products. The combination of social and scientific discovery has accelerated in recent years, enabling the creation of many social movement organizations and pushing for more protective government regulation and corporate reform. This movement continues to flourish even as it meets resistance in the Trump era.

The most complete examinations of contamination causes, impacts, and resolutions are done by transdisciplinary teams with a community-engaged approach. Our team's experience of this is guided by a framework centered in science-motivated and engaged social change. In our engaged environmental sociology, not all aspects of our project strictly conform to the principles of CBPR, in that not all our activities involve solely working with specific communities, and community members are not involved in all stages of our research process; however, we would argue that our research is always community engaged and oriented toward a dialogue with impacted publics.

Environmental sociology grew up in a milieu in which activism and scholarship have been commonly combined. We see increasing numbers of physical and life scientists now doing what many social scientists have done, and consider this a beacon for future efforts. Three recent large grants have provided strong support for academic–community collaborations that have a strong public policy approach, in addition to the scientific research. An $8 million Superfund Research Program (Sources, Transport, Exposure and Effects of PFASs; STEEP) Center established in 2017 at the University of Rhode Island brings together scientists from that university, Harvard, and Silent Spring Institute with communities on Cape Cod in a multi-project center with a strong Community Engagement Core, working to avert the human and environmental health impacts of PFAS exposure and disseminate lessons learned to help avoid similar contamination problems in the future. The PFAS Project team at Northeastern, in collaboration with Silent Spring Institute environmental chemist Laurel Schaider (who is also part of the above-mentioned STEEP Center) and Michigan State University epidemiologist Courtney Carignan, received in September 2018 a $2.6 million grant, in partnership with community groups Testing for Pease, Toxics Action Center, and Massachusetts Breast Cancer Coalition. That project will study how PFAS can lead to decreased immune response to vaccines in children; document the experiences of affected communities by conducting in-depth interviews and ethnographic research; conduct water testing; and create the "PFAS Exchange"

– an online resource center for the public as well as medical professionals. The website will include a variety of educational materials, web-based tools to help residents visualize and interpret their blood test results, and resources for connecting affected communities. Also in September 2018, the PFAS Project received a $500,000 grant from the National Science Foundation to study PFAS activism across the United States, using its unique Contamination Site Database. That project also includes Silent Spring Institute, Toxics Action Center, and Testing for Pease, and will also conduct water testing. Finally, all the above parties worked with community groups and scientists to organize two National PFAS Conferences in 2017 and 2019 that brought together the whole range of players dealing with PFAS to learn from impacted communities and hear the latest updates in PFAS science and regulation.

The PFAS Project's website (pfasproject.com) posts daily the many news stories of continuing and newly forming community groups that are pushing for action on PFAS, ranging from local and state pressure to federal pressure that has resulted in Congressional funding for major research. We are fortunate to be both observing and studying, as well as helping to shape, an exciting energy involving this class of chemicals in all of their manifestations.

References

Adams, C., Brown, P., Morello-Frosch, R., et al. 2011. Disentangling the exposure experience: The roles of community context and report-back of environmental exposure data. *Journal of Health and Social Behavior*, 52(2), 180–196.

Agyeman, J., Schlosberg, D., Craven, L., and Matthews, C. 2016. Trends and directions in environmental justice: From inequity to everyday life, community, and just sustainabilities. *Annual Review of Environment and Resources*, 41, 321–340.

Allen, B. L. 2003. *Uneasy Alchemy Citizens Experts in Louisiana's Chemical Corridor Disputes*. Cambridge, MA: MIT Press.

Berg, J., Campbell, P., et al. 2018. Joint statement on EPA proposed rule and public availability of data. *Science*, 360(6388).

Bove, F., Ruckart, P., Maslia, M., and Larson, T. 2014. Mortality study of civilian employees exposed to contaminated drinking water at USMC Base Camp Lejeune: A retrospective cohort study. *Environmental Health*, 13, 68.

Brody, J. G., Morello-Frosch, R., Zota, A., et al. 2009. Linking exposure assessment science with policy objectives for environmental justice and breast cancer advocacy: The Northern California Household Exposure Study. *American Journal of Public Health*, 99, S600–S609. DOI: 10.2105/AJPH.2008.149088.

Brown, P. 1987. Popular epidemiology: Community response to toxic waste-induced disease in Woburn, Massachusetts. *Science, Technology & Human Values*, 12(3/4), 78–85.

Brown, P. 2007. *Toxic Exposures: Contested Illnesses and the Environmental Health Movement.* New York: Columbia University Press.

Brown, P., Brody, J. G, Morello-Frosch, R., Tovar, J., Zota, A. R., and Rudel, R. A. 2012. Measuring the success of community science: The Northern California Household Exposure Study. *Environmental Health Perspectives*, 120, 326–331.

Brown, P. and Masterson-Allen, S. 1993. The toxic waste movement; A new type of activism. *Society & Natural Resources*, 7(3), 269–286.

Brown, P., McCormick, S., Mayer, B., et al. 2006. A lab of our own: environmental causation of breast cancer and challenges to the dominant epidemiological paradigm. *Science, Technology, and Human Values*, 31, 499–536.

Brown, P. and Mikkelsen, E. J. 1990. *No Safe Place: Toxic Waste, Leukemia, and Community Action.* Berkeley: University of California Press.

Brown, P., Morello-Frosch, R., and Zavestoski, S. 2012. *Contested illnesses: Citizens, Science, and Health Social Movements.* Berkeley: University of California Press.

Brown, P., Zavestoski, S., McCormick, S., et al. 2001. A gulf of difference: Disputes over Gulf War-related illnesses. *Journal of Health and Social Behavior*, 42, 235–257.

Bullard, R. 1990. *Dumping in Dixie: Race, Class, and Environmental Quality.* Boulder, CO: Westview Press.

Bullard, R. 2008. *The Quest for Environmental Justice: Human Rights and the Politics of Pollution.* San Francisco, CA: Sierra Club Books.

C8 Science Panel. www.c8sciencepanel.org/publications.html (last accessed January 22, 2020).

Carson, R. 1962. *Silent Spring.* Boston, MA: Houghton Mifflin.

Casarett, L., Doull, J., and Klaassen, C. D. 2001. *Casarett and Doull's Toxicology: The Basic Science of Poisons* (6th edn). New York: McGraw-Hill.

Centers for Disease Control and Prevention. 2017. Per- and Polyfluorinated Substances (PFAS) Factsheet. Available at www.cdc.gov/biomonitoring/PFAS_FactSheet.html (last accessed January 22, 2020).

Centers for Disease Control and Prevention. 2018. *Fourth National Report on Human Exposure to Environmental Chemicals, Updated Tables March 2018*, Volume 1C. Atlanta, GA: Centers for Disease Control and Prevention.

Corburn, J. 2005. *Street Science: Community Knowledge and Environmental Health Justice.* Cambridge, MA: MIT Press.

Cordner, A. 2016. *Toxic Safety: Flame Retardants, Chemical Controversies, and Environmental Health.* New York: Columbia University Press.

Cordner, A. and Brown, P. 2013. Moments of uncertainty: Ethical considerations and emerging contaminants. *Sociological Forum*, 28(3), 469–494r.

Cordner, A., Richter, L., and Brown, P. 2016. Can chemical-class based approaches replace chemical-by-chemical strategies?: Lessons from recent FDA regulatory action on per-fluorinated compounds. *Environmental Science & Technology*, 50(23), 12584–12591.

Cordner, A., Richter, L., and Brown, P. 2019. Environmental chemicals and public sociology: Engaged scholarship on highly fluorinated compounds. *Environmental Sociology*, 5(4), 339–351.

Danish Ministry of the Environment. 2015. Short-chain polyfluoroalkyl substances (PFAS). A literature review of information on human health effects and environmental fate and effect aspects of short-chain PFAS. Available at www2.mst.dk/Udgiv/publications/2015/05/978-87-93352-15-5.pdf (last accessed January 22, 2020).

Dillon, L., Sellers, C., Underhill, V., Shapiro, N., Ohayon, J. L., Sullivan, M., Brown, P., Harrison, J., Wylie, S., and EPA Under Siege Writing Group. 2018. The Environmental Protection Agency in the early Trump administration: Prelude to regulatory capture. *American Journal of Public Health*, 108(S2), S89–S94.

Dodson, R. E., Rodgers, K. M., Carey, G., et al. 2017. Flame retardant chemicals in college dormitories: Flammability standards influence dust concentrations. *Environmental Science & Technology*, 51(9), 4860–4869. DOI: 10.1021/acs.est.7b00429.

Edelstein, M. R. 1988. *Contaminated Communities: The Social and Psychological Impacts of Residential Toxic Exposure*. Boulder, CO and London: Westview Press.

Environmental Working Group. 2017. Mapping a contamination crisis. Available at www.ewg.org/research/mapping-contamination-crisis#.WlpvRZO7_Uo (last accessed January 2, 2020).

Faber, D. 2008. *Capitalizing on Environmental Injustice: The Polluter-Industrial Complex in the Age of Globalization*. London: Rowman & Littlefield.

Finn, S. and Collman, G. 2016. The pivotal role of the social sciences in environmental health sciences research. *New Solutions*, 26(3), 389–411.

Frickel, S., Gibbon, S., Howard, J., Kempner, J., Ottinger, G., and Hess, D. 2010. Undone science: Charting social movement and civil society challenges to research agenda setting. *Science, Technology, & Human Values*, 35(4), 444–476.

Frickel, S. and Gross, N. 2005. A general theory of scientific/intellectual movements. *American Sociological Review*, 70(2), 204–232.

Frickel, S. and Moore, K. 2006. *The New Political Sociology of Science*. Madison: University of Wisconsin Press.

Frisbee, S. J., Brooks, A. P., Maher, A., Flensborg, P., et al. 2009. The C8 health project: Design, methods, and participants. *Environmental Health Perspectives*, 117(12), 1873–1882. DOI: 10.1289/ehp.0800379.

Gibbs, L. 2011. *Love Canal and the Birth of the Environmental Health Movement*. Washington, DC: Island Press.

Gieryn, T. 1983. Boundary-work and the demarcation of science from non-science: Strains and interests in professional ideologies of scientists. *American Sociological Review*, 48(6), 781–795.

Guo, Z., Liu, X., and Krebs, K. 2009. Perfluorocarboxylic acid content in 116 articles of commerce. EPA/600/R-09/033. Office of Research and Development, National Risk Management Research Laboratory, US Environmental Protection Agency: Research Triangle Park, NC.

Hagerty V. 2018. Could 140 ng/L limit for GenX increase? *Star News Online*, February 18.

Harrison, J. 2011. *Pesticide Drift and the Pursuit of Environmental Justice*. Cambridge, MA: MIT Press.

Helm, J. S., Nishioka, M. N., Brody, J. G., Rudel, R. A., and Dodson, R. E. 2018.

Measurements of endocrine disrupting and asthma-associated chemicals in hair products used by black women. *Environmental Research*, 165, 448–458. DOI: 10.1016/j.envres.2018.03.030.

Hess, D. 2009. The potentials and limitations of civil society research: Getting undone science done. *Sociological Inquiry*, 79(3), 306–327.

Hoover, E., Renauld, M., Edelstein, M., and Brown, P. 2015. Social science contributions to transdisciplinary environmental health. *Environmental Health Perspectives*, 123, 1100–1106. DOI: 10.r1289/ehp.1409283.

Houlihan, J., Wiles, R., Thayer, K., and Gray, S. 2003) *Body Burden: The Pollution in People*. Washington, DC: Environmental Working Group.

Interstate Technology Regulatory Council. 2018. Available at www.itrcweb.org (last accessed January 20, 2020).

Irwin, A. 1995. *Citizen Science: A Study of People, Expertise and Sustainable Development*. London: Routledge.

Jasanoff, S., Markle, G., Peterson, J., and Pinch, T. 1995. *Handbook of Science And Technology Studies*. Thousand Oaks, CA: Sage.

Kempler, J., Merz, J. F., and Bosk, C. L. 2011. Forbidden knowledge: Public controversy and the production of nonknowledge. *Sociological Forum*, 26, 475–500.

Kinchy, A. J. 2010. Anti-genetic engineering activism and scientized politics in the case of "contaminated" Mexican maize. *Agriculture and Human Values*, 27, 505–517.

Kinchy, A. J. 2017. Citizen science and democracy: Participatory water monitoring in the Marcellus shale fracking boom. *Science as Culture*, 26(1), 88–110.

Kinchy, A. J. and Kleinman, D. L. 2003. Organizing credibility: Discursive and organizational orthodoxy on the borders of ecology and politics. *Social Studies of Science*, 33, 869–896.

Kleinman, D. L. and Suryanarayanan, S. 2012. dying bees and the social production of ignorance. *Science, Technology & Human Values*, 38, 492–517.

Kotthoff, M., Müller, J., Jürling, H., Schlummer, M., and Fiedler, D. 2015. Perfluoroalkyl and polyfluoroalkyl substances in consumer products. *Environmental Science and Pollution Research*, 22(9), 14546–14559. DOI: 10.1007/s11356-015-4202-7.

Krimsky, S. 2000. *Hormonal Chaos: The Scientific and Social Origins of the Environmental Endocrine Hypothesis*. Baltimore, MD: Johns Hopkins University Press.

Kroll-Smith, J. S. and Couch, S. R. 1990. *The Real Disaster Is Above Ground: A Mine Fire and Social Conflict*. Lexington: University of Kentucky Press.

Lau, C. 2015. Perfluorinated compounds: An overview. In J. C. DeWitt (ed.), *Toxicological Effects of Perfluoroalkyl and Polyfluoroalkyl Substances*. Cham: Springer.

Lerner, S. 2012. *Sacrifice Zones*. Cambridge, MA: MIT Press.

Levine, A. 1982. *Love Canal: Science, Politics, and People*. Lexington, MA: Lexington Books.

Lindstrom, A. B., Strynar, M. J., and Libelo, E. L. 2011. Polyfluorinated compounds: Past, present, and future. *Environmental Science & Technology*, 45(19), 7954–7961.

Liu, X., Guo, Z., Folk, E. E., and Roache, N. F. 2015. Determination of fluorotelomer alcohols in selected consumer products and preliminary investigation of their fate in the indoor environment. *Chemosphere*, 129, 81–86. DOI: 10.1016/j.chemo sphere.2014.06.012.

Lyons, C. 2007. *Stain-Resistant, Nonstick, Waterproof, and Lethal: The Hidden Dangers of C8.* Westport, CT: Praeger.

MacKendrick, N. 2018. *Better Safe Than Sorry: How Consumers Navigate Exposure to Everyday Toxics.* Berkeley: University of California Press.

Malkan, S. 2003. Chemical trespass: The chemical body burden and the threat to public health. *Multinational Monitor*, 24(4), 8.

Markowitz, G. E. and Rosner, D. 2002. *Deceit and Denial: The Deadly Politics of Industrial Pollution.* Berkeley: University of California Press.

Martini, E. 2012. *Agent Orange: History, Science, and the Politics of Uncertainty.* Amherst: University of Massachusetts Press.

Matz, J., Brown, P., and Brody, J. 2016. Social science-environmental health collabora- tions: An Exciting new direction. *New Solutions*, 26, 349–358.

Maxwell, N. I. 2009. *Understanding Environmental Health.* Boston, MA: Jones and Bartlett Publishers.

Michaels, D. 2008. *Doubt Is Their Product: How Industry's Assault on Science Threatens Your Health.* New York: Oxford University Press.

Michaels, D. and Monforton, C. 2005. Manufacturing uncertainty: Contested science and the protection of the public's health and environment. *American Journal of Public Health*, 95, S39–48.

Mitro, S. D., Chu, M. T., Dodson, R. E., et al. 2018. Phthalate metabolite exposures among immigrants living in the United States: Findings from NHANES, 1999–2014. *Journal of Exposure Science & Environmental Epidemiology.* DOI:10.1038/s41370-018-0029-x.

Mohai, P., Pellow, D. N., and Roberts, J. T. 2009. Environmental justice. *Annual Review of Environment and Resources*, 34, 405–430.

Moore, K. 2008. *Disrupting Science: Social Movements, American Scientists, and the Politics of the Military, 1945–1975.* Princeton, NJ: Princeton University Press.

Moore, K., Kleinman, D., Hess, D., and Frickel, S. 2011. Science and neoliberal globaliza- tion: A political sociological approach. *Theory and Society*, 40, 505–532.

Morello-Frosch, R., Brody, J., Brown, P., Altman, R. G., Rudel, R. A., Perez, C. 2009. Toxic ignorance and right-to-know in biomonitoring results communication: A survey of scientists and study participants. *Environmental Health*, 8, 6.

Morello-Frosch, R. and Brown, P. 2014. Science, social justice, and post-Belmont research ethics: Implications for regulation and environmental health science. In D. Kleinman and K. Moore (eds), *Handbook of Science, Technology, and Society.* London: Routledge.

Morello-Frosch, R., Zavestoski, S., Brown, P., Altman, R. G., McCormick, S., and Mayer, B. 2006. Embodied health movements: Responses to a "scientized" world. In S. Frickel and K. Moore (eds), *The New Political Sociology of Science: Institutions, Networks, and Power.* Madison: University of Wisconsin Press, pp. 244–271.

New Jersey Drinking Water Quality Institute. 2015. New Jersey Drinking Water Quality Institute. Health-Based Maximum Contaminant Level Support Document:

Perfluorononanoic Acid (PFNA). Available from http://www.nj.gov/dep/watersup ply/pdf/pfna-health-effects.pdf (last accessed January 22. 2020).

O'Fallon L. and Dearry A. 2002. Community-based participatory research as a tool to advance environmental health sciences. *Environmental Health Perspectives*, 110, 155–159.

Oreskes, N. and Conway, E. M. 2010. *Merchants of Doubt: How a Handful of Scientists Obscured the Truth on Issues from Tobacco Smoke to Global Warming.* New York: Bloomsbury.

Organisation for Economic Co-operation and Development. 2018. *Toward a New Comprehensive Global Database of Per- and Polyfluoroalkyl Substances (PFASs).* Environmental Directorate. Available at www.oecd.org/officialdocuments/publicdisplaydocumentpd f/?cote=ENV-JM-MONO(2018)7&doclanguage=en (last accessed January 22, 2020).

Ottinger, G. 2010. Buckets of resistance: Standards and the effectiveness of citizen science. *Science, Technology, and Human Values*, 35, 244–270.

Paris, B. S., Dillon, L., Pierre, J., Pasquetto, I. R., Marquez, E., Wylie, S., Murphy, M., Brown, P., Lave, R., Sellers, C., Mansfield, B., Fredrickson, L., Shapiro, N., EDGI. 2017. *Pursuing A Toxic Agenda: Environmental Injustice in the Early Trump Administration.* Available at https://envirodatagov.org/publication/pursuing-toxic-agenda (last accessed January 22, 2020).

Pérez F., Nadal, M., Navarro-Ortega A., et al. 2013. Accumulation of perfluoroalkyl substances in human tissues. *Environment International*, 59, 354–362.

Post, G. B., Cohn, P. D., and Cooper, K. R. 2012. Perfluorooctanoic acid (PFOA), an emerging drinking water contaminant: a critical review of recent literature. *Environmental Research*, 116, 93–117.

Proctor, R. and Schiebinger, L. 2008. *Agnotology: The Making and Unmaking of Ignorance.* Stanford, CA: Stanford University Press.

Rae, J. C., Craig L., Slone T. W., et al. 2015. Evaluation of chronic toxicity and carcinogenicity of ammonium 2, 3, 3, 3-tetrafluoro-2-(heptafluoropropoxy)-propanoate in Sprague–Dawley rats. *Toxicology Reports*, 2, 939–949.

Redfield, S. E. 1984. Chemical trespass: An overview of statutory and regulatory efforts to control pesticide drift. *Kentucky Law Journal*, 73(3), 855–918.

Richter, L., Cordner, A., and Brown, P. 2018. Non-stick science: Sixty years of research and (in)action on fluorinated compounds. *Social Studies of Science*, 48(5), 691–714.

Rosenmai, A. K., Taxvig, C., Svingen, T., et al. 2016. Fluorinated alkyl substances and technical mixtures used in food paper-packaging exhibit endocrine-related activity in vitro. *Andrology*, 4(4), 662–672.

Rudel, R. A., Camann, D. E., Spengler, J. D., Korn, L. R., Brody, J. G. 2003. Phthalates, alkylphenols, pesticides, polybrominated diphenyl ethers, and other endocrine-disrupting compounds in indoor air and dust. *Environmental Science & Technology*, 37(20), 4543–4553. DOI: 10.1021/es0264596.

Rudel, R. A., Dodson, R. E., Perovich, L. J., Morello-Frosch, R., Camann, D. E., Zuniga, M. M., Yau, A. Y., Just, A. C., and Brody, J. G. 2010. Semivolatile endocrine disrupting compounds in paired indoor and outdoor air in two northern California communities. *Environmental Science & Technology*, 44(17), 6583–6590. DOI:10.1021/ es100159c.å

Rudel, R. A., Seryak, L. M., and Brody, J. G. 2008. PCB-containing wood floor finish is a likely source of elevated PCBs in residents' blood, household air and dust: A case study of exposure. *Environmental Health*, 7(2). DOI: 10.1186/1476-069X-7-2.

Schafer, K. S., Reeves, M., Spitzer, S., and Kegley, S. E. 2004. *Chemical Trespass: Pesticides in Our Bodies and Corporate Accountability*. Pesticide Action Network North America.

Schaider, L. A., Balan, S. A., Blum, A., et al. 2017. Fluorinated compounds in U.S. fast food packaging. *Environmental Science & Technology Letters*, 4(3), 105–111. DOI: 10.1021/acs.estlett.6b00435.

Schlosberg, D. 2009. *Defining Environmental Justice: Theories, Movements, and Nature*. Oxford: Oxford University Press.

Shamasunder, B. and Morello-Frosch, R. 2016. Scientific contestations over "toxic trespass": Health and regulatory implications of chemical biomonitoring. *Journal of Environmental Studies and Science*, 6, 556–568.

Silent Spring Institute. 2018. DeTox Me Action Kit. Available at https://silentspring.org/detoxmeactionkit/ (last accessed January 22, 2020).

Sullivan, M. 2018. *Addressing Perfluorooctane Sulfonate (PFOS) and Perfluorooctanoic Acid (PFOA)*. Available at https://partner-mco-archive.s3.amazonaws.com/client_files/1524589484.pdf (last accessed January 22, 2020).

Sun, M., Arevalo, E., Strynar, M., et al. 2016. Legacy and emerging perfluoroalkyl substances are important drinking water contaminants in the Cape Fear River Watershed of North Carolina. *Environmental Science & Technology Letters*, 3(12), 415–419.

US EPA 2006. United States, U.S. Environmental Protection Agency, Office of Pollution Prevention and Toxics. 2010/15 PFOA Stewardship Program: Guidance on Reporting Emissions and Product Content, p. 3.

US EPA. 2009. Provisional health advisories for perfluorooctanois acid (PFOA) and perfluorooctane sulfonate (PFOS). Available at https://www.epa.gov/sites/production/files/2015-09/documents/pfoa-pfos-provisional.pdf (last accessed March 6, 2020).

US EPA. 2016a. US Environmental Protection Agency – Office of Water. Health Effects Support Document for Perfluorooctanoic Acid (PFOA).

US EPA. 2016b. US Environmental Protection Agency – Office of Water. Drinking Water Health Advisory for Perfluorooctanoic Acid (PFOA).

US EPA 2017. PFOA Stewardship Program Baseline Year Summary Report. Available at https://www.epa.gov/assessing-and-managing-chemicals-under-tsca/pfoa-stewardship-program-baseline-year-summary-report (last accessed January 22, 2020).

US EPA 2018. Third Unregulated Contaminant Monitoring Rule. Available at https://www.epa.gov/dwucmr/third-unregulated-contaminant-monitoring-rule (last accessed January 22, 2020).

Wallerstein, N., Duran, B., Oetzel, J., and Minkler, M. (eds) 2017. *Community-Based Participatory Research for Health: Advancing Social and Health Equity* (3rd edn). New York: Wiley.

Washburn, R. 2013. The social significance of human biomonitoring. *Sociology Compass*, 24, 162–179.

Wasserman, H. and Solomon, N. 1982. *Killing Our Own: The Disaster of America's Experience with Atomic Radiation*. New York: Delacorte Press.

Wylie, S. and Thomas, D. 2014. New tools for detecting and communicating environmental exposures and risks associated with oil and gas extraction. In publication of Annual Meeting of Partnerships for Environmental Public Health, September 22, 2014.

Zota, A., Singla, V., Adamkiewicz, G., Mitro, S., and Dodson, R. 2017. Reducing chemical exposures at home: Opportunities for action. *Journal of Epidemiology and Community Health*, 71(9), 937–940.

2

Making effective participatory environmental health science through collaborative data analysis

Barbara L. Allen

Introduction

Recent politics has amplified, albeit in stark terms, some simmering issues with the frame of participatory science. For example, when claims of environmental injustice are raised, citizen groups often produce a different set of data from that used by industry or the state to back up their assertions – "alternative facts," if you will, to borrow a term from the contemporary political arena. This is part of epistemic modernization (Hess 2007; Moore et al. 2011) or epistemic democratization (Sismondo 2017) whereby laypeople and social movement groups participate in shaping the science and enacting the scientific agendas that impact them (Hess 2015; Hess et al. 2017). However, as I will argue in this chapter, the kinds of new knowledge that residents of environmentally compromised communities produce, while different from the science they are arguing against, are substantively and categorically opposite from the popular press version of "alt facts" in our post-truth era. By this I refer to the recent right-wing political demagoguery, bent on "inflaming anger and resentment" (Hoffman 2018, 449) and willing to invent and disseminate new "facts" as needed for coercion and confusion in the name of proto-authoritarian political gamesmanship. This so-called populism is not the same as public participation in the creation of science, which involves "arrangements that facilitate the active involvement of outsiders" (Marres 2018b, 454) toward a rich and reflexive "knowledge democracy" (Marres 2018a). Before discussing the ways in which relevant and rigorous alternative science is produced by residents in contested regions, it would be helpful to explain what exactly constitutes participatory or citizen science today.

Dividing citizen science into a four-level classification scheme, Alan Irwin (2015, citing Haklay 2013) has attempted to link participation to depth of engagement with making scientific knowledge. Level 1 citizen science covers crowdsourcing and other activities that engage citizens in gathering specific kinds of information such as wildlife counting and other types of empirical data gathering for expert-devised projects. "Distributed intelligence" defines level 2 citizen science, where laypeople are interpreting scientific issues prepackaged by experts such as citizen juries and consensus conferences. Level 3 citizen science is termed "participatory science," defined as lay inclusion in both problem definition and data collection. This could include some forms of popular epidemiology and resident-initiated data collection such as water and air sampling to expose contamination. The final classification, level 4 citizen science, Haklay calls "extreme" participation in science, but I will call it "strongly participatory" science following Harding's concept of "strong objectivity"[1] (Harding 1991, 2015). Strongly participatory science is knowledge-making that is collaborative all the way down – from the problem definition, methodological considerations and data collection, to the final analyses (Allen 2018). What "demarcates citizen science activities (of whatever sort) from more conventional science is that they build not only on the active participation of citizens but, also, and explicitly, on their *expertise*" (Irwin 2015, 35, italics in original).

Drawing on a participatory health survey I conducted in an industrial area zone near the port of Marseille, France, I will demonstrate how citizen science constructed for policy influence can be made even stronger (Allen et al. 2016). First, working with the residents and local doctors, my team and I developed a health questionnaire. We then randomly and systematically sampled 8.3% of the households in two of the most pollution-impacted towns. We produced cross-sectional epidemiological data on a myriad of illnesses with prevalence well above comparative national statistics. Our study countered the findings of the French health service (Santé Publique France) that had reported few health issues in this region. Holding dissemination meetings throughout all phases of the project, as well as over 30 focus groups to analyze the data with residents, we produced a health report with the residents. By deeply contextualizing the epidemiology data with the local people, the health study became a more relevant and useful tool for their purposes. The group analysis process enabled citizens to meaningfully interpret the data and align their own analytical assessments with the statistical outcomes. Furthermore, by including their narratives of living with illness and pollution as an integral part of the final report, the document became a robust voice for the local population and is currently being used by them successfully to promote environmental change in a variety of ways.

In what follows, I will provide a discussion and rationale for strongly participatory science, particularly expanding on the last phase of this process: analyzing data with local people in focus groups. Using a case study from the Étang de Berre industrial region in France, I will demonstrate how quantitative survey statistics can be effectively linked to qualitative data obtained from interviews and workshops. In conclusion, my study will show that embodied, contextualized knowledge can be a useful tool to amplify citizen voices, thus enabling them to better shape their environments.

Democratization and socially robust knowledge

When people for whom the science matters are able to participate in its making, this leads to greater contextualization of knowledge. Some science policy scholars have argued that "the more socially robust one's knowledge claims, the more empirically reliable they will be. That is, the more scientific research projects engage with their social environments in egalitarian discussions, the higher the quality of the results of that research" (Harding 2008, 97). I argue that strongly participatory science, science where citizens are more than simply observers or data collectors but are involved in the development of science from start to finish, will be a powerful tool for implementing their choices (Allen 2017, 2018). The strongest science in terms of usefulness and efficacy for local residents is the science that they want to have for answering questions about their environments and their health. This is the knowledge that would enable them to make decisions about their families or pressure policy makers, regulators, and elected officials to do the right thing in the interests of citizens. Thus, social integration of knowledge leads to stronger and more relevant results compared to its weaker version, universal science or socially remote knowledge. Often this kind of science does not speak to laypeople and the ways in which they live and navigate their neighborhoods and places of work. An instructive way to view this is through the lens of environmentally distressed communities. Residents of these places often have many questions, few of which are answered by decontextualized, socially segregated science. Last summer, I met with a member of the scientific council of a major international environmental organization discussing approaches to citizen science. He told me that "we got it wrong" in the past. Trained as a scientist, he explained that the organization thought if you provide the local people with the best natural science produced by unaffiliated or unbiased scientists, and you gave that science to the people, they would act. But this did not happen. Citizens given possession of "good environmental science," even by an organization they perceiveed as trustworthy, did not compel action.

Furthermore, other scholars have studied participatory citizen science whereby citizens collect samples of air or water from their environments. The debates with regulatory and corporate officials that ensue over standards of measurement or veracity of data do not necessarily lead to change (Ottinger 2010, 2013; Kinchy 2016). As a scholar of citizen–scientist collaboration for the last two decades, I am interested in what kind of science can serve as "change-agent" knowledge – what are the ingredients that can facilitate action?

My hypothesis, which I tested with a recent project conducted in a polluted French region, is that science that answers the questions that local residents are vociferously asking tended to produce more "action" leading to potential change. While contested communities are often barraged by official data stem-ming from facility-permitting applications and state regulatory agencies, this data is often in the form of amount of substance released or amount of permis-sible release, listed substance by substance. Citizens, however, are interested in the total amount of toxic substances impacting their daily lives: home, schools, parks, and other public spaces. But even this data, while concerning, can fail to sufficiently motivate strong civic voices and bring about positive change as defined by the residents, themselves.

I argue that what motivates people living in polluted communities to act are perceived problems with human health – their health and that of their families. While general data about toxins in the environment can elicit concern, evidence of elevated disease and chronic conditions tend to motivate people to speak out and act. This is because one's body provides an intimate and visceral level of empirical knowledge, a kind of "chemical sublime" (Shapiro 2015), as each individual is an expert on their own health and disease experience. Plus, well-ness, or lack thereof, has an immediate impact on the day-to-day lives of people, a constant reminder that everything is not all right. Relevant health science is deeply contextualized knowledge, knowledge that I argue can be the impetus to speak out and to act.

Case study and methodology

Following several years of fieldwork, culminating in a participatory environ-mental health study, this chapter focuses on addressing the questions of resi-dents in two polluted towns in the Étang de Berre industrial region in France: Fos-sur-Mer (Fos) and Port-Saint-Louis-du-Rhône (PSL) (see Figure 2.1). In

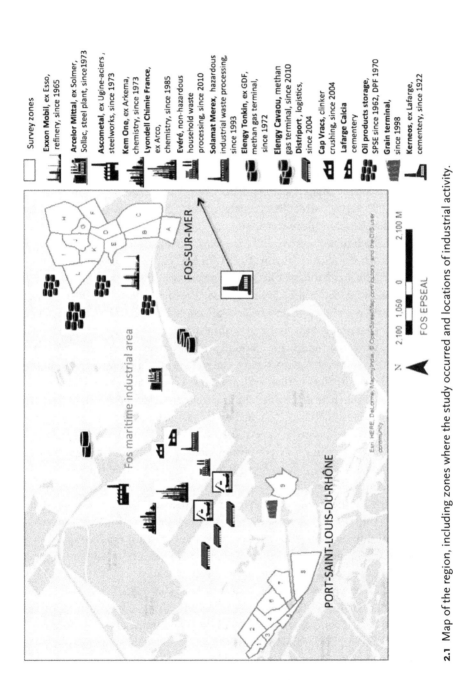

Survey zones

☐

Exxon Mobil, ex Esso, refinery, since 1965

Arcelor Mittal, ex Solmer, Sollac, steel plant, since1973

Ascometal, ex Ugine-aciers, steelworks, since 1973

Kem One, ex Arkema, chemistry, since 1973

Lyondell Chimie France, ex Arco, chemistry, since 1985

Everé, non-hazardous household waste processing, since 2010

Solamat Merex, hazardous industrial waste processing, since 1993

Elengy Tonkin, ex GDF, methan gas terminal, since 1972

Elengy Cavaou, methan gas terminal, since 2010

Distriport, logistics, since 2004

Cap Vracs, clinker crushing, since 2004

Lafarge Calcia cementery

Oil products storage, SPSE since 1962, DPF 1970

Grain terminal, since 1998

Kerneos, ex Lafarge, cementery, since 1922

FOS-SUR-MER

Fos maritime industrial area

PORT-SAINT-LOUIS-DU-RHÔNE

Esri, HERE, DeLorme, MapmyIndia, © OpenStreetMap contributors, and the GIS user community

N

2.100 1.050 0   2.100 M

FOS EPSEAL

2.1 Map of the region, including zones where the study occurred and locations of industrial activity.

1965, this area was classified a special development zone of the port of Marseille and all commercial siting decisions were removed from local governments and ceded to a public–private port authority (Garnier 2001). In more recent years, local residents fought against unpopular projects such as the location of a Gaz de France depot on the Fos public beach (opened 2005) and the construction of an incinerator designed to burn all the garbage from the city of Marseille (opened 2010) (Allen 2014). While losing these battles, the disputes raised local awareness about the impacts of industrial pollution, most notably on human health. In response to these concerns, the state conducted over a dozen environmental health and risk studies, all concluding there were few, if any, health problems (Allen et al. 2017b). Many local residents deemed these findings non-credible and attempted creative strategies to obtain health data, from "occupying" the terraces of the French health service building in Marseille and signing petitions, to trying to hack into the service's data repository. Even a local doctor expressed frustration at his inability to obtain data given his concern regarding an inordinate number of chronic illnesses he was seeing in local children.

My interviews with local residents, medical professionals, and government agency officials were part of an earlier NSF-funded project (National Science Foundation) examining how policy-relevant science was shaped in chemical regions.[2] My idea to conduct a community-based participatory environmental health (CBPEH) survey arose from the concern of my local informants about the lack of relevant health data in their communities. I successfully applied for funding from a new French health agency for environmental and occupational health[3] to conduct the study and hired Yolaine Ferrier, a local resident of the industrial zone (who had worked with me previously as a translator), as project manager (Allen et al. 2016). Numerous concerned citizens and environmental leaders volunteered to participate in helping with the study and donated space for meetings. Further interviewing local people to be sure we had an exhaustive list of all their health questions, my team epidemiologist, Alison Cohen, designed the health survey tool.[4] In 2015, we spent six months going door to door, randomly and systematically sampling a cross-section of the population until we had surveyed 8.3% of the population with a 45% response rate for those answering the door (Cohen et al. 2017). For illnesses (asthma, cancers, diabetes, etc.) the survey question was phrased: "Have you ever been diagnosed by a doctor with _____?" Additionally, we asked questions about chronic conditions that residents had expressed concern about (such as skin conditions, eye irritation, nose and throat irritation, etc.) (see Table 2.1).

In June 2016, we held a series of public meetings in the two towns to disseminate our broad findings about the elevated prevalence of cancer, asthma, diabetes, and other illnesses compared to the French population as a whole. But

Table 2.1 Health issues in the Fos EPSEAL study and relevant comparison populations. Barbara Allen adapted from Cohen et al. (2017)

Health outcome	Respondents (n = 818)	France
Self-rated health	Excellent: 15%	Very good: 25%
	Good: 57%	Good: 43%
	Poor: 19%	Somewhat good: 23%
	Very poor: 7%	Very bad: 1%
Chronic conditions		
At least one condition	63%	37%
Chronic skin problems	26.80%	9.40%
Asthma	All: 15.1%	10.20%
Cancer	11.80%	4.10%
Endocrine disease (other than diabetes)	13.40%	5–10%
Diabetes	12.9% (11.5% type I,76.9% type II, 11.5% unknown)	5% (5.6% type I, 91.9% type II, 2.5% unknown)

Note: The prevalence of smoking in the French population is 34% and in our study was 30%. When multiple prevalences are reported, these are from separate studies.

our work making participatory science with the townspeople did not stop with epidemiological statistics. At the public meeting in PSL, a resident and local environmental activist raised his hand and commented, "This data is not us – our lives are not charts and figures." Our work with the citizens to produce rigorous, relevant science was not yet complete. There was a final step, and maybe the most important one, that was yet to come: building a recognizable context in which the data was relevant and had local meaning.

Contextualizing data: from health statistics to residents' science

Making deeply contextualized science that is empirically strong and valid for communities requires further work on the part of the researcher. Strongly participatory science needs to start from the questions that the local people actually have about their health and their environment, but it must go further than simply producing numeric data and statistics. While relevant data does represent the production of "undone science" in contested places, more needs to happen before the lay population have strong science that can become change-agent knowledge.

Along with a community's quest for science come other effects of the power differential that led to the lack of science in the first place. Often the making of science, "… indeed, what comes to count as legitimate knowledge – does not occur on a symmetrical field, but rather in a complex structure of relations of domination and subordination … [wh]ere dominant scientific cultures define what counts as legitimate knowledge acquisition methods, data, and analysis" (Suryanarayanan and Kleinman 2012: 219, citing Wynne 2003). Typically, the local population had suspicions about illnesses in their community, only to be told otherwise by state officials (Allen 2003, 2014). In the case of France there were no less than a dozen environmental health studies conducted for the benefit of the local residents living in the Étang de Berre industrial region, all showing there was little cause for concern or that there was too much uncertainty in the results such that more studies needed to be done (Allen et al. 2016). There were no studies verifying the illnesses that the local residents and their doctors saw on a regular basis. This gave the citizens a less than clear voice as they tried to explain why they did not trust or believe the studies. The state, over many years, was in effect telling the people that they were imagining or exaggerating their conditions. In a documentary film about health problems in the region, *Tumeurs et Silences* (2013), an epidemiologist from the regional French health service office in Marseille says, "I've never been to Fos but those reported cancers are hearsay not substantiated facts and figures."

Hermeneutical injustice occurs when there is a collective gap in fully understanding the issues, even when there is an underlying feeling that something is wrong – something that is fully in their interests to make communicable. According to Fricker, "relations of unequal power can skew shared hermeneutical resources so that the powerful tend to have appropriate understandings of their experiences … [and] the powerless are more likely to find themselves having … experiences through a glass darkly, with at best ill-fitting meanings to draw on in the effort to render them intelligible" (2007, 148). Often the language of science, and more specifically regulatory science, exacerbates the injustice because those who cannot speak that language are left on the outside, looking in to a knowledge arena that they would do well to understand and participate in.

Additionally, for people of color and those in poor and working-class communities, there is the added marginalization of testimonial injustice whereby their experiences and observations about their health and environment are treated as less credible or not relevant in matters of regulation. Both testimonial and hermeneutical injustices have left people searching for a voice with which to represent what they knew empirically but could not really manifest in a way to be heard by policy makers. Years of prejudice in the "economy of credibility" (Fricker 2007, 1) left the residents of the Étang de Berre both frustrated and distrustful of the state, particularly the French health service. The lack of belief

2.2 Residents analyzing data in focus groups.

or willingness to properly investigate on the part of the state left people without words as they were continually told that what they were seeing and saying was not true.

To situate the data in the local context, we held over 30 focus group meetings with five to ten participants over a 10-week period. These were open, voluntary, and widely advertised in the two towns (Figure 2.2). Given the history of mistrust and lack of credibility of the previous health studies in the region, how we presented the data on the reports was an important discussion item. We wanted their feedback on how best to represent the epidemiological statistics for clarity and understanding. The residents knew from their own experience that people were ill and that their environment was polluted, but their voices were ignored and they were left feeling abandoned. The analyses and grounding of the statistics in local experience was one of the main purposes of the focus group discussions. We included quotes from the residents adjacent to the health statistics charts in the relevant sections of the final report. Thus, the relationship of numerical data is clearly aligned with local narratives even to outside readers, policy makers, and the press.

In the case of surprising or contradictory findings, the groups were useful in making sense of confusing data. For example, the discussions provided a lens with which to examine the conceptualization and management of chronic illness and discomfort. The study revealed that 37% of the French population reported at least one chronic condition, as compared to 63% of the study's respondents. However, the local residents and the French population's self-reported wellness indicators were about the same with approximately 70% of both groups reporting their perceived overall health to be between "excellent" and "good." In discussing the statistics, the residents arrived at the idea of the "normalization of illness" in their communities. Further discussion revealed that some residents maintained their perception of "wellness" through prescription medication. One woman remarked that "we are artificially healthy by managing our conditions."

Respiratory issues were common topics for discussion in the focus groups (Figure 2.3 shows the proximity of industry to housing). Asthma in adults was reported in over 15% of the residents compared to only 10.2% of the French population. Over 40% of the adult population and 23% of the children suffered from at least one form of chronic non-asthma respiratory illness including bronchitis, emphysema, and respiratory allergies not related to hay fever, as compared to 7% of the French population. This increased prevalence was an issue with the participants, especially given that smoking was somewhat lower than in the French population: 30% as compared to 34%. Additionally, 48% of the respondents with asthma in the study said their disease began in adulthood. This is unusual since asthma begins most often in childhood and, over time, this and related respiratory illnesses are less pronounced in adults (Jacquemin et al. 2015). Discussion among the participants led to their conclusions that air pollution was more likely the culprit. My team would follow up their hypotheses by searching for recent medical publications and would often come back to the participants to confirm their ideas with published studies. In the case of air pollution, my team found that some scientists suggest that atmospheric pollutants have a role in triggering adult-onset asthma (ibid.) Having asthma affected people's daily lives: 28% of those who reported having asthma missed school or work because of their illness, and 25% had been hospitalized because of it. In the study, neither income nor education level could account for hospitalization due to asthma, so social disparities was not an explanation. Discussion led to

2.3 Homes and industry in Fos-sur-Mer.

the conclusion that hospitalization could be due to the duration and intensity of attacks or in relation to a person's first attack.

A pneumologist from Arles who had once practiced in Port-Saint-Louis expressed interest in, and attended, the local group focused on asthma. She was verbally working out her understanding of the asthma phenomena as she participated in the group discussion:

> It is not surprising to find more respiratory diseases in a region where there are factories because there are emissions … that makes sense … But there are things I cannot put into words and I thought of coming to your working groups … What is interesting for me in your study are the nose–throat symptoms, which are not usually listed and I have the impression that in twenty years we will say that they are precursors of certain diseases …

Participants explained how their bodies and lives are disrupted during "bad air days":

> I have been on cortisone for the past fifteen days [when an air alert was in effect] and I could not go out of my house. If the focus group had taken place yesterday, I could

not have come as there was no wind and it was unbreathable. I get coughing fits in my sleep and am awakened … sometimes I am afraid as I cannot seem to take a breath. (Asthma group participant)

In July 2015 during an air alert period, I had trouble breathing. It was a crisis for me and the fireman had to come to my house. It was during the holidays … (Fos-sur-Mer participant)

I have a tingling in my throat and choking sensations at night with difficulties swallowing. It happens at least once a month when there is no wind [to blow the pollution away] … (Fos-sur-Mer participant)

Children's sports and personal exercise habits were topics of discussion around air pollution. One mother described her son, who did not have asthma but who experienced breathing difficulties and "whistles" when playing soccer on a field directly adjacent to industrial sites:

Are refineries not able to adjust their off-gassing to not coincide with children's soccer schedules and off-gas only on windy days? Basically, I think the plants off-gas according to performance requirements, and not according to the weather … The football field, with brand new synthetic turf, is right on the trajectory of the smoke. Could they not have found a better place in town to practice football? (Fos-sur-Mer participant)

The impossible cohabitation between outdoor exercise and industrial practices was a point of frustration and adaptation. A cyclist mentioned that he puts his bike in his car and begins his touring 20 to 30 kilometers north of the city. A jogger noted that on cloudy days it is more difficult to breathe at the end of his usual loop than in clear weather. Explains another Port-Saint-Louis participant: "We are advised not to do too much sport when it is polluted, but it is hard to live that way."

There are also other ways that the townspeople dealt with the heavy load of pollutants on their bodies. Numerous participants mentioned going to cleaner environments for vacations as much as possible – and noted how well they could breathe and how much better they felt when they came back. One participant said (echoing others), "We go twice a year for two weeks in the Pyrenees, and twice a year for two weeks in the southwest too – we go there to breathe." Another respondent explained that "we have to go to the mountains and when we're there, it's better, and we breathe – and as soon as we come back here, we feel the difference."

The view of many participants was that particularly noxious releases happened at night:

The first year here I thought I'd go crazy at night, with the noise of factories that does not stop for a moment. Sometimes I wear earplugs. I wake up always tired in the morning. (A resident recently settled in Fos-sur-Mer)

Yesterday I returned at four-o'clock in the morning and it was fireworks. The plants were flaring as when they have to release more pollution ... and I do not know why it happens so often at night. Yesterday it was at Esso, spitting out from everywhere and we could see these smoke clouds. (Port-Saint-Louis participant)

The representative of Air PACA (the air monitoring association) indicated that the factories are operated on a continual basis, around the clock, for economic reasons. However, some residents mentioned feeling greater effects of pollution at night, when their windows were open or when they were outside. This local belief could be because in calm weather the pollution stagnates closer to the ground, which is cooler at night. The increased visibility of the flares at night also reinforces the belief about more flaring after dark, thus bolstering the distrust the citizens feel about industry.

Cancer was another common topic among participants trying to make sense of the health data. While the prevalence of cancer in the towns was 11.8% compared to 4.1% for the French population, it was much higher for women (14.5%) as compared to men (8.3%) in our study. Furthermore, while the most common cancers in the living population in France were breast, prostate, and colon, in our study uterine cancer was in third place, displacing colon cancer in prevalence. The residents and local doctors in our groups discussed this alarming data:

Of course the uterus should not be there as normally gynecological cancers are further down in the rankings ... so it is striking to see the uterus as it is a serious disease ... and one dies from it. (Oncologist participant in the cancer focus group)

Our workshop leaders checked and confirmed what the oncologist had said: cancer of the uterus is serious as the 10-year survival rate is estimated at 68% (Grosclaude et al. 2013, 4). Another doctor in the group mentioned the possibility that uterine cancer may have even been under-reported as women having hysterectomies did not always report a cancer, which may have been present, or have developed later. Participants discussed the endocrine-disrupting nature of some of the polluting chemicals as a possible reason for elevated cancers in hormone-dependent areas of the body, noting that thyroid cancer was also elevated. Other ideas that emerged were that women's cancers (such as breast cancer) generally have a good prognosis and can be managed over time and survived. They also hypothesized that women were more likely to seek treatment early and be vigilant in their medical regimes.

Noting the absence of certain cancers with poor prognoses (i.e., lung and pancreas), focus group participants wondered whether men might be more impacted by these diseases. We explained that their absence does not mean that they do not exist, but that either our numbers were too low for inclusion (i.e., fewer than 10 cases for privacy and statistical reasons) or that people with these illnesses were too sick to answer our survey. The two Fos EPSEAL (*Étude participative en santé environnement ancrée localement sur le front industriel de Fos-sur-Mer et Port-Saint-Louis-du-Rhône*) team members relayed to the participants that at least once a day while they were collecting the door-to-door surveys someone would respond, "I am too ill to speak with you," or "It's too difficult to talk as my husband is in the middle of dealing with cancer," or, "Thank you mademoiselle, but I am seriously ill and do not want to talk about it." We explained to the participants that mortality studies are often better at capturing the prevalence of fast-acting cancers.

Another anomaly in the study was that 15% of residents who reported having cancer also reported having or having had more than one type of cancer (two to four cancers per person). A cumulative number of cancers in the same person can sometimes happen, but the doctors, including an oncologist, in our groups felt that the frequency of this phenomenon in the study, as well as the nature of the associated cancer sites, seemed atypical. Dr. Vincent Besin, a recently retired local physician in Port-Saint-Louis who attended some of the focus groups, explained his professional view in an earlier interview:

> You have different stages of illness in this area. First, are the immunological diseases (lupus, *vascularites*/phlebitis, skin disease, respiratory illness, chronic bronchitis) followed by cancers such as immunological cancers, and then sarcomas of the lung, lymph, and different kinds of pharynx/throat cancers. Finally, in some cases, the same person has a multiple cancers and/or cardiac disease or attacks. My wife (also a local physician) and I consider that there are three stages in time for a pathology here, on a period of twenty years: (1) small incidents stage; (2) strange disease stage where it looks like the disease you've studied in text books, but with always a little difference; and (3) catastrophic stage with cancers, strokes.[5]

Some of the groups focused on particular neighborhoods where residents wanted to better understand the data in context. At the beginning of our health survey, there were a number of residents in Fos-sur-Mer who had told us they thought the Carabins neighborhood had more serious health problems, specifically cancer, than the rest of the town (see Figure 2.1; Carabins delineated by area I and J). In order to collect neighborhood-specific data during the collection phase of our project, each town was divided into a grid, such that health outcomes could be assessed by zone. Our survey data did show that the Carabins neighborhood had nearly double the cancer prevalence than Fos-sur-Mer and Port-Saint-Louis, which themselves had almost double the cancer prevalence of the French population. This was discussed in the groups with the goal of trying to better understand this negative health outcome. First, our team ruled out socioeconomic disparities as this neighborhood was the least economically depressed in our study with only 4% of the population living in poverty as compared to 20% in Port-Saint-Louis or 10% in Fos-sur-Mer. Additionally, the number of Carabins residents exposed to industrial pollution in their current jobs is lower than the study average and about the same as the other two towns in previous employment, thus occupational exposure is not an explanation on the face of it. However, the residents' reflection on the history of the neighborhood yielded some possible explanations. People recalled that many men from this neighborhood worked in the steel plant, spending hours in very demanding locations such as the coking plant, the blast furnaces, and welding. This was also one of the least transient neighborhoods in Fos-sur-Mer, with residents living there 25 years, on average. According to one resident of that area:

> It's true that in the neighborhood there was a lot of illness. One of our neighbors had two sons both die of cancer at about thirty years old. One had a brain tumor, the other I don't know. On our street there were other brain tumors … I do not know if it's a coincidence, but it's true in our neighborhood that a lot of cancer exists and it really worries us.

The groups' last hypothesis was the location of the Carabins neighborhood relative to air pollutants as, regardless of which way the wind was blowing, the area was engulfed in a toxic plume. A scientist from Air PACA attended one of the focus groups and expressed doubts about differentiated air quality within the zone. He first said that the air pollutants impacting the zones were more or less homogeneous. However, during a discussion with the residents he acknowledged that the exposure profile to air pollutants was more clearly industrial in Fos, with a particular cumulative exposure to pollutants in the air of the Carabins neighborhood.

Reflexively speaking, some group participants questioned whether meeting to share stories about chronic illness was advised. One woman said that she felt she might be ill and the discussion groups made her more worried. Other residents expressed concern that our focus group meetings could further normalize their pathologies and thus make complaints banal or citizens less inclined to take action. Others felt that the normalization of illness could be seen as a form of resilience in that they perceive themselves as living well and closer to nature compared to their urban counterparts.

People also wanted more reliable and accurate information, with sources considered legitimate locally, about the possible impacts of their environment on their health. The inhabitants were conscious of living in a specific environment that required a more detailed and contextualized attention, particularly in view of the power asymmetry of the forces involved. The lack of intellectual honesty of the industrialists in their communication with the inhabitants engendered a climate of distrust that sustained local controversies and suspicions:

> You have to have data to know what you are talking about … except perhaps to challenge the visual observations … When I was working at Sollac, I expressed my opinion to my colleagues, on the pH levels of the water in the basin, because of the color … Well I was right, they had to re-calibrate the device that had made a wrong measurement … Also what astonishes me in Fos is the Blue Flag! [referring to the public air quality alert system, blue indicating the air is clean] (Fos-sur-Mer participant and retired industrial worker)

Discussion

Lack of representation of the local people in earlier studies conducted by the state served to "misframe" the health issues of the population and, thus, "misrecognize" the problems the citizens had been trying to convey, leading to a sense of environmental injustice (Fraser 2010). This led to a deep mistrust among citizens of the French health service since they were treated as if their voices did not matter when it came to their own health – a testimonial injustice. Given that trust and credibility are relational, the exclusionary protocols and behavior of the state agents all but ensured a negative rapport with local citizens (Wynne 1992).

While our project also collected data about health, unlike the state, we started with local health questions to build a participatory survey and rigorous epidemiology data. This was a "scientized" response to the many state studies that showed little or no evidence of increased illness in the region. This approach has potential pitfalls. On a cautionary note, explain Kimura and Kinchy (2016, 349): "In a context where regulatory agencies will only respond to scientific data, rather than in a community's widely-held knowledge of environmental illness, it may be necessary to present grievances in the form of scientific data, but this devalues the knowledge of non-scientists and minimizes questions of social justice." I argue, however, that the knowledge of laypersons can be embedded in the kinds of statistical data that are policy ready. Situated science, knowledge inclusive of the lay public's voice, can become an incredible tool for shaping local and even national environments.

The key to hybridizing data is collaborative analysis. In our project, the linking of quantitative to qualitative data has increased the relevance of the study results to both residents and local medical professionals. The participants in the analysis workshops discussed the data, making sense of the numbers from their perspective. All of the quotations from residents and local doctors in the preceding section were included in the final 72-page report for our health survey, called Fos EPSEAL (Allen et al. 2017a). In the various sections divided by illness type, these stories and hypotheses of the local residents and medical professionals were presented side by side with the statistical data. This served, in the report, to structurally align the qualitative data with its quantitative counterpart, engendering greater interpretive representativeness and thus ownership of the study by the citizens.

The final report was presented to the residents and then to a large public audience in Marseille in January 2017 and the data published soon after (Allen et al. 2017a; Cohen et al. 2017). Immediately after, the report was available online and received a lot of attention from the local and national media over the course of the next year. Within months, there had been over 100 newspaper/magazine articles, medical journal discussions, radio programs, and television reports about the health outcomes revealed by the Fos EPSEAL study. The coverage often featured several local residents and doctors speaking authoritatively about their local health issues, using the study as evidence. The media buzz also generated numerous requests from other polluted towns in France, wanting a similar study. Generally, these towns were also the beneficiaries of official government health studies telling them that little or nothing was wrong with them even though, like Fos and PSL, they had empirical evidence that told them otherwise.

The French health service was contacted by the press after the release of our study. They were asked to comment on why their multiple studies did not align with ours and instead revealed few, if any, health problems in the region. Their response was to conduct an evaluation of our study and methodology, releasing it in early 2018 (Rapport 2018). Their rhetoric when speaking publicly about the project was to frame our project as "opinions" or "perceptions" of the residents. We continually corrected them by explaining that we were measuring prevalence of illness based on self-reporting and emphasized that many of our questions began with, "Have you ever been diagnosed by a doctor with …?"

In the end, the French health service report was mostly positive and their main disagreements with our study – the representativeness of the sample, the indicators used, and the types of data standardization – were, according to our team epidemiologist, typical disagreements within the field itself. However, one of their critiques of something very important to our methodology caught our attention. The health service stated that:

> After data collection, the quantitative results of the study were discussed with the local people. In drafting the report, to ensure a clear presentation, a rigorous structuring separating the statistical results from their local interpretation is necessary. (Rapport 2018, 16)

In a meeting we had with the French health service, following their report, they reiterated their displeasure that our Fos EPSEAL report presented the health outcomes data alongside the residents' interpretation of that data including their hypotheses regarding causation.[6] However, their report continues:

> The effort and resources devoted to the discussion of the final results with the population is a strong point of the Fos EPSEAL study ... The explanatory hypotheses put forward by the inhabitants was analyzed with the disciplinary knowledge of the medical professionals invited to the focus groups, in order to refine them ... The purpose of these discussions was to increase the impact of results, particularly in local decision-making, engaging the community ... (Rapport 2018, 18)

Though the health service had some typical disciplinary disagreements with our study, they realized that the hybridization of data, even though it made them uncomfortable, was the actual strength of the Fos EPSEAL study. Following the initial study, we hosted an ANSES-funded training workshop to teach 25 French scholars and health professionals how to conduct a CBPEH survey similar to ours. Several professionals from the French health service enrolled. Additionally, following a presentation of our project's participatory approach at the French health service's 2018 "Public Health Days," one of their lead epidemiologists asked if we would be willing to lead a similar training for them, which is a positive sign for the future of this resident-inclusive methodology at the institutional level in France. In a final meeting between my team and a group of French health service officials, they said that while a "declarative" study such as ours could be complementary to their work, it did not supplant their own studies from "medico-administrative data."[7]

Conclusion

Since the study was released, it has been used in a number of important ways to pressure for positive change. Mayor Renaudi of Fos has used the survey to try to stop the expansion of the incinerator that burns all the garbage from the city of Marseille. In a letter to Mayor Gaudin of Marseille, the second largest city in France, Renaudi states: "We have data." Additionally, politicians of PSL have used the study to try to stop excess release permits by industry. Doctors of the nearby hospital have applied for funding to study some of the connections between health outcomes uncovered by the Fos EPSEAL study. At the end of every focus group we asked the participants to come up with "next steps" now that they have the data they have been wanting. They came up with dozens of ideas, including better air quality warning systems, indoor play facilities for schools, local access to medical specialists, better public transportation to discourage auto traffic, and dissemination of recommendations and "best practices" for local food consumption. Other ideas for city administrators were suggested, such as ending mechanical blowing for street cleaning, reducing pesticide spraying for mosquitos, and adding charging stations to promote electric cars. The townspeople were energized and, in 2018, seven citizen groups, several workers' unions, and 260 citizens filed both civil and criminal lawsuits against the state and industry for endangering their health – a first in France (Nossiter 2020).

In thinking about the transferability of this epidemiology-based, strongly participatory approach to other sites, nationally and internationally, both difficulties and potentials come to mind. One of the criticisms of our study from the regional prefecture, faced with citizen groups wanting a similar health study, was its cost, approximately €200,000. This included door-to-door surveying done by post-docs as well as a US-based epidemiologist and project director. The cost could be lowered by having volunteer or student surveyors and only hiring graduate students or post-docs to run the focus groups. Additionally, having locally based epidemiologists and project directors would decrease travel costs. There is also the issue of funding sources, as even if the cost could be cut in half, it is still prohibitive for many communities.

Another barrier to transferability of this kind of study is the way in which the questions were asked. We ascertained illness prevalence by asking residents if they had been so diagnosed by a doctor. In countries such as the United States and developing nations, where healthcare may not be available to everyone, questions would have to be framed differently, possibly expanded to capture symptoms and chronic conditions. While there is clearly work to be done in developing an approach that is accessible to vulnerable communities worldwide, there is some additional promise to consider. Often, communities exposed to industrial pollution witness a number of rare diseases, such as pediatric cancer, that are hard to assess with anecdotal (e.g., disease clusters) or statistical tools given their small numbers. However, with a non-state controlled participatory study, health outcomes data could be aggregated across inhabited areas with similar pollutant exposures in multiple countries producing statistically significant results. This has the potential of showing correlations between specific illnesses and particular pollutants, something that single site studies typically cannot reveal.

In conclusion, the public, such as residents in polluted communities, have salient knowledge about their health and environment that needs to be taken seriously. This is important knowledge-in-context, health seen from the perspective of those that live it daily. If the only people who are allowed to be experts of people's health are people sitting in offices far from the polluted towns and sites, and if the "disembodied" science that they create is the only measure of health, then we do not have a robust health outcome picture. Furthermore, if only outside experts with political power and authority get to define the health and environmental issues to be addressed and select the terms of deliberation, then democracy has not been well served. However, in making the case for "knowledge democracy" (Marres 2018a) or "knowledge justice" (Allen 2018) today we must be clear that we are not aligning with anti-science or anti-intellectual viewpoints evident on the political right. Expanding the realm of expertise to include embodied public knowledge, specifically what residents of environmentally degraded environments observe on a daily basis, strengthens science. Broadening what can be known about the places that we live in beyond the authority of experts, to further empirical public validation, is not playing into deception and demagoguery of populism and post-truth politics (Hoffman 2018). Instead, as the Fos EPSEAL project has demonstrated, the robust inclusion of local people in the making of environmental health science – from the questions asked to the in-depth collaborative analyses of the data collected – leads to more relevant and effective science in contested regions.

Funding note: This research was supported the Agence Nationale de Sécurité Sanitaire de l'alimentation, de l'environnement et du travail (ANSES) (award number: PNREST Anses, Cancer ITMO AVIESAN, 2014/1/023 and EST/2017/1/035), and also received support from the Institut Méditerranéen de Recherches Avancées (IMéRA) in Marseille, France.

Notes

1   Strong objectivity is about transparency and inclusiveness in the making of scientific knowledge. On one hand, it is about including the observations and hypotheses of diverse stakeholders in the shaping of science, and on the other hand, it is about revealing voices and interests that have been hidden from view in traditional science, also termed by Harding (2015) "weakly objective science."

2   During this project, I conducted over 45 semi-structured interviews focusing on citizen inclusion or exclusion in the environmental policy process. Written consent was obtained where names are used, and the interviews were transcribed and translated into English.

3 ANSES (Agence Nationale de Sécurité Sanitaire de l'Alimentation, de l'Environnement, et du Travail) is a relatively new French agency for food, environmental, and occupational health.

4 Alison Cohen was at the time a doctoral candidate in epidemiology at the University of California, Berkeley. She had experience in designing and conducting CBPEH studies in polluted communities in California (Cohen et al. 2012).

5 Vincent Besin, retired physician, interviewed by Barbara Allen and Yolaine Ferrier (translator), in Port-Saint-Louis-du-Rhône, December 9, 2013.

6 Our process with regard to the local participants' theories of disease causation or correlation was to follow up by searching in the peer-reviewed literature for studies verifying their ideas. Oftentimes we found such studies and brought them back to the focus groups in subsequent meetings. We also invited medical specialists to our group meetings and they hypothesized with the residents, adding their opinions where appropriate.

7 From distance meeting with Santé Publique France, March 21, 2018.

References

Allen, B. 2003. *Uneasy Alchemy: Citizens and Experts in Louisiana's Chemical Corridor Disputes.* Cambridge, MA: MIT Press.

Allen, B. 2014. The social construction of non-knowledge. *Perspectives: Journal Réseau français des Instituts détudes avancées*, 12(Winter), 9. Available at http://rfiea.fr/articles/social-construction-non-knowledge (last accessed January 23, 2020).

Allen, B. 2017. A successful experiment in participatory science for promoting change in a french industrial region. *Engaging Science, Technology, and Society*, 3, 375–381.

Allen, B. 2018. Strongly participatory science and knowledge justice in an environmentally contested region. *Science, Technology and Human Values*, 1–25. DOI: 10.1177/0162243918758380.

Allen, B., Cohen, A., Ferrier, Y., Lees, J., and Richards, T. 2016. Redesigning a participatory health study for French industrial context. *New Solutions: A Journal of Environmental and Occupational Health Policy*, 26(3), 458–474.

Allen, B., Cohen, A., Ferrier, Y., and Lees, J. 2017a. *FOS EPSEAL: Etude participative en santé environnement ancrée localement sur le front industriel de Fos-sur-Mer et Port-Saint-Louis-du-Rhône.* Available at https://fosepseal.hypotheses.org/rapport-de-letude-fos-epseal-janvier-2017 (last accessed January 23, 2020).

Allen, B., Ferrier, Y., and Cohen, A. 2017b. Through a maze of studies: Health questions and "undone science" in a French industrial region. *Environmental Sociology*, 3(2), 134–144.

Cohen, A., Lopez, A., Malloy, N., et al. 2012. Our environment, our health: A community-based participatory environmental health survey in Richmond, California. *Health Education & Behavior*, 39(2), 198–209.

Cohen, A., Richards, T., Allen, B., Ferrier, Y., Lees, J., and Smith, L. 2017. Health issues in the industrial port zone of Marseille, France: The Fos EPSEAL community-based cross-sectional survey. *Journal of Public Health*, 26(2), 235–243. DOI: 10.1007/s10389-017-0857-5.

Fraser, N. 2010. *Scales of Justice: Reimagining Political Space in a Globalizing World*. New York: Columbia University Press.

Fricker, M. 2007. *Epistemic Injustice: Power and the Ethics of Knowing*. Oxford: Oxford University Press.

Garnier, J. 2001. *L'évolution du complexe industriel de Fos/Lavéra/Etang de Berre*. Aix-en-Provence: Laboratoire d'Economie et de Sociologie du Travail, CNRS.

Grosclaude, P., et al. 2013. Survie des personnes atteintes de cancer en France, 1989–2007. *Etude à partir des registres des cancers du réseau Francim*. Synthèse, Institut national de Veille Sanitaire, Paris: Santé Publique France.

Haklay, M. 2013. Citizen science and volunteered geographic information: Overview and typology of participation. In D. Sui, S. Elwood, and M. Goodchild (eds), *Crowdsourcing Geographic Knowledge*. New York: Springer, pp. 105–122.

Harding, S. 1991. *Whose Science? Whose Knowledge?: Thinking from Women's Lives*. Ithaca, NY: Cornell University Press.

Harding, S. 2008. *Sciences from Below: Feminisms, Postcolonialities, and Modernities*. Durham, NC: Duke University Press.

Harding, S. 2015. *Objectivity and Diversity: Another Logic of Scientific Research*. Chicago: University of Chicago Press.

Hess, D. 2007. *Alternative Pathways in Science and Industry: Activism, Innovation, and the Environment in an Era of Globalization*. Cambridge, MA: MIT Press.

Hess, D. 2015. Undone science and social movements: A review and typology. In M. Gross and L. McGoey (eds), *Routledge International Handbook of Ignorance Studies*. New York: Routledge, pp. 141–154.

Hess, D., Sulfikar, A., Frickel, S., Kleinman, D., Moore, K., and Williams, L. 2017. Structural inequality and the politics of science and technology. In U. Felt, R. Fouché, C. Miller, and L. Smith-Doerr (eds), *Handbook of Science and Technology Studies*. Cambridge, MA: MIT Press, pp. 319–347.

Hoffman, S. 2018. The responsibilities and obligations of STS in a moment of post-truth demagoguery. *Engaging Science, Technology, and Society*, 4, 444–452.

Irwin, A. 2015. Citizen science and scientific citizenship: same words, different meanings? In B. Schiele, J. Marec, and P. Baranger (eds), *Science Communication Today*. Nancy: Presses Universitaires de Nancy, pp. 29–38.

Jacquemin, B., et al. 2015. Ambient air pollution and adult asthma incidence in six European cohorts (ESCAPE). *Environmental Health Perspectives*, 123(6), 613–621.

Kimura, A. and Kinchy, A. 2016. Citizen science: Probing the virtues and contexts of participatory research. *Engaging Science, Technology, and Society*, 2, 331–361.

Kinchy, A. 2016. Citizen science and democracy: Participatory water monitoring in the Marcellus shale fracking boom. *Science as Culture*. DOI: 10.1080/09505431.2016.1223113.

Marres, N. 2018a. Why we can't have our facts back. *Engaging Science, Technology, and Society*, 4, 423–443.

Marres, N. 2018b."Response to Steven Hoffman's "The Responsibilities and Obligations of STS in a Moment of Post-Truth Demagoguery". *Engaging Science, Technology, and Society*, 4, 453–457.

Moore, K., Hess, D., Kleinman, D., and Frickel, S. 2011. Science and Neoliberal Globalization. *Theory and Society*, 40, 505–532.

Nossiter, A. 2020. "One of Europe's Most Polluted Towns Stages a Noisy Revolt". *New York Times*, April 1. https://www.nytimes.com/2020/04/01/world/europe/france-pollution-fos-sur-mer.html (last accessed May 1, 2020).

Ottinger, G. 2010. Buckets of resistance: Standards and the effectiveness of citizen science. *Science, Technology & Human Values*, 35(2), 244–270. DOI: 10.1177/01622439093371 21.

Ottinger, G. 2013. *Refining Expertise: How Responsible Engineers Subvert Environmental Justice Challenges*. New York: NYU Press.

Rapport d'analyse de l'etude Fos-EPSEAL. 2018. Saisine No. 17-DSPE-0217-1513-D. Saint-Maurice: Santé Publique France. http://invs.santepubliquefrance.fr/Publications-et-outils/Rapports-et-syntheses/Environnement-et-sante/2018/Rapport-d-analyse-de-l-etude-Fos-Epseal (last accessed January 24, 2020).

Shapiro, N. 2015. Attuning to the chemosphere: Domestic formaldehyde, bodily reasoning, and the chemical sublime. *Cultural Anthropology*, 30(3), 368–393.

Sismondo, S. 2017. Post-truth? *Social Studies of Science*, 47(1), 3–6.

Suryanarayanan, S. and Kleinman, D. 2012. B(e)ecoming experts: The controversy over insecticides in the honey bee colony collapse disorder. *Social Studies of Science*, 43(2), 215–240.

Winderberger, J. 2013. *Tumeurs et Silences* (film).

Wynne, B. 1992. Misunderstood misunderstanding: social identities and public uptake of science. *Public Understanding of Science*, 1(3), 281–304.

3

Crude justice: Community-based research amid oil development in South Los Angeles

Bhavna Shamasunder, Jessica Blickley,
Marissa Chan, Ashley Collier-Oxandale,
James L. Sadd, Sandy Navarro, Nicole J. Wong,
and Michael Hannigan

The public health consequences and environmental injustices stemming from oil development in densely populated urban environments are of increasing concern to residents surrounding oil and gas development facilities. The Los Angeles Basin contains one of the highest concentrations of crude oil in the world, with over 5,000 active oil wells in Los Angeles County. Oil was struck in the Los Angeles Basin in the 1890s and reached its production peak in the 1930s, making up nearly half of California's oil production at the time and nearly one quarter of the world's oil output. Oil development shaped, and oftentimes dominated, Los Angeles's development as a global city (Pratt et al. 2014). Today, although oil wells are scattered across the city and county, it is poor communities and communities of color that live closer to wells, have outdated emissions equipment, and have the oil fields near to homes uncovered rather than enclosed (Reyes 2016). The legacy of decision making over oil drilling in Los Angeles is that thousands of active wells in the greater Los Angeles area are located among a dense population of more than 10 million people. Seventy percent of active oil wells in the city are located within 1,500 feet (457 meters) of a home or sensitive land use such as a school, playground, or hospital – places where people live, work, and play (Sadd and Shamasunder 2015).

Oil development in Los Angeles grew side by side with urbanization. In some communities, such as the South Los Angeles neighborhood of West Adams, residences were destroyed to make room for oil development operations, and houses now sit adjacent to the 36-well field site. The city and counties of Los Angeles require no setback distances, allowing houses to sit adjacent to an oil field wall and as close as 60 feet (18 meters) from operating wells.

Oil industry operations in Los Angeles benefited from a history of more than a century of coordination among state and local governments to smooth the way for ongoing oil production, even as the city's population grew and despite periods of public scrutiny or protest (Sabin 2004; Quam-Wickham 2015; Shamasunder 2018). This coordination took place in the years before the passage of major US environmental legislation in the 1970s and continued into the present, as oil field permits were grandfathered[1] in and so avoided new regulatory mandates. As communities have increasingly raised concerns about nearby wells, regulatory agencies and industry have argued there is insufficient data to affirm the merits of their concern and compel regulatory agencies, the state, and corporations to respond. As connected to the larger post-truth stories presented in this volume, strong scientific evidence on an issue (such as climate change) (Oreskes and Conway 2011) may be weighed alongside efforts to cast doubt on existing knowledge or call for ever more data collection as a way to delay or deter action.

In Los Angeles, today's environmental justice struggles to address health hazards from oil contamination in neighborhoods are inherited from decades of environmental justice activism in the region (Shamasunder 2018). Community-led efforts by a coalition of frontline organizations have brought attention to the consequences of active oil development near a dense urban population. Communities facing long-standing enforcement disparities and a fragmented regulatory landscape have an uphill battle to shed light on the contradiction of California's portrayal as a climate change leader while neighborhood oil development continues unabated (Koseff 2018). STAND-LA (Stand Together Against Neighborhood Drilling) has been working to address impacts from oil development on neighborhood health and quality of life in environmental justice neighborhoods, and to achieve a distance setback from oil field operations and sensitive land uses such as childcare centers, schools, playgrounds, and houses. This chapter details a community-based study conducted by neighborhood organizations within the coalition in partnership with researchers to systematically collect neighborhood-level health data near to two wells that could be compared with city- and county-wide health data as well as to gain a stronger understanding of how residents experienced living near to oil development. The project is detailed below.

Community-based science amid urban oil development

The environmental justice (EJ) movement in the United States has, since the 1980s, moved forward an agenda of environmental protection through a racial justice and civil rights framework. Struggles by environmental justice communities argued that residents are entitled to clean and healthy environments in places where they live, work, play, and pray regardless of race, ethnicity, or socioeconomic status. Frontline communities often live in neighborhoods with multiple environmental hazards. The health consequences of exposure to these hazards can be compounded by social and economic vulnerabilities of race, poverty, age, and linguistic isolation, among other factors, thereby constituting a cumulative impact (Office of Environmental Health Hazard Assessment 2014).

Environmental justice activists have taken a multi-pronged approach to confronting environmental inequalities that leverage tactics inside and outside of government, with one strategy of collaborating with academics to generate relevant data that can contribute to improved state response (Morello-Frosch et al. 2005). However, some scholars have argued for the movement activists to deploy more diverse and multi-scalar methodological approaches with attention to strategies outside of regulatory relief, to recognize the role of the state in perpetuating injustice and find new avenues to confront entrenched inequality and systems of oppression (Pulido 2016; Pellow 2017). Yet, community-based participatory research (CBPR) and citizen science efforts have remained vital, though not singular, components of on-the-ground environmental justice efforts, with research designed around the "3Rs" – rigor, reach, and relevance – being critical to scientific findings (Balazs and Morello-Frosch 2013). While many of these struggles are rooted in political contest, the local state still relies on scientific data in decision-making processes, making the knowledge-making and fact-establishing process maintain continued relevance, despite these limitations (Jasanoff 1987).

EJ community organizations have historically documented health and environmental consequences from polluting industries and other incompatible land uses located near their homes, schools, and playgrounds. Poor communities of color that are impacted by multiple sources of pollution often actively seek information and gather data to demonstrate the hazards and risks they face, and to inform policy and decision making (Brown 1992; Cole and Foster 2001). In Los Angeles, residents near oil development sites have routinely reported health symptoms such as nosebleeds and headaches. These symptoms have also been described in other oil and gas production areas around the country (Witter et al. 2013). Oil production and drilling is associated with exposure to hazardous air pollutants (HAPs) and toxicants, such as BTEX chemicals (benzene, toluene, ethylbenzene, and xylene) (Macey et al. 2014). In addition, secondary drilling and production enhancement practices inject fluids into oil and gas reservoir rocks to enhance recovery of hydrocarbon products. In Los Angeles, acidizing is routinely used, where large volumes and high concentrations of hydrochloric acid, hydrofluoric acid, or other chemicals are injected underground, mixing and reacting with other well fluids, most of which lack adequate hazard evaluations. Oil development facilities within the South Coast Basin submit chemical use reports for certain well activities, and these reports show chemical ingredients with known air toxics such as hydrogen chloride, xylene, hydrofluoric acid, and ethylbenzene used as part of standard well development and maintenance acidizing practices (Abdullah et al. 2017; Stringfellow et al. 2017).

In the South Los Angeles neighborhood of West Adams, the Jefferson oil field wall is 3 feet (1 meter) away from the nearest home, and the field itself constitutes a complex of more than 60 active oil wells. For members of this primarily black and Latino neighborhood, where over 60% of residents live below the poverty line, information about the oil field, ongoing operations, and on-site hazards are hard to obtain. Chemical combinations trucked into closed compounds are shrouded in trade secret protections, and community residents must remain vigilant to learn about plans and activities at the field (Redeemer Community Partnership 2016). In June 2016, West Adams residents filed a petition for nuisance abatement to enclose the field and afford them some of the same protections found in wealthier neighborhoods (Petition for Abatement of Public Nuisance 2016). Such disparities in the enforcement and regulation of oil industry operations have prompted communities to raise questions about systemic environmental injustice by city and county agencies.

Neighborhood oil drilling health survey

In 2012 and 2013, residents of the University Park neighborhood in South Los Angeles complained of foul emissions and reported nosebleeds, headaches, and respiratory problems. These complaints coincided with increased oil production in the nearby field, where production rose 400% in one year following the purchase of the facility by AllenCo Energy Inc (from 4,178 barrels in 2009 to 21,239 barrels in 2010) (Sahagun 2013). Subsequently, the EPA (Environmental Protection Agency) fined and closed AllenCo. The facility is temporarily closed with plans to reopen once it installs emissions control equipment and receives state approval. Other extraction facilities in this and many other densely populated Los Angeles neighborhoods continue to operate.

Following resident complaints and prior to AllenCo's closure, the community embarked on a health survey that grew into a broader academic–community collaboration, on which the research for this chapter is based. Our partnership includes a coalition of residents living nearby the AllenCo and Jefferson oil fields, *promotoras de salud* (community health workers), students, and academic researchers, who came together to examine health consequences from oil development through a self-reported community health survey. We also gathered qualitative information about community knowledge of the oil field and experiences of living nearby. Our findings demonstrate adverse health impacts for asthma and respiratory harm in excess of that seen further from the well site and as compared to residents in the broader city of Los Angeles. We also found that residents often lacked knowledge of the well itself and many did not know how to report symptoms or odors, a challenge that reveals the extent of oil company obfuscation of their presence in the community and lack of regulatory attention to making community reporting to regulatory authorities transparent and accessible.

Ongoing research on health impacts from living nearby oil and gas development suggests an important spatial dimension, with residents who live closer to active wells experiencing greater adverse impacts. Residents living within half a mile (0.8 kilometers) of a gas well, compared with residents living further away from such active gas development, have worsened health consequences from exposure to emissions (Meng and Ashby 2014). Greater density and proximity of natural gas wells to maternal residences (within a 10 mile / 16 kilometer radius) were associated with adverse birth outcomes (McKenzie et al. 2014). Residential proximity has also been associated with skin and respiratory conditions in residents near natural gas extraction activities with distances typically measured at less than 0.6 to 0.12 miles (1–2 kilometers) from well to residence (Rabinowitz et al. 2014).

Proximity of residents to active oil development

Since studies of oil and gas development suggest proximity to emissions as central to considerations of public health impacts, policy relief routinely suggest setbacks or buffers as one possible public health protection (Haley et al. 2016). Los Angeles requires no buffers or setbacks, which permits very close distances between residents and extraction sites. Responding to community complaints, in April 2017 Los Angeles City Council introduced a motion for the city to study the possibility of a safety buffer (Southern California Public Radio 2017). Seventy percent of active wells in Los Angeles are located within a 1,500 foot (457 meter) distance from "sensitive land uses," such as a home, school, childcare facility, urban park or playground, or senior residential facility, as defined by Cal EPA (California Air Resources Board 2005) (Table 3.1). Setbacks have

Table 3.1 Sensitive land uses in selected areas hosting oil production facilities.

Location	Number of schools	Childcare facilities	Schools per 10,000 people	Childcare per 10,000 people	Childcare per sq. mile
LA County	3,036	3,903	3.09	3.98	1.6
LA City	1,087	1,385	2.88	3.67	2.9
Within 1,500 ft. of an active LA City well	40	29	3.25	2.35	1.5
University Park: AllenCo oil field	5	2	7.83	3.13	8.0
Historic West Adams: Jefferson oil field	1	2	1.29	2.59	8.0
Historic West Adams: Murphy oil field	3	1	5.44	1.81	4.0
Wilmington: Warren E&P oil field	0	1	0.00	2.35	2.4
Baldwin Hills: Inglewood oil field	2	7	3.64	2.35	4.4

been enacted in municipalities in Colorado, Pennsylvania, and Texas to separate oil and gas development from residences for health and safety protections. We conducted a random sample household survey of residents living within a 1,500 foot radius of oil development sites. We compared resident self-reported health within that radius to resident health in Service Planning Area 6 (SPA6), the Los Angeles County Department of Public Health designated area in which South Los Angeles is located, and to Los Angeles County residents overall.

In partnership with residents, we also piloted the use of an open-source low-cost air quality monitoring system during the survey period in West Adams (Jefferson oil field) as a pilot site. While these sensors present challenges in terms of lower accuracy/precision compared with conventional monitoring equipment (Piedrahita et al. 2014), they have led to more affordable and accessible tools that can complement existing monitoring by state agencies and serve as a screening method for concerned communities, which may be in neighborhoods that lack regulatory agency monitors. In recent years, much work has gone into understanding the capabilities of low-cost sensors (Mead et al. 2013) and they have been utilized in a variety of applications from personal exposure monitoring to high-density networks designed for monitoring in complex urban environments (Eugster and Kling 2012). In addition to providing community residents with new options for data collection, low-cost sensors allow researchers and residents to examine high time-resolution data alongside community-member knowledge, which offers another way to engage community expertise to better understand the potential impact of local emission sources, such as oil and gas operations.

The West Adams and University Park neighborhoods

The West Adams and University Park neighborhoods in South Los Angeles host well-established fields with sustained and active oil development. Community partners included Esperanza Community Housing and Redeemer Community Partnership, both member organizations of STAND-LA. Esperanza is a long-standing community organization in the University Park area, where the AllenCo oil site is located. The neighborhood is predominantly Latino (76%) with 72% of residents living 200% below the poverty line and 81% renters. Redeemer Community Partnership has been a community development corporation in the West Adams neighborhood for over 25 years and has been organizing the community around the Jefferson drill site. The neighborhood is 87% residents of color, with 58% Latino and 20% African American. Twenty percent of the population is under the age of five (as compared to 7% for Los Angeles County), 68% of residents live 200% below the poverty line, and 69% of residents are renters (Table 3.2).

Table 3.2 Demographics of West Adams and University Park within the 1,500 foot buffer.

Population	West Adams buffer area, 1,500 ft. around Jefferson oil field	University Park buffer area, 1,500 ft. around AllenCo oil field	City of Los Angeles
Total population	6,641	5,401	2,546,606
% Age 5 or under	20.90%	5.31%	7.63%
% Age 65 or older	9.92%	6.94%	6.95%
% People of color	87.82%	84.17%	72.85%
% Non-Hispanic black	20.86%	8.17%	9.99%
% Non-Hispanic white	12.18%	15.83%	27.15%
% Hispanic	58.20%	76.00%	50.85%
% Linguistically isolated	23.42%	39.21%	12.37%
% Less than high school	42.49%	46.72%	18.91%
Per capita income	$11,194	$11,203	$18,839
Median household income	$23,912	$20,115	$37,723
Poverty (< 150%)	51.51%	59.39%	20.57%
Poverty (< 200%)	64.88%	72.30%	27.57%
% Renters	68.77%	81.13%	34.70%
Median household size	2.7	3.4	1.7

Adapted from the US Census Bureau American Community Survey 5-year data set 2009–2013 2014.

Study area and sample selection

The study areas were defined to represent the neighborhoods surrounding the wells and production facilities at two locations that produce oil from the Las Cienegas oil field (Figure 3.1). Study areas were defined by constructing a circular buffer using ArcGIS (Esri, Redlands, CA, USA), with a 1,500 foot radius, surrounding the outer perimeter of the two oil production sites (Figure 3.1). The Jefferson drill site (Jefferson) is located in the West Adams neighborhood, and the AllenCo drill site (AllenCo) is located in the University Park neighborhood of Los Angeles. We chose a 1,500 foot (457 meter) buffer based on distances considered by other urban cities, such as Dallas (Austin and Zeeble 2013). Based on analysis of the population within the buffer, we selected a target minimum sample size of 76 households around AllenCo and 84 households around Jefferson, conducting the surveys at the addresses identified using a random sampling algorithm to ensure systematic sample coverage.

Community-centered research methods as a community organizing strategy

Health surveys are a recognized method of community organizing in an environmental justice context (Cohen et al. 2012). The survey provided a vehicle for community education about issues of concern in the neighborhood. Residents were able to provide their contact information if they wanted to participate in report-back from survey results or other community events. In partnership with Esperanza's trained network of community health workers, Promotoras de Salud in Action, we conducted the door-to-door surveys of residents in Spanish and English. *Promotoras de salud* live and work in the community, engage in long-term community building, and have a baseline of trust in the neighborhood. *Promotora de salud* networks are have long been recognized as community health experts within environmental justice research (Minkler et al. 2010). *Promotoras* were agile at accessing residents, many of whom work in service sector jobs, the night shift, or have other non-traditional working hours. We also trained four bilingual Occidental College students to conduct surveys alongside *promotoras*. Using the addresses generated from the random household sample, we visited each household on our list, starting in March 2016 and continuing through May 2016. If we could not find anyone at home, we returned on different days and at different times until we could complete the survey. Residents would also become interested as they saw surveyors in conversation with other residents. These residents' surveys supplemented the random sample surveys if the address

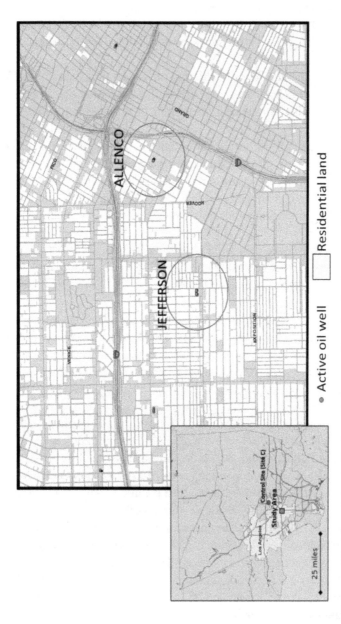

3.1 Location map. Study area is located in the mid-city area of Los Angeles, just west of downtown. Circles are 1,500-foot (457 meter) radius buffers surrounding active wells. Note active oil wells in other nearby residential neighborhoods.

fell within the 1,500 foot buffer. Through these methods, we were able to achieve a high survey response rate.

In addition to asthma and respiratory health, we asked questions about infertility and birth outcomes: community organizers were interested in these variables as many women had reported miscarriages and other adverse birth outcomes. We provided this self-reported information back to the community but we do not include an analysis of this data in published materials as we did not have specific enough data to do a birth outcomes analysis, and had informed residents in advance. Thus, that information served to inform community data collection efforts moving forward.

Esperanza Community Housing, Redeemer Community Partnership, and researchers collaboratively designed the survey to ask questions of community importance, such as ratings of the environmental quality of their neighborhood, feelings of safety living in the neighborhood, resident knowledge and experience of the site, health insurance and uninsured numbers, asthma rates, and asthma hospitalization. For detailed methods and results, see Shamasunder et al. (2018). We surveyed 84 households comprising 315 residents in University Park and 119 households comprising 498 residents in West Adams. In both sites, more than 50% of surveyed households had incomes of $20,000 or less (University Park: 57.1%, West Adams: 53.7%). Median household income according to census data (2010–2015 ACS 5-year rollup) for West Adams is $25,980, and for University Park is $20,115. This data demonstrates higher poverty levels and lower incomes as compared to the city. There is also an absence of regulatory agency monitoring nearby the operating wells. The use of low-cost sensors was piloted in this study to help provide community-level monitoring data.

A pilot of low-cost sensor use for community-based research

Low-cost sensor systems are typically small and low power, which makes them fairly easy to deploy at potential sites within the community (e.g., homes, schools, or businesses). This flexibility allows researchers and community members to work together in choosing sites that will best inform the research question. In this pilot study, the monitors were set up and maintained by community-based research partners at three field sites. These sites include three residences – one near an active drill site, one across the street from an inactive drill site, and one in an area with no drilling (our control site). Sites A and B were located in the Study Area (Figure 3.1), whereas Site C was located roughly seven miles away in Northeast Los Angeles. Site C was intended to serve as a comparison for the low-cost sensor data portion of the study, and no other measures were taken at this location. All sites were relatively similar in terms of land use and proximity to other major pollution sources (e.g., highways). The sites were selected to provide a preliminary example of what sensors can tell us regarding the differences in methane levels/trends in areas with drilling versus those without drilling. These results were preliminary and intended to explore the potential for this technology in the context of community-based participatory research (CBPR), an area where low-cost sensors are increasingly of interest in communities with little access to air monitoring, and in this instance in a cumulatively burdened, environmental justice context.

Community-based survey and low-cost sensor findings

Our random household sample and exposure monitoring within 1,500 feet of oil development sites is the first study in partnership with residents living in very close proximity to oil development in Los Angeles. It is also the first study, to our knowledge, to compare the self-reported health of residents within 1,500 feet of oil development to residents in the broader area of South Los Angeles (SPA6) and Los Angeles County. In over one hundred years of oil development in Los Angeles, with residences placed side by side with oil fields, there has been little research on the public health consequences of these land use choices. We see this study as a first step to considering community concerns.

In our results, many residents (University Park: 45.8%, West Adams: 38.9%) living within 1,500 feet of active oil development did not know that a field was located in the neighborhood. This is likely due to tall walls and landscaping surrounding both sites, and visible signage of private property and no trespassing. Indeed, the oil industry in Los Angeles made significant investment in order to limit their visibility as the region's population grew. Around the region, oil companies have built tall hedges around walls and planted landscaped gardens. For example, in 1965 a consortium of companies hired famed Disney theme park architect Joseph H. Linesch to design $10 million THUMS Island (named for the consortium of companies Texaco, Humble (now Exxon), Union, Mobil, and Shell) (Gougis 2015). The complex is a set of four artificial islands built to camouflage drill rigs with landscaping, waterfalls, and tall structures to hide from view 42 acres of oil fields and 1,100 wells in a vast underground oil field (Schoch 2006). These same strategies have been employed, to a lesser extent, around the Jefferson and AllenCo fields.

From our survey, one of the main burdens appeared to be odors, which some respondents reported as preventing daily activities (University Park: 15.7%, West Adams: 27.5%). However, only a few respondents said they had reported odors or any health symptoms to the gas company, the Los Angeles Department of Public Health, the South Coast Air Quality Management District, or any other entity, as most responded that they lacked information about how to report. Further, since most residents are unaware of these activities, they may attribute symptoms to allergies or general poor air quality.

Oil and gas development is associated in the scientific literature with degraded air quality and exposure to air pollution as well as exacerbated respiratory conditions and asthma (Rasmussen et al. 2016; Webb et al. 2016). For both University Park and West Adams, compared with SPA6, resident-reported asthma prevalence was significantly higher. Respondents in West Adams (15.5%) and University Park (12.1%) reported experiencing asthma symptoms of coughing and wheezing on a weekly or daily basis. Decreases in ambient pollution levels in southern California have been associated with statistically significant decreases in asthma-related symptoms in children (Rabinowitz et al. 2014). Children under the age of five living within the West Adams buffer area represent 20% of the population as compared to 7% of residents in the city of Los Angeles, and this group is more biologically sensitive to air pollution health impacts.

Through sensor monitors, we found that spatial differences occurred at a fine temporal scale. These differences occurred with periods of elevated methane lasting from approximately 10 minutes to up to 3 hours. These events included differences in methane between the two sites greater than 1.0 ppm (parts per million), well above the calibration site. Given that these events occurred at one site and not the other, they were likely the result of an emission source nearer to Site A. This was even more evident for the events that occurred during daytime hours when more atmospheric mixing is typically taking place (Bamberger et al. 2014). Additional measurements would aid in further narrowing down the source of these events. For example, wind speed and direction information combined with data from multiple sensors might point to the origin of emissions.

A benefit of utilizing low-cost sensors in a CBPR context is that local experience, such as observations about local activities or odors, can improve interpretations of the data. On one day, nearby residents reported seeing heavy equipment in use at the active drill site. If similar methane spikes were observed every time this activity occurred, it would indicate a correlation worthy of further investigation. Examining this qualitative data alongside quantitative data provided by low-cost sensors may result in a more robust and comprehensive understanding of the community's experiences, be responsive to community concerns, and in turn carry through and inform community-based action or policy recommendations.

Conclusion

Oil development has proceeded in Los Angeles for more than one hundred years with little attention to public health consequences of these long-lived facilities. Environmental justice communities living near active oil development are burdened by multiple polluting sources. It is difficult to examine oil-development-related impacts in cumulatively burdened neighborhoods, near freeways, diesel pollution, and other industrial sources, but it is critical to do so given the consistent reports from residents living nearby. The academic–community study detailed here is just one step in a longer, community-determined agenda. This research centers resident health concerns and the rights of residents to have knowledge about their communities and supports hypothesis generation for future air monitoring or health studies. It points to the need for regulatory agencies to provide clear, transparent, and actionable reporting structures with sustained community education on how residents can report problems such as odors, nosebleeds, or headaches. Our study leads to additional questions that require more complex scientific design and raises the imperative that centers community knowledge as new research proceeds.

Studies on oil and gas development have associated distance with worsened air pollution, an issue of significant concern in Los Angeles. Buffers or setbacks are well recognized as protective by regulatory authorities such as local air districts and should be incorporated into neighborhood oil development sites to protect community health (Penning et al. 2014). This early research helped support an infrastructure for further efforts related to oil and gas development in Los Angeles.

Los Angeles hosts the entirety of the oil supply chain, from extraction through refining, and continues to be a top oil producing hub. Community concerns over the public health consequences of oil development are deep seated, with considerable attention in environmental justice neighborhoods. Los Angeles also has a long history of environmental justice organizing and community-engaged environmental justice research. Data collection is a single prong of a larger strategy toward policies that will improve community health, making community–academic collaborations of continued relevance in on-the-ground struggles for justice.

On May 15, 2019, the city of Los Angeles announced that it is officially requiring the Jefferson oil field, owned by Sentinel Peak Resources, to close and clean up the neighborhood drill site. The field is one of the closest in the city to residences, just feet away, as well as 130 feet (40 meters) from a church and 730 feet (222 meters) from an elementary school. The city found ongoing nuisances from the drilling operation and ordered them to clean up the site in addition to closing it down. Community efforts to address the hazards from this field have been years long, and they hope the closed site can be transformed into a library or a park that will benefit the community.

Acknowledgments

This research was supported by the 11th Hour Project, a program of the Schmidt Family Foundation. Additional support for air quality monitoring was provided through the NSF-SRN AirWaterGas Project (CBET: 1240584) and the MetaSense Project (NSF grant CNS-1446912). We thank students Sofia Polo, Edgar Galicia, Daniela Borquez, and Alison Salazar and Promotoras de Salud in Action, a program of Esperanza Community Housing, for their dedication and ongoing work in the community. The contents of this article are solely the responsibility of the authors and do not necessarily represent the official views of the funders.

Note

1 "Grandfather clauses either exempt or create more lenient standards for existing facilities. The stricter standards imposed by the legislation apply only to new facilities, while grandfathered facilities may be permitted to continue polluting at prior levels. The new environmental standards may therefore do little to improve environmental quality for those living near grandfathered facilities" (Kaswan 1997, 270).

References

Abdullah, K., Malloy, T., Stenstrom, M. K., and Suffet, I. H. 2017. Toxicity of acidization fluids used in California oil exploration. *Toxicological and Environmental Chemistry*, 99(1).

Austin, B. J. and Zeeble, B. 2013. Dallas City Council approves more restrictive gas drilling ordinance. *StateImpact Texas*, December 11. Available at https://stateimpact.npr.org/texas/2013/12/11/dallas-city-council-approves-more-restrictive-gas-drilling-ordinance/ (last accessed February 13, 2020).

Balazs, C. L. and Morello-Frosch, R. 2013. The three Rs: How community-based participatory research strengthens the rigor, relevance, and reach of science. *Environmental Justice*, 6(1), 9–16.

Bamberger, I., Stieger, J., Buchmann, N., and Eugster, W. 2014. Spatial variability of methane: Attributing atmospheric concentrations to emissions. *Environmental Pollution*, 190.

Brown, P. 1992. Popular epidemiology and toxic waste contamination: Lay and professional ways of knowing. *Journal of Health and Social Behavior*, 33(3), 267–281.

California Air Resources Board. 2005. *Air Quality and Land Use Handbook: A Community Health Perspective* (April 2005).

Cohen, A., Lopez, A., Malloy, N., and Morello-Frosch, R. 2012. Our environment, our health: A community-based participatory environmental health survey in Richmond, California. *Health Education and Behavior*, 39(2), 198–209.

Cole, L. W. and Foster, S. 2001. *From the Ground Up: Environmental Racism and the Rise of the Environmental Justice Movement*. New York: NYU Press.

Eugster, W. and Kling, G. W. 2012. Performance of a low-cost methane sensor for ambient concentration measurements in preliminary studies. *Atmospheric Measurement Techniques*, 5(8).

Gougis, M. 2015. THUMS oil islands: Half a century later, still unique, still iconic. *Long Beach Business Journal*, October.

Haley, M., McCawley, M., Epstein, A. C., Arrington, B., and Bjerke, E. F. 2016. Adequacy of current state setbacks for directional high-volume hydraulic fracturing in the Marcellus, Barnett, and Niobrara shale plays. *Environmental Health Perspectives*, 124(9).

Jasanoff, S. S. 1987. Contested boundaries in policy-relevant science. *Social Studies of Science*, 17(2), 195–230.

Kaswan, A. 1997. Environmental justice: Bridging the gap between environmental laws and "justice." *American University Law Review*, 47(2). Available at https://ssrn.com/abstract=1012388 (last accessed February 14, 2020).

Koseff, A. 2018. "It's literally drill, baby, drill": Did Jerry Brown's climate crusade give Big Oil a pass? *Sacramento Bee*, September 13.

Macey, G. P., Breech, R., Chernaik, M., Cox, C., Larson, D., Thomas, D., and Carpenter, D. O. 2014. Air concentrations of volatile compounds near oil and gas production: A community-based exploratory study. *Environmental Health*, 1, 82.

McKenzie, L. M., Guo, R., Witter, R. Z., Savitz, D. A., Newman, L. S., and Adgate, J. L. 2014. Birth outcomes and maternal residential proximity to natural gas development in rural Colorado. *Environmental Health Perspectives*, 122(4), 412–417.

Mead, M. I., Popoola, O. A. M., Stewart, G. B., Landshoff, P., Calleja, M., Hayes, M., Baldovi, J. J., McLeod, M. W., Hodgson, T. F., Dicks, J., Lewis, A., Cohen, J., Baron, R., Saffell, J. R., and Jones, R. L. 2013. The use of electrochemical sensors for monitoring urban air quality in low-cost, high-density networks. *Atmospheric Environment*, 70, 186–203.

Meng, Q. and Ashby, S. 2014. Distance: A critical aspect for environmental impact assessment of hydraulic fracking. *The Extractive Industries and Society*, 1(2), 124–126.

Minkler, M., Garcia, A. P., Williams, J., LoPresti, T., and Lilly, J. 2010. Sí Se Puede: Using Participatory research to promote environmental justice in a Latino community in San Diego, California. *Journal of Urban Health*, 87(5), 796–812.

Morello-Frosch, R., Pastor, M., Sadd, J., Poras, C., and Prichard, M. 2005. Citizens, science, and data judo: Leveraging community-based participatory research to build a regional collaborative for environmental justice in southern California. *Methods for*

Conducting Community-Based Participatory Research in Public Health. Available at https://dornsife.usc.edu/tools/mytools/PersonnelInfoSystem/DOC/Faculty/GEOG/publication_1013240_3882.pdf (last accessed January 27, 2020).

Office of Environmental Health Hazard Assessment. 2014. *California Communities Environmental Health Screening Tool, version 2.0* (2014).

Naomi O. and Conway, E. M. 2011. *Merchants of Doubt: How a Handful of Scientists Obscured the Truth on Issues from Tobacco Smoke to Global Warming*. New York: Bloomsbury.

Pellow, D. N. 2017. *What is Critical Environmental Justice?* Cambridge; Medford, MA.

Penning, T. M., Breysse, P. N., Gray, K., Howarth, M., and Yan, B. 2014. Environmental health research recommendations from the Inter-Environmental Health Sciences Core Center Working Group on Unconventional Natural Gas Drilling Operations. *Environmental Health Perspectives*, 122(11), 1155–1159.

Petition for Abatement of Public Nuisance. 2016. Available at https://earthjustice.org/sites/default/files/files/Petition%20to%20Department%20of%20Planning%20–%20Final%20(Electronic).pdf (last accessed February 13, 2020).

Piedrahita, R., Xiang, Y., Masson, N., Ortega, J., Collier, A., Jiang, Y., Li, K., Dick, R. P., Lv, Q., Hannigan, M., and Shang, L. 2014. The next generation of low-cost personal air quality sensors for quantitative exposure monitoring. *Atmospheric Measurement Techniques*, 7(10).

Pratt, J. A., Melosi, M. V., and Brosnan, K. A. 2014. *Energy Capitals: Local Impact, Global Influence*. Pittsburgh, PA: University of Pittsburgh Press.

Pulido, L., Kohl, E., and Cotton, N.-M. 2016. State regulation and environmental justice: The need for Strategy reassessment. *Capitalism Nature Socialism*, 27(2).

Quam-Wickham, N. 2015. "Sacrificed on the Altar of Oil": Los Angeles' uneasy relationship with petroleum. *American Institute for Progressive Democracy*, 23: special issue #2 (February).

Rabinowitz, P. M., Slizovskiy, I. B., Lamers, V., Trufan, S. J., Holford, T. R., Dziura, J. D., Peduzzi, P. N., Kane, M. J., Reif, J. S., Weiss, T. R., and Stowe, M. H. 2014. Proximity to natural gas wells and reported health status: Results of a household survey in Washington County, Pennsylvania. *Environmental Health Perspectives*, 123(1), 21–26.

Rasmussen, S. G., Ogburn, E. L., McCormack, M., Casey, J. A., Bandeen-Roche, K., Mercer, D. G., and Schwartz, B. S. 2016. Association between unconventional natural gas development in the Marcellus Shale and asthma exacerbations. *JAMA Internal Medicine*, 176(9) .

Redeemer Community Partnership. 2016. *Odor Control Chemical spotted at Jefferson Drill Site*. (March).

Reyes, E. A. 2016. Community group petitions city to enclose South L.A. drilling site. *Los Angeles Times*, June 9.

Sabin, P. 2004. *Crude Politics: The California Oil Market, 1900–1940*. Berkeley: University of California Press.

Sadd, J. and Shamasunder, B. 2015. Oil extraction in Los Angeles: Health, Land use, and environmental justice consequence. *Drilling Down: The Community Consequences of Expanded Oil Development in Los Angeles* (Fall), 7–14.

Sahagun, L. 2013. Chemical odor, kids' nosebleeds, few answers in South L.A. neighborhood. *Los Angeles Times*, September 21.

Schoch, D. 2006. Toasting industry as art. *Los Angeles Times*, September 13.

Shamasunder, B. 2018. Neighborhood oil drilling and environmental justice in Los Angeles. In B. Sarathy, V. Hamilton, and J. Farrell Brodie (eds), *Inevitably Toxic: Historical Perspectives on Contamination, Exposure, and Expertise*. Pittsburgh, PA: University of Pittsburgh Press.

Shamasunder, B., Collier-Oxandale, A., Blickley, J., Sadd, J., Chan, M., Navarro, S., Hannigan, M., and Wong, N. J. 2018. Community-based health and exposure study around urban oil developments in South Los Angeles. *International Journal of Environmental Research and Public Health*, 15(1).

Southern California Public Radio. 2017. LA to study banning oil production around homes, schools, parks. *Southern California Public Radio* (39:23 700).

Stringfellow, W. T., Camarillo, M. K., Domen, J. K., Sandelin, W. L., Varadharajan, C., Jordan, P. D., Reagan, M. T., Cooley, H., Heberger, M. G., and Birkholzer, J. T. 2017. Identifying chemicals of concern in hydraulic fracturing fluids used for oil production. *Environmental Pollutution*, 2J., 20, Part A.

Webb, E., Hays, Dyrszka, L., Rodriguez, B., Cox, C., Huffling, K., and Bushkin-Bedient, S. 2016. Potential hazards of air pollutant emissions from unconventional oil and natural gas operations on the respiratory health of children and infants. *Review of Environmental Health*, 31(2).

Witter, R. Z., McKenzie, L., Stinson, K. E., Scott, K., Newman, L. S., and Adgate, J. 2013. The use of health impact assessment for a community undergoing natural gas development. *Amercan Journal of Public Health*, 103(6), 1002–1010.

4

Environmental injustice in North Carolina's hog industry: Lessons learned from community-driven participatory research and the "people's professor"

Sarah Rhodes and KD Brown, Larry Cooper, Naeema Muhammad, and Devon Hall

A vignette of life in hog country

Imagine a house. This house may have been owned by your family for generations or is one that you worked very hard to purchase. Now imagine that, unbeknownst to you, an industrial hog operation[1] with over 5,000 hogs and a football field-sized waste pit containing hog feces and urine has been permitted by the state government to be built across the street. The odor is overwhelming. You taste it in your food and smell it on your clothes and furniture. Worried about the waste overflowing when it rains, you learn that the state-sanctioned solution to manage these pits is to spray the feces on nearby fields using mechanized sprinkler systems. You look from your window in dread as fecal mist floats onto your property, saturating your line-dried clothes, your car, and your house. You close all the windows to protect yourself, even though it's beautiful outside.

Matters become worse when you notice a dumpster covered in flies and vultures at the entrance to the hog operation. A garbage truck speeds down your street, stops and picks up the dumpster, and dumps its contents into the back. Large, bloated hog corpses heave out, their liquefied viscera and rot splattering down the sides of the box and into the street. As the truck pulls away, you notice the same liquid spilling out from the bottom, marking a continued and discernable path along the road and into the distance. All you want to do is work in your garden and enjoy the sunshine, but the smell of decomposing flesh mingles with smell of hog feces, causing you to gag and retreat into your home. You feel angry and depressed.

You think about selling your house, but the proximity and smell of the hog operation causes your property value to drop. The barbeques you once loved are impossible due to swarms of flies, and your children can't play outside because it's too hard to breathe. Your own asthma worsens. You call everyone you can think of about the smell, the waste sprayers, the boxes full of dead hogs, and the damage to your home. You talk to your town and local representatives. You call the governmental agency responsible for permitting and regulating the hog operation. You call the police. You call the local health department. You call everyone associated with the operation, but to no avail. Few return your calls, and even fewer provide solutions. That evening, you're confronted in the grocery store parking lot by strangers who advise you to "not make trouble for yourself." You find out later that one of the government officials you spoke to about the smell shared your phone number and name with the owner of the industrial hog operation.

You're scared, but also angry at being ignored, marginalized, and betrayed by institutions responsible for your protection and health. You notice that these operations are not commonly located in predominantly wealthy, white communities, and more and more hog operations appear with legal permission in low-income communities and communities of color, including your own. One day, you hear about a local community group that is conducting research on the potential impacts of industrial hog production on public health. You attend one of their monthly meetings and are inspired by their stories and objectives. They want to monitor the air for toxic gases and document your experiences with the industry. Even though you are afraid of more retaliation, you invite the community group to your home to set up an air monitor in your yard. Finally, you have the opportunity to collect evidence that may explain why you are sick. For now, only your neighbors believe you. But soon, all of that will change.

Introduction and background

This vignette represents an amalgam of real-life stories told to, and witnessed by, the authors of this chapter, embodying the collective experiences of community members pursuing dignified lives and livelihoods at the epicenter of industrial pork production in the United States. Tucked away in rural eastern North Carolina (NC), Duplin and Sampson Counties have the highest density of hogs in the United States, with 2.0 and 1.9 million hogs, respectively (USDA and NCDACS 2018). Close to half of the population in both counties are people of color (26% black and 23% Hispanic in Duplin; 27% black and 20% Hispanic in Sampson). Additionally, an estimated 20% of the population in both counties lives below the federally designated poverty line (US Census Bureau 2018).

What may be more important than these social demographics, however, is the role state government has played in legitimizing the disproportionate concentration of industrial hog operations (IHOs) in low-income communities and communities of color. The North Carolina Department of Environmental Quality (NCDEQ) has legally permitted IHOs in these communities for decades, despite myriad and rigorous scientific research demonstrating its hazardous public and environmental health impacts. To interpret this permitting as anything other than government-sanctioned violence and racial capitalism ignores the racist history of the NC "Black Belt" (Robinson 1997). The Black Belt is a geopolitical region expanding across several states in the southeastern United States, with large present-day African American populations living in areas with centuries-long histories of slave- and plantation-based economies. The modern-day siting of hog operations and their waste in these same communities demonstrates the continued necropolitical power leveraged by the NC government and industry to deem who deserves, or does not deserve, to live a healthful life (Mbembé and Meintjes 2003).

Environmental justice can be defined as "equal access to a healthful environment, regardless of race, ethnicity, or income" (Guidry et al. 2018, 324). The modern environmental justice (EJ) movement began in Warren County, NC in response to the siting of a hazardous waste landfill in a rural African American community, and it continues today with industrial animal production in Duplin and Sampson Counties (Guidry et al. 2018). This chapter will explore the work of Dr. Steve Wing, an epidemiologist at the University of North Carolina who devoted his life to conducting community-driven participatory research (CDPR) on environmental justice issues in North Carolina until his untimely death in 2016 (Guidry 2017). Steve understood the political and historical entanglements of EJ and worked in equitable collaboration with community partners to enumerate and scientifically validate environmental injustice, including environmental racism, perpetuated by the NC government and transnational, multibillion-dollar livestock industries.

Steve was known by his collaborators as the "people's professor," a moniker that evokes his dedication to elevating community voices in public health and legal action by critically confronting corporate influence on scientific knowledge production and environmental management. This chapter is dedicated to his memory and aims to build on the important lessons embedded within the community-driven participatory research that he conducted in partnership with communities. It is presented in three parts. In the first section, we examine the expansion, impact, and political influence of IHOs in eastern NC. In the second section, we unpack particularly influential CDPR projects on environmental justice and the NC hog industry to elucidate how researchers and communities can work in concert to generate rigorous and objective systems of inquiry that do not rely on exploitative methodologies. In the third section, we present explicit lessons learned from these CDPR studies for use by academics and community-based organizations (CBO) to improve and sustain their partnerships.

This chapter is written from the perspectives and experiences of seasoned community organizers and academic researchers deeply involved in environmental justice work in the American South. Our authors represent a group of community–academic partners from the Rural Empowerment Association for Community Help (REACH), the North Carolina Environmental Justice Network (NCEJN), and the University of North Carolina at Chapel Hill (UNC).

History and structure of North Carolina industrial hog operations

Hog production in North Carolina is a multibillion-dollar industry and a critical piece of the state's economy and culture. Historically, family farms across the state raised small hog herds (< 25 hogs) on open pasture and sold the meat directly at local markets (Furuseth 1997; Thompson 2000). However, in the 1980s, the hog industry abruptly shifted to a vertically integrated, industrial-scale production model, where industry-owned hogs are raised in confinement at high density (> 250 hogs) in IHOs, otherwise known as concentrated animal feeding operations (CAFOs) (Wing et al. 2002). As a result of the state's rapid agro-industrialization, NC is currently the second-highest producer of hogs in the United States and is home to over 2,000 IHOs and 9 million hogs (USDA and NCDACS 2018) (see Figure 4.1).

This rapid agro-industrialization was facilitated in part by the election of pork industry affiliates to local and state governments. Wendell Murphy, an agricultural lobbyist and pork producer, served for 10 years in the NC General Assembly, where he pushed forth laws (known as "Murphy's laws") that benefited IHOs at the expense of community and environmental health (Sill et al. 1995). These "right to farm" laws ensured that IHOs, despite documented impacts on health, were exempt from taxation, "environmental regulations, zoning laws, labor regulations, and nuisance suits" (Ladd and Edward 2002). The systematic passing of pro-IHO legislation has secured the long-standing stronghold of the hog industry, strategically undermining local communities fighting for improved

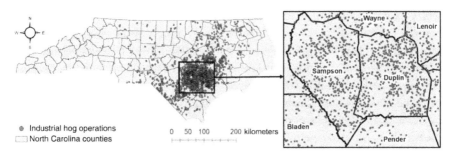

4.1 Industrial hog operations sited in eastern North Carolina. The figure was created using Esri® ArcGIS® software version 10.3.1. The industrial hog operation locations were provided by the Environmental Working Group and Waterkeeper Alliance (Environmental Working Group & Waterkeeper Alliance, 2016).

operational practices and against industry expansion (Julius L. Chambers Center for Civil Rights, 2018).

Today, the few multinational corporations that dominate NC industrial hog production are Smithfield Foods, Inc. (owned by WH Group) and its subsidiary, Murphy-Brown LLC, and Prestage Farms, Inc. These large, vertically integrated companies operate across their supply chains, hiring local contract growers (i.e., farmers) to raise industry-owned hogs on growers' land. The companies control everything from growth to slaughter, as well as product delivery to grocery stores (Wing 2002). Growers sign contracts, which specify guidelines regarding the animal husbandry practices that they must implement – for instance, antibiotic administration via feed. These contracts can require growers to make large investments to build and staff their operations (MacDonald and McBride 2009). Because the growers do not own the animals, and often do not receive financial or legal support from the overseeing company for issues related to waste management, they can face financial instability and feel like "indentured servants" (Braun and Braun 1998; Farmers' Legal Action Group 2003). As Larry Cooper from REACH explains:

> The contract growers are between a rock and a hard place due to the strategy of the "powers that be." They have to jump when they are told to jump, the "powers that be" control their destiny. That strategy pits the contract grower against people like us and similar organizations because they feel we stand in their way of making a living. They don't understand our true purpose and as a result they fear us. We are not anti-hogs, we simply want things done the right way; that's all. (Interview, 2018)

To further understand the impacts of industrialization and associated contracts, it is important to understand the architecture of typical North Carolina

IHOs, which consist of confinement barns, waste lagoons, and waste spray-fields. Confinement barns are designed to raise hundreds to thousands of hogs in densely packed pens. To reduce accumulation of harmful gases from hog excrement as well as animal overheating, barns are often ventilated by exhaust fans or rooftop chimneys. Barn floors consist of tightly spaced metal slats for drainage of hog waste, which is then funneled to uncovered, outdoor cesspools called "lagoons." Hog lagoons can be as large as a football field, depending on the number and life stage of the hogs. The purpose of lagoons is to treat waste via anaerobic decomposition; however, these lagoons cannot effectively contain and treat the waste without stringent maintenance and monitoring (Wing et al. 2000; EarthJustice 2014).

Therein lies an important stipulation of industrial livestock contracts that con-tributes to the degradation of community and environmental health: the grow-ers' responsibility for the treatment and storage of waste. Corporations legally own the animals but contract growers own the animal waste, limiting corporate liability associated with regulatory compliance related to waste management (Wing 2002; Farmers' Legal Action Group 2003). Contract growers, especially poultry growers, are at risk of becoming indebted to the industry (RAFI-USA 2017) and often do not have the financial capacity to install advanced treatment systems, such as those used for the treatment of human waste. Therefore, the majority of contract growers use the most affordable (e.g., lagoon/sprayfield system), as opposed to the most protective, waste management systems.

At an industrial magnitude, hog waste is a major source of greenhouse gases, pathogenic microbes, and nutrient pollution (Cole et al. 2000). The existing precarity of communities living near IHOs is only further complicated by the increased occurrence and intensity of hurricanes, including Hurricanes Floyd (1999), Matthew (2016), and Florence (2018). Uncovered lagoons contain mil-lions of gallons of waste and are vulnerable to overflow during heavy rain events, potentially contaminating nearby environments, as well as ground and surface waters (Wing et al. 2002). To prevent this, it is standard practice to periodically remove waste and apply it to crop sprayfields as a fertilizer using high-powered, mechanized sprinkler systems. This practice is dependent upon soil infiltration, which can lead to contamination of surface and groundwater in regions with high water tables like the NC coastal plain (Guidry et al. 2018). As a regulatory tool, the NCDEQ requires IHOs to apply for waste disposal permits, which track the cover crop of sprayfields and the frequency of spraying to assess nutri-ent balance and prevent environmental contamination (Christenson and Serre 2017). However, these permits do not require microbial analysis of waste prior to spraying, nor do they require public notice in the case of a potentially harmful discharge event (EarthJustice 2014).

The proximity of IHO lagoons and sprayfields to neighboring homes and communities is striking. There are 4,145 swine lagoons in NC, with 37 lagoons located within half a mile of a school, 136 within half a mile of a public water well, and 170 within the state's 100-year flood plain (Environmental Working Group & Waterkeeper Alliance 2016). Due to the high density and proximity of IHOs to communities, the public can be exposed to hog waste via spray aerosolization, lagoon leachate, and lagoon overflow. Further, harmful gases and malodor can be generated via spraying of hog waste, off-gassing of lagoons, and use of barn exhaust fans, leading to increased stress (Horton et al. 2009) and potential negative impacts on respiratory health and neurological function (Schinasi et al. 2011; Kilburn 2012).

Residents living close to industrial hog operations have frequently expressed incredulity at the actions of the corporations. For example, as Devon Hall of REACH recalled: "One time, a friend said, 'How could another Christian do to a fellow Christian what Murphy Brown is doing to the community?'" (interview, 2018). In 2014, after decades of organizing and research to illuminate these issues, NCEJN, REACH, and the Waterkeeper Alliance filed a Title VI complaint against the NC Department of Environmental Quality for:

> issuing a general permit that allows industrial swine facilities in NC to operate with grossly inadequate and outdated systems of controlling animal waste and little provision for government oversight, which has an unjustified disproportionate impact on the basis of race and national origin against African Americans, Latinos and Native Americans in violation of Title VI of the Civil Rights Act of 1964. (EarthJustice 2014)

This case is revolutionary and represents a major success for the EJ movement, as it is only the second time in the history of the US Environmental Protection Agency where disproportionate impact was confirmed and a settlement agreement was signed, proving discriminatory practices by the government to benefit industry (Julius L. Chambers Center for Civil Rights 2018). This work could not have been done without the scientific knowledge produced by NC community groups partnering with Steve Wing and others. The following sections will focus on Wing's legacy and lessons learned from scientific research rooted in community power.

Community-driven participatory research (CDPR) and the "people's professor"

Though the Title VI complaint was submitted in 2014, this work truly began in the 1980s when CBOs, with members including authors of this chapter, began to resist the rapid expansion of IHOs in low-income communities of color in eastern NC. The Concerned Citizens of Tillery (CCT), NCEJN, and REACH were among the first organizations to expose environmental injustice and environmental racism in the NC hog industry through political mobilization and organizing tactics, including advocacy, empowerment, education, direct action, litigation, and finally, community-driven participatory research.

In the 1990s, Steve Wing began attending community meetings held by the Concerned Citizens of Tillery, a CBO in Halifax County that "promotes social justice and self-determination for rural African American communities" (Wing et al. 2008a), to learn about industrial animal production from the perspective of neighboring communities. There, he met Gary Grant (CCT), A. Nan Freeland (CCT; NC Central University), and Naeema Muhammad (Black Workers for Justice), with whom he would later form the NCEJN (Guidry 2017). Steve listened carefully and documented the human health concerns raised by the community at these meetings. For the next two decades, Wing conducted scientifically rigorous research on issues related to industrial animal production in collaboration with community partners. His groundbreaking work inspired generations of researchers and activists and continues through his collaborators and students. Reflecting on the depth of his influence, Naeema Muhammad of NCEJN stated: "Steve Wing was the greatest researcher to ever walk the halls of any university" (interview, 2018). Wing was particularly admired for inspiring people to use community-driven research as a tool for change, while simultaneously recognizing its limitations. For example, Devon Hall of REACH recalls a particularly insightful conversation: "Steve Wing once said to me, 'I don't know if this research will do you any good.' And something lit up inside me – it will. Just knowing, getting the data, learning what we are being exposed to ... I can learn how to protect myself. I can give that information to someone else ... because knowledge is power" (interview, 2018). The following section attempts to synthesize the key findings of the research conducted by impacted communities alongside Steve Wing and his mentees, and to provide lessons learned from their work at the forefront of the environmental justice movement.

In 2000, Wing, in collaboration with CCT, conducted one of the first community-driven participatory research (CDPR) studies to address community concerns about hog industry practices and siting. The specific objective of the study was to assess the "extent to which hog CAFOs are located dispropor-tionately in communities with high levels of poverty, high proportions of non-white persons, and high percentages of households dependent on well water" (Wing et al. 2000). The study showed that hog CAFOs are disproportionately located in low-income communities and communities of color across the state. The results validated community member observations and provided scientific data and informative maps to support their claims of systemic environmental injustice and racism. This work became the antecedent for a very influential CDPR study called "Community Health Effects of Industrial Hog Operations," or CHEIHO.

The CHEIHO study investigated health outcomes and quality of life factors associated with exposure to CAFO-related air pollutants, while simultaneously sharing scientific knowledge with participants and promoting social and envi-ronmental justice (Wing et al. 2008a). The CCT recruited 102 participants who lived within 1.5 miles (2.4 kilometers) of an IHO from 16 communities to participate in a 2-week sampling effort. A trailer containing air monitors and weather tracking devices was set up in participant neighborhoods to con-duct real-time monitoring, including assessment of pollutants and environmen-tal factors like particulate matter, hydrogen sulfide, temperature, wind speed, humidity, and rainfall. Simultaneously, participants were asked to categorically rate the strength of odor outside their homes (on a scale of 1 to 9), record any respiratory issues, and take blood pressure and lung function measurements. Finally, semi-structured interviews were conducted before and after the study to gauge participants' quality of life perception before and after IHO expansion as well as during the data collection process (Wing et al. 2008a).

This study was groundbreaking in its design and scientific assessment of physi-ological and psychological impacts of malodor. The community led the design and recruitment and provided valuable knowledge on regional sociopolitical dynamics, including the hog industry's intimidation tactics. Participants' con-cerns, comfort, trust, and anonymity were explicitly prioritized within the design, such as holding training sessions at participants' homes, churches, and other local venues as opposed to research institutions. At these sessions, food, childcare, and educational brochures were provided and community organizers were available to "bridge cultural divides by translating technical data collection concepts into meaningful local language" (Wing et al. 2008a).

A rich and unique data set was created, and several important community-driven questions about the impacts of IHO air pollution on health and well-being were addressed. The CHEIHO study results found prevalent odor in the region on half of the study days, in concert with high concentrations of PM10 in the air (Wing et al. 2008b). Results found it was common for participants to change their daily activity and have increased self-reported stress in response to malo-dor (Tajik et al. 2008; Horton et al. 2009). Results also showed that increased hydrogen sulfide gas exposure (a biomarker for hog waste) was associated with elevated blood pressure of participants (Wing et al. 2013). Interestingly, increasing industry awareness of the study impacted the data collection process using the mobile trailers. Several participants reported suspicions that IHO operators learned of the trailers' purpose and temporarily changed their practices, potentially reducing odor during the study period (Wing et al. 2008a).

The CHEIHO database is still in use today. Steve's students and colleagues continue to analyze CHEIHO data as well as create new research on emerging questions in partnership with CBOs. For example, Steve's students – the authors of this chapter among them – have collaborated with REACH to investigate the emergence of antibiotic-resistant bacteria within IHOs related to the industry's administration of antibiotics to hogs for growth promotion, disease prevention, and disease treatment. This work has shown that antibiotic-resistant, livestock-adapted bacteria are present on North Carolina IHOs and have the potential to spread from hogs to IHO workers, community residents, and to the environment (Rinsky et al. 2013; Hatcher et al. 2016a, 2016b; Davis et al. 2018). Additionally, this research has shed light on the need for improved working conditions and workplace protections for IHO workers. Some of this work was later cited in the 2014 Title VI Civil Rights Act complaint filed by CBOs against the NCDEQ.

Additional studies that were inspired by Steve Wing's work on North Carolina IHOs have investigated (1) environmental racism in the Mississippi hog industry (Wilson et al. 2002), (2) hydrogen sulfide exposure in children attending school near NC IHOs (Guidry et al. 2016), and (3) presence of fecal indicator bacteria and pig-specific microbial fecal markers downstream proximal to IHOs (Heaney et al. 2015). For more information, the *North Carolina Medical Journal* provides a comprehensive summary of the pollutants and health impacts that are associated with IHOs, as documented by Wing and community partners, his mentees, and other researchers from North Carolina and beyond (Guidry et al. 2018). Notably, in a 2016 interview, Steve reflected on the extensive body of research that has been conducted by the community over multiple decades, posing that: "The evidence of impact is so overwhelming that we don't need more research. We need action to protect people and the environment" (Wing, interview in Robinson 2016).

Lessons learned from CDPR and the "people's professor"

By considering the history and philosophy of their disciplines, practicing researchers can increase the rigor, objectivity, and social responsibility of environmental health science. Steve Wing (Wing 2003)

As awareness of EJ grows and is applied outside the United States, it is important to pay homage to its lineage in NC and recognize the breadth of lessons still to be learned from the community organizing and CDPR conducted there. The following section presents a selection of lessons learned from the extensive body of CDPR studies described above. These lessons were derived from a series of reflective group interviews conducted by KD Brown and Sarah Rhodes with Devon Hall, Larry Cooper, and Naeema Muhammad (all authors of this chapter). We intersperse our lessons learned with selected quotes from our conversations. It is our hope that these lessons can be operationalized by academic researchers interested in becoming involved with CDPR and by CBOs who may be interested in pursuing scientific research as an education and organizing tool. Table 4.1 at the end of the section sums up the lessons learned.

1. Promote research equity

Academic researchers are trained to become "experts" in their field. A side effect of this pedagogy is the creation of a hierarchy of power, where academia is the keeper of knowledge and the public is a naive entity in need of education. In the context of this work, this style of pedagogy generates dangerous narratives about EJ communities that focus on victimization rather than honoring community triumph and capacity in the face of oppression. Research is often posed as a "capacity-building" tool within impacted communities, obscuring their self-determination and autonomy. The implicit hierarchy of academic knowledge production must be deconstructed in order to conduct equitable, community-driven research. If researchers are not members of the impacted community, they do not have requisite expertise and should defer to community partners as experts of their own lived experiences. CDPR studies are often only possible through partnership with community members who have deep roots in the study community or region. The power of the community must be acknowledged and venerated, just as the privilege of academic researchers and institutions must be challenged in order to establish a partnership based in equity and respect.

Researchers, don't come in and say "this is what we're going to do." You need to come in with a draft to discuss and edit together with the community. Devon Hall, REACH (interview, 2018)

2. Engage in participatory research design and budgeting

Impacted community members should be involved in every step of the research process, from the drafting of research questions and project plans to report-backs of research results. Further, it is important to adequately compensate community members for their involvement in research. However, research funding is often temporary and should not be the primary source of funding for CBOs, as this often strips them of their capacity to engage in other organizing. Collectively writing grants is very welcome, but the ultimate goal should be to ensure that CBOs have financial autonomy apart from research funding. Participatory budgeting at the nascent stages of grant writing is exceptionally important to sustainable collaborations.

3. Respect non-research objectives of community partners

Academic researchers must be careful not to demand too much time of CBOs. These organizations have other priorities that are equal to, if not more important than, research. Similarly, CBOs should set clear boundaries for researchers regarding the amount of time and personnel they can dedicate. Research should always be driven by, protective of, and relevant to communities and their objectives. Academics must iteratively ask themselves "Can my research influence or be used in legal action, organizing, education, or policy efforts?" If not, rethink your approach by directly consulting with your community partners on how to better align your work with theirs. Remember, scientific research is important, but should remain secondary to CBOs' empowerment and mobilization efforts.

4. Acknowledge historic mistreatment of communities of color by research institutions

Mistrust of research institutions can be pervasive in EJ communities, as academia has a long history of systemic discrimination and subjugation of communities of color (Wing et al. 2008a). Researchers must respectfully accept when people decline or cease involvement in research. Informed consent and data confidentiality procedures must be clearly defined and provided verbally and in writing, as the participants' lives and livelihoods may be threatened if their involvement is discovered. If extra protection is needed, researchers should apply for a Certificate of Confidentiality administered by the US Department of Health and Human Services, or a similar entity in their home country. This is especially relevant to our work in North Carolina, as the pork industry yielded influence over the governing body of Steve Wing's academic institution, subpoenaing his work to demand he turn over de-identified participant records to attorneys representing the Pork Council, potentially endangering his research participants (Wing 2002).

5. Acknowledge the impact and limitations of research studies

It is important to stress that absence of scientific evidence does not mean that health impacts are not being experienced or are not meaningful. It is necessary to explain and understand the limitations and impact of research from both sides, as results do not always align with publishing goals or community experiences of chronic illness. In addition, one must contextualize and iteratively reflect on the social and political implications of research, as science is limited in its capacity to enumerate lived experiences and trauma but powerful in its ability to discredit them.

6. Establish trust and prioritize community comfort

Academic researchers and CBOs must work together to ensure community members feel safe, as they may be at risk of intimidation and economic retaliation for their participation in research. Creating a culture of trust and comfort can come in many forms, including providing extensive information about plans for anonymization and secured storage of personally identifiable data, such as names and phone numbers. Academics must prioritize and acknowledge the working schedules of their community partners and research participants, adjusting their own needs to meet the needs of their collaborators. Further, it is important for researchers to provide culturally appropriate food (check in with your partners) and services, such as babysitting, at meetings. Finally, the spaces in which meetings are held are incredibly important. Workshops and meetings led by academics are often designed to impress and comfort their peers, not their community partners. Fancy hotels and conference centers may be intimidating, inaccessible, and unwelcoming to attendees who do not benefit from institutional privilege. If there is a meeting venue located within the community, use it.

> This is white privilege at its best. Furthermore, I'm not trying to be nobody's token. You bringing me out to all of this eloquence and I'm working with communities who are dying every day.
> Naeema Muhammad, NCEJN (interview, 2018)

7. Cultivate an inclusive language base

An inclusive and intentional language base must be cultivated and shared in order to move forward as an intersectional collective of environmental justice researchers. Language that is not accessible or that is dominated by acronyms is useless outside of an academic context. Institutional language, both private and public, comes from a place of top-down privilege and is potentially violent for marginalized communities. Consequently, researchers must be very intentional in how they speak about environmental justice issues and to whom they speak.

> *Yeah, I have a PhD. It stands for Poor, Hungry, and Determined.* Larry Cooper, REACH (interview, 2018)

8. Support and respect the formation of community review boards

After years of conducting research alongside academic institutions, REACH established a community review board composed of community leaders that meets to determine whether becoming involved with new research studies will serve the community's needs. These community review boards are essential to ensuring that community groups do not become involved in exploitative research that does not support their broader mission and organizing objectives.

Conclusion

This chapter celebrates EJ communities who have triumphed over state-sanctioned environmental injustice. When the North Carolina government failed to conduct rigorous surveillance of industrial pollution and document associated health burdens, the community produced their own knowledge. This extensive body of CDPR was operationalized in increased organizing efforts and litigation to hold the government and industry accountable. The resulting Title VI and nuisance complaints have far-reaching implications for other extractive industries benefiting from the "post-truth" era where scientific evidence is silenced. EJ communities will continue to face new challenges, including climate change and the growing waste crisis. Steve Wing's legacy provides a framework to address burgeoning environmental health issues through equitable, extramural science that elevates community power and resistance to oppression, influencing both the local and global environmental justice movement. Reflexive in our approach, we build on Wing's call for the need for community-driven *action* as well as *research*. Moving forward, we are dedicated to creating accessible

Table 4.1 Lessons learned from community-driven participatory research conducted in North Carolina.

Lesson	Example
Promote research equity	Community members are experts, not victims, and should be treated as such by academic allies.
Engage in participatory research design and budgeting	Community members should co-direct the entirety of the research process, from grant writing to research report-backs.
Respect the non-research objectives of community partners	Research studies should facilitate, not eliminate, a CBO's capacity for other critical organizing efforts.
Acknowledge the historic mistreatment of communities of color by research institutions	Researchers must clearly define informed consent and remain transparent about the ways in which they benefit from institutionalized racism.
Acknowledge the impact and limitations of research studies.	Research findings do not always align with community members' experiences. It is important to note that absence of scientific evidence does not equate to evidence of absence of health impacts.
Establish trust and prioritize community comfort	Academics should take time to learn culturally appropriate language and conduct research in spaces where community members feel safe.
Cultivate an inclusive language base	Terms such as "community-driven research" can be used in place of "citizen science" to maximize inclusivity.
Support and respect the formation of community review boards	CBOs can create community review boards composed of community leaders who determine whether research will serve the community's needs.

research summary materials for use in education and empowerment efforts and are taking the lead from youth, women, LGBTQIA2S+ (lesbian, gay, bisexual, transgender, queer and/or questioning, intersex, asexual, two-spirit, etc.) community, and other under-represented voices in the EJ movement. We continue to learn new lessons each day from impacted community members, animal operation workers, contract growers, and other partners. United, we face the enduring and ever-changing issues of environmental injustice and environmental racism in North Carolina as we work collectively to build a just future.

Note

1   A "hog" is a type of pig. By definition, hogs are domestic pigs bred to be heavier for use in pork production (Wikipedia 2020). Thus, "industrial hog production" in North Carolina is comparable to what may be referred to as "industrial pig production" or "industrial pig

farming" in other regions of the world; however, the North Carolina industry is distinct due to the high density of production and environmental injustice concerns associated with it.

References

Braun J. and Braun, P. 1998. Inside the industry from a family hog farmer. In K. Thu and E. Durrneberger (eds), *Pigs, Profits, and Rural Communities*. Albany, NY: State University of New York Press, pp. 39–56.

Christenson, E. C. and Serre, M. L. 2017. Integrating remote sensing with nutrient management plans to calculate nitrogen parameters for swine CAFOs at the sprayfield and sub-watershed scales. *Science of the Total Environment*, 580, 865–872.

Cole, D., Todd, L., and Wing, S. 2000. Concentrated swine feeding operations and public health: A review of occupational and community health effects. *Environmental Health Perspectives*, 108(8), 685–699.

Davis, M. F., Pisanic, N., Rhodes, S. M., Brown, A., Keller, H., Nadimpalli, M., … Heaney, C. D. 2018. Occurrence of Staphylococcus aureus in swine and swine workplace environments on industrial and antibiotic-free hog operations in North Carolina, USA: A One Health pilot study. *Environmental Research*, 163, 88–96.

EarthJustice. 2014. NCEJN et al. Complaint Under Title VI of the Civil Rights Act of 1964, 42 U.S.C. § 2000d, 40 C.F.R. Part 7. Available at https://earthjustice.org/sites/default/files/files/North-Carolina-EJ-Network-et-al-Complaint-under-Title-VI.pdf (last accessed January 27, 2020).

Environmental Working Group & Waterkeeper Alliance. 2016. Exposing fields of filth: Data and methodology. Available at https://www.ewg.org/research/exposing-fields-filth/data-and-methodology (last accessed January 27, 2020).

Farmers' Legal Action Group (FLAG) 2003. Livestock production contracts: Risks for family farmers. 2-4. Available at http://www.flaginc.org/publication/livestock-production-contracts-risks-for-family-farmers/ (last accessed January 27, 2020).

Furuseth, O. J. 1997. Restructuring of hog farming in North Carolina: Explosion and implosion. *The Professional Geographer*, 49(4), 391–403.

Guidry, V. T. 2017. In memoriam: Steve Wing. *Environmental Health Perspectives*, 125(1), A1–A2.

Guidry, V. T., Kinlaw, A. C., Johnston, J., Hall, D., and Wing, S. 2016. Hydrogen sulfide concentrations at three middle schools near industrial livestock facilities. *Journal of Exposure Science and Environmental Epidemiology*, 27(2), 167–174.

Guidry, V. T., Rhodes, S. M., Woods, C. G., Hall, D. J., and Rinsky, J. L. 2018. Connecting environmental justice and community health: Effects of hog production in North Carolina. *North Carolina Medical Journal*, 79(5), 324–328.

Hall, D., Cooper, L., and Muhammad, N. 2018. *Group Interview: CDPR in Hog Country*. Interviewers: K. M. Brown and S. M. Rhodes, February and August 2018.

Hatcher, S. M., Myers, K. W., Heaney, C. D., Larsen, J., Hall, D., Miller, M. B., and

Stewart, J. R. 2016a. Occurrence of methicillin-resistant Staphylococcus aureus in surface waters near industrial hog operation spray fields. *Science of the Total Environment*, 565, 1028–1036.

Hatcher, S. M., Rhodes, S. M., Stewart, J. R., Silbergeld, E., Pisanic, N., Larsen, J., … Heaney, C. D. 2016b. The prevalence of antibiotic-resistant Staphylococcus aureus nasal carriage among industrial hog operation workers, community residents, and children living in their households: North Carolina, USA. *Environmental Health Perspectives*, 125(4), 560–569.

Heaney, C. D., Myers, K., Wing, S., Hall, D., Baron, D., and Stewart, J. R. 2015. Source tracking swine fecal waste in surface water proximal to swine concentrated animal feeding operations. *Science of the Total Environment*, 511, 676–683.

Horton, R. A., Wing, S., Marshall, S. W., and Brownley, K. A. 2009. Malodor as a trigger of stress and negative mood in neighbors of industrial hog operations. *American Journal of Public Health*, 99 Suppl 3, S610–615.

Julius L. Chambers Center for Civil Rights. 2018. *Environmental Justice: Duplin County, NC*. Available at https://chambersccr.org/2018/10/19/chambers-center-releases-duplin-county-environmental-justice-report/ (last accessed January 27, 2020).

Kilburn, K. H. 2012. Human impairment from living near confined animal (hog) feeding operations. *Journal of Environmental and Public Health*, 2012, 565690.

Ladd, A. E. and Edward, B. 2002. Corporate swine and capitalist pigs: A decade of environmental injustice and protest in North Carolina. *Social Justice*, 29(3 (89)), 30–31.

MacDonald, J. M. and McBride, W. D. 2009. The transformation of US livestock agriculture: Scale, efficiency, and risks. *Economic Information Bulletin* 43. Economic Research Service, US Department of Agriculture.

Mbembé, J. A. and Meintjes, L. 2003. Necropolitics. *Public Culture*, 15(1), 11–40.

RAFI-USA. 2017. *Viewer's Guide: Under Contract – Farmers and the Fine Print*. Available at https://rafiusa.org/blog/undercontract/ (last accessed January 27, 2020).

Rinsky, J. L., Nadimpalli, M., Wing, S., Hall, D., Baron, D., Price, L. B., … Heaney, C. D. 2013. Livestock-associated methicillin and multidrug resistant Staphylococcus aureus is present among industrial, not antibiotic-free livestock operation workers in North Carolina. *PloS one*, 8, e67641.

Robinson, C. J. 1997. *Black Movements in America*. New York: Routledge.

Robinson, C. 2016. *W4F – Duplin County - Life Under the Waste Sprayer*: Vimeo. Available at https://vimeo.com/165758267 (last accessed January 27, 2020).

Schinasi, L., Horton, R. A., Guidry, V. T., Wing, S., Marshall, S. W., and Morland, K. B. 2011. Air pollution, lung function, and physical symptoms in communities near concentrated swine feeding operations. *Epidemiology*, 22(2), 208–215.

Sill, M., Stith, P., and Warrick, J. 1995. Boss hog: The power of pork, North Carolina's pork revolution. Compilation. *The News & Observer*, Feb.–March. Raleigh, NC Available at https://www.pulitzer.org/winners/news-observer-raleigh-nc (last accessed January 27, 2020).

Tajik, M., Muhammad, N., Lowman, A., Thu, K., Wing, S., and Grant, G. 2008. Impact of odor from industrial hog operations on daily living activities. *New Solutions*, 18(2), 193–205.

Thompson, M. D. 2000. This little piggy went to market: The commercialization of hog production in eastern North Carolina from William Shay to Wendell Murphy. *Agricultural History*, 74(2), 569–584.

US Census Bureau. 2018. Quick Facts: North Carolina (V2018). Available at https://www. census.gov/quickfacts/ (last accessed January 27, 2020).

USDA (US Department of Agriculture) and NCDACS (North Carolina Department of Agriculture and Consumer Services). 2018. *2018 North Carolina Agricultural Statistics*, vol. 219, ed. K. Krueger. US Department of Agriculture.

Wikipedia. 2020. Domestic pig. Available at https://en.wikipedia.org/wiki/Domestic_ pig (last accessed February 20, 2020).

Wilson, S. M., Howell, F., Wing, S., and Sobsey, M. 2002) Environmental injustice and the Mississippi hog industry. *Environmental Health Perspectives*, 110 Suppl 2, 195–201.

Wing, S. 2002. Social responsibility and research ethics in community-driven studies of industrialized hog production. *Environmental Health Perspectives*, 110(5), 437–444.

Wing, S. 2003. Objectivity and ethics in environmental health science. *Environmental Health Perspectives*, 111(14), 1809–1818.

Wing, S., Cole, D., and Grant, G. 2000. Environmental injustice in North Carolina's hog industry. *Environmental Health Perspectives*, 108(3), 225.

Wing, S., Freedman, S., and Band, L. 2002. The potential impact of flooding on confined animal feeding operations in eastern North Carolina. *Environmental Health* Perspectives, 110(4), 387–391.

Wing, S., Horton, R. A., Muhammad, N., Grant, G. R., Tajik, M., and Thu, K. 2008a. Integrating epidemiology, education, and organizing for environmental justice: Community health effects of industrial hog operations. *American Journal of Public Health*, 98(8), 1390–1397.

Wing, S., Horton, R. A., Marshall, S. W., Thu, K., Tajik, M., Schinasi, L., and Schiffman, S. S. 2008b. Air pollution and odor in communities near industrial swine operations. *Environmental Health Perspectives*, 116(10), 1362–1368.

Wing, S., Horton, R. A., and Rose, K. M. 2013. Air pollution from industrial swine operations and blood pressure of neighboring residents. *Environmental Health Perspectives*, 121, 92–96.

Part II

Sensing and witnessing injustice

Introduction to Part II

Thom Davies

Pollution surrounds us all. From the clothes we wear, to the way we travel, to our consumption choices, we are all – in highly *uneven* ways – creators and repositories of environmental damage. Toxicants have become increasingly ubiquitous in everyday life, and toxic potential suspends itself between absolute mundanity and perpetual threat. Yet despite the ever-present realities of contamination and environmental damage, pollution is often very difficult to sense or witness. Hazardous substances, for example, are often impossible to observe with the naked eye. According to the dominant narrative (see Kuchinskaya 2014), the dangers of chemical spills, radioactive particles, and air pollution, for example, would all be rendered imperceptible without the intervention of scientific devices; chemical sensors, Geiger counters, air meters, and so on. The human body alone, it seems, is not equipped to grapple with the agencies of late-modern discard. But what is it about pollution that gives it this uncanny characteristic? And moreover, does this narrative of sensorial ignorance correspond with the actually existing experience of living with pollution?

Toxic pollution is occluded from our senses in two primary ways: through *scale* and through *temporality*. Geographically, the impacts of toxic things can transcend the widest of scales: from the sphere of microbiology – operating at the cellular level within the borders of the polluted body – to a global reach, where toxic pollution spreads invisibly, ignoring geopolitical boundaries in the land, sea, and air. From the impacts of nuclear disasters to the spread of microplastic pollution, the silent mobility of pollution is no respecter of national borders, state lines, or passport control. At the scale of the individual, pollution can render human and more-than-human bodies "open," exposing the permeability of skin, tissue, and bone. Put simply, pollution is often too *tiny* or too *vast* to be fully comprehended. Scale and distance can conspire to make pollution enigmatic from a human perspective.

Thinking beyond space, *time* can make pollution unknowable in other ways, too. Temporally, environmental hazards may linger and accumulate as toxic lag, taking generations to make an impact, and allowing past pollution to transfer its harmful presence to the future (Nixon 2011; Murphy 2015; Boudia et al. 2018; Davies 2018). The gradual velocity of pollution creates a temporal blind spot, drip-feeding its toxic violence across the distance of months, years, or even lifetimes. Time obscures the possibility of knowing, for example, if a particular substance from the past has caused a particular cancer today. It conceals the impacts of our environmental decisions from those who are destined to inherit our pollution in the future. Time hides pollution from plain view, making it difficult to sense or make sense of. In the most extreme cases, the impacts of toxic pollution will only reveal themselves years later, in the illnesses and deaths of those who are exposed (Davies 2019). Even then, it takes political *work* – often by environmental justice activists – to transform a sick body into a political fact (Armiero and Fava 2016). In some polluted communities, the only witnesses to years of environmental damage can be found in fenceline stories of mysterious sickness and lost relatives, with the graveyard becoming a reluctant archive of contested and occluded exposure.

And herein lies the problem: How can individuals, when faced with the peculiar opacity of pollution, bear witness to its impacts? Which senses do we rely upon when we are confronted by toxic hazards? Moreover, which perspectives and epistemologies are silenced in environmental justice struggles, and how might we broaden our framework of creating toxic truths? These questions are put into sharp relief in an age of post-truth, where expertise of all kinds is being diminished, undermined, and questioned. In this section – drawing on case studies from Ecuador, Ghana, and Brazil – the authors take up the challenge of how to make "sense" of pollution and witness its impacts, by looking at different ways that pollution is being voiced and observed by the public.

But how can you witness pollution if it is invisible? As we saw in the previous chapter, where we encountered the cesspits and pig shit of North Carolina's hog industry, not all pollution is unsenuous. As countless frontline communities around the world testify, pollution can also be embodied, viscous, acrid, and uncanny. It can stick in the back of your throat and cling to your nostrils. It can bring you out in rashes or leave you short of breath. For those living in highly toxic geographies, such as Louisiana's "Cancer Alley," pollution can also catch you off-guard and wake you up in the middle of the night (Davies 2018). Pollution can also be witnessed in the hospital records of fenceline communities, and in the memories of those who have survived toxic accidents, such as Bhopal, Chernobyl, and Fukushima. But it can also be witnessed in mundane ways: as anyone who has visited any coastline on this planet in the last few decades can testify, pollution can be found in the waves lapping against the shore, in the form of unruly plastic flotsam.

In a world beset by an increasing toxic presence, perhaps the invisibility of pollution has been overplayed within discard studies (Peeples 2011; Kuchinskaya 2014). Instead of focusing our attention solely on the *invisibility* of technological hazards – which has dominated environmental thought for some time – we should extend our attention to the myriad ways that individuals *do* notice, sense, and witness the circulation and accumulation of pollution (Balayannis 2019; Davies 2019). The era of post-truth has made us more attentive to the importance of stories, narratives, and emotions within political struggles. Paradoxically – and in line with the idea of progressive populism (Bosworth 2019) – this may offer new opportunities to take the knowledge claims of local communities much more seriously. By refocusing our attention on the body as an environmental sensor, for example, a new wave of academic research has sought to understand pollution via the experiences of those who actually live with it. Recent environmental justice scholarship has highlighted the importance of "slow observations" (Davies 2018), "bodily reasoning" (Shapiro 2015), and "resigned activism" (Lora-Wainwright 2017) as key modes of understanding pollution that may otherwise be dismissed or overlooked. These approaches do not fit neatly into definitions of "citizen science," but they do display an expertise about pollution that demands to be taken seriously.

In this part of the book, the authors bring to task the assumption that pollution is non-sensory. In the chapter by Amelia Fiske, we will see how a *touching* toxicity plays an important role in making pollution tangible for lawyers, activists, and tourists who go on toxic tours in the Ecuadorian rainforest. Fiske focuses on the role of a simple auger – a tool for removing a small core of soil from contaminated ground – highlighting how witnessing the sticky materiality of oil extraction can bring questions of injustice to the surface. By inviting participants to *touch* the toxic sludge, and *smell* its acrid notes, it becomes impossible to ignore the reality that certain people are exposed to the burden of pollution in the name of capitalist profit. During the toxic tours, the dirty "stink and stickiness" of oil becomes both the message and the medium for seeking environmental justice. Using the auger to collect samples of contaminated soil, Fiske explains, mimics the scientific practices of formal experts – but instead of creating "data" about pollution, it creates a story, exposing environmental injustice as viscous, fetid, and unmissibly *there*.

The challenge of making pollution present is also taken up by Peter C. Little and Marina Da Silva, who both focus on visual dimensions of pollution. Little takes us to one of the world's largest e-waste dumps, in Agbogbloshie, a district in Accra, the capital of Ghana. He explores how workers who recycle e-waste in this vibrant urban market are able to make their injuries and toxic working conditions visible by sharing digital photographs. Little describes how his participatory visual methods allowed his participants to show a side of Agbogbloshie not often witnessed by outsider photographers, who often represent e-waste extraction through the predictable prism of misery and spectacle. In the next chapter, Da Silva discusses the issue of visuality in a different way through the notion of "visual pollution." In her exploration of the world's first "clean city law" (*Lei Cidade Limpa*) in São Paulo, Brazil, she reveals how the anti-graffiti and anti-advertisement law has been interpreted and manipulated by regressive urban governors. Situated within the anti-environment populism of President Bolsonaro, Da Silva demonstrates how – in line with other types of contamination – what *counts* as visual pollution is a highly political decision.

Together, the chapters in this section of *Toxic Truths* provide a useful counterbalance to imaginations of pollution as "invisible" without the aid of scientific knowledge and devices. They push back against the tendency to frame discussions of pollution from the starting point of sensorial ignorance and move away from reducing local knowledge to narrow data entry points in citizen science projects. Rather, here we will read about how living with pollution can be a highly sensed, witnessed, and embodied experience.

References

Armiero, M. and Fava, A. 2016. Of humans, sheep, and dioxin: A history of contamination and transformation in Acerra, Italy. *Capitalism Nature Socialism*, 27(2), 67–82.

Balayannis, A. 2019. Toxic sights: The spectacle of hazardous waste removal. *Environment and Planning D; Society and Space*, 1–19.

Bosworth, K. 2019. The people know best: Situating the counterexpertise of populist pipeline opposition movements. *Annals of the American Association of Geographers*, 109(2), 581–592.

Boudia, S., Creager, A. N., Frickel, S., Henry, E., Jas, N., Reinhardt, C., and Roberts, J. 2018. Residues: Rethinking chemical environments. *Engaging Science, Technology, and Society, Society for Social Studies of Science*, 4, 165–178.

Davies, T. 2018. Toxic space and time: Slow violence, necropolitics, and petrochemical pollution. *Annals of the American Association of Geographers*, 108(6), 1537–1553.

Davies, T. 2019. Slow violence and toxic geographies: "Out of sight" to whom? *Environment and Planning C: Politics and Space.* DOI: 10.1177/2399654419841063.

Kuchinskaya, O. 2014. *The Politics of Invisibility: Public Knowledge about Radiation Health Effects after Chernobyl.* New York: MIT Press.

Lora-Wainwright, A. 2017. *Resigned Activism: Living with Pollution in Rural China.* New York: MIT Press.

Murphy, M. 2015. Chemical infrastructures of the St Clair River. In N. Jas and S. Boudia S. (eds), *Toxicants, Health and Regulation since 1945.* London: Routledge, pp. 103–115.

Nixon, R. 2011. *Slow Violence and the Environmentalism of the Poor.* London: Harvard University Press.

Peeples, J. 2011. Toxic sublime: Imaging contaminated landscapes. *Environmental Communication: A Journal of Nature and Culture*, 5(4), 373–392.

Shapiro, N. 2015. Attuning to the chemosphere: Domestic formaldehyde, bodily reasoning, and the chemical sublime. *Cultural Anthropology*, 30(3), 368–393.

5

The auger: A tool of environmental justice in Ecuadorian toxic tours

Amelia Fiske

The well platform is quiet in the afternoon heat of the Amazon. Two school-aged children in matching uniforms wander across the empty dirt rectangle carved out of the forest on their way home. I am with a group of photographers, on a "Toxic Tour" to document the pollution left in the soil after two decades of extraction by the Texaco Company[1] in Ecuador. Although Texaco left the country in the 1990s, oil extraction has since continued with the state and other foreign companies that operate in the region today. Donald, our guide, has brought the group to this site in order to illustrate the ways that residents' lives are entangled with industry and struggles for justice. Here it is common to find houses that are immediately adjacent to, or sometimes even located on top of, waste pits of buried crude oil.

Heading toward the house bordering the well platform, we walk through a narrow passage in the fence. Signs of life – outgrown shoes, a stray tunafish can – litter the yard. A sheep bleats in the brush. Donald indicates with his hand a depression in the land just a few meters from the house; it is a rectangular indentation as though years ago an old swimming pool had been dug, filled in, and then overgrown with grass. This will be today's operating theater, and we are the spectators. Setting up a small plastic table in one corner, Donald and his assistants begin to dig with a hand auger, a metal tool for extracting shallow, subsurface soil cores. At first, the dirt resists, and then gives way under their effort. One core sample is pulled up, then another, and another – each approximately 12 inches long. The samples are laid out, length-wise, in order of their extraction on a sheet of plastic prepared on the table. As each sample is added to the next, a color gradient begins to appear – from rocky gray to red to deep browns – as they probe deeper into the earth.

When the auger pulls up rock or soil, it scrapes loudly against the metal frame of the corer. But when the auger pulls up mud – or dirt that has been heavily contaminated with oil – the auger makes a sucking sound as it disengages from the hole. The next core slides out with a telltale squeak: *Aha!* There is an immediate, collective recognition of the contents. Camera shutters fire rapidly as Donald rights the auger and scrapes the core into position on the table. One of the participants leans in to smell the sample. Through whispers and photographs, smells and manual inspection with gloves, there is a public dissection of the remnants of oil extraction from decades before. It is a moment of reckoning, of realization that just a few feet beneath the land on which we are standing and upon which this family lived, are the buried contents of an old waste pit. At this site, one of many along the toxic tour, Donald exhumes traces of pollution for our collective confirmation. The auger allows for the shared recognition of the presence of pollution.

This chapter follows the use of the auger outside of official domains in regulatory inspections and lawsuits, in order to examine its role in matters of environmental justice. The use of soil coring tools in geology, archaeology, and other official regulatory domains is common; however, the work of the auger in the realms of social or environmental activism has been overlooked. Of particular interest is the way in which the auger enrolls participants as witnesses in the "discovery" of contamination through a range of visceral engagements on the toxic tour: the nostril-curling smell of the samples, the squish of oily muds between the fingers, or the telltale, incandescent sheen of hydrocarbons. In the process, the buried legacies of old industrial practices (such as the dumping of crude oil and industrial waste in unlined pits in the jungle) are brought to the surface in publically negotiated, personally convincing, acts of toxic revelation.

In a place marked for decades by a contentious lawsuit that has scrutinized the validity of various scientific, legal, and social means of apprehending environmental harm, what constitutes "evidence" of contamination and wrongdoing changes as we follow the auger out of official forums to the unofficial, collective moments of the toxic tour. In querying the multiple registers of evidence that the auger makes possible, and in an era where scientific expertise is increasingly under attack, what can we learn from citizen-led practices such as soil coring? At first blush, it might seem that the use of the auger is simply an expert tool that has been "borrowed" and applied to a sociopolitical cause. Yet, as I will show throughout this chapter, there is more to toxic tours than simply mock exhibitions of expert practices. Rather, by taking a technique that normally exists within the domain of natural sciences or legal arbitration, and using it to publicly interpellate the soil as contaminated, soil coring emerges as a technique for sensing injustice. It demonstrates that "toxicity is not only about quantifiable concentrations embodied in bioscientific ways of knowing, but is also about cultural understandings of it" (Calvillo 2018). A scientific demonstration of the presence of toxicants in these soils cannot be divorced from the questions of injustice that such toxicity implies. The auger makes the toxic histories of oil extraction tangible for the lawyers, students, tourists, and activists present on the tours.

This chapter brings the auger to bear on the public discernment of contamination and accountability, offering an opportunity to explore how questions of industrial contamination are adjudicated publicly, and what these tools of knowledge production illuminate and what they occlude (Murphy 2006). Following the auger from official to lay realms is instructive in a moment where expertise is increasingly scrutinized amid what has been debated as an era of "post-truth" (Sismondo 2017). Yet, rather than collecting robust scientific evidence, the use of the auger in the context of toxic tours aims to enroll the public in witnessing environmental injustice – an objective which sidesteps debates over the success or failure of scientific initiatives (including citizen-led practices) to focus on the continued production of toxic inequality in places like the Amazon. This move underscores the need for recognition of environmental justice struggles in the face of failed or incomplete attempts at distributional or procedural justice (Schlosberg 2007), a matter which is crucial given ongoing legal struggles over Texaco operations in the Amazon. The auger makes old contamination evident, and thus actionable, for participants in ways that buried crude is not. By exhuming contamination, participants grasp an essential part of residents' stories of harm that has been obscured by the production of contested scientific evidence and stories of fraud and collusion in the legal case: the very *obviousness* of the contamination that residents encounter in their daily lives.

Judicial inspections in the *Aguinda v. Texaco* lawsuit and toxic tours

Oil operations began in the northeastern corner of the Ecuadorian Amazon in the 1960s, through a joint venture between the Ecuadorian state and the Texaco Company. Over the course of twenty years of operations, Texaco drilled 339 wells and built 18 production stations, to extract an estimated 1.5 billion barrels of crude oil (Kimerling 2006, 449). Widespread dumping of crude oil and production fluids into local rivers and streams and the routine burning of oil by-products from waste pits resulted in massive environmental contamination as well as health problems for indigenous and settler communities. In 1993, a group of lawyers filed a lawsuit against Texaco on behalf of 30,000 Amazonians who were living in the Concession area at the time (*Aguinda v. Texaco*). Claiming environmental, health, and cultural damages, the subsequently convoluted path of the lawsuit brought unprecedented international attention to the region. In 2011, the court found Chevron (which purchased Texaco in 2001) guilty and fined the company $9.5 billion. Following Texaco's exit from Ecuador in 1993, national and foreign oil companies have expanded operations, and extraction emerged as an object of political and social controversy. After two decades of operations, in the 1990s Ecuador introduced its first comprehensive environmental regulations, resulting in new audit practices and increased state oversight of the industry. At the time of the fieldwork for this text, the government of Rafael Correa relied heavily on extractive industries to generate revenue for social and educational programs. Ongoing activism has called for cleanup, compensation, and conservation in light of continual problems with contamination.

Toxic tours started as a civic forum for educating the public and bringing about social change in the form of expeditions to polluted spaces in the United States. Tours were largely led by residents of communities that had been historically disadvantaged and thus carried an undue burden of industrial contamination (Pezzullo 2009). Emerging in conjunction with the environmental justice movement in the mid-1980s, activists began to articulate the associations between race, class, and environmental assault. The movement theorized the production of particular spaces as "appropriately polluted" (Higgins 1994) or as "human sacrifice zones" (Bullard and Benjamin 1999), pointing out the patterned siting of toxic waste sites in low-income communities of color (Commission for Racial Justice and United Church of Christ 1987). The idea of a toxic tour was to invite outsiders to places they would not normally go, forging connections across spatial, political, racial, and affective distance by giving participants an intimate experience in places where the "other" lived, worked, and played.

In 2003, the *Aguinda* lawsuit returned to Ecuadorian courts after nearly 10 years in the United States judicial system. With the arrival of the case, journalists, lawyers, and students began to arrive in Lago Agrio with questions, and asking to see the disputed Texaco sites. Often, they were referred to the Frente de Defensa de la Amazonía (FDA, Amazon Defense Front), the most prominent national nongovernmental organization supporting the case at the time. There they met Donald Moncayo, who had grown up in the first oil camp drilled by Texaco in Ecuador, just outside Lago Agrio. Donald knew the region intimately. As a child he had watched Texaco's early operations unfold. He knew which streams had been contaminated by spills and which old waste pits had been covered over. At first his activities were largely informal, volunteering to show visitors around when someone arrived with questions. As he began to conduct tours more regularly, this task became his vocation. As Donald told me, one journalist suggested the name "Toxic Tour," and that is the term by which these events are known now. Today, Donald's principal role at the non-profit is to run the tours. There is no fee charged for the tour itself, and participants are only responsible for paying the transportation for the day. Donald conducts tours alone as well as with the collaboration of others, including indigenous leaders, plaintiffs in the *Aguinda* lawsuit, or in the company of his young daughter.

I attended dozens of these tours between 2011 and 2013 as part of field research on the matter of harm resulting from oil production in the provinces of Sucumbíos and Orellana. Donald principally conducted tours in the Concession area that was previously operated by Texaco and the state company, PetroEcuador. Although each tour was designed to speak to the specific interests of the group participating (lawyers, students, tourists, or activists), in general, the tours had several key components that were always present. Opening with a historical narrative describing the beginning of oil exploration in the Amazon, Donald would then discuss the technical practices of Texaco operations and their resulting contamination of the surrounding soils and water. This narrative was interwoven with a review of the *Aguinda* lawsuit as groups visited different sites; sometimes he showed them the endless bookshelves of documents related to the lawsuit held in the plaintiff lawyer's office, other times he indicated well-known photos of the region (Dematteis and Szymczak 2008), or recounted the stories of individuals who had lost family members or become ill from exposure to toxicants related to oil production. While the order of these different components would vary, the tours always included at least one, most often several, first-hand encounters with contamination. Tours were designed to include an itinerary of sites that would illustrate a range of infrastructure, from pipelines to waste pits, wells, spill sites, or gas flares. Whether observing the sheen of oil in streams, listening to the crunch under foot of thousands of dead bugs that accumulate beneath a roaring gas flare, or inspecting with a gloved finger the buried crude present in poorly remediated sites, going on a toxic tour was always an intense sensory experience. In the process, Donald and his collaborators worked to produce their own forms of evidence to convince viewers on the spot of the personal weight of toxic legacies – not evidence that could be entered into a court case, but evidence of the profound injustice borne in the name of corporate profit and the carbon-based present.

The auger as a tool of justice

A central aim of the toxic tour is to provide an opportunity for those who do not have quotidian, personal knowledge of oil contamination to begin to comprehend what it is like to live alongside operations. To facilitate these encounters, Donald employed several objects to assist visitors in seeing, smelling, and touching oil pollution for the first time: a glove, a long stick, a large recycled water bottle, and a hand auger. These assorted tools work together to enable a direct engagement with the materiality of toxicity and legacies of extraction that would not otherwise be possible. In other circumstances, tools like the auger produce soil samples that are inscribed through calibrated forms of scientific testing, in order to produce scientific or legal evidence – a register that does not aim to produce a public response. Crucially, by unearthing contamination in situ in the toxic tour, the samples produced with the auger aim to convince observers through the tactility of toxicity rather than through official forms of inscription. It is in this manner that the auger moves from being a tool of scientific sampling to a tool of justice.

An auger is an instrument designed to bore a hole into the earth and bring up columns of soil in the form of soil cores. Generally used in the natural sciences, a hand auger is a relatively inexpensive technology (in the range of $100–200 per device). It has a T-shaped body, with extendable lengths that can be added for deeper samples. A hollow encasement holds the soil sample, with a sharp pointed end. A remarkably fluid and adaptable technology (de Laet and Mol 2000), it is most useful at relatively shallow depths of a few meters – albeit with considerable sweat on the part of the operator! Augers are part of a repertoire of technical, expert-led practices, and results are usually recorded as part of regulatory documentation (such as an environmental impact assessment) or scientific studies (climatology, archaeology, geology), and rarely in sociopolitical or advocacy forums. In all cases, the auger makes it possible to see and analyze the layered sediments of the past.

In the mid-2000s, toxic tours emerged as an increasingly common means for the plaintiffs to communicate their story to outsiders. During this time, the *Aguinda* lawsuit moved into the "fact-finding" phase where the facts of contamination were generated. As part of the judicial inspections in Ecuador, the courtroom became mobile: the judge, lawyers, technical experts, and administrative staff traveled to 54 former Texaco sites[2] (wells, production facilities, spill sites) across the Concession.[3] Both parties nominated sites to be scrutinized in front of the judge. In the inspections, technicians for the plaintiffs and the defendant took samples of soil and water, which each party later analyzed. Once concluded, a panel of court-appointed experts reviewed the results that both parties submitted for the judge to consider. While a complete account of the *Aguinda* proceedings is beyond the scope of this chapter, here I would like to highlight the otherwise understated role that the hand auger played in these site inspections.

Described as more "theatre" (Tavares 2011) and "circus" (Barrett 2014) than legal proceeding, the judicial inspections were attended by an assorted flock of media, food vendors, environmental activists, security forces, and Chevron supporters, as well as lawyers, technical teams, the judge, and his assistants. In early inspections, technicians donned white Hazmat suits complete with facemasks to take soil cores and samples. The jungle heat quickly made wearing such suits untenable and they were later abandoned. When you look at images of these early inspections, the auger is often present – or, if not in the frame, one can spot its presence through the neatly encapsulated soil cores. In one photo, men covered in white suits, hard hats, and green surgical gloves sustain a soil core from an auger for inspection by the plaintiff and defendant lawyers (Tavares 2011, 102). Captured mid-examination, the technicians seem akin to surgeons, as though they were carefully extracting infected tissue in an operation. Like the scalpel, the auger is at once absolutely essential to the operation, and at the same time, totally absent from discussion of the evidence that results.

During the inspections, arguments by the lawyers went on at length, making for long days beneath the equatorial sun. Although there was no verbal testimony in the lawsuit, when residents were present for inspections on their land, they too offered accounts of operations and their comments were included in the court proceedings. During my fieldwork, I spoke with many such individuals who gave testimony of what was apparent to them from living in the Amazon: that oil exploitation had poisoned their water, land, farms, and those beings – human and animal – who lived there (Fiske 2016). For residents who lived through the first several decades of oil in Ecuador, no legal or scientific validation of the overwhelming presence of toxicity was necessary, even if it remained central to other forms of advocacy and legal dispute in the context of the *Aguinda* lawsuit. Thus, despite the long, convoluted trail of the lawsuit, replete with allegations of "made-up facts" (The Amazon Post 2015), for many living in this region the "proof" of contamination was never in question. It is this obviously harmful nature of contaminated sites, coupled with outrage at the resulting suffering and impunity with which companies operated, that is mobilized in the toxic tours today.

Toxic tours and the theatre of inspection

It's another tour in the Amazon. The students are gathered around Lago Agrio 1, the first oil well perforated by Texaco in Ecuador 1967. This site marks the beginning of the commercial oil industry in the country. It's hot and the students have just gotten off the bus from their university in the Andes; for many of them it is their first time in the Amazon. It is also their first toxic tour. Donald directs the group to gather around the well, their shadows distorted against the oily water accumulated at its base. Emergildo, a member of the Cofán nationality, who often accompanies Donald in leading the tours, begins to tell part of his story:

> Good morning, compañeros … In 1964, we, the Cofán nationality, lived along the banks of the Aguarico river. We went everywhere; we weren't in the habit of living in just one place. So that's why we would travel upstream, downstream, spending one year, two years, three years, and that's how we lived. In 1967, the Company arrived here in the Amazon to drill this well, Lago Agrio 1. We saw the helicopter that arrived in the air, and we were scared. We hid in the jungle, because we had never seen a helicopter flying in the air. After a few months, then we began to hear noises, and we didn't know what it was that was making this noise here in the jungle. We walked over here to see, but it wasn't like this [as it is today]. It was 10 hectares that had been completely cleared of all the trees. Completely cleared.

When Emergildo and his family returned home to the Aguarico after that first encounter, it was only a few months before black crude began floating downstream from the Lago Agrio 1 well:

> And a few months later, the oil spills started. The oil spilled down the Aguarico where we lived and our feet were stained because there was nowhere to walk because we would go to the edge of the river and you would step in the oil spill … We tried to wash it off with water and we scraped it with sand, but that's how we lived, suffering for many years … And then the diseases started, diseases of the skin, stomach pain, because all of the contamination went into the river. Before, when there wasn't any contamination, we got water directly from the Aguarico and drank it.

This is a story that Emergildo has told many times, not only to students, but also to lawyers, tourists, Chevron shareholders, politicians, and documentary film directors (Berlinger 2009). The students hold out their cell phones, recording as he tells them how his first child was born unable to develop properly and died a week after birth – which he explains was because his wife drank contaminated water while pregnant. This was an era, he says, when nobody knew that petroleum was toxic. Nobody understood what oil operations would come to mean for the region.

He recounts the story of a second child, who, after bathing in the Aguarico river following a spill, began vomiting uncontrollably. The child died the following morning before they were able to get him to the closest health center, which was then staffed by the missionaries at Limoncocha. His story condenses decades of suffering, colonization, and industrialization into several minutes. Yet, he is quick to remind the students that his story, while personal, is not singular: "I'm not the only one," he says, "many other families suffered as well. Not just Cofanes, but Secoyas, Sionas too."[4] The students are silent. It's an intimate narrative crafted from a lifetime spent alongside oil development; an account of a survivor of this toxic legacy (Fassin 2008). For some, the recounting of these painful histories has become an additional burden of toxicity that comes with life alongside extraction (Fiske 2018). During my research, there were often several toxic tours in any given week. Over the years, people like Emergildo and Donald have become accustomed to telling their story to visitors. First-person accounts like this give participants an impression of the lived experiences of loss and sickness that are intertwined with the history of this industry, providing essential narratives for those who come to visit the waste pits and observe the extraction of soil samples. Soil samples, like the ones we opened with, would not carry the same weight without these first-hand accounts of guides.

Motioning for the students to follow him, Donald leads the group across the cleared area of the platform, crossing over the smaller tubes that connect the storage tank to the ubiquitous pipelines that follow nearly all Amazonian roads here. The suspended tubes are wobbly – giving beneath your weight just enough to make you wonder if they might rupture. Lean your ear close enough and you can hear the contents hissing by, with the pipe hot to the touch. Just beyond the pipelines, on the other side of a low bank, lies an old pit. An abandoned gas flare is located toward one end of the pit – a rusted triangular configuration of pipelines used to burn off excess gas produced from the well.

The pit is overgrown with dead grass and pondweeds, the pooled water tinted here and there with the bluish sheen of oil. The tour participants are lined up along the pit's bank, as though standing along the steps of an improvised amphitheatre, with Donald below. The pit has been covered over with dirt, so it is firm enough to stand on. Picking up the auger, he announces to the group: *Here I am going to dig down one meter deep to start to take out what is hidden below. You all will realize what it is when you see it.*[5]

The auger screws clockwise into the mud, scraping rocks, and sucking reluctantly as Donald pulls out the first mud core. Knocking the auger on the ground, he dumps out the surface mud and screws it in deeper. Inspecting the second core, he looks up: *Get your noses ready!* Less than a meter down, the cores of mud begin to take on a dark tint. He removes a clump of mud, and with gloved hands passes it off to the student on his left. The students lean in to inspect the mud. *You can smell it from all the way over here!* says one, reluctant to get closer. Donning gloves, the students pass the mud around, smashing it between their fingers, holding it up for friends to smell or take pictures of. The mud is black and iridescent, glinting in the light.

Taking out an old 5-gallon water bottle that he has brought along for this purpose, Donald cuts it in half with a machete to form a makeshift bowl. *Now this you can see*, he says, *is clear plastic. And the water here is clean too.* Picking up a clump of mud taken from the sample of the pit, he drops it in the water, mixing it until it dissolves. The water turns a dark black, leaving a rainbow stain as it sloshes up the sides of the bottle. The students lean in to get a better look. With a clean, gloved hand, Donald skims the surface of the water with his palm, holding it out to face the students. The glove is black and shiny with oil. *This*, he says, *is the remediation done by Texaco.*[6]

The auger is a tool for uncovering what lies below now covered-over pits; of excavating, as an archaeologist might, the material remains of Texaco activities. As he holds out the oily mud for inspection, Donald states unequivocally: *This is the discovery of the lie told by Texaco.* The act of screwing the auger down and pulling up oily mud for participants to examine is to continually "rediscover" – as though for the first time, for audience after audience – contamination. In doing so, the tour reveals the stratigraphy of toxicity: how toxicants in the soil are intertwined with histories of injustice, with operational practices used in Ecuador that were outlawed in Texas, legal battles, and stories of children lost. Acts of sampling in the context of toxic tours resist simple bifurcations of science and advocacy: these contaminated soils are products of profit, intentions, and neglect. Soil coring shows us that all scientific facts, just like first-hand witness accounts, are situated. Sampling with the auger is informed by personal experience of life alongside the oil industry and of the suffering it has brought; indeed, Donald knows where to dig because he knows the industrial history of these sites. Likewise, the auger is able to enroll the audience as witnesses because they are present, on the banks of this pit, in the moment that the sample is extracted. Yet, sampling with the auger in toxic tours cannot be reduced to spectacle alone: the presence of crude oil in the soil samples refutes any simplistic negation of the material presence of contamination through this palpable, evidentiary, moment of toxic discovery.

The use of an auger in toxic tours mimics scientific and legal techniques for producing evidence of contamination in the *Aguinda* case, in which experts also used augers for sample collection. As an instrument usually employed in scientific practices, and retaining a specific history within the legal case that has defined oil operations in this region, the auger operates in a space on the toxic tours between what is evident (in the sense of being viscerally apparent to observers) and what is evidence (the figures, studies, maps, measures, and other official forms of legal or scientific proof) of pollution in this region. Recall, for instance, the soil samples that were extracted on the tour that opened this chapter: as the auger sucked away from the mud of the hole, there was a collective recognition of the contamination of the soil. The contamination was evident to those watching, indicated by their audible gasps, wrinkled noses, and outraged comments. Yet, soil that smells of petroleum to the human nose is not scientific or legal evidence until it has been sampled according to specific procedures, submitted to a series of laboratory protocols, evaluated, compared to other samples, and interpreted for the court by an appropriate expert. In the process of becoming a scientific fact admissible in a courtroom, many things are excluded. By the end of this chain of transformations, those initially telling features of that soil – its smell, its consistency, its iridescent glint under the Amazonian sun, the story of the family that lived alongside it – are no longer relevant. Yet, in the toxic tour, the stink, stickiness, or sheen of the muds, and the narratives that accompany them, are retained as central features of this public evidentiary process.

The process of sampling is what Latour refers to as the creation of "inscriptions," whereby something like a soil sample is transformed into an object that can be acted upon: extracted from the earth, transported under specific conditions to a laboratory, and then compared, analyzed, interpreted, and circulated as a number, figure, or map in a court record, newspaper article, or scientific study (Latour 1986, 2004). Attending to inscriptions is a reminder that the making of scientific and legal evidence requires a great deal of coordinated effort that extends far beyond the "collection" of naturally existing objects. It also points our attention to what is lost when the inscriptions become mobile, released from the ground in which they were extracted. Yet, for the farmer whose crops grow in that soil, or for the family who lived on top of the pit that opened this article, pre-inscription elements such as the smell of the earth already are evidence of contamination. The same is true for the observer on the toxic tour. If these samples weren't so heavily contaminated with the visible, smellable presence of crude oil, perhaps they wouldn't be so convincing. But here, the blackness of crude or the sensations of nausea after walking beneath a gas flare convince through their viscerality; no further testing is necessary in order for contamination to be apparent.

The soil cores discussed in this chapter were never carefully bagged, labeled, or taken to a lab to be measured for TPH, HAPs, pH, salinity, or heavy metals

– although hundreds of other samples were tested and found to be well above the legal limits (Zambrano Lozada 2011). They weren't compared to other mud samples, or written up as part of a scientific study or a legal complaint. But the contaminated samples extracted by the auger did travel in other ways. In the process of seeing, smelling, and touching on the tours, harm took shape with increasing clarity. Captured on smartphones, written up in blogs, newspaper articles, and school reports, recounted verbally in interviews or to families and friends when participants arrived home, the results of sampling with the auger on toxic tours were carried far beyond this one spot in the Amazon. In the process, witnesses were made and a sample taken in one spot was made to speak to broader histories of environmental injustice.

Conclusion

Science and law purportedly adjudicate matters of fact, establishing truth and, in the case of law, ascertaining wrongdoing. *Aguinda* was expected to determine if Texaco was responsible for harm to the environment and people who lived in the Ecuadorian Amazon during its twenty years of operations. Yet, more than two decades after the lawsuit was initiated, the matter of who to hold responsible for contamination, or how to document and measure contamination remain fiercely contested despite the proliferation of scientific and legal evidence. These disputes are part of a broader narrative in which scientific expertise on the effects of extractive industries is increasingly suspect, or held to unreasonable standards of certainty in light of demonstrated harm. As others have demonstrated, industry mobilizes disagreements over the "facts" to create the perception that no consensus exists (Oreskes and Conway 2011) or to insist on "high-proof" positions of certitude on contested environmental matters (Edwards 1999; Sismondo 2017). As I have argued here, corporate and state denials of toxic responsibility are in tension with the obviousness of contamination in this highly industrialized region, a pattern which holds true across the globe – whether for survivors of disasters like Bhopal or those suffering from the long-term effects of air pollution in Pennsylvania (Fortun 2001; Davis 2003). The presence of contamination is a persistent, undeniable reality. Given the contested space in which both public and expert forums seek to determine accountability for extensive environmental damage, citizen-led practices such as soil coring on toxic tours have an important role to play, not only in advancing struggles for environmental justice through the mobilization of ordinary tools, but also as a critical counter to calls to divorce science from advocacy. Importantly, the auger emerges a tool for achieving recognition in a broader struggle for environmental justice in the region, even in spite of a continued lack of distributional justice following the *Aguinda* lawsuit. By turning to the context of injustice – present in the stories of Emergildo or the scent of contaminated muds beneath a family's home – rather than narrowly focusing on verifying the presence of hydrocarbons and toxicants where they should not be (Fraser 1997), the making of evidence in these toxic tours retains the crucial component of what is deeply *evident* for those living with decades of oil contamination.

In this chapter I have marshaled one object – the auger – in order to tell a story about the contingencies involved in building an evidentiary assemblage, in which the scientific and the social, senses and memory, are entangled in the production of knowledge of environmental harm. By contingencies, I mean that knowledge is produced through relations with other human and nonhuman actors (that can fail or surprise in a variety of ways) that form social-material engagements that give the world specific material form (Barad 2007, 91). Attention to contingencies – to relationships, technicalities, and unknowns – emphasizes the positionality, coordination, and the fragility of such engagements. What emerges in this case is one account of how the presence of contamination is established through toxic tours. Here a common tool, when assembled with narrative accounts from residents, within the context of a place with abundant soil pollution from oil operations that is open for the inspection of participants on the tours, becomes a means of producing evidence of harm and inspiring political action.

In bringing the auger to bear on the matter of contamination in toxic tours, questions of justice are brought to the fore. In the toxic tour, the act of digging up old crude oil and inviting participants to smell, touch, and see it with their own eyes makes it impossible to ignore questions of why ordinary people have been made to bear the burden of contamination in the name of corporate or state profit. The questions that augers were brought to bear on in other contexts like the judicial inspections (Is there contamination on this site? How much? Has it migrated outside the boundaries of the waste pit? Who is responsible?) materialize in the toxic tour with new saliency. These demands remain at the forefront rather than becoming submerged in ongoing allegations of fraud and bribery which have diverted attention away from matters of environmental justice in this case (see Barrett 2014). Just like the soil that retains its smell when inspected by students on the toxic tour, the soil also retains matters of suffering, responsibility, and justice that are bifurcated when soil is "inscribed" as a statistic to be debated.

Questions of justice are embedded in scientific questions. What to sample, where to sample, how to interpret evidence of contamination in relation to broader inequalities of wealth, power, and pollution are also present in the judicial inspections of the *Aguinda* lawsuit – but in the toxic tour they retain a remarkable lucidity. Perhaps what the toxic tour leads us to ask is: How we can use our tools – augers, samples, senses – for good? "The point," following Haraway, "is to make a difference in the world, to cast our lot for some ways of life and not others" (Haraway 1997, 36). The toxic tour invites us all to take a turn at screwing the auger into the mud, and in so doing to throw our weight behind struggles for justice in the Amazon and beyond.

Notes

1 In 2001, Texaco and Chevron merged to become ChevronTexaco.
2 Originally 122 sites were named, but ultimately only 54 sites were inspected because the process took too long and the plaintiffs petitioned the judge to conclude the inspections and move to an appraisal by an independent expert. The resulting "Technical Summary Report" (2008) by Engineer Richard Cabrera Vega was subsequently thrown out after Chevron alleged inappropriate collaborations between Cabrera and the plaintiff team.
3 "The Concession" refers to the area operated by the consortium of Texaco and the Ecuadorian state between 1972 and 1992.
4 The region opened for oil operations under the first concessions is the ancestral territory of the Indigenous nationalities of Cofán, Sekoya, Siona, and Waorani, and home to the Kichwa.
5 Speech in italics indicates text reconstructed from footnotes. While I have done my best to accurately recreate the content and feel of Donald's tours, direct quotations should not be taken as such unless indicated.
6 The most iconic image of the toxic tour is the extended, crude-covered hand. Donald's picture, face out of focus and obscured behind his black hand, regularly accompanies articles in newspapers and magazines and has made countless appearances on activist websites and blogs. The dirtied hand makes contamination – which, when sitting in the mud at the bottom of a stream or distributed across the surface of water can be evasive – visible for the viewer. It is a striking, personal gesture that denounces the legacy of oil (Fiske 2018).

References

Barad, K. 2007. *Meeting the Universe Halfway: Quantum Physics and the Entanglement of Matter and Meaning*. Durham, NC: Duke University Press.
Barrett, P. M. 2014. *Law of the Jungle: The $19 Billion Legal Battle Over Oil in the Rain Forest and the Lawyer Who'd Stop at Nothing to Win*. New York: Crown.
Berlinger, J. 2009. *Crude: The Real Price of Oil*. DVD. New York: First Run Features.

Bullard, R. D. and Benjamin, C. 1999. *Confronting Environmental Racism: Voices from the Grassroots*. Boston, MA: South End Press.

Cabrera Vega, R. 2008. *Technical Summary to the Court of Nueva Loja*. Available at chevrontoxico.com/assets/docs/cabrera-english-2008.pdf (last accessed January 27, 2020).

Calvillo, N. 2018. Political airs: From monitoring to attuned sensing air pollution. *Social Studies of Science*, 48(3), 372–388.

Commission for Racial Justice, and United Church of Christ. 1987. Toxic Wastes and Race in the United States: A National Report on the Racial and Socio-economic Characteristics of Communities with Hazardous Waste Sites. Public Data Access, Inc. Available at https://www.nrc.gov/docs/ML1310/ML13109A339.pdf (last accessed January 27, 2020).

Davis, D. 2003. *When Smoke Ran Like Water: Tales of Environmental Deception and the Battle Against Pollution*. New York: Basic Books.

de Laet, M. and Mol, A. 2000. The Zimbabwe bush pump. *Social Studies of Science*, 30(2), 225–263.

Dematteis, L. and Szymczak, K. 2008. *Crude Reflections / Cruda Realidad: Oil, Ruin and Resistance in the Amazon Rainforest*. Bilingual. San Fransisco, CA: City Lights Publishers.

Edwards, P. N. 1999. Global climate science, uncertainty and politics: Data-laden models, model-filtered data. *Science as Culture*, 8(4), 437–472.

Fassin, D. 2008. The humanitarian politics of testimony: Subjectification through trauma in the Israeli–Palestinian conflict. *Cultural Anthropology*, 23(3), 531–558.

Fiske, A. 2016. *Crude Assemblages: Oil and Harm in the Ecuadorian Amazon*. Chapel Hill, NC: University of North Carolina at Chapel Hill.

Fiske, A. 2018. Dirty hands: The toxic politics of denunciation. *Social Studies of Science, Toxic Politics*, 48(3), 389–413.

Fortun, K. 2001. *Advocacy after Bhopal: Environmentalism, Disaster, New Global Orders*. Chicago, IL: University of Chicago Press.

Fraser, N. 1997. *Justice Interruptus: Critical Reflections on the "Postsocialist" Condition*. Abingdon: Routledge.

Haraway, D. J. 1997. *Modest_Witness@Second_Millennium.FemaleMan_Meets_OncoMouse: Feminism and Technoscience*. New York: Routledge.

Higgins, R. R. 1994. Race, pollution, and the mastery of nature. *Environmental Ethics*, 16(3), 251–264.

Kimerling, J. 2006. Indigenous peoples and the oil frontier in Amazonia: The case of Ecuador, ChevronTexaco, and *Aguinda v. Texaco*. *New York University Journal of International Law and Politics*, 38, 413.

Latour, B. 1986. Visualization and cognition: Drawing things together. *Knowledge and Society*, 6, 1–40.

Latour, B. 2004. *Politics of Nature: How to Bring the Sciences into Democracy*. Cambridge, MA: Harvard University Press.

Murphy, M. 2006. *Sick Building Syndrome and the Problem of Uncertainty: Environmental Politics, Technoscience, and Women Workers*. Durham, NC: Duke University Press.

Oreskes, N. and Conway, E. M. 2011. *Merchants of Doubt: How a Handful of Scientists Obscured the Truth on Issues from Tobacco Smoke to Global Warming*. New York: Bloomsbury.

Pezzullo, P. C. 2009. *Toxic Tourism: Rhetorics of Pollution, Travel, and Environmental Justice*. Tuscaloosa: University Alabama Press.

Schlosberg, D. 2007. *Defining Environmental Justice: Theories, Movements, and Nature*. Oxford: Oxford University Press.

Sismondo, S. 2017. Post-truth? *Social Studies of Science*, 47(1), 3–6.

Tavares, P. 2011. Murky evidence: Environmental forensics in the age of the Anthropocene. *Cabinet*, Fall (43 Forensics), 101–105.

The Amazon Post. 2015. When Steven Donziger doesn't find evidence against Chevron … he creates it. *The Amazon Post*, September 15. Available at http://theamazonpost.com/donziger-quote-1/ (last accessed January 27, 2020).

Zambrano Lozada, N. 2011. *Aguinda et al. v. Chevron Corporation* 188. Provincial Court of Justice of Sucumbíos.

6

Witnessing e-waste through participatory photography in Ghana

Peter C. Little

Introduction

Drawing on extended ethnographic research in Agbogbloshie, an urban scrapyard in Accra, Ghana that has become the subject of a contentious electronic waste (e-waste) narrative, this chapter explores the extent to which citizen[1] photography and similar participatory visual research efforts augment contemporary toxic studies in general and e-waste studies in particular. Attuned to the visual promises, politics, and possibilities of photography in toxic landscapes (Peeples 2011; Davies 2013; Barnett 2015; Rosenfeld et al. 2018), the chapter contends that engaging with participatory visualization and documentation can provide vital contextualization for debates grappling with the toxic injustices and environmental politics of e-waste labor. I explore how and why visual techniques in participatory action research matter in global environmental justice studies in general and postcolonial e-waste studies in Ghana in particular. This participatory e-waste visualization project accounts for the critical role of researcher positionality and reflexivity in efforts to bear witness to and make sense of lived experiences of e-waste. Taking a participatory photography approach that recognizes embodied ways of knowing e-waste, this project attempts to go beyond the massive archive of contentious natural and humanist photography focused on Africa and the "prism of misery" (Keane 1998, 2) that too often typifies transatlantic and North-to-South visions of environmental destruction in Africa.

Amid air monitoring technologies, risk mitigation machines, optimistic NGOs (nongovernmental organizations), journalists, environmental and social scientists, makerspace engineers, slum tourists, and photographers, Agbogbloshie is a vibrant urban scrap-metal market. It is a space and place where workers engage in hazardous metal extraction to supply global copper and aluminum markets. For most who have turned to Agbogbloshie as a site of e-waste research, there is an effort to somehow extend an ethos of care for those living and working in this notorious West African hot spot of "toxic colonialism" (Koné 2009).[2] But, what seems less common in projects focused on Agbogbloshie are efforts to showcase how these workers are creative postcolonial agents actively documenting and communicating their own lived experience, pollution situation, and e-waste vitality. In short, the chapter asks: what happens when e-waste workers are involved image makers? What does this participatory photography do to and for representations of Agbogbloshie? To what extent can this alternative visualization shift understandings of a place and space that has become a central node of global e-wasteland and digital pollution narratives? Moreover, how does engagement with this alternative approach to witnessing and knowing e-waste draw attention to or renew critical discussion of researcher positionality and ethnographic reflexivity?

Workers in this site, for example, have too often been understood as e-waste recycling laborers who foreground their experience of pollution and environmental health risk. But, representations of Agbogbloshie as a site of e-waste toxicity and ruination are not the only stories being told. Lived experiences of e-waste, it turns out, are far more complicated. In light of this, the chapter navigates how e-waste "perceptual regimes" (Poole 1997) can be reconfigured and meshed with the overlapping projects of environmental justice (EJ) and toxics knowledge production. It will be argued that e-waste worker images advance contemporary and future e-waste and digital pollution studies by providing much-needed perceptual inversion and representational plurality (Bleiker and Kay 2007). They teach us new ways of seeing and visioning e-waste contextualization and perhaps even the environmental justice challenges experienced in Agbogbloshie (Akese and Little 2018). My aim here, then, is to turn to a participatory photography project in Agbogbloshie to stimulate critical discussion of the ways in which alternative e-waste visioning can transform how e-wasteland politics in Ghana are told, seen, and responsibly contextualized. Participatory photography, in this way, offers a critical perspective on embodied ways of knowing and practices of bearing witness to e-waste pollution, Furthermore, photography itself offers a compelling counterpoint to systemic post-truth politics in the Trump era. For example, one of the most powerful uses of photography-for-proof in recent times was on January 20, 2017, the day of Donald Trump's inauguration. The image spread quickly. Visual proof concluded that Barak Obama was the obvious champion of recent inaugural turnout statistics, despite the Trump Administration's efforts to convince the public otherwise. In short, the citizen showing for Obama's inauguration on January 20, 2009 was clear evidence of victory. This visual proof sparked a debate that highlighted the first of many disappointments with and opposition to techniques of visualization coming from the Trump White House. This all dovetails with recent trends in post-truth politics. As Lyons (2017) points out:

> The "post-truth" environment we live in seems, at least in part, to be a function of the current confusing information flow and how politicians, governments and others use it towards their own ends. It remains to be seen what longer term effects this will have on journalism generally and photojournalism in particular but the power of the still image remains undeniable, even if some choose to ignore inconvenient truths. (Lyons 2017, 2)

This contemporary reorientation of the power of visualization can provide a platform for "making new sense" (Hastrup 1995) of the complexities and confusion that come with current and future representations of the e-waste pollution problem that put Agbogbloshie on the global toxics map.

Situating Ghana in the global e-wasteland narrative

The globalization of electronic discard is a robust and growing domain of scholarship and activism (Lepawsky 2018). The places where this discard shows up – most notably China, India, Bangladesh, and Ghana – are often described by academics and activists as digital dumping grounds and high-tech slums where informal economies and ecologies are marked by a tangle of toxic substances, contentious state oversight and NGO intervention, local corruption, extreme poverty, and scrap-metal market politics. One such place is Agbogbloshie, an urban scrap market in Accra, Ghana, that has attracted numerous international environmental NGOs, makerspace activists, environmental health scientists, slum tourists, journalists, photographers, and social scientists. Visitors can witness what they have been told about this place and space of digital "wastelanding" (Voyles 2015). They encounter a smoky scrap market zone of intense metal recovery, a site where the burning of e-waste to recover valuable metals, especially copper and aluminum, is an everyday activity. It is a space of ram-

pant toxicity, an environment of lead, mercury, cadmium, PCBs (polychlorinated biphenyls), and airborne contaminants, including polybrominated diphenyl
ethers (PBDEs) that present numerous environmental health risks (Caravanos
et al. 2011, 2013; Feldt et al. 2014; Wittsiepe et al. 2015; Kyere et al. 2016).
Agbogbloshie is also a place of contentious green NGO risk mitigation intervention that tends to overlook the complex lived experience of the postcolonial
bodies and subjectivities navigating the web of social, environmental, and economic risks associated with toxic e-waste recycling (Little 2016).

Located on the banks of the Korle lagoon in Accra, Ghana, the Agbogbloshie
scrapyard is located within a vibrant informal settlement and economy where
commercial, industrial, and residential zones overlap and land rights struggles persist. Adjacent to the scrap market is the biggest fresh food market in
Accra, the Agbogbloshie market. Old Fadama, an informal settlement, also
sits to the east of the scrap market. Opposite the scrap market and along the
Abossey Okia road are a host of industrial and commercial enterprises including a paint factory, a brewery, a Pepsi bottling plant, a timber market, a meat
market, branches of various banks, and a commercial bus depot. About 90% of
the roughly 5,000 workers at Agbogbloshie also make the nearby Old Fadama
informal settlement their home (Prakash et al. 2010). Old Fadama residents are
constantly threatened by the Accra Metropolitan Assembly (AMA), an urban
authority that has recently been the focus of public scrutiny after the AMA forcefully evicted residents following the disastrous flooding of the Korle lagoon in
May 2015. The flooding killed nearly 300 people and caused an explosion at a
gas station that made international headlines.

While the broader Agbogbloshie and Old Fadama area has a deep history
of land management politics dating back to the colonial period (Grant 2006;
Afenah 2012; Stacey and Lund 2016), the establishment of the scrap market
dates to the early 1990s when city authorities, in an attempt to decongest the
central business district of Accra, relocated hawkers and Accra's yam market to
the edge of the Korle lagoon. The relocation of Accra's yam market in 1993 laid
the ground for the scrapyard as various services such as vehicle repair and spare
parts trading, welding, auto mechanics, and tire servicing were crucial to the
operation of the yam trucks (Grant 2006). With diminished agricultural opportunities and compounding intertribal conflicts in Ghana's northern territory,
people moved south to Accra in search of alternative livelihoods. However, in
the absence of job opportunities in the formal sector and in the niche parts of the
informal sector, and in addition to rising housing costs and rent in Accra for the
urban poor, most of these migrant labors found residency in Agbogbloshie
or Old Fadama. In a time marked by rapid population growth in the wider
Agbogbloshie area, truck repair and ancillary services transformed into a major

scrap market which now also serves as the major hub for e-waste processing and employs about 5,000 people (Prakash et al. 2010).

Agbogbloshie's contentious visual economy

Despite widely circulated journalistic accounts of Agbogbloshie as a dump-site for the world's electronic discard, it is much more than an e-wasteland. Workers, for example, talk about Agbogbloshie as a market, not a landfill. Despite this representational confusion, toxic e-waste recycling is ongoing and continues to be a source of critical environmental health risk in Agbogbloshie, as workers spend long hours each day engaging in market metal extraction that is highly toxic. When discarded electronics and electrical equipment end up in Agbogbloshie, the discard containing copper and aluminum is collected, but not as raw copper. Workers first extract the electrical components from the range of exhausted machines that end up at the scrapyard, such as junked cars, buses, and delivery trucks which contain copper-based wires. The quickest and easiest way to extract the copper embedded in these forms of waste is to burn it. The process involves igniting petroleum-based materials, like discarded tires or refrigerator insulation, and tossing bundles of copper wire on the flame until all the plastic insulation disappears. These workers burn the e-waste at several designated burn sites at Agbogbloshie. Locally described as "the burners," they face all the bodily risks of the "burning class," as Marx and today Peter Sloterdijk would have it. Their toxic labor comes with a body burden cost. For example, epidemiological studies have shown that workers experience significant expo-sures to lead, mercury, cadmium, PCBs, and PBDEs (Caravanos et al. 2013; Grant et al. 2013; Wittsiepe et al. 2015).

After an international team of epidemiologists "scientifically" confirmed the risks of this wage labor, an international solutions-based environmental NGO came on the scene, an organization called Pure Earth (formerly Blacksmith Institute; www.pureearth.org). Their primary mission: "eliminating burning" at Agbogbloshie and developing a scrap worker health promotion campaign. While there is no shortage of NGO critique to highlight in the case of Pure Earth, I want to single out Pure Earth's approach to formalizing e-waste recycling in Ghana. I suggest the organization actually further marginalizes the workers who do the burning for several reasons. First, the workers don't have direct access to the facility and do not receive training in how to use the granulators for strip-ping the wires. Second, using the granulators slows down the copper extraction process. Third, since the granulators run on electricity – a constant energy infra-structure challenge in Ghana – it costs money to use the facility. Lastly, since the

6.1 An urban authority fire. Photo by Peter Little.

facility primarily processes waste electrical equipment, usually large-diameter cables, coming from Ghana's electrical utility company, the facility seems to only serve clients who either have a "formal" relation with Pure Earth or who have a direct supply of large-diameter cables. The burners lose out on this business opportunity because the e-waste collected by those working directly with the burners only have the capacity to extract small-diameter cables from junked machines in the scrapyard. Without the ability to deliver large-diameter cables to the facility, the burners are left out of the purported "economic development" goals of the e-waste recycling project.

Agbogbloshie exhibits a unique case of "electronic pyropolitics" (Little 2016, forthcoming) – a postcolonial struggle over toxic fire, burning, and extreme open-air incineration. It is always ablaze, always smells of burning plastics and metals, and it happens to be the case that it is not always workers engaged in copper extraction who are responsible for these highly toxic fires. One photograph I took in July 2016 (see Figure 6.1) depicts a fire started by the Accra Metropolitan Assembly (AMA), an urban agency that, ironically, has a mission "to improve the quality of life of the people of the city of Accra, especially the poor, vulnerable and excluded, by providing and maintaining basic services and facilities in the areas of education, health, sanitation and other social amenities, in the context of discipline, a sense of urgency and commitment to excellence."

This image tells a complex postcolonial and "pyropolitical" story (Minter 2016; Little forthcoming; see also Marder 2015). It signals the state-based disciplinary forces at play in Agbogbloshie. The image tells the all-too-common story of violent displacement and demolition.[3] It cracks open the incineration politics of social and environmental justice, and exposes and sustains the politics of confusion and paradoxical nature of state and non-state interventions of risk mitigation. One could deconstruct this image further, but what is perhaps most interesting is that when e-waste workers engage in pollution visioning and documentation, they capture and focus on the usual toxic suffering of classic Agbogbloshie imagery. But, on the other hand, these workers also witness and document radically different things and lived experiences. They raise awareness about that which is in their everyday material environment. That perceptual difference makes a difference, especially for how one witnesses, experiences, and knows e-waste pollution and violence in Ghana's urban margins.

Vital e-waste contextualization and the work of worker images

I never intended to develop a project centered on e-waste participatory photography. Rather, this interest emerged from my own ethnographic research experience in Agbogbloshie. During fieldwork in Agbogbloshie in the summer of 2016, I was talking to a group of workers about the risks they face when burning e-waste to extract copper. We sat under a makeshift shelter made from the roof of a junked *trotro*, the minibuses many Ghanaians use to travel. They began by talking about the smoke from burning e-waste and how it impacts their breathing and sleeping, but they also started to show me their hands, feet, arms, and legs. They pointed to wounds, especially burns, on their bodies, an experience that shifted my own visual ethnographic focus and feeling: that maybe it was best that the workers take their own photos and share them with me if they felt comfortable doing so. What transpired was a grassroots participatory photography emphasis that was not my original goal. Following this fieldwork experience, workers began using their cell phones to snap pictures of their wounded bodies. Workers would send me images of their cuts and burns on a weekly basis, and the more they shared these images with me, the more I started to realize that this practice of image sharing was changing my own vision of Agbogbloshie and the workers making a living there. While their burnt and cut bodies became a medium of self-expression, it is important to consider how even these worker images are mediated by my own positionality as an American anthropologist and clear outsider. The fact of the matter is that the audience of the shared images is as powerful as the images themselves (Rose 2016). As the white American researcher, I was clearly the primary audience of these images. But, nevertheless, the practice of sharing these images was a way to make sure I knew that bodily harm from toxic e-waste extraction was still ongoing. On a return fieldwork trip in 2018, I asked the workers why they sent me these photos, and one of the burners explained: "it helps you see what we do here. This is how it is here. We know this. We send photos to tell you how it is here. You understand?" On the one hand, this response made perfect sense to me, but it also never did help clarify for me *why* workers continued to send me photos. The workers never tell me directly that they send images to help raise awareness about the toxic injuries they face as e-waste burners in Agbogbloshie, but they are explicit about teaching me something with their own images, even if that means turning the camera toward torched copper wires, burnt bodies, or even more playful group selfies. What I came to realize is that sustaining connection and keeping in touch with me – the American anthropologist in Agbogbloshie – had a lot to do with it, but not exactly everything to do with it.

When e-waste workers engage in this toxic risk documentation they are actively contextualizing, communicating, and indexing the embodied social and environmental health risks they face. One might call this a process of vital e-waste contextualization. Showing and marking vital signs of toxic risk contextualizes the experience of toxic burden, victimization, and marginalization within Ghana's e-waste recycling sector. But as visual anthropologists have pointed out, image making is a political practice with various consequences. Reminiscent of the "crisis of representation" (Marcus and Fischer 1986) critique emerging in the 1980s in anthropology, multiple problems and politics of representation emerge when privileged outsiders (usually white and from the global North) create representations of marginalized populations (usually dark and from the global South) in order to expose inequalities and disparities in social, political, and economic systems. There is an overwhelming sense that image making always risks being a practice of image *taking*, a way of doing representational appropriation in a "contact zone" (Pratt 1992) where vibrant power relations persist. All representational strategies, that is, directly or indirectly serve the interests of the image makers, no matter the shifts in representational ethos and edits to practices of objectification and dehumanization. Even the emergence of participatory photography in my ethnographic research serves my own interests as an anthropologist attempting to better understand the lived experience of e-waste workers in Ghana. Like others studying toxic environments, I am caught in a familiar conundrum. A front-and-center challenge, it seems, is that even while trying to find new ways to represent our toxic world, we confront, no matter our representational strategies, the risks of "hazardous aesthetics" (Rosenfeld et al. 2018) and challenges of "visual interventions" (Pink 2007; Peeples 2011; Harper 2012; see also Harper 2002).

More recently, visual anthropologists contend that

> relying on images of suffering bodies as a visual strategy of depicting injustice or inequality is at odds with making systemic social, economic, and political oppression visible … [I]mages of suffering bodies tend to naturalize connections between violence and already marginalized peoples. Furthermore, they do not ultimately work to make structural violence visible by (1) obscuring the mechanisms and perpetrators of violence, (2) not disrupting dominant conceptual frameworks, and (3) not leaving room for solutions. (Stone 2015, 179)

Beyond simply a technology of documentation, taking photos can have intended and unintended self-serving consequences that can dehumanize e-waste laborers in Agbogbloshie, even for photographers emphasizing humanistic portraiture. For example, during an interview focusing on his project *Agbogbloshie: Digital Wasteland*, the German photographer Kevin McElvaney noted that, "At first, Agbogbloshie caught my attention because it's really photogenic, but the environmental, socio-economic, political and ethical problems there forced me to see it with my own eyes. I don't like to judge things when I haven't seen it for real and everything I found about Agbogbloshie on the web seemed so unreal, but after I'd been there, I realized that it's even worse" (Donson 2014).

What I want to suggest here is that e-waste worker images, as a representational strategy for exploring environmental health risk, labor, and life in Agbogbloshie, are not simply toxic "shock value" images, but instead new forms of everyday life documentation and cultural vitality that make Agbogbloshie a place and space that is *more than* e-waste toxicity. What these workers face is what they digitally capture and what they face can be many things, but it is rarely the burning piles of copper wire that constitute the dominant optic of circulating narratives on Agbogbloshie. Each worker image I receive inspires me to ask what workers key into, what they account for, and why they share the images they share. Additionally, this grassroots e-waste visualization experience has inspired me to take more seriously the extent to which participatory photography can provide a new platform for bearing witness to e-waste struggle in a toxic, urban, and postcolonial scrapyard landscape, especially at a time when emergent forms of instrumentalization, computation (Gabrys 2016), and digitization are shaping how we make sense of and understand environmental problems. In this way, my interests in e-waste visualizations draw inspiration from recent discussion and theory in "digital anthropology," or doing ethnography in a contemporary world that "accounts for how the digital, methodological, practical and theoretical dimensions of ethnographic research are increasingly intertwined" (Pink et al. 2016, 1).

Amid the toxic smoke, it is critical to remember that Agbogbloshie is Ghana's most active scrap metal market, with iron, steel, brass, copper, and aluminum

6.2 Workers showing their collected copper wires. Photo by Abdul Rahim.

being the most sought-after market metals. The workers making up the informal labor force here come mostly from villages in northern Ghana where economic hardships caused by colonialism have long been known to be a stimulus for southward labor migrations (Plange 1979). As shown in Figure 6.2, when these workers turn the camera on themselves, they purposively emphasize their copper wire collections. In this image, taken by one the sub-chiefs or managers of a primary group of copper burners, pre-scorched copper wires, objects with market value, are made to be the center of attention. As Jacob, one of the longtime workers among this group of copper burners told me during my visit in July 2017, "Copper is why we here. We be here for dat. All dis be copper. No work in north. This be work." Given this dominant metal in the scrapyard, it is easy to see why copper is foregrounded in this image. Copper is also a major reason why these workers migrate to Agbogbloshie from their villages in the north. When this image was taken, the price of copper was US$2.10 a pound, a commodity that is significantly more valuable than the ground nuts that many of these workers' families farm in Ghana's northern region.

For me, these e-waste worker images are not simply additives to the ethnographic method, but instead represent "an emerging platform for collecting, exploring, and expressing ethnographic materials" (Hsu 2014, 1). Many, if not most, ethnographies of pollution and environmental justice today involve a complex political ecology of data, what some in the digital humanities call our age of "augmented empiricism" (Hsu 2014) and what Trump critics signal as an age of "environmental data justice" (Dillon et al. 2017). Of course, the turn to the visual and visual data is nothing new in the social sciences, nor is it new for discard studies focusing on the global e-waste trade and its local manifestation in spaces and places like Agbogbloshie. If anthropological debates over the ethnographic use of images in toxic postcolonial spaces actually reproduces or risks the reproduction of colonialism or colonial acts of representation, then what do citizen-based images really do? What do these marginalized urban e-waste worker images do? What visual standpoint epistemologies and ontologies do they offer? What politics of representation do these images generate and communicate? Perhaps more importantly, what politics of representation do or can these images circumvent? Researchers have discussed Agbogbloshie as a symbolic reminder of "toxic colonialism," but how might participatory photography operate as a method of visual decolonization, a technique of vital contextualization that can augment understandings of labor and social life in electronic "discardscapes" (Lepawsky 2018)?

Other worker photos help communicate and translate the "blessing" of the scrap metal market itself, a topic that no studies of Agbogbloshie account for. Agbogbloshie workers have a primary meeting place for metal market meetings, negotiations, and blessings that they call "Gaza." As shown in Figure 6.3, one worker named Ibrahim took my camera and waited for a good time to take a shot during a meeting and blessing at Gaza. I didn't immediately ask why he spontaneously took my camera, but I later learned that it was because it would have been inappropriate or disrespectful for me to take a picture because many of the meeting attendees did not know who I was. Soon after, Ibrahim returned to where I was sitting and I learned that the meeting and blessing had nothing to do with e-waste. It had nothing to do with praying for greater pollution control or government waste management policy and action. Instead the gathering occurred to discuss and voice worker opinions, concerns, and ideas about the

6.3 Scrap worker meeting and market blessing. Photo by Ibrahim Akarima.

social, political, spiritual, and economic management of the scrap market. As Ibrahim told me, "The workers want the copper here. The iron and the aluminum here. We bless it so it come here." After taking a few more pictures of the meeting and blessing, Ibrahim repeated: "They be blessing the copper. Blessing the market."

They were not debating and discussing lead and cadmium exposures and body burdens, nor were they organizing a meeting to respond to NGO interventions to control pollution emitting from Agbogbloshie. Again, this "other" story matters. Even while critical relations between toxic bodies and environments (Roberts and Langston 2008) ought to remain a concern of e-waste studies in Agbogbloshie, these relations must also consider the dominant role of Muslim cultural, religious, and hereditary chieftaincy dynamics at play. This is what sustains social life in the market and what ultimately informs North–South labor migrations, movements, and experiences of people navigating the actual political ecology of e-waste risk. Inspired by Beck's (2006) idea that "Without techniques of visualization, risks are nothing at all," we need to make on-the-ground facts visible to fully visualize and come to terms with the actual toxic reality experienced in and among those making a living in Agbogbloshie.

Still images of e-waste workers in Agbogbloshie do many things. They communicate postcolonial waste management, inequities in the global toxic waste trade, but also friendship, tribal relations, and bodily distress. The latter topic has had a strong focus within photo-ethnographic work in medical anthropology. For example, medical anthropologist Paul Farmer has been criticized for his use of images of sick bodies to make visible what he calls "structural violence."[4] He admits that "the use of such images is problematic but sometimes necessary in order to stir privileged populations to do something about global systems of inequality" (Stone 2015, 180). The logic of this angle is that "the problem of making structural violence visible is that social, political, and economic structures that are to blame for the violence are very difficult to photograph because they are very difficult to see" (2015, 180). One could argue that citizen visioning practices like participatory photography don't necessarily "capture" experience (images are powerful, but don't replace bare life experience itself), but they do "expose" or "share" lived *context* to the world of observers and those bearing witness. Furthermore, images can and often do generate empathy. When workers share photos they are, in some fast digital way, "sharing" their life experience with me. These images are shared by the purported "victims" of e-waste toxicity, but a problem emerges when images of suffering bodies are deployed "to illustrate injustice or structural violence locates all of the violence, the shame, and the danger of the violence in the suffering body of the victim rather than the assailant for the simple reason that the assailant is nowhere to be seen" (Stone

2015, 183). But, what happens when postcolonial subjects are the image makers and those bearing witness to e-waste pollution and contextualization? What happens when Agbogbloshie workers themselves visualize "landscapes of affect" (Moore et al. 2003: 31), when they themselves enable us to better understand "the simultaneous imagination and fabrication of inner selves, social bodies, and environmental milieu" (ibid.)? These are important questions for advancing not only e-waste studies, but environmental ethnographies of environmental justice and toxics citizen science writ large.

Conclusion

In this chapter, I have tried to show how in the process of making and sharing images, e-waste workers in Agbogbloshie are engaging in a participatory photography practice that accounts for the multiple ways of witnessing and knowing e-waste. Ultimately, their images stretch and go beyond the usual e-wasteland narrative. As an ethnographer *being shown* what matters, and especially what matters beyond the "singular story" (Mkhwanazi 2016) of toxic digital destruction and extraction so common in representations of Agbogbloshie, I have begun to find these images to be necessary tools for making sense of Agbogbloshie. Ironically, the digital devices we use as research tools might eventually end up back in Agbogbloshie or another toxic wasteland as salvageable digital discard. But, while not knowing where these tools may end up, I do know that these workers turn to images, including selfies, to share what matters of concern matter to them. Accordingly,

> Rather than paralyze representational practices … visual depiction of structural violence need not settle for a qualified visual strategy heavily bolstered by written or spoken analysis. Ethnographic reflexivity (in toxic studies) is a good strategy for many reasons, but it is not the only option. As the robust traditions of feminism and visual anthropology have argued, we should take the lead from the marginalized peoples who already work to make the abstract forces of [toxic] structural violence visible. (Stone 2015, 180)

How these workers show and share their experience of toxic suffering and violence is complicated by the fact that they don't necessarily turn the camera toward the postcolonial state nor toward objects of toxic destruction to communicate their "environmental" experience. For example, the workers didn't send me images of urban authorities evicting workers attempting to dwell in the Agbogbloshie scrapyard or shelters being demolished in Old Fadama, the adjacent settlement, to mitigate the risks of annual flooding along the Korle lagoon.

In short, the e-waste worker images validate an on-the-ground lived experience that can be overlooked and lost amid the prism of toxicity and misery images that dominate the e-wasteland narrative of Agbogbloshie.

My ongoing e-waste participatory photography project, in this sense, speaks to an ethos of "pluralist photography" (Bleiker and Kay 2007, 168) attuned to power. As Bleiker and Kay (ibid.) put it, "Human relations cannot exist outside power. But the nature of pluralist photography minimizes the oppressive effects of these relations by consciously problematizing representation. The collaborative and dialogical nature of pluralist photography can provide ways through which multiple perspectives may be seen and validated." In light of this, I have come to realize that there are many benefits and even more challenges of doing participatory photography or collaborative photo-ethnography in Agbogbloshie. To start with, using photography to bear witness to e-waste lived experience is not necessarily a difficult thing to do. Taking pictures is a rather easy observational technique that even the poorest and most marginalized of the global South can engage. For the workers I engage with in Agbogbloshie, this is an easy way to participate in the visual storytelling that takes place in Agbogbloshie. On the other hand, the turn to grassroots participatory photography does not escape criticism nor necessarily lead to more ethical e-waste ethnography. In fact, anthropologists have rightly cautioned that visions of marginality and the practice of recycling the production of these representational strategies and visions can sustain marginality itself (Ferguson 2006). Some have even engaged with this important issue more directly in Ghana by encouraging consideration of the always contentious nature of ongoing "Black transatlantic visions" (Holsey 2013). These are research and representational concerns that have informed my way of thinking about and doing participatory photography in Agbogbloshie. Working in collaboration with Agbogbloshie workers to visualize Agbogbloshie was never my intended goal, but it became a focus once workers themselves began to voluntarily snap shots and send me images of their own making. In the process, I have experienced a personal transformation in how to position myself as a researcher. I am not just finding new ways to forge relationships with e-waste workers, but also learning how to relate to the images they share with me. For sure, worker images help me translate my own ethnographic experience and narrative. They help me find a way to understand and possibly make better sense of Agbogbloshie. Without a doubt, they draw attention to things I don't see. In the process of being shown what I don't see and therefor know about e-waste, they have helped me become more aware, self-critical, and reflexive as a researcher. Finally, participatory photography taught me about unforeseen ethics of research and representation that can emerge when navigating politics of pollution, participation, and the various environmental injustices of global electronic discard.

As I have noted, most depictions of Agbogbloshie's e-waste workers high-light toxic labor practices (e.g., burning copper wires) and do so to expose the contentious nature of e-waste recycling matters of concern in Ghana and other "discardscapes" (Lepawsky 2018) of the global South. These e-waste representa-tions, it turns out, have a charismatic quality and force that has consequences for contemporary waste theory and action (Lepawsky 2018; see also Liboiron 2016). In other words, "what makes e-waste charismatic is its capacity to act as an allegory of contemporary environmental crisis" (Lepawsky 2018, 6). The e-waste environmental justice politics emerging in Agbogbloshie, then, are as much about environmental health crisis as they are shaped by a complex crisis of representation. What I am hoping to illustrate in my turn to workers' photo-graphs of life and labor in Agbogbloshie is that these visualizations showcase the actual involvement of postcolonial agents in documenting their own lived expe-rience.[5] They also provide an example for how e-waste workers visually explore their own toxic e-waste situation and lived experience. This other technique of risk visualization can help advance critical and creative environmental health studies, synthesize the democratization of science and EJ advocacy efforts, and push the boundaries and intentions of visual ethnography in sites of toxic elec-tronic discard more broadly. While participatory photography will certainly not fix all the problems and politics of representation in e-waste studies, this form of visualization can certainly lead to more creative research and action partner-ships. At the very least, it opens up alternative epistemic possibilities within an ever-changing landscape of mixed-media pollution and discard studies.

Notes

1   In this chapter, I follow the approach to "citizenship" taken up by Ellison (1997), which suggests that citizenship is "a form of social and political practice born of the need to establish new solidarities across a range of putative 'communities' as a defense against social changes which continually threaten to frustrate such ambitions" (Ellison 1997, 712).

2   One of the first writings on e-waste dumping in Africa appeared in the late 1980s (see Brooke 1988), which emerged amid other works on "toxic terrorism" in Africa writ large (O'Keefe 1988).

3   For a description of the demolition campaign in Agbogbloshie and Old Fadama in 2015, see Lepawsky and Akese (2015).

4   The term originally comes from Galtung (1969).

5   Emerging scholarship on toxicological science and contamination politics in Senegal similarly highlights this need for greater attention to postcoloniality (Tousignant 2018).

References

Afenah, A. 2012. Engineering a millennium city in Accra, Ghana: The Old Fadama intractable issue. *Urban Forum*, 23, 527–540.

Akese, G. and Little, P. C. 2018. Electronic waste and the environmental justice challenge in Agbogbloshie. *Environmental Justice*, 11(2), 77–83.

Barnett, J. T. 2015. Toxic portraits: Resisting multiple invisibilities in the environmental justice movement. *Quarterly Journal of Speech*, 101(2), 405–425.

Beck, U. 2006. Living in the world risk society. *Economy and Society*, 35(4), 329–345.

Bleiker, R. and Kay, A. 2007. Representing HIV/AIDS in Africa: Pluralist photography and local empowerment. *International Studies Quarterly*, 51, 139–163.

Brooke, J. 1988. Waste dumpers turning to West Africa. *New York Times*, July 17. http://www.nytimes.com/1988/07/17/world/waste-dumpers-turning-to-west-africa.html?pagewanted=all (last accessed February 3, 2020).

Caravanos, J., Clark, E. E., Fuller, R., and Lambertson, C. 2011. Assessing worker and environmental chemical exposure risks at an e-waste recycling and disposal site in Accra, Ghana. *Journal of Health and Pollution*, 1, 16–25.

Caravanos, J., Clarke, E. E., Osei, C. S., and Amoyaw-Osei, Y. 2013. Exploratory health assessment of chemical exposures at e-waste recycling and scrapyard facility in Ghana. *Journal of Health and Pollution*, 3, 11–22.

Davies, T. 2013. A visual geography of Chernobyl: Double exposure. *International Labor and Working-Class History*, 84, 116–139.

Davis, J.-M., Akese, G., and Garb, Y. 2019. Beyond the pollution haven hypothesis: Where and why do e-waste hubs emerge and what does this mean for policies and interventions? *Geoforum*, 98, 36–34.

Dillon, L. et al. 2017. Environmental data justice and the Trump Administration: Reflections from the Environmental Data and Governance Initiative. *Environmental Justice*, 10(6), 186–192.

Donson, T. 2014. Agbogbloshie: Digital wasteland. *Dazed Magazine*, February 26.

http://www.dazeddigital.com/photography/article/19008/1/agbogbloshie-digital-wasteland (last accessed February 3, 2020).

Ellison, N. 1997. Towards a new social politics: Citizenship and reflexivity in late modernity. *Sociology*, 31(4), 697–717.

Feldt, T., Fobil, J. N., and Wittseipe, J. 2014. High levels of PAH-metabolites in urine of e-waste recycling workers from Agbogbloshie, Ghana. *Science of the Total Environment*, 369–376.

Ferguson, J. 2006. *Global Shadows: Africa in the Neoliberal World Order*. Durham, NC and London: Duke University Press.

Gabrys, J. 2016. *Program Earth: Environmental Sensing Technology and the Making of a Computational Planet*. Minneapolis: University of Minnesota Press.

Galtung, J. 1969. Violence, peace, and peace research. *Journal of Peace Research*, 6(3), 167–191.

Grant, R. 2006. Out of place? Global citizens in local spaces: A study of the informal settle-ments in the Korle Lagoon environs in Accra, Ghana. *Urban Forum*, 17, 1–24.

Grant, K., Goldizen, F., and Sly, P. 2013. Health consequences of exposure to e-waste: A systematic review. *The Lancet Global Health*, 1(6), 350–361.

Harper, D. 2002. Talking about pictures: A case for photo elicitation. *Visual Studies*, 17, 13–16.

Harper, K. 2012. Visual interventions and the "crisis in representation" in environmental anthropology: Researching environmental justice in a Hungarian Romani neighbor-hood. *Human Organization*, 71(3), 292–305.

Hastrup, K. 1995. *A Passage to Anthropology: Between Experience and Theory*. London and New York: Routledge.

Holsey, B. 2013. Black Atlantic Vvsions: History, race, and transnationalism in Ghana. *Cultural Anthropology*, 28, 504–518.

Hsu, W. F. 2014. Digital ethnography toward augmented empiricism: A new methodologi-cal framework. *Journal of Digital Humanities*, 3(1), 1–5.

Keane, F. 1998. Another picture of starving Africa: It could have been taken in 1984, or 1998. *Guardian*, June 8.

Koné, L. 2009. Pollution in Africa: A new toxic waste colonialism? An assessment of com-pliance of the Bamako Convention in Côte d'Ivoire. LLM dissertation, University of Pretoria.

Kyere, V. N., Greve, K., and Atiemo, S. A. 2016. Spatial assessment of soil contamination by heavy metals from informal electronic waste recycling in Agbogbloshie, Ghana. *Environmental Health and Toxicology*, 31.

Lepawsky, J. 2018. *Reassembling Rubbish: Worlding Electronic Waste*. Cambridge, MA: MIT Press.

Lepawsky J. and Akese, G. 2015. Sweeping away Agbogbloshie again. *Discard Studies* (blog). https://discardstudies.com/2015/06/23/sweeping-away-agbogbloshie-again (last accessed February 3, 2020).

Liboiron, M. 2016. Redefining pollution and action: The matter of plastics. *Journal of Material Culture*, 21(1), 87–110.

Little, P. C. 2016. On Electronic pyropolitics and Pure Earth friction in Agbogbloshie. *Toxic News*, November 8.

Little, P. C. Forthcoming. *Burning Matters: Life, Labor, and E-Waste Pyropolitics in Ghana*. New York and Oxford: Oxford University Press.

Lyons, S. 2017. The purpose of photography in a post-truth era. *Time*, January 26. http://time.com/4650956/photojournalism-post-truth/ (accessed February 3, 2020).

Marcus, G. E. and Fischer, M. M. J. 1986. *Anthropology as Cultural Critique: An Experimental Moment in the Human Sciences*. Chicago: University of Chicago Press.

Marder, M. 2015. *Pyropolitics: When the World is Ablaze*. London and New York: Rowman & Littlefield.

Minter, A. 2016. The burning truth behind an e-waste dump in Africa. *Smithsonian*, January 13. http://www.smithsonianmag.com/sciencenature/burning-truth-behind-e-waste-dump-africa-180957597 (last accessed on February 3, 2020).

Mkhwanazi, N. 2016. Medical anthropology in Africa: The trouble with a single story. *Medical Anthropology*, 35(2), 193–202.

Moore, D. S., Pandian, A., and Kosek, J. 2003. The cultural politics of race and nature: Terrains of power and practice. In. D. S. Moore, J. Kosek, and A. Pandian (eds), *Race, Nature, and the Politics of Difference*. Durham, NC and London: Duke University Press, pp.1–70.

O'Keefe, P. 1988. Toxic terrorism. *Review of African Political Economy*, 15(42), 84–90.

Peeples, J., 2011. Toxic sublime: Imaging contaminated landscapes. *Environmental Communication: A Journal of Nature and Culture*, 5(4), 373–392.

Pink, Sarah (ed.) 2007. *Visual Interventions*. New York: Berghahn Books.

Pink, Sarah et al. (eds) 2016. *Digital Ethnography: Principles and Practice.* London: Sage.

Plange, N.-K. 1979. Underdevelopment in northern Ghana: Natural causes or colonial capitalism? *Review of African Political Economy*, 6, 4–14.

Poole, D. 1997. *Vision, Race, and Modernity: A Visual Economy of the Andean Image World.* Princeton, NJ: Princeton University Press.

Prakash, S. et al. 2010. *Socio-economic Assessment and Feasibility Study on Sustainable e-Waste Management in Ghana.* Report by Ghana EPA, Green Advocacy Ghana, NVMP, VROM-Inspectie, and the Institute for Applied Ecology.

Pratt, M. L. 1992. *Imperial Eyes: Travel Writing and Transculturation.* London: Routledge.

Roberts, J. A. and Langston, N. (eds) 2008. Toxic bodies/toxic environments: An interdisciplinary forum. *Environmental History*, 13(4), 629–703.

Rose, G. 2016. *Visual Methodologies: An Introduction to Researching with Visual Materials.* London: Sage.

Rosenfeld, H., Moore, S., Nost, E., Roth, R. E., and Vincent, K. 2018. Hazardous aesthetics: A "merely interesting" toxic tour of waste management data. *GeoHumanities*, 4(1), 262–281.

Stacey, P. and Lund, C. 2016. In a state of slum: Governance in an informal urban settlement in Ghana. *Journal of Modern African Studies*, 54(4), 591–615.

Stone, L. K. 2015. Suffering bodies and scenes of confrontation: The art and politics of representing structural violence. *Visual Anthropology Review*, 31(2), 177–189.

Tousignant, N. 2018. *Edges of Exposure: Toxicology and the Problem of Capacity in Postcolonial Senegal.* Durham, NC: Duke University Press.

Voyles, T. B. 2015. *Wastelanding: Legacies of Uranium Mining in Navajo Country.* Minneapolis: University of Minnesota Press.

Wittsiepe, J., Fobil, J. N., and Till, H. 2015. Levels of polychlorinated dibenzo-p-dioxins, dibenzofurans (PCDD/Fs) and biphenyls (PCBs) in blood of informal e-waste recycling workers from Agbogbloshie, Ghana, and controls. *Environment International*, 79, 65–73.

7

Making sense of visual pollution: The "Clean City" law in São Paulo, Brazil

Marina Da Silva

Introduction

The impact of human activity on the Earth has been a central environmental concern throughout contemporary history. One of the main challenges of the Anthropocene (Crutzen and Stoermer 2000) is to reverse the damage we are doing to the planet through climate change and industrial pollution (National Research Council 2012). The focus of this chapter is on a perhaps less known type of harm – visual pollution. Unlike other forms of sensory pollution, such as noise and light pollution, visual pollution has not been extensively studied, nor have its impacts been assessed. Despite this, the term "visual pollution" has been increasingly used in the Americas and it is central to São Paulo's "Clean City" law (Lei Cidade Limpa).

The "Clean City" law was enacted in April 2007. The legislation requires the removal of commercial advertisements in public areas. It also restricts the use of signage on building facades and prohibits graffiti in order to "protect citizens' rights to clean public spaces" free of visual pollution (law no. 14.223, 2006; Harris 2007). Pollution, as understood within toxicity studies, is a by-product of society's industrial and economic development and its ensuing impact on nature and society. However, it is important to question the specificity of visual pollution as these visualities are often the cultural output of a given society: "Now

more than ever, nature cannot be separated from culture; in order to comprehend the interactions between ecosystems, the mechanosphere and the social
and individual Universes of reference, we must learn to think 'transversally'"
(Guattari 2014, 29). Perhaps one of the main challenges of this kind of pollution
is to think about the methodologies that can consider the problem "transversally," and therefore analyze the intersection between pollution, culture, and
society.

In this chapter, I will demonstrate the urgent need for this type of transversal
thought, especially since Brazil's election of Jair Bolsonaro as president in late
2018. Since coming into power, Bolsonaro's political measures have given rise
to national indignation (Phillips 2019). However, it was his Amazon exploration proposal at the World Economic Forum meeting in Davos that caused
international outrage (Shear and Haberman 2019). Bolsonaro's discourse on
the environment and his ideas on the commercialization of the Amazon show the
dangers of post-truth politics, not only by acting as a climate change denier but
also by undermining the agencies responsible for environment protection: the
president's response to criticism of the policy was to state that "What is damaging Brazil's image is the permanent and well-orchestrated defamation campaign
by NGOs and supposed experts, within and outside of Brazil" (Kaiser 2019).

Bolsonaro's post-truth discourse demonstrates the need for a stronger understanding of the relationship between pollution, culture, and society; this will
be further exemplified as I follow Clean City's fight against visual pollution
and discuss how each political administration in São Paulo has understood the
law – and subsequently visual pollution – given the lack of framework around
the legislation and the concept itself. This analysis is crucial as these different
understandings of visual pollution have an impact on São Paulo's residents, both
as producers of visual pollution and those experiencing it (Figure 7.1).

For my conclusion, I will discuss the methodology used during qualitative
research done in São Paulo in 2014 and how new and innovative ways of sensing
the city, including the use of citizen science as a methodological practice, can
help investigate how different structures of experience are perceived within the
same urban reality. The multidisciplinary approach to the research presented
in this project is a technique critical for assessing the impact of visual pollution,
consequently informing frameworks to regulate the use of the public space.

Clean City law and São Paulo's fight against pollution

In 2007, São Paulo received media attention around the world as the first
global city to ban advertisements (The Economist 2007). The Clean City law,

7.1 São Paulo's buildings with covered billboards, graffiti, and pixo, found at Via Elevado Pres. João Goulart where the author conducted some of the interviews. Photo by Marina Da Silva.

approved by mayor Gilberto Kassab, was part of a "bigger" fight against the city's pollution. Arguably, São Paulo is better known for its air and water pollution problems. To contextualize this environmental paradox, air pollution, which is caused by the city's severe car traffic issues, causes more deaths per year than car accidents (globo.com 2013). Water pollution from São Paulo's main rivers – Pinheiros and Tietê – not only added to the city's unpleasant smell but also aggravated the unprecedented drought in São Paulo back in 2015 (Romero 2015). Despite the evident need to address air and water pollution in São Paulo, Mayor Kassab started his "fight" on pollution by dealing with what he described as "the most conspicuous sector – the visual" (Bevins 2010).

The Clean City law was acknowledged and celebrated all over the world, winning awards in China (Expo Shanghai, 2010), the United States (Emotional Branding Visionary Award, 2011), Germany (Werkbund-Label, 2012), and the United Kingdom (Brit Insurance Design of the Year, 2008). São Paulo's Clean City law seemed to have started an urban design revolution, but how does it relate to the idea of pollution more broadly? In other words, if visual pollution has not been assessed or measured as per other kinds of pollution present in the city, such as air and water, it is safe to assume that neither has its impact, on both the social and natural environment. Therefore it is important to question the criteria used by São Paulo's government to decide which pollution to deal with first.

Clean City was radical and unique in its absolutist stance: the changes required by this law had to be actioned within 60 days (law no. 14.223, 2006). Interestingly, São Paulo was not the first to impose such measures; other places, including Hawaii (the 1920s), Vermont (1968), Maine (early 1980s), and Alaska (1998) have taken similar actions (Mahdawi 2015). However, unlike other legislation, Clean City was the first to officially classify these visualities as *pollution* and such an advertisement ban was unprecedented in a global city.

It is important to note that despite classifying advertisements, signage, and graffiti as visual pollution, the term itself *is not defined* in Clean City, nor has any research been done regarding the possible impact on the environment. Currently, the most extensive analysis on the topic is by Adriana Portella, in *Visual Pollution: Advertising, Signage and Environmental Quality* (2014). Portella describes visual pollution as "an established expression commonly used to describe the degradation of the visual quality of places by signage" (Portella 2014, 1). However, what Clean City classifies as "visual pollution" seems to suggest that the degradation of public space also occurs as a result of advertisements and graffiti, visualities often found in a typical globalized urban space.

How is visual pollution situated within other types of sensory pollution?

Visual pollution, as a type of multimodal environmental degradation, should be analyzed in relation to other types of sensory pollution commonly found in the urban environment, such as light (Longcore and Rich 2004) and noise pollution (Fong 2016). Light pollution impacts the behavior of humans and animals by interfering with their circadian rhythms and physiological behavior; noise pollution (from transport, industry, and neighbors) disrupts complex task performance, modifies social behavior, and causes annoyance (Stansfeld and Matheson 2003). Unlike other types of sensory pollution, visual pollution cannot be easily measured since the *visual* element of this kind of pollution has not been agreed upon and therefore no threshold has been determined. This is now particularly problematic due to the expansion of targeted advertising and the blurred lines created by the commodification of culture (Jameson 2009) between graffiti, street art, and advertisement.

Extensive studies have shown the negative impact of air and water pollution on the quality of life in São Paulo, yet we do not see any radical ban on vehicles or tougher regulations on industrial waste disposal. The same can be said for light and noise pollution, so how can legislation be approved on such an unknown type of pollution? The impact of advertising (Baudrillard 1998; Cronin 2010), signage (Sennett 1990; Klein 2009), and graffiti (Cresswell 1992; Ferrell 1995) has been widely discussed, albeit these visualities as a collective – and more importantly, *as a sensory pollution* – have not been analyzed. Arguably more important and tractable pollution issues have been sidelined or avoided by São Paulo's government in focusing both their own and the public's attention on this issue instead. I believe it is important to analyze how visual pollution is being understood by those who enforce Clean City in order to understand how the political agenda is shaping São Paulo's urban space.

How has "visual pollution" been understood by different administrations in São Paulo?

My research has looked into how the different political administrations interpreted Clean City and how this has impacted the idea of visual pollution. Since the law's enactment, the city's urban space has changed dramatically. The law was originally developed by the urban planner Regina Monteiro to allow the creation of *a single* visual order in a city that grew up quickly and without a defined urban plan (Estadão 2013).

Clean City was meant to redefine the city's visual public space by banning advertisements, controlling the sizing of signage, and removing graffiti. These visualities, commonly found in post-industrialized metropolitan areas, were then meant to be reintroduced, albeit in an organized form, creating a better balance between the city's visual communication and the urban space. The enforcement of Clean City and the understanding of visual pollution has changed across different political administrations. In the age of post-truth, where expert analyses have been continuously and openly ridiculed, how can the different interpretations of visual pollution ever be solved? This is particularly pertinent in the era of President Bolsonaro, who has denigrated the role of experts in relation to several pertinent environmental issues. Below I will detail the contrasting interpretations of the law accordingly to each political mandate and the issues around it.

Gilberto Kassab, the mayor who officialized Clean City, came to power on March 31, 2006. With the promise to address the city's pollution, Clean City's visual cleanse seemed to fit the bill. The law was then appropriated under Gilberto Kassab's fight against the city's pollution; Clean City seemed to be the first step against the commercialization of public space (Sennett 1990; Klein 2009), which seemed to be against Kassab's economic agenda that focused on economical liberalism.

By enforcing Clean City, Kassab was in direct conflict with small businesses owners, billboard printers, and media agencies, with many claiming that the legislation was going to destroy their lives (Folha de São Paulo 2007). Ironically, the only sector that did not seem to mind the advertising ban was advertising. They not only embraced the legislation but also praised it: Claudio Lima, head of Ogilvy Advertising, said that despite the losses, "Clean City was ultimately a good idea for the city." A possible explanation for this is that the billboard removal was happening simultaneously with an increased use of social media and tailored advertising. In an interview for the *Financial Times* in 2010, Marcio Oliveira, Lew'Lara/TBWA's vice president of operations said: "The internet was the really big winner" (Bevins 2010).

However, advertising was not the only kind of visuality to be banned by Clean City; there are still discussions on what types of graffiti are allowed. São Paulo is world reference for graffiti art, with its two distinctive styles: there are the famous colorful illustrations, but there is also a distinct kind of graffiti called "pixo," which is a type of tagging. Pixo is overwhelmingly present in the city's urban landscape and started to appear in the 1980s as a protest against the military dictatorship. Pixo is now seen as a tool of resistance against the disenfranchisement created by São Paulo's wealth disparity.

A crucial question, then, is who decides which of the above is graffiti art or vandalism? São Paulo's visual pollution removal is currently outsourced at great public cost; the lack of defined guidelines in the legislation allows the "cleaning" company the responsibility for that distinction as they remove what they personally consider visual pollution to be. This controversy over "Clean City" was documented in the film *Cidade Cinza* (Grey City, 2013) by Marcelo Mesquita and Guilherme Valiengo. The documentary follows the discussion about the usage of São Paulo's public space and the role of graffiti as art and as social expression, culminating in the removal of a 75-foot-long (23 meters) mural created by a street art collective without warning under the enforcement of Clean City; this decision was taken by the cleaning company, not by city hall. This happened while "osGemeos" (two artists from the collective) were exhibiting at the Tate Modern, which was used as an argument to show the cultural value of this type of visuality. The media coverage was extensive and supportive of the mural and, in the end, Kassab was forced to recommission a new mural.

At the same time, "pixo" is removed on a daily basis without any front-page news. The documentary *Pixo* (2010), directed by João Wainer and Roberto T. Oliveira, is similar to *Grey City*, in that it follows *pixadores* (pixo artists) in order to understand their views on urban space ownership and how the act of "spraying" is a way to be seen in a society that ignores their social class. The pixadores want to intervene in the public space by "marking" the city. According to the film, unlike graffiti artists, their aim is not to create but to destroy.

The distinction between these two types of graffiti was once more made official by another piece of legislation created after Clean City, namely law no. 12.408 distinguishing pichação (vandalism) from graffiti as street art in São Paulo. This validates the general understanding that one kind is street art and the other is visual pollution (Dias 2016). Interestingly, graffiti and street artists have been allowed by the government to be sponsored by companies, once again blurring the line between art and advertisement.

Kassab's successor, Fernando Haddad (mayor 2013–2016, Workers' Party [Partido dos Trabalhadores, PT]), presented a manifesto focused on the social aspect of the city, which included a series of cultural proposals. The most controversial cultural measure of Haddad's administration was the authorization of a historical space called "Arcos do Jânio" (Jânio's Arches) to be used for street art. Haddad aimed to make São Paulo the world's biggest "open-air street art museum." The reappropriation of this place for a democratic purpose seemed to be a positive action. However, there is no public record of the parameters for how the artists and artworks were selected, adding once again to the problem of artistic validation of the different types of graffiti present in São Paulo.

As well as housing the biggest open-air museum, São Paulo also boasts South America's largest LED screen building facade, which can be found adorning the FIESP Cultural Center in Avenida Paulista. In 2016 the building facade was used to protest against former president Dilma Rousseff; the building is managed by Paulo Skaf, a member of PMDB-SP and opposed to Rousseff's government. Skaf authorized the use of the screen facade to protest against the government, which was a direct violation of Clean City, as the law states that no ideological message can be displayed in the public space. The removal of the protest artwork was interpreted by the media as an action taken by Haddad to protect Rousseff, as they shared the same party, and not because it is stipulated by the law.

Despite Haddad's commitment to the cultural development of São Paulo's urban space, it was also during his management that Clean City was "softened." Brands were allowed to "sponsor" bus shelters, meaning they were permitted to have advertisements on the side of the shelters while being responsible for the maintenance of the structure. Haddad's interpretation of Clean City and visual pollution was contradictory: he allowed São Paulo's residents to own the space that had been reclaimed by Clean City, but he also allowed the introduction of advertisements and corporate sponsorship.

The next mayor was João Dória (mayor 2017 to the time of writing, member of the Brazilian Social Democracy Party [Partido da Social Democracia Brasileira, PSDB]). His first public commitment was to implement an operation called "Cidade Linda" (Beautiful City) which he described as the "largest action towards the visual rehabilitation of the city." Dressed as a refuse collector at an organized press conference, he promised to clean the streets once a week. His first "cleaning" lasted 10 seconds (Exame 2017).

Beautiful City aims to protect and clean the city's urban space, which also includes landscaping the city's green areas. It is important to point out that this program actively includes public participation in the maintenance of sidewalks by organizing "multirões," which can be translated as "community collective effort." During one of his multirões, he covered a series of graffitied walls with grey paint. He also authorized the removal of the graffiti art from Jânio's Arches without any consent from the cultural preservation sectors of the government; the open-air museum created by Haddad has been closed. As tension grew, so did the fines for whoever was caught "spraying" on the walls.

Dória is also responsible for what has been described as the "biggest urban privatisation of São Paulo" (POPS) (Flynn and Simões 2017). If Clean City was softened during Haddad's administration, under Dória's new program it will become virtually nonexistent. He plans to allow advertising on all privatized areas of São Paulo. What this essentially means is that São Paulo's public space will become privately owned, and this will give grounds to allow private authorization of the visual material in the city. Who will be deciding what constitutes visual pollution then? The company that owns that space or the city? How will the changing views on visual pollution interfere with its citizens' rights?

This question becomes particularly relevant when discussing perhaps the most contested measure toward São Paulo's beautification authorized by Dória: the cover-up of areas inhabited by the homeless community below São Paulo's viaducts. This action, according to the mayor, was meant to protect them from the weather. However, reports from within his government suggest that this was actually done to hide them from the rest of São Paulo's urban space. We can, then, speculate on how the idea of visual pollution can be exploited and how it can impact on important issues such as the environmental justice of São Paulo's population. The number of homeless people has grown 10% in four years (Veja 2015). What these examples demonstrate is that visual pollution needs to properly assessed in order to understand its impact on the social and natural environment.

Is visual pollution more than a sensory issue?

Despite their very disparate political ideologies, São Paulo's mayors seem to have one overall point in common: the beautification of São Paulo's urban space. Perhaps this fixation with the beautification of São Paulo has its roots in the rivalry with Rio de Janeiro, *Cidade Maravilhosa*, translated as "the marvellous city." Rio de Janeiro is known for its *natural* beauty, unlike São Paulo, which is better known for its "concrete jungle." But are these urban projects connected to pollution at all?

What São Paulo's example demonstrates is that visual pollution, *as a term*, has been widely accepted, even though it has not been understood as pollution per se. By including the term in Clean City, Gilberto Kassab has officialized visual pollution in the mainstream of environmental discourse, albeit as a normative concept. In other words, we may all have a general understanding about what is the visual and what is pollution, but not what they mean together.

Clean City highlights an issue already anticipated by Georg Simmel in 1903 in his seminal essay "Metropolis and the Mental Life" in which he discusses the effect of hyper-visual stimulation in a metropolis – the "Blasé outlook" – which is the point where the individual can no longer react to new stimulation (1976). Simmel's argument, which is framed within theories of consumerism, is that this stimulation would reach its peak with the concentration of purchasable goods, and that would generate an outlet of nervous energy where the individual could no longer react to new stimulation. The critique of mental invasion by advertising has been widely discussed (Baudrillard 1998; Klein 2009; Cronin 2010). But are we being over visually stimulated only by advertisements?

São Paulo's law is creating a new urban identity: a "clean" space free from commercial communication, signage, and graffiti. Yet this radical urban cleansing does not consider how the classification of cultural production impacts the different creators of these visualities and their relation to the social space. Given how the production of space is a politically contested field that determines who we are as a society (Lefebvre 1991), it is essential to question who decides what a "visually clean" urban public space is and how this type of ban affects society.

The Clean City law raises questions about how the visual appearance and experience of a city comes about (Sennett 1990) and how this sensory pollution is affecting and shaping the urban environment and, more importantly, society. The lack of definition or theoretical frameworks leaves the idea of visual pollution vulnerable to personal interpretation as well as possible misuse, as seen in São Paulo's different administrations. This suggests the importance of understanding the specificity of framing or classifying these elements as pollution, and how visual pollution is made to exist and subsequently experienced as such. As Eriksen (1995, 246) explains, "Systems of classification allow us to mentally structure our surroundings to understand its relation to socially pre-defined categories and types." How this classification impacts the categories where these visualities are embedded gives us essential understanding of how we perceive the impact of visual pollution, especially as the idea of a visual quality can be related to judgments of taste (Bourdieu 1984), and how pollution functions as a social symbol of order (Douglas 1966), thus making the aesthetic perception and the classification as pollution both political and ideological issues.

In order to understand the role of these visual stimuli, we need to reconsider what kinds of methods can be put in place to investigate the physiological and sociological effect of visual pollution. The creation of such methods requires citizen participation. Perhaps the most relevant process for this type of inquiry is considering a multimodal approach to research, including citizen science, qualitative research, and ethnography as a way to analyze how classification as pollution impacts different actors and their agencies.

Visual pollution and the city: Sensing different modes of experience

In 2014, I conducted a series of urban walks in São Paulo in order to analyze residents' impressions of a hypothetical urban space without visual pollution.

Moreover, I was hoping to understand whether the removal of adverts and graffiti had had an impact on their experience of that space. And São Paulo's space is a unique one: the "concrete jungle" holds the world's 12th largest population, and it is formed by a total of 7,216 high-rise buildings, almost double the number in London, which has 3,216 (Emporis 2018). It is therefore important to think about what a visual-pollution-free dense urban space might look like.

Walking through this urban jungle was not easy; most *paulistanos* (a term used to describe São Paulo's residents), drive or use public transport (which is mainly determined by their economic status) as the city is spread over a vast area. Driving gives a completely different sensorial experience of the city. Performing this urban sensory ethnography was a way to understand how people sense the space, and more importantly, to explore if the removal of visual pollution had made São Paulo's space less sensorily overloaded.

The advertisements had been removed, but everything else banned by Clean City could still be seen in São Paulo's public space. The main method of research I used were "city walks," which is an immersive type of mobile interview (Ingold and Vergunst 2008). The participants were randomly chosen and represented different sociocultural backgrounds. The walks took place in Consolação Avenue, from metro station Paulista to metro República. This path was chosen because it connects the city's main avenue (Avenida Paulista), to República Square, which is the beginning of São Paulo's historical center and one of the most deprived areas of the city. Consolação Avenue was chosen as it has a mixture of residential and commercial spaces, where you can witness different types of visualities, all of which are banned by Clean City.

During the walks, I invited the participants to perform their own visual ethnography of São Paulo's urban space. They could photograph it, draw it, film it, or merely describe it as a way to immerse them in São Paulo's urban space. The approach was particularly relevant due to São Paulo's residents' specific relationship to the city: the city has little pedestrian infrastructure, so most people do not dwell in the urban space, often experiencing the city from inside their cars or from underground transport. Their behavior in the city is mediated; residents avoid urban noise (which São Paulo has in abundance) and do not experience the urban space from a pedestrian's viewpoint. City walking was a strategy used to make the participants explore the different types of stimuli present in the city's urban space, to help analyze how visual pollution can be defined and separated from other sensorial stimuli.

The elements photographed by the participants make this sensorial tension visible; it is an ongoing cultural negotiation present in Sao Paulo's public space, accepted and understood as part of the city's "chaotic" identity. The sensorial data showed that despite agreeing that Clean City was a positive measure, there was no agreement on what makes a specific visual communication a pollutant. For some, it was a quantitative issue – there were just too many advertisements – but for most, the classification as pollution was influenced by their personal taste, as per the extracts below:

> Visual pollution, in my opinion, is everything that makes what you see ugly or unattractive because we can't deny that beauty is good for the soul. (Sebastiana)

> Visual pollution is a visual intervention that shouldn't be there … like pixo, graffiti not so much, but pixo I think it's horrible, I get that it's a social movement … I guess it is something ugly on the top of something that is already awful, the city is ugly. (Oscar)

The photographs taken by the participants suggest that their judgment of taste influence their definition of visual pollution. However, that judgment is accompanied by a general understanding of visual pollution as a social expression. Therefore, São Paulo's society is "visually polluting" the built environment (either with graffiti or "pixo") as way to resist the harm done by the economic and political system. The idea of excess of visual elements in São Paulo's urban space could be a way to narrow the idea of visual pollution and to encourage reflections about the city's public space ownership and social agency. Interestingly, this same excess, chaos, and mess construct São Paulo's multiple identities.

If we agree that aesthetic judgments are connected to one's personal views and therefore subjective, should we try to understand these judgments from the point of view of their agency? This, perhaps, is a better angle for analysis, as per Max Liboiron's research on plastic pollution in oceans, where she affirms that "objects have agency and they influence other things around them and in relation to each other. Objects also have politics and are entangled in struggles of power and meaning" (Latour 2007; Coole and Frost 2010; Liboiron 2015). In order to understand the relation between the meaning of these visuals and their impact, it is essential to analyze the agency of advertisements with regard to other types of visual pollution (e.g., commercial signage and graffiti as in Clean City), and its relation to the public space to assess its harmful effect on society.

Previous research into visual pollution has focused on the mapping of visual communications, which are mainly billboards and signage. A group of researchers in Poland aims to give citizens the chance to collect and inform data on the subject (Chmielewski et al. 2016) by allowing the mapping of visual pollution using phone apps and feeding the results into an open-source website. The app is defined on their website as a type of citizen science, but are these citizen sensing practices showing new modes of experience or just cataloguing the quantity of advertisements?

How can citizen-gathered sensing be used to significantly impact environmental politics? Given the importance of public space in social relations (Lefebvre 1991) and in environmental issues (Wolch et al. 2014), it is important to reflect on the relational cause between the different visualities present within it, and – more importantly – how this can be translated. São Paulo's municipal law is a unique opportunity to observe visual pollution, to understand the consequences of such a classification (Douglas and Hull 1994), and to collect data to develop frameworks for its application.

How can we expand the methodology used and distributed to the public in order to understand this unique type of pollution? My research aims to solve this by being multidisciplinary and inventive (Lury and Wakeford 2012) and deploying different sensory methods (Rose 2001) such as photography, videos, and soundscapes.

The data analysis is not only textual but also visualized as an immersive installation (borrowing from art techniques) in order to explore different modes of existence in the city, to speculate on the connection between the individual's perception of public space and the social dynamics created by visual communication in the cityscape, and investigate how different structures of experience and consciousness are visualized within the same urban realities. The installation, informed by the fieldwork data, creates a physical, embodied, situated experience and is an attempt to encourage the audience to critically reflect on how different actors are influencing the choices made in São Paulo's public space and therefore how society's changing views on "visual pollution" can interfere with the democratic use and creation of the public space.

Conclusion

São Paulo's case study demonstrates empirically the issues caused by the lack of frameworks on visual pollution, and furthermore how other, better-understood pollution issues have not been dealt with due to the politicians' populist environmental agenda in São Paulo, which is now echoed in wider national politics in Brazil. The different interpretations of Clean City suggest that the term *visual pollution* has not been properly investigated or assessed.

This becomes evident through analysis of the initial enforcement of Clean City by Gilberto Kassab (2006–2013), where all advertising was removed, to the next mayor, Fernando Haddad, who supported the legislation (despite allowing advertisements to be reintroduced) but did not consider graffiti to be visual pollution, and, finally, the time of the current mayor, João Dória (2017–present), where all types of graffiti are considered pollution (unless sponsored by known brands), adding a further layer to the aestheticization of São Paulo's urban space through the creation of the new program, Beautiful City, which included, for some, the covering up of the homeless in the city.

The never-ending quest for a more "beautiful" São Paulo shows how complex and potentially misunderstood the concept of visual pollution is. The politics behind the classification of visual communication as pollution reveals social and spatial inequalities, including social exclusion and marginalization of its producers. Which voices count in the debate about graffiti as street art or as vandalism? More importantly, it is essential to ask whether the law actually protects citizens' rights for clean urban spaces or whether it is affecting their sense of environmental justice, as speculated in the example of the "cleaning up" of homelessness in São Paulo.

It is undeniable that the urban environment has become saturated with all kinds of visualities, billboards, graffiti, street art, and even buildings. However, how we understand these visual stimuli as pollution has not yet been fully researched. The larger and more populated the urban environment becomes, the more we will notice the increasing amount of pollution that impact our senses, and ultimately health, both physically and mentally. Arguably, certain sensory pollutions (light and noise) can be measured in relation to an average perception of that stimulation and changing behavioral patterns. However, the assessment of visual pollution presents many challenges; the contrasting perceptions of visual cultural production calls for a set of inventive methodologies to measure and understand the different impacts of these visual stimuli, not only quantitatively, but also qualitatively.

The empirical work done in São Paulo's public space in 2014 raises questions about the continuous negotiation that the different types of visualities and their producers have in the production of that space (Lefebvre 1991), and therefore how the control of such visuals impacts this new space. The data collected during the initial fieldwork raised important questions on the understanding of these visuals as a collective and in degradation (pollution?) of the urban space, on the role that graffiti played in São Paulo's urban spaces, and how this relates to other environmental issues. The sensorial ethnographic data from the "city walks" was used on an installation that reinterpreted modes of experience of the urban space, as an attempt to incite the audience to critically reflect on society's (changing) views on visual pollution and how different structures of experience are perceived within the same urban reality.

The rise of visual pollution in the Anthropocene seems understandable since we are living in a time where visual cultural production is increasingly prioritized. Therefore, understanding how this phenomenon could be causing us harm is crucial, especially when the term comprises different problematics. São

Paulo's law validated a new concept – visual pollution – and in doing so has acted as a controlling tool on the public space, infringing on ideas of freedom and environmental justice. Clean City demonstrates the urgent need to further expand the concept of pollution and to understand other types of sensorial pollution – not only how to measure visual pollution but also how visual pollution impacts society.

References

Baudrillard, J. 1998. *The Consumer Society: Myths and Structures*. London: Sage.

Bevins, V. 2010. São Paulo advertising goes underground. *Financial Times*. Available at https://www.ft.com/content/5ad26f14-b9e6-11df-8804-00144feabdc0 (last accessed February 11, 2014).

Bourdieu, P. 1984. *Distinction*. Cambridge, MA: Harvard University Press.

Chmielewski, S., Lee, D., Tompalski, P., Chmielewski, T., and Wezyk, P. 2016. Measuring visual pollution by outdoor advertisements in an urban street using intervisibilty analysis and public surveys. *International Journal of Geographical Information Science*, 30, 801–818. DOI: 10.1080/13658816.2015.1104316.

Cidade Limpa 2015. ww2.prefeitura.sp.gov.br, (2015). *Cidade Limpa*. Available at https://www9.prefeitura.sp.gov.br/cidadelimpa/conheca_lei/conheca_lei.html.

Coole, D. and Frost, S. 2010. *New Materialisms*. Durham, NC: Duke University Press.

Cresswell, T. 1992. The crucial "where" of graffiti: A geographical analysis of reactions to graffiti in New York. *Environment and Planning D: Society and Space*, 10(3), 329–344.

Cronin, A. M. 2010. *Advertising, Commercial Spaces and the Urban*. Basingstoke: Palgrave Macmillan.

Crutzen, P. J. and Stoermer, E. F. 2000. The Anthropocene. IGBP *Global Change Newsletter*, 41, 17–18.

Dias, T. 2016. Tem um "pixo" num grafite assinado. E isso agradou muita gente. *Nexo* [online]. Available at https://www.nexojornal.com.br/expresso/2016/02/12/Tem-um-%E2%80%98pixo%E2%80%99-num-grafite-assinado.-E-isso-agradou-muita-gente (last accessed February 4, 2020).

Douglas, M. 1966. *Purity and Danger*. New York: Praeger.

Douglas, M. and Hull, D. (eds) 1994. *How Classification Works*. Illustrated edition. Edinburgh: Edinburgh University Press.

Emporis 2018. London | Buildings | EMPORIS. [online] Available at https://www.emporis.com/city/100637/london-united-kingdom (last accessed February 4, 2020).

Eriksen, T. H. 1995. *Small Places, Large Issues: An Introduction to Social and Cultural Anthropology*. London: Pluto.

Estadão 2013. Como era São Paulo sem Plano Diretor. Available at http://acervo.estadao.com.br/noticias/acervo,como-era-sao-paulo-sem-plano-diretor,9276,0.htm (last accessed February 4, 2020).

Exame 2017. *Doria varreu o chão por menos de 10 segundos em ato*. Available at https:// exame.abril.com.br/brasil/doria-varreu-o-chao-por-menos-de-10-segundos-em-ato/ (last accessed February 12, 2020).

Ferrell, J. 1995. Urban graffiti. *Youth & Society*, 27(1), 73–92.

Flynn, D. and Simões, E. 2017. Sao Paulo to launch $2.3 billion privatization plan this year: Mayor. *Reuters*. Available at https://www.reuters.com/article/us-brazil-politics-doria-privatisations/sao-paulo-to-launch-2-3-billion-privatization-plan-this-year-mayor-idUSKBN17731Z (last accessed February 4, 2020).

Folha de São Paulo 2007. *Folha Online – Cotidiano – Justiça derruba liminar que permitia empresa manter outdoors em SP*. January 30. Available at https://www1.folha.uol.com. br/folha/cotidiano/ult95u131145.shtml (last accessed August 19, 2012).

Fong, J. 2016. Making operative concepts from Murray Schafer's soundscapes typology: A qualitative and comparative analysis of noise pollution in Bangkok, Thailand and Los Angeles, California. *Urban Studies*, 53(1), 173–192.

globo.com. 2013. Estudo aponta que poluição mata mais que o trânsito em São Paulo. Available at http://g1.globo.com/sao-paulo/noticia/2013/09/estudo-aponta-que-poluicao-mata-mais-que-o-transito-em-sao-paulo.html (last accessed February 4, 2020).

Guattari, F. 2014. *The Three Ecologies*. London: Bloomsbury Academic.

Harris, D. E. 2007. São Paulo: A city without ads. Adbusters, August 3.

Ingold, T. and Vergunst, J. 2008. *Ways of Walking*. Aldershot: Ashgate.

Jameson, F. 2009. *Postmodernism, or, The Cultural Logic of Late Capitalism*. London: Verso.

Kaiser, A. 2019. "Exterminator of the future": Brazil's Bolsonaro denounced for environmental assault. *Guardian*, May 9. Available at https://www.theguardian.com/world/2019/may/09/jair-bolsonaro-brazil-amazon-rainforest-environment (last accessed February 4, 2020).

Klein, N. 2009. *No Space, No Choice, No Jobs, No Logo*. Toronto: Vintage Canada.

Latour, B. 2007. *Reassembling the Social*. Oxford: Oxford University Press.

Lefebvre, H. 1991. *The Production of Space*. Oxford: Blackwell.

Liboiron, M. 2015. Redefining pollution and action: The matter of plastics. *Journal of Material Culture*, 21. DOI: 10.1177/1359183515622966.

Longcore, T. and Rich, C. 2004. Ecological light pollution. *Frontiers in Ecology and the Environment*. Available at https://esajournals.onlinelibrary.wiley.com/doi/full/10.1890/1540-9295(2004)002[0191:ELP]2.0.CO;2 (last accessed February 4, 2020).

Lury, C. and Wakeford, N. 2012. *Inventive Methods*. London: Routledge.

Mahdawi, A. 2015. Can cities kick ads? Inside the global movement to ban urban billboards. *The Guardian*, August 12. Available at https://www.theguardian.com/cities/2015/aug/11/can-cities-kick-ads-ban-urban-billboards (last accessed February 12, 2020).

National Research Council. 2012. *Science for Environmental Protection: The Road Ahead*. Washington, DC: The National Academies Press.

Phillips, T. 2019. Diehard Bolsonaro supporters prepare to march as criticism of his rule intensifies. *Guardian*, May 24. Available at https://www.theguardian.com/world/2019/may/24/brazil-president-jair-bolsonaro-calls-for-street-rallies-as-criticism-of-his-rule-intensifies (last accessed February 4, 2020).

Portella, A. 2014. *Visual Pollution: Advertising, Signage and Environmental Quality*. Farnham: Ashgate.

Romero, S. 2015. Taps start to run dry in Brazil's largest city. *New York Times*. Available at https://www.nytimes.com/2015/02/17/world/americas/drought-pushes-sao-paulo-brazil-toward-water-crisis.html?_r=0 (last accessed February 4, 2020).

Rose, G. 2001. *Visual Methodologies*. London: Sage.

Sennett, R. 1990. *The Conscience of the Eye*. New York: Knopf.

Shear, M. D. and Haberman, M. 2019. For Trump, Brazil's president is like looking in the mirror. *New York Times*, March 19. Available at https://www.nytimes.com/2019/03/19/us/politics/bolsonaro-trump.html (last accessed February 4, 2020).

Simmel, G. 1976. The metropolis and mental life. In *The Sociology of Georg Simmel*. New York: Free Press.

Stansfeld, S. A. and Matheson, M. P. 2003. Noise pollution: Non-auditory effects on health, *British Medical Bulletin*, 68(1), 243–257. DOI: 10.1093/bmb/ldg033.

The Economist 2007. Visual pollution. October 11. Available at https://www.economist.com/business/2007/10/11/visual-pollution (last accessed February 11, 2020).

Veja São Paulo 2015. População de rua cresce 10% em quatro anos, mostra censo. Available at https://vejasp.abril.com.br/cidades/censo-mostra-quais-sao-os-bairros-com-mais-moradores-de-rua-em-sao-paulo/ (last accessed February 4, 2020).

Wolch, J., Byrne, J., and Newell, J. 2014. Urban green space, public health, and environmental justice: The challenge of making cities "just green enough." *Landscape and Urban Planning*, 125, 234–244.

Part III

Political strategies for seeking environmental justice

Introduction to Part III

Alice Mah

Science and politics are impossible to disentangle within environmental justice (EJ) struggles. What counts as legitimate data, and whose voices count? How can local communities that face disproportionate toxic burdens effectively mobilize science to support their campaigns for environment justice? Scientific evidence of toxic exposure is often not sufficient to ensure adequate compensation, remediation, or recognition (Boudia and Jas 2014). As the epidemiologist and environmental justice activist Steve Wing (2005, 55) argued, "The environmental justice movement has been led primarily by people of color, women, and people who live in communities that are adversely affected by environmental problems created by industry and government, the very institutions that are closest to science."

One of the key challenges within the environmental justice movement is the problem of quantifying the health risks of toxic exposure. Within epidemiology, there are established correlations between environmental exposure to particular chemicals and diseases. However, the levels of exposures are disputed (i.e., concentrations, duration, and measurement criteria), and these are notoriously difficult to isolate from other environmental factors (Tesh 2000; Vrijheid 2000). Debates about environmental health in contaminated areas are particularly controversial, reflecting competing and unequal interests between corporate profit, job security, environmental protection, and community health.

Corporations have frequently denied the health risks associated with toxic pollutants, emphasizing the uncertainty of science as a strategic use of ignorance (Markowitz and Rosner 2002; Michaels 2008; McGoey 2012). Moreover, contested forms of expertise have led to the problem of "undone science," whole avenues of scientific exploration that are too politicized to gain widespread support (Frickel et al. 2010; Hess 2016). Corporations are able to use scientific uncertainty over measurements of toxicity in order to move the goal posts, and thus ignore the "snapshots of chemical exposure" that citizen scientists are able to record (Murphy 2015, 110). The toxic yardsticks and standardized practices of science can become both a source of legitimacy for "fenceline" communities, but also the means of their downfall (Ottinger 2013).

The politicized nature of science has led academics and activists to call for the democratization of science and expertise, advancing forms of citizen science and participatory public interventions in science and policy (Irwin 1995; Fischer 2000; Carolan 2006). The community-based environmental justice research examples discussed earlier, in Part I of this book, exemplify some of the success stories of participatory citizen science while highlighting the need for enduring struggles. However, citizen-led environmental justice victories, where corporations or state actors are held legally responsible for costs of compensation, clean-up, or relocation, typically only occur in extreme cases of negligence (Bullard and Wright 2009). Following the uneven geography of toxic hazards, the environmental justice "wins" also correspond to "losses" in other places, as toxic hazards move to communities with weaker political voices.

Part III of *Toxic Truths* highlights the importance of context-specific environmental justice strategies, alongside crosscutting EJ concerns with political recognition (Schlosberg 2013) and the democratization of knowledge (Carolan 2006). The three chapters in this section foreground public engagements with science, rather than citizen science per se, drawing attention to the uses of science and how these have been mobilized strategically within different political contexts. Despite the well-documented public health consequences for people living and working close to contaminated sites around the world, the methodologies and strategies for addressing these problems are fragmented (see Pasetto and Iavarone, this volume). While there are systemic patterns of environmental injustice around the world, the social and political dynamics of interests, values, and actions are different in each case. These chapters highlight the political dilemmas of engaging with science for seeking environmental justice in different contexts in Spain, Italy, and China. In particular, the authors explore the challenges of addressing knowledge gaps about environmental health data; equitable participation and dialogue in environmental decision making; and effective local strategies of confrontation with industry and the state.

Miguel López-Navarro's chapter focuses on a local environmental organization's confrontational approach toward industry over air quality in the "northern petrochemical complex" in Tarragona, Spain. This chapter shows that
the organization's adversarial approach toward industry was more effective
than consensus-based approaches for changing the behavior of industry. The
regional and industrial context is important for understanding the efficacy of
this approach. The local environmental organization's confrontational approach
was bolstered by the perceived scientific legitimacy of the study among multiple
stakeholders. The absence of epidemiological studies and the limited number of
pollutants monitored by the regional government were key factors behind the
mobilization of the health study, which had been carried out by experts in which
civil society organizations had actively participated. This chapter also shows how
an environmental strategy based on confrontation does not necessarily exclude
dialogue, because, in this case, it led to the local organization's active participation in a multi-stakeholder deliberative process.

The lack of epidemiological studies is a significant barrier to seeking environmental justice, particularly on a systemic level. The chapter by Roberto Pasetto
and Ivano Iavarone addresses this issue from another angle, by examining the
environmental justice implications of a national epidemiological monitoring
system in Italy, where the health profile of populations who live in close proximity to Italian National Priority Contaminated Sites (NPCS) has been periodically assessed. The authors argue that the national epidemiological monitoring
system could help contaminated communities in their struggles for environmental justice by identifying and communicating the environmental health risks
that are concentrated in particular neighborhoods. In other words, the chapter
seeks to address gaps in "epistemic injustice" (Fricker 2007) or "knowledge justice" (Allen, this volume) through the production and communication of official
national epidemiological data, as a public resource for local communities. The
authors conclude with a reflection on the widespread public health implications of living in close proximity to industrially contaminated sites around the
world, yet the lack of common epidemiological methodologies or frameworks.
They argue that there is an urgent need to promote international cooperation
to identify appropriate strategies and methods to deal with these issues more
systematically.

The case of China demonstrates the political barriers to such aspirational
models of international cooperation on the epidemiology of toxic contaminated
sites. Echoing the case of Tarragona in Spain, but on a much wider scale, polluted industrial sites in China also lack epidemiological data and reliable air
quality monitoring. Air, water, and land pollution are pervasive throughout
China, often at very high and alarming concentrations well above international

standards for acceptable thresholds. However, toxic pollution in China comes from multiple sources, and it is often difficult, if not impossible, to attribute it to a single industry. Furthermore, in most cases, having scientific data about toxic exposure risks would not be sufficient for seeking compensation or justice in China (see Van Rooij et al. 2012; Mah and Wang 2019). As Xinhong Wang and Yuanni Wang discuss in their chapter, civil society organizations face severe constraints in China, and environmental NGOs tend to adapt their work to avoid direct confrontation with the state. In contrast with López-Navarro's chapter, Wang and Wang argue that strategies of "soft confrontation" have been more successful than direct confrontational strategies for addressing environmental problems in Hunan Province in China. The authors demonstrate how Green Hunan, a local environmental volunteers' organization, has operated strategically to avoid direct confrontation while advocating for environmental protection, for example through the use of the media and lobbying rather than protests.

Participatory citizen science is one method for seeking environmental justice, and bearing witness through embodied experience is another. However, it is important to recognize the need for diverse citizen-led strategies for seeking environmental justice based on different contexts. Questions of power, including the role of the state, corporate interests, and civil society, are crucial in debates about the science of environmental justice. With the world beset by an increasing number of seemingly unsolvable environmental problems, the "uneasy alchemy" (Allen 2003) of citizen–expert alliances is all too often the social fallout of battles over scientific expertise. The stakes of this fallout are high in a post-truth age, where the interplay of science and politics is increasingly unpredictable.

References

Allen, B. L. 2003. *Uneasy Alchemy: Citizens and Experts in Louisiana's Chemical Corridor Disputes.* Cambridge, MA: MIT Press.

Boudia, S. and N. Jas. 2014. Introduction: The greatness and misery of science in a toxic world. In by S. Boudia and N. Jas (eds), *Powerless Science? Science and Politics in a Toxic World.* New York: Berghahn Books, pp. 1–28.

Bullard R. D and Wright B. 2009. *Race, Place, and Environmental Justice after Hurricane Katrina.* Boulder, CO: Westview Press.

Carolan, M. S. 2006. Science, expertise, and the democratization of the decision-making process. *Society and Natural Resources*, 19(7), 661–668.

Fischer, F. 2000. *Citizens, Experts, and the Environment.* Durham, NC: Duke University Press.

Frickel, S. et al. 2010. Undone science: Charting social movement and civil society challenges to research agenda setting. *Science, Technology & Human Values*, 35(4), 444–473.

Fricker, M. 2007. *Epistemic Injustice: Power and the Ethics of Knowing*. Oxford: Oxford University Press.

Hess, D. 2016. *Undone Science: Social Movements, Mobilized Publics, and Industrial Transitions*. Cambridge, MA: MIT Press.

Irwin, A. 1995. *Citizen Science: A Study of People, Expertise, and Sustainable Development*. Abingdon: Routledge.

Mah, A. and Wang, X. 2019. Accumulated injuries of environmental injustice: Living and working with petrochemical pollution in Nanjing, China. *Annals of the American Association of Geographers*. DOI: 10.1080/24694452.2019.1574551.

Markowitz, G. E. and Rosner, D. 2002. *Deceit and Denial: The Deadly Politics of Industrial Pollution*. Berkeley: University of California Press.

McGoey, L. 2012. Strategic unknowns: Towards a sociology of ignorance. *Economy & Society*, 41(1), 1–16.

Michaels, D. 2008. *Doubt Is Their Product: How Industry's Assault on Science Threatens Your Health*. Oxford: Oxford University Press.

Murphy, M. 2015. Chemical infrastructures of the St. Clair river. In S. Boudia and N. Jas (eds), *Toxicants, Health and Regulation since 1945*. London and New York: Routledge, pp. 103–115.

Ottinger, G. 2013. *Refining Expertise: How Responsible Engineers Subvert Environmental Justice Challenges*. New York and London: NYU Press.

Schlosberg, D. 2013. Theorising environmental justice: The expanding sphere of a discourse. *Environmental Politics*, 22(1), 37–55.

Tesh, S. N. 2000. *Uncertain Hazards: Environmental Activists and Scientific Proof*. Ithaca, NY: Cornell University Press.

Van Rooij, B., Wainwright, A. L., Wu, Y., and Zhang, Y. 2012. The compensation trap: The limits of community-based pollution regulation in China. *Pace Environmental Law Review*, 29(3), 701–745.

Vrijheid, M. 2000. Health effects of residence near hazardous waste landfill sites: A review of epidemiologic literature. *Environmental Health Perspectives*, 108(1), 101–112.

Wing, S. 2005. Environmental justice, science and public health. *Environmental Health Perspectives*, 113, 54–63.

8

Legitimating confrontational discourses by local environmental groups: The case of air quality monitoring in a Spanish industrial area

Miguel A. López-Navarro

Introduction

The escalating role of the firm at the expense of the public authorities' function as guarantors of citizens' rights may have helped drive the increased political authority of nongovernmental organizations (NGOs)[1] as representatives of civil society (Hahn and Pinkse 2014). In the business and society literature, there is a growing body of research on firm–NGO relationships (Dahan et al. 2010; Kourola and Laasonen 2010). Studies exploring the firm's new political role – influenced by developments in political theory, particularly Habermas's concept of "deliberative democracy" – place participation and consensus at the heart of the governance discourse and identify collaboration between firms, governments, and civil society as the way forward (Baur and Palazzo 2011; Laasonen et al. 2012). The dominant articulation in the business and society discourse on firm–NGO relationships revolves around collaboration, and systematically undervalues the constructive role that confrontation and conflict can play (Laasonen et al. 2012).

One stream in the literature on business–NGO interaction is concerned with large multinational corporations that operate in multiple locations and generate negative externalities on a global scale (e.g., de Lange et al. 2016). However, a great deal of activism takes place at the local level, particularly on environmental issues. As Grant and Vasi (2017, 100) point out, "the strong local orientation of many activists reflects the specific environmental damages that companies cause to specific geographical areas in the form of toxic dumping, destruction of lands and resources, and air pollution." Many local environmental NGOs, with limited resources and a focus on a specific geographical area, share characteristics with grassroots activist movements and are more likely to be confrontational than cooperative (Leon-Zchout and Tal 2017). These local NGOs often find it difficult to legitimize their activities; their work is frequently challenged by political and business powers, and even by many citizens, on the grounds that they are raising barriers to the economic development of the region.[2] Legitimizing their strategy is therefore a key factor in their survival.

In a context in which cooperation among actors is the dominant articulation, our study goes some way to responding to calls from authors such as Laasonen et al. (2012) for further research favoring greater recognition of the constructive role confrontational strategies can have. The need for a better understanding of how NGOs construct their discourses and manage their adversarial relationships, and for analysis of the conditions under which confrontation can lead to the most favorable solutions are research questions also raised in the work of Baur and Palazzo (2011). Specifically, the present chapter draws on a case study in a Spanish industrial region to analyze how a local environmental group articulates and legitimizes a confrontational strategy based on a scientific study instigated by the group, in collaboration with local town councils, and carried out by independent experts. We also assess industry and regional government responses to this strategy, particularly the extent to which it is bringing about improvements in responsible industry behavior and making advances that may favor the health of the local communities affected by the industrial activity. The question of regional government response is especially relevant, since public bodies are often perceived as being aligned with industry interests by local communities (Espluga et al. 2010).

This chapter contributes to the literature in several ways. First, it highlights the value of the confrontation strategy, while identifying the key elements that have favored the group's legitimacy and the effectiveness of its actions: a strategy based on scientific knowledge and acceptance of the industry's role in contributing to the development of the region. Second, it shows how a strategy based on confrontation does not necessarily exclude dialogue or, more specifically in this case, the possibility of actively participating in a multi-stakeholder deliberative process.

NGO–business relations

Like any other organization, NGOs develop strategies with which to achieve their objectives. In their efforts to improve issues of public health and the environment, they face the dilemma of either challenging the status quo or working within the frame of conventional channels to achieve improvements (Dalton et al. 2003). At a conceptual level, many authors classify NGOs into two main groups according to whether their strategies follow a conflictive or a consensual line (Michaelson 1994; Dryzek et al. 2003). Conflict NGOs are usually characterized by some level of activism that challenges the status quo, whereas consensus NGOs are more collaborative and acknowledge the legitimacy of the establishment (Leon-Zchout and Tal 2017). Although these strategies are posed generically, environmental groups operate under the restrictions and opportunities found in the political context in which they operate (Kadirbeyoglu et al. 2017). Thus, NGOs in advanced industrial democracies –the context in which our research takes place – must consider the question of adopting strategies of confrontation or collaboration, taking into account that both options are accepted within the limits established by the democratic framework. However, in unconsolidated or consolidating democracies, where dissent is not generally accepted, the most confrontational movements are usually restricted (Dalton 2005).

These two logics of confrontation and cooperation may also coexist in what Covey and Brown (2001), for example, define as *critical cooperation*. Indeed, the same organization may follow confrontational or cooperative strategies in different circumstances, and it is the frequency and intensity with which they use these tactics that define their strategic orientation (Leon-Zchout and Tal 2017).

The role of NGOs has traditionally been associated with pressurizing companies to meet their responsibilities and respond to social and environmental problems. Contributions from stakeholder theory have considered NGOs as key stakeholders in influencing organizational behavior (van Huijstee and Glasbergen 2010; Sprengel and Busch 2011). Social movement theory has also been applied in the organizational field to analyze how activist movements determine corporate changes (den Hond and de Bakker 2007; King 2008; Gómez-Carrasco and Michelon 2017).

Yet recent developments in the business and society literature have emphasized partnerships between companies and NGOs, in pursuit of collaboration and consensus (van Huijstee and Glasbergen 2010; Baur and Palazzo 2011; Laasonen et al. 2012; Hahn and Pinkse 2014). According to Laasonen et al. (2012, 537–538), business and society discourse interacts with social movements discourse and governance discourse in the following ways: it attempts to (1) co-opt social movements through partnership and collaborative articulations, (2) suppress those accounts of social movements theory that are still focused on adversarial relationships, and (3) place business at the center of governance discourse notably through articulations that draw on "deliberative democracy" and the "post-political" perspective.

This trend toward greater collaboration is justified as a consequence of the increasing complexity of the problems facing society, and the search for "win–win" solutions for all parties[3] (Olk 2013; Bitzer and Glasbergen 2015). The interconnections between social, economic, political, and ecological factors require interaction, stable continuous relationships, and dialogue among all agents in order to reduce tensions and reach agreements that benefit society. By participating in these partnerships, companies and NGOs come to know each other's views of the problem in question, smoothing the way for responses to present and future social and environmental challenges. Collaboration can grant legitimacy to participating NGOs, since firms and public authorities recognize their ability to contribute constructively to social change (Macdonald and Chrisp 2005).

Such partnerships are not, however, without their problems. Bonds are often forged in these relationships that engulf the NGOs in an institutional logic that favors the industry and contributes to slowing down social and environmental changes. On numerous occasions, firms use dialogue and cooperation to avoid criticism and gain social legitimacy, but without actually pursuing changes in their key processes (Burchell and Cook 2011). NGO co-optation through corporate partnerships may seriously undermine NGOs' credibility, since independence is crucial to their legitimacy (Baur and Schmitz 2012).

The constitution of firm–NGO collaboration as the dominant articulation in the business and society discourse can contribute to suppressing the narratives that continue to focus on relationships between adversaries, and largely ignores the role of NGOs that follow a non-collaboration strategy. Consigning non-cooperative relationships to the past is problematic because it ignores the fact that legitimate disagreement can be understood as a commitment to improving social problems (Laasonen et al. 2012). However, engaging in an adversarial relationship does not necessarily exclude dialogue. As we noted above, the literature has pointed out the coexistence, or alternative use, of confrontational and collaborative strategies (Covey and Brown 2001; Arenas et al. 2013; Kadirbeyoglu et al. 2017). Indeed, dialogue can transform manifestly hostile relationships into less conflictive forms of interaction without erasing the condition of adversaries underlying the relationship between the parties.

We focus our attention on the case of a local grassroots environmental group that adopts a confrontational strategy. These groups, as we noted in the introductory section, have problems of legitimacy, to the extent that they are questioned by the industry and public institutions – and possibly by a part of the local community – insofar as they may be holding back the economic growth of the region. As Berry points out (2003, 7), taking as reference the work of Kroll-Smith and Couch (1991), "corporations, industry groups, or government agencies often characterize grassroots activists or community groups that complain about contaminants and environmental risks as irrational or hysterical." In this context, the key issue is how the local environmental group articulates and legitimizes a confrontational strategy which opens the way to solutions that allow progress in solving environmental problems.

Case study

In this chapter, we refer to a case study to illustrate how a local environmental group articulates a confrontational strategy, and to analyze industry and regional government responses. Using a single case is a common method in qualitative research traditions (Alvesson and Deetz 2000), with the advantage that it allows the phenomenon of interest to be studied in depth. The data was gathered from various documentary sources. The process began with a thorough analysis of the websites of both the environmental group and Repsol, the main company involved. Newspaper, radio, and television interviews with the primary agents were also assessed. Other sources analyzed were documents from the working sessions of the deliberative platform set up by the regional government to find a solution to the controversy, and the technical reports from the air quality studies. Finally, we examined newspaper articles (from June 2014 when the environmental group presented the first study, up to August 2017) using the Factiva database to search for the name of the local environmental group. We concentrated on publicly available information because the justification and legitimization of the actors involved took place in the public sphere.

The industrial area

Tarragona (Spain) is the place of one of the largest petrochemical complexes in southern Europe. The complex is located on two sites 10 kilometers apart: the Southern Industrial Complex and the Northern Industrial Complex. Both sites occupy more than 1,400 hectares devoted to the chemical industry and generate approximately 10,000 direct jobs (6,000 generated by the companies of the

AEQT – Chemical Industry Association of Tarragona – and 4,000 generated by the companies of the AEST[4]) and over 30,000 induced jobs (AEQT 2013). To date, the local environmental group has centered its activities on the Northern Industrial Complex, where companies such as Repsol and Dow Chemical are located. As Espluga et al. (2014) note, the few citizen protests that have taken place in the area have essentially been in the form of legal actions filed in the courts against episodes of accidental pollution, although they have had little collective impact.

The local environmental group and the scientific study on air quality

The local environmental group "Cel Net" was formed at the end of 2008 to campaign for improvements in air quality for residents as a consequence of petrochemical industry activity. However, in 2014 the group gained influence after publishing the results of a scientific study (carried out between the end of 2012 and May 2014) into air quality in the area of the Northern Industrial Complex. This study forms the cornerstone of the case described in the present research, in that it generated some disruption of the established social order and, at the same time, provided the foundations for the local environmental group's confrontational strategy. According to statements from the group, the study arose from the situation of uncertainty about the air quality in the area. In this context, a proposal was made to the five local councils in the towns adjoining the northern complex with a request for funding to undertake an independent scientific study of the air quality. Four of these councils (El Morell, Constantí, Villalonga del Camp, and Perafort-Puigdelfí) gave their support to the proposal, while one (La Pobla de Mafumet) declined to participate. The study was carried out by the Environment Center Laboratory (Laboratori del Centre de Medi Ambient, LCMA) at the Polytechnic University of Catalonia (UPC). Members of the local environmental group and volunteers from the four municipalities involved participated in the social and chemical control activities of the study.

The study identified more than 200 compounds. Abnormally high values were found for some pollutants such as benzene and 1,3-butadiene – both compounds are included in group 1 of carcinogens of the IARC (International Agency for Research on Cancer) (IARC 2018). The methodology used in the study not only identified the components but also traced their path – the source of their emission. These findings generated considerable social debate on air quality in the area. A further two studies were subsequently carried out, the results of which were presented in November 2015 and February 2017. These studies were carried out in only one of the four municipalities (El Morell); in the latter study only 1,3-butadiene was analyzed, the pollutant that seems to have triggered the greatest social concern because of its toxicity and the high levels detected in the initial study. The platform attributes the lack of involvement in the follow-up studies by the other town councils to political and business pressure. In general terms, these later studies found lower emission levels of the pollutants than those detected in the first study.

The local environmental group's strategy and industry and regional government responses

As highlighted above, the study's results generated public controversy over the nature of the problem, its causes and its possible solutions. In what follows, we describe the response and the actions of the environmental group, which to a certain extent define its strategic orientation, and also the responses from the industry and the regional government.

For the environmental group, the study brought to light the problem of air quality that hitherto had remained hidden. The problem was attributed to insufficient efforts by the companies on environmental issues and to the limitations of the air quality monitoring network. As a result, the group made public demands for industry interventions to improve their environmental performance, together with stricter regulations and enhanced controls from the regional government. Both these demands align with what den Hond and de Bakker (2007) identify as the two complementary routes followed by activist groups to bring about change: regulatory modifications and changes in organizational behavior.

In the assessment of the study's results, published on its website (http://plataformacelnet.blogspot.com.es), the group explicitly stated its wish that the results would be a starting point for a commitment to a common objective by all parties involved: to improve the conditions of the lives, health, and work of the populations in the vicinity of the petrochemical complex. But at the same time, the results provided the keystone for the design of a confrontational strategy. A manifesto was drawn up specifying the group's demands, and they instigated a protest campaign titled "*Saps què respires?*" (Do you know what you are breathing?) (Figure 8.1). The results of the study were widely disseminated through presentations in the affected towns (with the collaboration of the scientists responsible for the study from the LCMA at the UPC) and through social media. A considerable effort was made to democratize the air quality information generated by the scientific studies. All these endeavors were designed to capture the attention of the mass media, raise the movement's public profile, and increase public pressure.

The group's strategy was clearly to put pressure on the industry through its demands for more responsibility and higher investment. As the platform's

8.1 Campaign image "*Saps què respires?*" Source: http://plataformacelnet.blogspot. com.es/.

spokesperson stated in a newspaper interview (Diari de Tarragona 2016), "The petrochemical [industry] is not transparent if it does not feel pressure from the community. Social media and the mass media also have a role to play. So the consequences for a brand's image can be very damaging." Social media was also used as a space in which to share information and audiovisual documentation reporting the incidents taking place in the industrial complex. The importance of social media in articulating social movements' confrontational strategies, helping to spread information at a relatively low cost, has been highlighted in the literature (Daubanes and Rochet 2016; Dahlberg-Grundberg and Örestig 2017). As examples of this, we reproduce two messages from the group's Facebook page, published after specific incidents that illustrate its critical orientation:

> Repsol invents the future. Its own future. A future in which polluting will be synonymous with benefit. In which sponsorship will be synonymous with public support. Meanwhile, the present is a reality punished to benefit the industry and cheated by its sponsorships. (April 18, 2017)

> The freedom to pollute is a condition granted by the passivity of the political class. (April 26, 2017)

However, in developing its confrontational strategy the group was fully aware of the industry's importance to the economic development of the region, and in parallel it continued to use the conventional channels of communication and dialogue, one example being its participation in Repsol's public panel.

The strategy of pressure also sought to bring about changes to air quality policies at regional government level. The results of the study openly challenged the legitimacy of the current public model for monitoring air quality. In fact, the experts responsible for the study from the LCMA at the UPC questioned the efficiency of the evaluation model used.

Local environmental groups are frequently small organizations with few resources and sometimes very little social credibility. Consequently, as described in the introduction, they find it difficult to legitimize their actions. In our case study, by instigating an independent scientific study – the results of which defined subsequent actions – the group gained a certain legitimacy. In parallel, support for the study from the local town councils probably also contributed to raising the group's credibility in the eyes of the public.

The relevance of the scientific study in legitimizing the group's strategy of confrontation is reaffirmed by the two subsequent studies referred to above. In a radio interview (Catalunya Radio 2015), the group's spokesperson described how these additional studies not only aimed to monitor levels of the pollutants identified in the first study and therefore assess whether any corrective measures had been implemented, but were also conceived to continue the pressure on the industry and the regional government. On the same lines, in collaboration with other environmental groups in the area, the group initiated a campaign in mid-2015 calling for an air quality study in the Southern Industrial Complex.

The industry response

The only firm considered in our analysis was Repsol, whose plant was identified as the origin of the most problematic toxic substances in the first study. The firm's discursive response in the public arena was scarce, and, when it did appear, was a combination of skepticism about the study's results and a message conveying its good intentions. The firm claimed the results did not coincide with its own internal measures, and suggested that there could be some confusion over the measurement parameters. Company representatives stated that although it is not required by European regulations, "in the plant we do control this parameter; if the exposure limit is 4.5 micrograms per cubic metre, our workers register between 0 and 4% of the maximum dose" (El Mundo 2015).

In the same newspaper article the company also acknowledged "a feeling in the area that there was a problem with air quality," and expressed its willingness to intensify efforts to reduce emissions of carcinogenic volatile organic compounds such as benzene or 1,3-butadiene. It also called for greater clarity from the regional government on the regulation of 1,3-butadiene, in order to avoid subjectivity and specify the circumstances for action when appropriate measures are taken. The company also expressed its willingness to assess the results of the study with members from the local environmental group, with whom they held a meeting at the firm's request. In line with their policy to keep channels of dialogue open, the group attended the meeting, where they called on the company to provide tangible and measurable facts.

With regard to the firm's statements on its willingness to intensify efforts to reduce emissions, the subsequent studies promoted by the environmental group, which to a certain extent can be considered as a base for control, in general terms found improvements in the air quality results. The local environmental group claimed this improvement was due to a process of self-control by the industry stemming from the higher levels of external control to which it was subjected. Indeed, some studies, such as Daubanes and Rochet (2016), have shown that opposition from NGOs can stimulate firms to implement self-regulation processes.

Companies' discursive responses become increasingly responsible, the more their legitimacy is threatened (Ählström 2010). In this vein, Repsol has introduced new environmental targets in its sustainability reports for the Tarragona plant. Its sustainability plan for 2015 introduced, for the first time, an air quality protection objective. In the frame of this objective, the sustainability plan for 2016 included specific studies for the compounds identified in the study instigated by the local environmental group: benzene and 1,3-butadiene. However, such behavior does not align with the postulates of what is known as "political corporate social responsibility" (Scherer and Palazzo 2011; Scherer et al. 2016), which hold that actions implemented by firms should be proactive. Repsol's reaction appears to be a response to social pressure in a specific location, since the new air quality objectives introduced in the Tarragona plant sustainability report are not included in reports for its other sites (with the exception of Puertollano). In turn, the firm's call for greater regulatory clarity from the regional government may simply indicate a desire for a reference framework within which to determine the scope of their investments.

The regional government response

The regional government's discursive response to the study and to the local environmental group's actions was more visible than that of the company. Although they strongly defended the public air quality monitoring network, they also accepted that some of the problems were due to the lack of suitable regulation for certain components, and also referred to inherent problems in appropriate communication of information and risks to the public.

The regional government's response to the controversy was conditioned by a resolution on the matter approved by the Catalan Parliament on March 25, 2015. This led to the creation in July of the same year of the multi-stakeholder deliberative platform on air quality with the participation of the main agents involved. The merit for the creation of the platform, explicitly recognized in its first working session, is largely attributable to the local environmental group, since the above-mentioned resolution[5] leading to its constitution corresponds almost entirely to the request made by the group through certain political parties. The deliberative platform was constituted with 52 members, including representatives from regional government, social organizations (including the local environmental group), the AEQT (Chemical Industrial Association of Tarragona), and other economic sectors and business associations. According to the deliberative platform website, its objective is "to exchange information about air quality and the effects of emissions from the chemical industry on people's health, to ensure the appropriate monitoring and research into the effects of the main pollutants from the petrochemical industry on human health, and to improve transparency" (TQACT 2018).

One of the deliberative platform's most significant initiatives, announced in the second working session, was to create three working groups to: (1) analyze legislation in other countries and examine the measures adopted in areas with similar characteristics; (2) analyze the studies carried out to date, both in terms of pollutants and of population health, in order to assess the data and draw up a projection of specific measures to adopt; (3) establish a communication plan for the data on air quality monitoring and data produced by the platform to improve communication with the public and enhance data dissemination.

Although the local environmental group participates in the deliberative platform and has positively evaluated its constitution, in which the group played a decisive role, the relationship has not been without its conflicts. One example was the group's decision not to attend the third working session on the grounds that it was held in the town that did not support the initial study. Instead, the group organized a protest outside the building used for the session. The second example is the decision by the LCMA of the UPC to leave the platform after the second session; the experts issued a public statement explaining that their decision was due to the lack of real "will" on the part of the regional government to improve environmental quality in the area. Over time, although the group positively values the efforts of the working groups, they have criticized the essence of the platform. The group's spokesperson stated that although they participate in the platform, because it "does not meet all our demands, we will continue to use all the options open to us" (Diari de Tarragona 2016). More specifically, in the public assessment of the results from the third study, and in reference to the lack of specific outcomes from the deliberative platform, the group criticized the platform, stating that,

> it is now an ineffectual body, marked by its lack of commitment and will, that only serves to evade the responsibilities of both the local governments and the government of Catalonia, and prolong the problem. It is unacceptable that, once again, we have to resort to the media and social networks to put pressure on them to convene the working groups; to ensure the governments do their job, assume their responsibilities and work towards solving this problem in favour of the people they represent.

As well as from the deliberative platform, other actions put in place by the regional government following the first study are also of note. Specifically, the number of air pollution monitoring stations increased to 13 from 10 stations in 2014 when the results of the first study were published. Similarly, as the general director of environmental quality explained in the third working session of the deliberative platform, the number of volatile organic compounds analyzed rose from 24 to 89 in the second half of 2016. Moreover, in February 2017 the Catalan Parliament approved a comprehensive study of air quality for the whole region. Although the regional government will undertake this study, consensus must first be reached on which methodology to use, an issue to be discussed in the deliberative platform's working groups. An additional complication is the political situation in Catalonia that arose in the last quarter of 2017, with the activity of many institutions being put on hold, and which may affect the pace at which this project is carried out.

Conclusion

This study is part of ongoing research into the problem of air quality in a Spanish petrochemical industrial area and the interactions between the actors involved. The preliminary findings from our case study suggest that although the business and society discourse considers cooperation and consensus between actors as the dominant logic in resolving social and environmental problems, significant advances can be made in spaces where confrontation prevails.

In our case study, the actions of a local environmental group, based mainly on confrontation, have to date helped to bring about some advances: the increased number of measurement stations, monitoring of a wider range of pollutants, and an apparent self-control by the industry (based on the results of studies instigated by the local environmental group). Other issues, such as advances in the regulatory measures or the study to evaluate air quality across the entire petrochemical area, should be dealt with in the future, taking into account the conclusions of the deliberative platform's working groups. A longer time horizon is therefore needed in order to judge the real extent of the achievements.

As well as shedding light on the value of confrontation, our study also contributes to the literature by identifying two key elements that have favored the group's legitimacy and the effectiveness of its actions:

1. *Strategy based on scientific knowledge.* The literature highlights the tensions produced between the perceptions of local communities, generally based on experience, and those of corporations, grounded on scientific knowledge that supposedly determines their behavior (Idemunia 2017). In our case, the group's strategy of confrontation was based on a series of independent scientific air quality studies, which gave it credibility in the eyes of the public. The group's efforts to democratize this knowledge among the population also contributed to building its legitimacy. In addition, the support of town councils in the first study, apart from the financial resources to fund it, may also have contributed to the recognition of the group's activity, by taking it out of the marginal situation where such small-sized local movements are frequently found.

2. *Acceptance of the industry in its role in contributing to the development of the region.* Although the petrochemical industry faces pressure to improve its environmental behavior, its crucial role in the economic development of the region is acknowledged. Under this premise, as noted in the previous section, confrontation was articulated from a stance that is reformist, pursuing changes in corporate behavior, rather than a radical/destructive position. As den Hond and de Bakker (2007, 903) observe, "reformative groups are taken to believe that although companies are part of the problem, they can also be part of the solution." This approach favors the acceptance of the group and its strategy in an area where the jobs of many local citizens depend on the petrochemical industry, but where the community also aspires to achieving satisfactory environmental conditions.

Over time, the group's activities have not been exclusively confrontational, as reflected in its participation in the multi-stakeholder deliberative platform, or in the determination to maintain spaces for dialogue with the industry in an attempt to influence its behavior through conventional channels (by taking part in public panel discussions, for example). However, the group's primary strategic orientation is confrontational. According to the literature, organizations may develop a variety of tactics, but it is the frequency and intensity with which they are used that determines the nature of their strategy (Leon-Zchout and Tal 2017). Dialogue with the industry may ameliorate the level of conflict in a relationship, but not necessarily remove the parties' condition as adversaries, nor confer the condition of partners. Although we understand the main orientation of the group to be confrontational, this confrontation is not grounded on radical actions that seek to destroy the adversary by, for example, closing down the industry. The group acknowledges the economic importance of the industry and its campaigns are designed to bring pressure on firms, through a critical narrative, to improve their environmental behaviors.

The way in which the confrontation strategy has been constructed – on the basis of scientific knowledge and industry acceptance – may indeed have contributed to the creation of the multi-stakeholder deliberative platform, largely attributable to the local environmental group pressure, and especially the group's inclusion in it. However, although the group participates in this deliberative platform, its critical attitude toward its institutional role – not so much toward the dynamics of the working groups – has also had a prominent role. There appears to be a suspicion that the platform can be used as an instrument to draw out the problem, causing it to dissipate over time. Indeed, the group does not limit its efforts to the deliberative platform arena, maintaining spaces for confrontation and limiting the chances of being co-opted by more powerful participants such as the industry or the regional government. In sum, the group's activities are firmly grounded on confrontation, and over time have been supplemented, not substituted, by participative actions in a multi-stakeholder deliberative process.

Notes

1   NGOs have been defined broadly as non-state, non-firm actors, and include environmental groups, human rights organizations, labor unions, consumer groups, and many others (Dahan et al. 2010).
2   Economic and environmental factors are dimensions that interact in citizens' evaluations of an industry's activity (López-Navarro et al. 2016, 2018).
3   In spite of this dominant articulation in the business and society discourse, signified in the research of Laasonen et al. (2012), confrontational relationships continue to play a prominent role in today's world. These confrontations range from actions to pressurize companies into improving their behavior on behalf of the interests the NGO defends, to movements that oppose the implementation of technologies such as fracking or new infrastructure projects (nuclear power plants, landfills, etc.) in their immediate environment.
4   The Association of Service Companies of Tarragona (AEST) integrates companies

providing industrial maintenance services. These companies are certified by an independent entity to carry out their activity in AEQT firms.

5   This resolution also urged the regional government to implement the necessary actions
to reduce levels of 1,3-butadiene and benzene, site 1,3-butadiene control points in
two of the towns where the study took place, and start the process that would allow
legislation existing in other EU countries to be applied in Catalonia.

References

AEQT 2013. Informe Público. Available at http://www.aeqtonline.com/media/AEQT-
Informe-P%C3%BAblic-2013-ESP.pdf (last accessed February 4, 2020).

Ählström, J. 2010. Corporate response to CSO criticism: Decoupling the corporate responsibility discourse from business practice. *Corporate Social Responsibility and Environmental
Management*, 17, 70–80.

Alvesson, M. and Deetz, S. 2000. *Doing Critical Management Research*. London: Sage.

Arenas, D., Sánchez, P., andd Murphy, M. 2013. Different paths to collaboration between
business and civil society and the role of third parties. *Journal of Business Ethics*, 115,
723–739.

Baur, D. and Palazzo, G. 2011. The moral legitimacy of NGOs as partners of corporations.
Business Ethics Quarterly, 21(4), 579–604.

Baur, D. and Schmitz, H. P. 2012. Corporations and NGOs: When accountability leads to
co-optation. *Journal of Business Ethics*, 106, 9–21.

Berry, G. R. 2003. Organizing against multinational corporate power in cancer alley: The
activist community as primary stakeholder. *Organization & Environment*, 16(1), 3–33.

Bitzer, V. and Glasbergen, P. 2015. Business–NGO partnerships in global value chains:
Part of the solution or part of the problem of sustainable change? *Current Opinion in
Environmental Sustainability*, 12, 35–40.

Burchell, J. and Cook, J. 2011. Banging on open doors? Stakeholder dialogue and the challenge of business engagement for UK NGOs. *Environmental Politics*, 20(6), 918–937.

Catalunya Radio 2015. Cel Net denuncia pressions de l'AEQT a la Universitat i ajunta-
ments. A la Carta, Informatius Catalunya Radio, April 13.

Covey, J. and Brown, L. D. 2001. Critical cooperation: An alternative form of civil society–
business engagement. *IDR Reports*, 17(1), 1–18.

Dahan, N. M., Doh, J. P., and Teegen, H. 2010. Role of nongovernmental organizations in
the business–government–society interface: Special issue overview and introductory
essay. *Business and Society*, 49(1), 20–34.

Dahlberg-Grundberg, M. and Örestig, J. 2017. Extending the local: Activist types and
forms of social media use in the case of an anti-mining struggle. *Social Movement Studies*,
16(3), 309–322.

Dalton, R. J. 2005. The greening of the globe? Cross-national levels of environmental group
membership. *Environmental Politics*, 14(4), 441–459.

Dalton, R. J., Recchia, S., and Rohrscheneider, R. 2003. The environmental movement and the modes of political actions. *Comparative Political Studies*, 36(7), 743–771.

Daubanes, J. and Rochet, J. C. 2016. *A Theory of NGO Activism*. MIT Center for Energy and Environmental Policy Research.

De Lange, D. E., Armanios, D., Delgado-Ceballos, D., and Sandhu, S. 2016. From foe to friend: Complex mutual adaptation of multinational corporations and nongovernmental organizations. *Business & Society*, 55(8), 1197–1228.

den Hond, F. and de Bakker, F. G. A. 2007. Ideologically motivated activism: How activist groups influence corporate social change activities. *Academy of Management Review*, 32(3), 901–924.

Diari de Tarragona 2016. La química solo es transparente si siente la presión ciudadana. July 29.

Dryzek, J. S., Downs, D., Schlosbert, D., and Hernes, H. K. 2003. *Green States and Social Movements, Environmentalism in the United States, United Kingdom, Germany, & Norway*. Oxford: Oxford University Press.

El Mundo 2015. Repsol se compromete a reducir las emisiones en Tarragona. April 17.

Espluga, J., Farré, J., Gonzalo, J., and Prades, A. 2014. Factors inhibiting the social mobilization: The case of the petrochemical area of Tarragona. *Revista Española de Investigaciones Sociológicas*, 146, 191–216.

Espluga, J., Prades, A., and Gonzalo, J. 2010. Communicating at the edge: Risk communication processes and structural conflicts in highly industrialized petrochemical areas. *Catalan Journal of Communication & Cultural Studies*, 2(2), 231–251.

Gómez-Carrasco, P. and Michelon, G. 2017. The power of stakeholders' voice: The effects of social media activism on stock markets. *Business Strategy and the Environment*, 26(6), 855–872.

Grant, D. and Vasi, I. B. 2017. Civil society in an age of environmental accountability: How local environmental nongovernmental organizations reduce U.S. power plants' carbon dioxide emissions. *Sociological Forum*, 32(1), 94–115.

Hahn, T. and Pinkse, J. 2014. Private environmental governance through cross-sector partnerships: Tensions between competition and effectiveness. *Organization & Environment*, 27(2), 140–160.

IARC 2018. List of classifications. World Health Organization. https://monographs.iarc.fr/list-of-classifications-volumes/ (last accessed February 4, 2020).

Idemudia, U. 2017. Shell–NGO partnership and peace in Nigeria: Critical insights and implications. *Organization & Environment*. DOI: 10.1177/1086026617718428.

Kadirbeyoglu, Z., Adaman, F., Özkaynak, B., and Paker, H. 2017. the effectiveness of environmental civil society organizations: An integrated analysis of organizational characteristics and contextual factors. *Voluntas*, 28(4), 1717–1741.

King, B. G. 2008. A political mediation model of corporate response to social movement activism. *Administrative Science Quarterly*, 53(3), 395–421.

Kourula, A. and Laasonen, S. 2010. Nongovernmental organizations in business and society, management, and international business research. *Business & Society*, 49(1), 35–67.

Kroll-Smith, J. S. and Couch, S. R. 1991. Technological hazards, adaptation and social change. In S. R Couch and J. S. Kroll-Smith (eds), *Communities at Risk: Collective Responses to Technological Hazards*. New York: Peter Lang, pp. 293–320.

Laasonen, S., Fougere, M., and Kourula, A. 2012. Dominant articulations in academic business and society discourse on NGO–business relations: A critical assessment. *Journal of Business Ethics*, 109, 521–545.

Leon-Zchout, S. L. and Tal, L. 2017. Conflict versus consensus strategic orientation among environmental NGOs: An empirical evaluation. *Voluntas*, 28, 110-1134.

López-Navarro, M. A., Tortosa-Edo, V., and Castán-Broto, V. 2018. Firm–local community relationships in polluting industrial agglomerations: How firms' commitment determines residents' perceptions. *Journal of Cleaner Production*, 186, 22–33.

López-Navarro, M. A., Llorens-Monzonis, J., and Tortosa-Edo, V. 2016. Residents' behaviour as a function of cognitive appraisals and effective responses toward a petrochemical industrial complex. *Journal of Cleaner Production*, 112, 1645–1657.

Macdonald, S. and Chrisp, T. 2005. Acknowledging the purpose of partnership. *Journal of Business Ethics*, 59, 307–317.

Michaelson, M. 1994. Wangari Maathai and Kenya's Green Belt Movement: Exploring the evolution and potentialities of consensus movement mobilization. *Social Problems*, 41(4), 540–561.

Olk, A. 2013. Partnerships as panacea for addressing global problems? On rationale, context, actors, impact and limitations. In M. Seitanidi and A. Crane (eds), *Social Partnerships and Responsible Business: A Research Handbook*. London: Routledge, pp. 15–41.

Scherer, A. G. and Palazzo, G. 2011. The new political role of business in a globalized world: A review of a new perspective on CSR and its implications for the firm, governance, and democracy. *Journal of Management Studies*, 48(4), 899–931.

Scherer, A. G., Rasche, A., Palazzo, G., and Spicer, A. 2016. Managing for political corporate social responsibility: New challenges and directions for PCSR 2.0. *Journal of Management Studies*, 53(3), 273–298.

Sprengel, D. C. and Busch, T. 2011. Stakeholder engagement and environmental strategy – the case of climate change. *Business Strategy and the Environment*, 20, 351–364.

TQACT 2018. Official website. http://mediambient.gencat.cat/ca/05_ambits_dactuacio/atmosfera/qualitat_de_laire/qa-camp-tgn/taula-de-la-qualitat-de-laire-al-camp-de-tarragona/ (last accessed February 4, 2020).

Van Huijstee, M. and Glasbergen, P. 2010. Business–NGO interactions in a multistakeholder context. *Business and Society Review*, 115(3), 249–284.

9

Environmental justice in industrially contaminated sites: From the development of a national surveillance system to the birth of an international network

Roberto Pasetto and Ivano Iavarone

Sites highly contaminated by a variety of hazardous agents are found in almost all countries as contaminants are routinely or accidentally released into the environment either by active industrial sources or as toxic waste from current or past industrial activities. From a public health point of view, contaminated sites can be defined as, "Areas hosting or having hosted human activities which have produced or might produce environmental contamination of soil, surface or groundwater, air, food-chain, resulting or being able to result in human health impacts" (Martuzzi et al. 2014). Industrial activities – especially those related to large petrochemical plants, power generation, heavy industry such as steel mills, and mining – lead to environmental pressure, with potential adverse social and health effects on local communities through both occupational and residential influences (World Health Organization 2009).

In recent years, networking, research initiatives, and literature on industrial contamination and health have increased, following the need to acquire evidence for risk management and policy actions (World Health Organization 2013a). One of the public health priorities identified in the European Ministerial Conference on Environment and Health promoted by the World Health Organization in 2017 was to prevent and eliminate the adverse environmental and health effects, costs, and inequalities related to waste management and contaminated sites in the context of a transition toward a circular economy (World Health Organization 2017a). Moreover, the resulting "Ostrava Declaration" states that environmental degradation and pollution, climate change, exposure to harmful chemicals, and the destabilization of ecosystems threaten the right to health, and disproportionately affect socially disadvantaged and vulnerable population groups, thereby increasing and compounding inequalities. In this perspective, and in order to provide evidence for actions, in many contaminated sites scientists and decision makers need to adequately address issues such as contamination-related health risks, the prioritization of efforts for remediation, the cost-effectiveness of actions directly or indirectly promoting public health. Another aim is to explore the sphere of environmental justice (EJ).

Environmental justice emerged as a theme in the United States in the 1980s as result of grassroots activism of some African American communities fighting against the unfair association between race and poverty and the uneven spatial distribution of waste and industrial sites producing pollution (Bullard and Johnson 2000). The applications of environmental justice have been broadened over the years to a wide variety of environmental themes including their relationship with public health. At the time of writing, the EPA, the US Environmental Protection Agency, defines environmental justice in terms of

> the fair treatment and meaningful involvement of all people regardless of race, color, national origin, or income with respect to the development, implementation, and enforcement of environmental laws, regulations, and policies ... It will be achieved when everyone enjoys the same degree of protection from environmental and health hazards and equal access to the decision-making process to have a healthy environment in which to live, learn, and work. (www.epa.gov/environmentaljustice)

The debate on the meaning of environmental justice in academia has been intense, with different formulations around the concept of equal distribution for everyone of environmental risks and benefits. Among the different definitions and meanings, Schlosberg has stressed the need to focus on recognition, distribution, and participation as three interlinking, overlapping circles of concern: "Inequitable distribution, a lack of recognition, and limited participation all work to produce injustice, and claims for justice are integrated into a comprehensive political project in the global Environmental Justice movement" (Schlosberg 2004: 528–529). The subject of recognition is underlined by Schlosberg as a prerequisite for promoting environmental justice, since the different distribution of benefits and risks by ethnic and socioeconomic determinants among population groups and communities, together with the expression of their identities and cultural practices, are usually neglected in decision-making processes (Schlosberg 2004).

In this chapter, we refer to environmental justice, as summarized by Walker, in the intertwining between environment and social difference and how the justice of their interrelationship matters (Walker 2012), applying it to the topic of industrially contaminated sites. We describe the birth and evolution of a national epidemiological monitoring system, developed in Italy, to assess whether communities affected by environmental hazardous exposures from contaminated sites are also prone to be fragile in socioeconomic conditions (i.e., whether potential or actual risks from contaminated sites are unfairly distributed because of the concurrence in the same communities of environmental risks and socioeconomic fragilities). Then, we discuss how the above system can contribute to promoting awareness of risks to people and communities and empowering their involvement in decision-making processes linked to risk management. We also discuss strengths and limits connected to the national perspective on which the monitoring system has been developed: on one hand, it gives the opportunity of monitoring the health profiles and socioeconomic conditions of all communities at the national level, with the potential of identifying the areas with the greatest level of unfairness; on the other hand, it cannot describe the complexity of interconnection between different factors affecting health, and in each area, that are related to the peculiar history of each community. Notwithstanding the limits of a top-down perspective, we discuss how results from a national epidemiological monitoring system can contribute to identifying areas and priorities of interventions for improving public health in communities living close to industrially contaminated sites, thus promoting environmental justice in that context.

Finally, we describe how the experience developed at a national level can contribute to identifying approaches, methods, and tools to assess health risks and to implement primary interventions, accounting for local needs across a wide heterogeneous scenario of contaminated areas and communities across Europe and beyond.

Postwar industrialization and contamination from industrial areas in Italy

Italy's industrialization process can be described in three main phases in terms of its impact on the environment and health. The first phase, after World War II, witnessed the construction of major industrial complexes, in particular during the 1960s, the golden age of Italian manufacturing. In the second phase (1970s and 1980s), major efforts were directed at improving production efficiency, often accompanied by an increase in pollutant emissions into the environment. That was also when environmental legislation was first introduced. However, the implementation of laws was not monitored and relevant laws were sparsely applied, with the consequence of a growing contamination of the environment, mainly close to plants. The Seveso disaster occurred in 1976 in a small chemical manufacturing plant – leading to the exposure to 2,3,7,8-tetrachlorodibenzo-p-dioxin (TCDD) in the surrounding residential communities – and became an emblematic event of the time. The case led to numerous scientific studies and to standardized industrial safety regulations, including the first EU industrial safety regulation, known as the Seveso Directive (http://ec.europa.eu/environment/seveso/). In the third phase, beginning in the early 1990s, relevant authorities began documenting the effects of contamination on the health profile of populations residing close to industrial plants. Over the past decades, the impact of contamination on health has steadily grown and is still growing in areas without effective reclamation activities, and is now a major environmental health issue on the political agenda.

This was the context when, in the late 1990s and early 2000s, most of the main Italian industrial areas were listed as Sites of National Concern for Remediation (henceforth Sites). In the same period, the need for a better understanding of the impact of contamination on health grew, with requests coming from local and health authorities in the communities living close to contaminated areas.

The following case study has been chosen to illustrate the impact of socioeconomic factors and the sphere of environmental justice in Italian industrially contaminated areas.

The Gela case

Gela is a town in southeast Sicily, in the province of Caltanissetta, on the shores of the Mediterranean. Until the 1950s, Gela was the center of a thriving farming community; the sea was crystal clear and fishing plentiful, as it had been for generations. Local tourism was also on the rise in the area. In other words, Gela was a large farming and maritime community mainly producing cotton, wine, and sulphur from the inland area, as depicted by the local non-profit environmental association LegaAmbiente.[1]

In 1963 an industrial complex for the refining, processing, and storage of hydrocarbons was built in Gela. In addition, its purpose was to exploit the crude oil discovered in the nearby area, on the initiative of Enrico Mattei, President from 1953 to 1962 of the newly formed oil and gas public company (ENI – Ente Nazionale Idrocarburi). On its opening, Enrico Mattei declared the Gela complex the "largest petrochemical plant in Europe."

The idyllic description given by LegaAmbiente differs from the portrait of Gela in the 1960s provided by a sociological study:

Life in the city of Gela is partly determined by the overall underdevelopment of national agriculture and by the presence of a large petrochemical plant ... although it is on the sea, Gela turns its back to it and unlike most comparable towns, the sea does not appear to play an important part in its life ... alongside the new development following urbanisation and new arrivals, and the resulting construction of the village for the petrochemical workers of the plant, agriculture is still very poor: bare, empty housing, crumbling walls and even the public housing speak of the extremely basic living conditions of the community. (Hytten and Marchioni 1970, 18, 29–30)

Local literature and documents indicate that the town of Gela and its surroundings underwent major changes – in fact were completely transformed – in a matter of a few years following the discovery of oil fields in the district in 1956. The year of the plant start-up, 1962, was a watershed year, marking the beginning of a new era for the town, its surroundings, and its residents, separating the agricultural past from the industrial present. Within two decades, the population increased by more than 50%.

The petrochemical industrial complex in Gela hosted a large oil refinery, as well as thermoelectric power and petrochemical plants for production of organic and inorganic chemicals (Figure 9.1). In 1998, a part of Gela's municipal

9.1 The Gela petrochemical complex. View from the ancient acropolis of the town, now included in the archaeological museum district.

district – the entire petrochemical complex and an extended sea portion – was included among the Italian National Priority Contaminated Sites (Pasetto et al. 2012). Data gathered after 2000 by the Istituto Superiore di Sanità (ISS – the Italian National Institute of Health) documented heavy groundwater, soil, and air contamination (Zona et al. 2019). Healthwise, the residents of Gela suffered a number of critical problems highlighted in the mid-1990s and still present at the time of writing: they have a high risk for various diseases whose aetiological factors include the pollutants due to local contamination of industrial origin (Pasetto et al. 2012; Zona et al. 2019). Both the general population and the young age sub-groups suffer higher risks, and specific situations of congenital malformations have been documented (Zona et al. 2019).

The case of Gela was described as an example of "industrialization without development: a southern history," the title of Hytten and Marchioni's book (1970). The situation in Gela to a certain extent recalls industrialization processes promoted by transnational companies in recently industrialized low-income countries where processes promoted from the outside, rather than being the result of a progressive socioeconomic evolution of the local society, failed to induce local territorial and population development (LaDou 1992; Castleman 1995). For the purposes of the present chapter, we intend "development" as a sustainable process with the appreciation and not the deterioration of available resources in line with the principles of the sustainable development goals promoted by the United Nations (www.un.org/sustainabledevelopment/sustainable-development-goals/). Under this perspective, individuals and communities should develop capabilities to satisfy primary needs and to pursue their ambitions without undermining chances and conditions for future generations. The concept of development is thus strictly linked to the concept of "sustainability" as proposed by Agyeman, Bullard, and Evans: to "ensure a better of quality of life for all, now, and into the future, in a just and equitable manner, while living within the limits of supporting ecosystems" (Agyeman et al. 2003, 5).

In Gela, just like in many other cases, the industrialization process triggered mechanisms of societal acceptance of risky industries, mainly because it appeared to be the only viable option for people who feared unemployment and lacked better opportunities (Saitta 2012). Social contexts such as the ones mentioned may hamper the implementation of environmental monitoring and reclamation activities, leading to a deterioration of contamination with its resulting impact on the health of the population. Gela's case is an example of a community where the origin and the development of industrialization made it impossible for the population to become resilient and cope with the damage to the environment and the impact on the community's health resulting from industrial contamination. Furthermore, in Gela, as elsewhere, as time goes by, industrial processes become more automated, thus reducing the number of manual jobs and increasing unemployment. This has led to a higher level of individual and social conflicts affecting many parts of residents' lives: the economy, the environment, and the health services. As a result, the local situation has become increasingly chaotic and difficult to manage.

The epidemiological monitoring system of sites of national interest for remediation

In Italy, the situation of contaminated sites is not unique to Gela: throughout the past few years the Istituto Superiore di Sanità has received a growing number of requests by local authorities for help in understanding whether and to what extent the health of their residents was at risk in areas contaminated by the industries; they also requested advice on what could be done to eliminate or limit risks, as well as how to carry out decontamination and remediation work. In some cases, it was the epidemiological research implemented by ISS that enabled researchers to identify health risks from environmental pollution in areas that were eventually recognized as national priority contaminated sites (Bruno et al. 2015).

Starting in the 1990s, Italian epidemiologists began researching possible health risks due to contaminated sites more systematically, also thanks to specific contributions from WHO pointing to contaminated sites as an emerging environmental health priority (Cislaghi et al. 1997; Martuzzi et al. 2002). The ISS developed a system of epidemiological monitoring of the population thanks to a strict collaboration with WHO (Mudu et al. 2014) and to the experience gained in studying contaminated sites in several Italian regions. Data on resident communities living close to 44 contaminated sites of national interest earmarked for decontamination and remediation actions were used. The Sites included areas within the main Italian industrial complexes. The system is known as SENTIERI.[2] It was initially conceived as a study to describe the state of health of the communities residing close to the Sites, but subsequently it became a permanent epidemiological monitoring system. The system is essentially based on a descriptive approach and it has been progressively implemented, thus becoming methodologically more complex. Changes have been consistent with requirements for an area-based epidemiological monitoring of contaminated sites (Pasetto et al. 2016). In Italy, municipalities (*comuni*) are the administrative local authority and community basic unit, which is the main reason why SENTIERI used the population under municipal remit as its unit of observation. SENTIERI's approach has been described in detail by Pirastu and colleagues and by Comba (Pirastu et al. 2013a; Comba 2017). SENTIERI is based on an a priori definition of diseases to focus on when describing a health profile.

When performing epidemiological studies, especially descriptive studies, there is a risk that researchers become data driven. This can be the case when commenting on results for causes showing an increase, possibly on the sole basis of statistical significance. To control this problem at least partially, SENTIERI, for each monitored Site, focused on those diseases identified a priori, from the strength of their association with the sources of contamination in every contaminated site (Pirastu et al. 2013a) and, in the Sites where it was possible, also on the basis of the toxicological profiles of the main contaminants (Zona et al. 2015). In SENTIERI, possible relevant exposures were abstracted from legislative decrees – that is, administrative sources defining Sites' boundaries and coded on a productive sectors basis (e.g., petrochemicals and/or refineries, harbor areas, etc.). The choice was made because contaminated sites had different levels of environmental characterization (for some Sites, information on specific chemical contaminants were available, for others only productive plants were listed). Having once identified the environmental exposures of interest, researchers should examine the updated scientific literature to evaluate the associated health effects. To assess the strength of association between industrial sources of contamination and diseases, the SENTIERI study group defined a hierarchy in literature sources: sources expressing the epidemiological community consensus, evaluating scientific evidence by means of standardized criteria, weighting the study design and the occurrence of biased results (i.e., monographs of the International Agency for Research on Cancer, IARC; publications of World Health Organization, WHO; European Environment Agency publications, handbooks of environmental and occupational medicine). They were followed by quantitative meta-analyses. Multi-centric studies, systematic reviews, and single investigations were also considered. Consistency among sources was a criterion used to classify the strength of the causal association between sources of contamination and diseases. The final classification is used to select the list of diseases of a priori interest for each source of contamination.

SENTIERI's list of possible sources found in Italian Sites includes the following: chemical industry, petrochemical plants and refineries, steel mills, energy power stations, quarries, mines, ports, waste dumps/landfills, and incinerators. Epidemiological indicators are based on current statistics (mortality and hospitalization) or on data from Registries of Diseases (the cancer registries and the registries of congenital malformations) (Pirastu et al. 2014). SENTIERI uses a multidisciplinary, multi-phase approach to the contaminated areas, contributing to an epidemiological characterization of each Site. The system is also tailored to perform overall risk analysis in contaminated sites and comparative studies among various Sites with the same sources of contamination. In this regard, the first overall estimates of health impact resulting from SENTIERI monitoring showed an overburden for communities living close to the Sites. An excess of mortality was found in 44 Sites, with around 10,000 deaths more than expected among the 404,000 deaths observed (men and women combined) in a period of 10 years (Pirastu et al. 2011). Interestingly, about 3,600 among them were caused by diseases for which there was sufficient or limited a priori evidence of association with the sources of pollution present in the Sites. A subsequent overall analysis of cancer incidence data in 10 years, limited to the 23 Sites served by cancer registries, showed an overall excess of 9% in men and 7% in women (Comba et al. 2014).

SENTIERI reports started, in 2011, offering periodical updates of health profiles of the communities living close to Sites of national interest earmarked for decontamination and remediation (Pirastu et al. 2011, 2014; Zona et al. 2016, 2019). An integrated approach to available information makes it possible to suggest the best course of action to defend public health on a case-by-case approach. Specific investigations to gain a better understanding of unresolved issues are also suggested or carried out if so required. Given that it is a permanent monitoring system, SENTIERI can also track health profile trends and developments over time. It has the potential to assess the effectiveness of the actions undertaken in terms of the impact they have on public health.

Where possible, the relevant regional Departments of Public Health are involved in sharing the SENTIERI results. Results are then passed on to the national agencies (*Enti centrali*), first and foremost to the Ministry of Health and also to the relevant local authorities and local technical departments. Working Group Members take part in the projects to communicate results involving all stakeholders.

SENTIERI is an epidemiological monitoring system which can promote environmental justice for communities living close to industrially contaminated areas since it offers the same information nationally, supplying evidence and stimuli to carry out more in-depth studies and actions focusing on areas that have had fewer opportunities to be evaluated from a technical standpoint. In fact, the ability to carry out technical investigations on the environment and health differs greatly according to which of the twenty regions it is, because of their history and how the authorities and technical facilities able to identify the association between contamination and health were established. Hence, SENTIERI is able to supply the same information base in all contexts. The dissemination of epidemiological information collected by SENTIERI also has the potential to enhance awareness among local populations of the risks associated with contamination. Local and national decision makers are mostly aware of the SENTIERI program, and some resident associations and citizens have demanded that it should be applied in areas that are not yet under epidemiological monitoring.

The involvement of central and local administrative and technical agencies in producing the final reports, the efforts in spreading reports and results involving the national and local media, and the initiatives of communication to the local associations and residents are the hallmarks of the monitoring system and promote the fairness of the decision-making processes in contaminated sites (Marsili et al. 2017).

Socioeconomic Deprivation in Industrial Areas

SENTIERI has enabled us to gain a better understanding of the impact of socioeconomic differences in contaminated sites. Over the years, analyses have identified a range of approaches: in a first phase, socioeconomic deprivation indices were generated at a municipal level – that is, for the community. During that phase, socioeconomic indicators were used to correct health risk estimates as suggested by international literature on small-area epidemiological studies (Pasetto et al. 2010). In a second phase, the use of available socioeconomic indicators was tested considering a number of factors, such as the size of the population being studied, gender, and the differential association with dissimilar outcomes – such as mortality, hospitalization, incidence of cancer, and prevalence of congenital anomalies (Minichilli et al. 2017).

Such assessments made it possible to identify the limitations of the indicators being used, and specifically the following: which were only suited for small or medium sized populations; which were best suited for some areas of the country; and which displayed the associations between deprivation and health conditions more accurately in men than women.

In a third phase, socioeconomic conditions were analyzed in contaminated sites using area deprivation indicators as an additional description of risk indicators (Pasetto et al. 2017). Currently, we believe the most informative approach is not the generalized production of risk estimates corrected by socioeconomic indicators, but rather seeing how environmental exposure, and social, economic, and working conditions interact in determining risk profiles for populations living in the contaminated sites. The description of the socioeconomic characteristics of such communities is one of the preliminary steps for the analysis of the interactions among factors.

As previously mentioned, Gela is an exemplary case of "industrialization without development": the presence of an industrial complex did not become an opportunity to improve the socioeconomic conditions for the overall population living close by. Similar situations were observed in other sites contaminated by industrial plants. When implementing the SENTIERI system, we wondered whether all communities living close to the Italian Sites shared a similar situation. As a result, we tried to examine whether, as well as experiencing the disadvantages of living in a contaminated area, they were also socioeconomically vulnerable. Furthermore, we considered if, and if so to what extent, such unfavourable conditions impacted on their health profiles. Socioeconomic conditions were assessed using a multifactorial/multidimensional deprivation index based on census data: education (percentage of over 16-year-olds with primary school or lower education); employment (percentage of unemployed active residents); living conditions (percentage of rented accommodation and number of people per dwelling). A socioeconomic indicator was then developed using information on individuals. There are 298 communities living in the 44 contaminated sites monitored by the SENTIERI system. The distribution of the municipalities/ communities being monitored by deprivation level was asymmetrical (i.e., the higher the deprivation level, the larger the number): 12% of the municipalities fell into the least deprived quintile, 38% in the most deprived. All in all, 60% of the monitored municipalities (i.e., 179) fell into the two most deprived quintiles. Such a disadvantage highlights a distributive injustice, with a marked north/south divide evidencing worse conditions in the south and on the islands where nearly all the communities living close to the contaminated sites fell into the most deprived groups (Figure 9.2). In addition, when health risks were compared among residents of the various Sites, the more deprived ones appeared at greater risk for mortality for all causes and for all cancers (Pasetto et al. 2017). Analyses were influenced by the limitations of the indicator and did not enable us to identify which had been the conditions of deprivation at the time the industrial complexes had been established and opened. Existing knowledge makes it impossible for us to establish whether conditions deteriorated following industrialization and subsequent contamination. What is clear is that most communities close to contaminated sites belong to the most deprived groups in their region, and that this is especially true in southern Italy. In the south, iron and steel plants, oil refineries, and petrochemical plants were established, and accounted for most industrial jobs. However, the industrialization process failed to stimulate the growth of related networks in the surrounding areas that ended up as isolated enclaves, to the point they were nicknamed "cathedrals in the desert." In contrast, traditional manufacturing and tourism were neglected (Cento Bull 2016). Post World War II industrialization seems to have had a positive impact on socioeconomic conditions only where it started – that is, in the north of the country – and failed to do so in the south which had had a predominantly agricultural social organization and economy, prior to the postwar "industrial colonization."

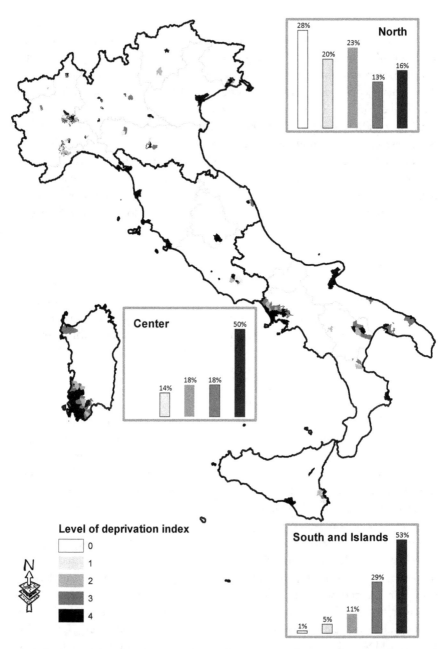

9.2 Italy. Percentage of communities living close to Sites of National Interest for decontamination and remediation by level of deprivation in macro-areas (North, Center, South and the Islands) (from Pasetto et al. 2017).

The above points contextualize the overall trend but are unable to fully explain the complexity of the relationship between the development or evolution of each industrial complex and their surrounding communities, in terms of their social profiles and health. Every Site and every community has its own history, which cannot be described by a national monitoring system. However, with such a system it is possible to improve the capability of monitoring socio-economic conditions that have an impact on health profiles and identify the areas with the greatest level of unfairness where one can implement action plans (Pasetto et al. 2017).

From local, national experience to the development of an international network

The Italian long-standing experience in evaluating the impact of contaminated areas using SENTIERI was one of the first steps in bringing environmental health issues related to contaminated sites to a wider international attention. The process was facilitated by the international networking consultations promoted by WHO with two expert meetings aimed at reviewing priorities, needs, data, and resources to address the question of contaminated sites and their health impact. A WHO publication on these meetings focuses on a number of European case studies, including the SENTIERI system, and summarizes the findings of the consultation, indicating opportunities, challenges, and a suggested way forward (World Health Organization 2013a). Another relevant improvement was the production of a specific training module, "Methods for risk assessment related to contaminated sites," which included a cross-sector training package developed by WHO for environment and health experts in Capacity Building in Environment and Health (World Health Organization 2013b). For the first time, the training course introduced concepts and guidance on how to deal with environmental health in contaminated sites using simple and frequently available vital statistics as proposed by the SENTIERI approach.

This experience led to the establishment of the key WHO Collaborating Centre on Environmental Health in Contaminated Sites in 2013 (WHO CC ITA97) at the ISS, in acknowledgment of its comprehensive activities in the field.

Since its creation, the WHO CC ITA97 has been operating in strict cooperation with WHO on:

- expanding and consolidating networks and mechanisms for the collection and dissemination of information on environment and health in contaminated

sites, through providing support in organizing WHO conferences, work-shops, training and dissemination activities, and other events; and
• contributing to WHO's efforts in identifying priorities on how to assess environmental health risks and to promote primary prevention interventions to protect public health in contaminated areas and environmental hotspots.

Activities coordinated by the WHO CC ITA97 importantly include the launch of a COST (European Cooperation in Science and Technology) Action on "Industrially Contaminated Sites and Health Network" (ICSHNet) in 2015 (http://www.icshnet.eu). The COST Action ICSHNet is supported by WHO, European Union, European Commission bodies, and the European Environment and Health Youth Coalition (EEHYC), and involves about 130 researchers and experts from public health institutions, universities, and environmental agencies of 33 countries.

Based on the experiences shared at international meetings with exchanges among experts from relevant institutions, and on some documents specifically devoted to the issue of environmental health in industrially contaminated sites (Martuzzi et al. 2014; Iavarone and Pasetto 2018), we currently have a more comprehensive picture of the issue.

In many circumstances, industrially contaminated sites can be attributed to the impact of development models rarely committed to sustainability, and of high concern at local, regional, and global scale. Moreover, industrial development and urbanization are proceeding rapidly in parallel.

Especially – but not exclusively – in low-income countries, environmental threats to health include traditional hazards as well as newer hazards such as urban air pollution, toxic chemicals such as lead, asbestos, mercury, arsenic, pesticides, and hazardous and electronic waste. The mix of traditional and modern hazards varies greatly across and within countries reflecting industrialization, urbanization, and socioeconomic forces, and affecting vulnerable population subgroups such, as children, more than others (Laborde et al. 2015; World Health Organization 2017a, 2017b).

In Europe, the percentage of people living close to contaminated sites is estimated to be quite substantial: about 342,000 sites require clean-up, corresponding, on average, to 5.7 estimated sites per 10,000 inhabitants. The pattern of key contaminants (heavy metals, aromatic hydrocarbons, and mineral oils) is similar in the liquid and the solid environmental matrices (Panagos et al. 2013). The main sources of contamination in these sites are directly or indirectly due to industrial activities, including industrial waste disposal and treatment; these estimates did not change greatly between 2006 and 2011 (van Liedekerke et al. 2014). Moreover, a recent Technical Report of the European Environment

Agency recognized that the environmental performance of European industry has improved in recent decades, but the sector is still responsible for significant amounts of pollution to air, water, and soil, as well as generation of waste (European Environment Agency 2015).

Several aspects may contribute to an industrially contaminated site (ICS) becoming a major public health issue. As ably described by Martuzzi and Matic (Martuzzi and Matic 2016), one distinctive feature shared by many contaminated sites is that they often involve marked health inequalities: since they are generally not located in pleasant residential areas, they tend to interest residents of a lower socioeconomic level and deprivation gradients can be observed in the surrounding areas. These authors also underline that due the concurrence of multiple contaminants, social disadvantage, and additional individual burden due to unhealthy lifestyles (alcohol consumption and smoking habits), contaminated sites can sometimes be seen as "hotspots" of generally bad environment and health, where pressures on health from different sources can produce peaks of bad health in otherwise healthy populations. Furthermore, society at large obviously benefits from the output of industrial activities, thus introducing an additional dimension of environmental injustice (World Health Organization 2010). For the above reasons, the issue of human health in ICS is best addressed with a strong sustainability perspective, by considering the evidence on health effects and impacts, as well as the broader context of environmental and ecosystem health, and the social environment – including the occupational opportunities that arise from industrial activities. The situation calls for a multi-pronged approach, and has to be seen as a part of social negotiation, where the legitimate needs and aspirations of vulnerable groups, residents, workers, investors, and business are taken into account, in a non-discriminatory process (Martuzzi and Matic 2016).

Economic development, social cohesion, poverty and social inequalities, environment and health management, gender, and human well-being are among the key aspects covered by the COST Action ICSHNet, as strongly related to industrially contaminated sites. Environmental justice is an issue of particular concern and is addressed with a focus on vulnerable social groups such as children, women, and disadvantaged communities: these people are thought to be among the priority target groups who will have major benefit from the ICSHNet. Disadvantaged groups are often disproportionally affected by the cumulative impacts of overall degraded environments and lack financial, educational, and cultural capacities to avoid such exposure, and poor environmental conditions tend to be spatially correlated with social stressors, though little is known about the combined and potentially synergistic health effects of stress and pollution (European Environment Agency 2013). While environment-related inequalities contribute to health inequalities, more work is needed to clarify the relationships and implications for policy (World Health Organization 2012).

The number and mix of ICSs, and the range of exposure scenarios and environmental social occupational settings, mean that an overall picture of the health impacts remains uncertain. Moreover, despite the expected considerable extent of the ICSs' potential health impact, and the availability of sound methodology for studying the health implications of living close to an ICS, a fragmentation of aims, methodologies, and assessment tools makes it difficult to identify common and standardized approaches. It is therefore urgent to promote international cooperation to identify appropriate strategies and methods to deal with this issue more systematically.

However, there are a number of commonalities across Europe such as the many legacies from past industrial activities that play a central role, large and strongly polluting industrial facilities built in the 1950s–1960s in western Europe that gradually improved to comply with increasingly stringent national and European Union legislation. In some cases, they can still pose serious health threats, like the Italian contaminated site of Taranto, one of the largest European steel factories (Pirastu et al. 2013b). In addition, plants from past industrial, mining, or military activities in areas of the former Soviet Union remain a reason of concern (Standring et al. 2009); waste landfills, especially hazardous and industrial waste, are ubiquitous and may affect human health – there preventive actions should support regulation and eliminate outdated and illegal practices of waste disposal (World Health Organization 2016; Fazzo et al. 2017). Several examples of local contexts were examined in a publication (Pasetto and Iavarone 2016) promoted by the ICSHNet reporting 17 case studies from the participating countries, especially eastern European countries, covering a wide range of issues from environmental health assessments related to industrial contamination: human bio-monitoring, risk management, remediation activities, as well as dealing with inequalities.

Conclusion

Contaminated industrial sites are a major environmental and health concern both in Italy and internationally. Both affect land and territorial management in the surrounding community. The communities in question are often overburdened by the accumulation of weaknesses ensuing from environmental risks in socially deprived contexts. The overall picture has to take into account complex interactions among the various pressure factors and their evolution. This requires adequate resourcing and a range of information, a combination which is unfortunately not very frequent. Some members of the communities living near contaminated sites are generally employed by the said industries, leading to social and individual conflicts. Furthermore, in several contaminated sites, inequality of environmental exposures and social differences and their impact on health can be greater in ethnic minority groups who are in jobs with a high level of exposure, or in vulnerable groups such as women and children. The picture may differ according to the geographical area and depending on whether it is an industrialized or a low-income country, thus expanding the notion of environmental justice to a range of contexts. If appropriately fine-tuned, national epidemiological monitoring programs can contribute to the promotion of environmental justice, offering the same opportunities to further develop and document the picture, especially in less favored areas. Such monitoring programs have a top-down environmental justice approach which enhances community awareness of the conditions of their area/territory by comparing their situation to the national picture, a process which will empower local communities in the decision-making process aimed at eliminating or reducing risks for the environment and health (De Castro et al. 2016).

Thanks to the establishment of an international network, experience accrued in specific Sites or in a given country can be shared and compared with others. As a result, this will favor local projects in countries that lack a background on the matter but have the need to deal with it. Both in Europe and elsewhere, industrial contaminations are long term, and are often found in socially and naturally deteriorated environments. Communities living in industrially contaminated sites lack the resources to plan a better future. Is there a way out? Remediation and decontamination may be an opportunity in such deteriorated environments. Remediation plans are a space to renew the social environment and its related symbols on top of reducing future health risks (Saitta 2012).

Finally, we would like to stress that a monitoring system like the one described can promote interconnection between top-down science-founded evidence coming from central institutions and bottom-up demands for environmental justice from local communities. This way of producing evidence is key to the development of trust of citizens in central public institutions.

Acknowledgments

Thanks to all colleagues of the Unit of Environmental and Social Epidemiology at ISS with whom we share daily discussions and research on industrially contaminated sites. Special thanks to Pietro Comba and Roberta Pirastu for their initial efforts in promoting SENTIERI and for their invaluable support over the years.

Notes

1   The Environmental League, an Italian national not-for-profit association with the aim of promoting environmental culture, new development, and widespread well-being (https://www.legambiente.it/english-page/).
2   In Italian, SENTIERI stands for "Studio Epidemiologico Nazionale dei Territori e degli Insediamenti Esposti a Rischio da Inquinamento" (National Epidemiological Study for Territories and Industrial Complexes at Risk of Contamination/Pollution). The acronym also means "paths" in Italian.

References

Agyeman, J., Bullard, R. D., and Evans, B. (eds) 2003. *Just Sustainabilities. Development in Unequal World*. London: Earthscan.

Bruno, C., Bruni, B., Scondotto, S., and Comba, P. 2015. Prevention of disease caused by fluoro-edenite fibrous amphibole: the way forward. *Annali Istituto Superiore di Sanità*, 51(2), 90–92.

Bullard, R. D. and Johnson, G. S. 2000. "Environmental justice: Grassroots activism and its impact on public policy decision making. *Journal of Social Issues*, 56(3), 555–578.

Castleman, B. 1995. The migration of industrial hazards. *International Journal of Occupational and Environmental Health*, 1(2), 85–96.

Cento Bull, A. 2016. *Modern Italy. A Very Short Introduction*. Oxford: Oxford University Press.

Cislaghi, C., Comba, P., Iavarone, I., Pirastu, R., Settimi, L., Di Paola, M., Mastrantonio, M., Forastiere, F., Michelozzi, P., and Nesti, M. 1997. Aree ad elevato rischio di crisi ambientale. In R. Bertollini, M. Faberi, and N. Di Tanno (eds), *Ambiente e Salute in Italia*. Rome: Il Pensiero Scientifico Editore, pp. 401–544.

Comba, P. 2017. The Italian experience on contaminated sites and health. In R. Pasetto and I. Iavarone (eds), *First Plenary Conference. Industrially Contaminated Sites and Health Network (ICSHNet, COST Action IS1408). Istituto Superiore di Sanità. Rome, October 1–2, 2015*. Rome: Istituto Superiore di Sanità. Rapporti ISTISAN 16/27, pp. 31–35.

Comba, P., Ricci, P., Iavarone, I., Pirastu, R., Buzzoni, C., Fusco, M., Ferretti, S., Fazzo, L., Pasetto, R., Zona, A., Crocetti, E. 2014. ISS-AIRTUM Working Group for the study of cancer incidence in contaminated sites. Cancer incidence in Italian contaminated sites. *Annali Istituto Superiore di Sanità*, 50(2), 186–191.

De Castro, P., Pasetto, R., Marsili, D., and Comba, P. 2016. Fostering public health awareness on risks in contaminated sites. Capacity building and dissemination of scientific evidence. *Annali Istituto Superiore di Sanità*, 52(4), 511–515.

European Environment Agency 2013. *Environment and Human Health. Joint EEA-JRC Report*. Luxembourg: Publication Office of the European Union.

European Environment Agency 2015. *The European Environment – State and Outlook 2015: Synthesis Report*. Copenhagen: European Environment Agency.

Fazzo, L., Minichilli, F., Santoro, M., Ceccarini, A., Della Seta, M., Bianchi, F., Comba, P., and Martuzzi, M. 2017. Hazardous waste and health impact: A systematic review of the scientific literature. *Environmental Health*, 16(1), 107.

Hytten, E. and Marchioni, M. 1970. *Industrializzazione Senza Sviluppo. Gela: Una Storia Meridionale*. Milan: Franco Angeli.

Iavarone, I. and R. Pasetto, R. (eds) 2018. Environmental health challenges in contaminated sites. *Epidemiologia e Prevenzione*, 42(5–6), suppl. 1.

Laborde, A., Tomasina, F., Bianchi, F., Bruné, M. N., Buka, I., Comba, P. … Landrigan, P. J. 2015. Children's health in Latin America: The influence of environmental exposures. *Environmental Health Perspectives*, 123(3), 201–209.

La Dou, J. 1992. First World exports to the third world-capital, technology, hazardous waste, and working conditions – Who wins? *Western Journal of Medicine*, 156(5), 553–554.

Marsili, D., Fazzo, L., Iavarone, I., and Comba, P. 2017. Communication plans and in contaminated areas as prevention tools for informed policy. *Public Health Panorama*, 3(2), 261–267.

Martuzzi, M. and Matic, S. 2016. Industrially contaminated sites and health: Challenges for science and policy. In R. Pasetto and I. Iavarone (eds), *First Plenary Conference. Industrially Contaminated Sites and Health Network (ICSHNet, COST Action IS1408). Istituto Superiore di Sanità. Rome, October 1–2, 2015*. Rome: Istituto Superiore di Sanità. Rapporti ISTISAN 16/27, pp. 6–8.

Martuzzi, M., Mitis, F., Biggeri, A., Terracini, B., Bertollini, R., & Working Group Environment and Health in Italy 2002. Environment and health status in the population of the areas at high risk of environmental crisis in Italy. *Epidemiologia e Prevenzione*, 26(6) suppl.

Martuzzi, M., Pasetto, R., and Martin-Olmedo, P. 2014. Industrially contaminated sites and health. *Journal of Environment and Public Health*, 198574.

Minichilli, F., Santoro, M., Bianchi, F., Caranci, N., De Santis, M., and Pasetto, R. 2017. Evaluation of the use of the socioeconomic deprivation index at area level in ecological studies on environment and health. *Epidemiologia e Prevenzione*, 41(3–4), 187–196.

Mudu, P., Terracini, B., and Martuzzi, M. (eds) 2014. *Human Health in Areas with Industrial Contamination* (Copenhagen, World Health Organization Regional Office for Europe,).

Panagos, P., Van Liedekerke, M., Yigini, Y., and Montanarella, L. 2013. Contaminated sites in Europe: Review of the current situation based on data collected through a European network. *Journal of Environment and Public Health*, 158764.

Pasetto, R. and Iavarone, I. (eds) 2016. *First Plenary Conference. Industrially Contaminated Sites and Health Network (ICSHNet, COST Action IS1408). Istituto Superiore di Sanità. Rome, October 1–2, 2015*. Romae: Istituto Superiore di Sanità. Rapporti ISTISAN 16/27.

Pasetto, R., Martin-Olmedo, P., Martuzzi, M., and Iavarone, I. 2016. Exploring available options in characterising the health impact of industrially contaminated sites. *Annali Istituto Superiore di Sanità*; 52(4), 476–482.

Pasetto, R., Sampaolo, L., and Pirastu, R. 2010. Measures of material and social circum-stances to adjust for deprivation in small-area studies of environment and health: Review and perspectives. *Annali Istituto Superiore di Sanità*, 46(2), 185–197.

Pasetto, R., Zengarini, N., Caranci, N., De Santis, M., Minichilli, F., Santoro, M., Pirastu, R., and Comba, P. 2017. Environmental justice in the epidemiological surveillance system of residents in Italian National Priority Contaminated Sites (SENTIERI Project). *Epidemiologia e Prevenzione*, 41(2), 134–139.

Pasetto, R., Zona, A., Pirastu, R., Cernigliaro, A., Dardanoni, G., Addario, S. P., Scondotto, S., and Comba, P. 2012. Mortality and morbidity study of petrochemical employees in a polluted site. *Environmental Health*, 18(11), 34.

Pirastu, R, Comba, P., Conti, S., Iavarone, I., Fazzo, L., Pasetto, R., Zona, A., Crocetti, E, and Ricci, P. (eds) 2014. SENTIERI - Epidemiological study of residents in National Priority Contaminated Sites: Mortality, cancer incidence and hospital discharges. *Epidemiologia e Prevenzione*, 38(2), suppl. 1.

Pirastu, R, Pasetto, R., Zona, A., Ancona, C., Iavarone, I., Martuzzi, M., and Comba, P. 2013a. The health profile of populations living in contaminated sites: SENTIERI approach. *Journal of Environmental and Public Health*, 939267.

Pirastu, R, Comba, P., Iavarone, I., Zona, A., Conti, S., Minelli, G., Manno, V., Mincuzzi, A., Minerba, S., Forastiere, F., Mataloni, F., and Biggeri, A. 2013b. Environment and health in contaminated sites: The case of Taranto, Italy. *Journal of Environmental and Public Health*, 753719.

Pirastu, R., Iavarone, I., Pasetto, R., Zona, A., Comba, P., and SENTIERI Working Group 2011. SENTIERI Project. Mortality study of residents in Italian polluted sites: Results. *Epidemiologia e Prevenzione*, 35(5–6), suppl. 4.

Saitta, P. 2012. History, space, and power. Theoretical and methodological problems in the research on areas at (industrial) risk. *Journal of Risk Research*, 15(10), 1299–1317.

Schlosberg, D. 2004. Reconceiving environmental justice: Global movements and political theories. *Environmental Politics*, 13(3), 517–540.

Standring, W. J. F., Dowdall, M., and Strand, P. 2009. Overview of dose assessment devel-opments and the health of Riverside residents close to the "Mayak" PA facilities, Russia. *International Journal of Environmental Research and Public Health*, 6(1), 174–199.

van Liedekerke, M., Prokop, G., Rabl-Berger, S., Kibblewhite, M., and Louwagie, G. 2014. *Progress in the Management of Contaminated Sites in Europe*. Luxembourg: Joint Research Centre, Report EUR 26376.

Walker, G. 2012. *Environmental Justice: Concepts, Evidence and Politics*. New York: Routledge.

World Health Organization 2009. *Manual for the Public Health Management of Chemical Incidents*. Geneva: World Health Organization.

World Health Organization 2010. *Environment and Health Risks: A Review of the Influence and Effects of Social Inequalities*. Copenhagen: World Health Organization, Regional Office for Europe.

World Health Organization 2012. *Environmental Health Inequalities in Europe, Assessment Report*. Copenhagen: World Health Organization, Regional Office for Europe.

World Health Organization 2013a. *Contaminated Sites and Health. Report of Two WHO Workshop:*

Syracuse, Italy, 18 November 2011 and Catania, Italy, 21–22 June 2012. Copenhagen: World Health Organization Regional Office for Europe.

World Health Organization 2013b. *Capacity Building in Environment and Health (CBEH) Project. Report of the International Training Workshop on CBEH. 19–23 March 2012 Riga, Latvia.* Copenhagen, World Health Organization Regional Office for Europe.

World Health Organization 2016. *Waste and Human Health: Evidence and Needs. WHO Meeting Report. 5–6 November 2015. Bonn, Germany*. Copenhagen: World Health Organization Regional Office for Europe.

World Health Organization 2017a. *Declaration of the Sixth Ministerial Conference on Environment and Health* 2017a. Available at http://www.euro.who.int/__data/assets/pdf_file/0007/341944/OstravaDeclaration_SIGNED.pdf?ua=1 (last accessed February 5, 2020).

World Health Organization 2017b. *Inheriting a Sustainable World? Atlas on Children's Health and the Environment*. Geneva: World Health Organization.

Zona, A, Fazzo, L., Binazzi, A., Bruno, C., Corfiati, M., and Marinaccio, A. 2016. SENTIERI- Epidemiological study of residents in National Priority Contaminated Sites: Mesothelioma incidence. *Epidemiologia e Prevenzione*, 40(5), suppl. 1.

Zona, A, I. Marcello, M. Carere, E. Beccaloni, F. Falleni, M.E. Soggiu. In press. "Priority index contaminants, target organs and human exposure in contaminated sites" in D. Marsili, R. Pasetto (eds) *Italy-Latin America Cooperation. Health Impact of Contaminated Sites: Methods and Applications*, (Rome, Rapporti ISTISAN 15/32, 2015).

Zona, A, Pasetto, R., Fazzo, L., Iavarone, I., Bruno, C., Pirastu, R., and Comba, P. (eds) 2019. SENTIERI epidemiological study of residents in National Priority Contaminated Sites: Fifth report. *Epidemiologia e Prevenzione*, 43(2–3), suppl. 1.

10

Soft confrontation: Strategic actions of an environmental organization in China

Xinhong Wang and Yuanni Wang

Introduction

The increasingly complex and extensive existence of environmental problems in China has made environmental protection a public issue that concerns almost everybody. In China, despite the obstacles to the existence of a truly independent civil society, environmental organizations have been playing important roles in environmental governance, from promoting environmental education to initiating environmental campaigns. Moreover, as representatives of the public interest, environmental organizations have also formed a crucial bridge for public participation in environmental matters in China (Yang 2005). However, differing from most civil society organizations in the Western world which can freely participate in street protests and political demonstrations, organizations in China have to restrain their actions within government tolerable limits. In China, environmental organizations have generally chosen to act in a form of "embedded activism" (Ho 2007) in the semi-authoritarian context, facing mixed signals and political ambivalence regarding public participation (Stern and O'Brien 2012; Stern 2013). In other words, their activities have been in line with government policies, and their framing and tactics are generally depoliticized and collaborative. Environmental organizations in China also have close relationships with government institutions. This is reflected in the official registration requirement for civil organizations in China to be affiliated with a supervising parent institution, such as a public institution or a government agency (Hildebrandt 2011). As Ho (2001) argued, environmentalism in China, encompassing the various forms of green NGOs (nongovernmental organizations) that we see in the West and the ex-socialist states of Eastern and Central Europe, is different in its reluctance to openly confront the government. Hence, are Chinese organizations merely collaborating with the government in compromising and non-confrontational ways?

In this chapter, we analyze the strategies adopted by Green Hunan, a local environmental volunteers' organization in Hunan Province, China, and propose "soft confrontation" (柔性抗争 *rouxing kangzheng*) as a new concept to critically examine actions and strategies of environmental organizations in China. The case of Green Hunan shows that organizations can adopt measures that are both collaborative and confrontational for the sake of environmental protection. Adapting soft strategies (Chakib 2014) such as media campaign and lobbying instead of hard ones such as environmental protests and road blocking, Green Hunan has maintained its legitimacy in its fight for the environment and the public interest. Yet, in an authoritarian state, using soft strategies such as disseminating information to create public outcry can be considered confrontational as well. Instead of being oppositional or radical, the confrontation is persistent yet resilient, reflecting its particular ways of interacting with the local government against China's restrictive political background, as we will illustrate in the following section.

Earlier studies on environmental civil society in China mainly focused on organizations that have obtained more social resources – either established in Beijing or with official state-acknowledged backgrounds – such as Friends of Nature, Global Village, and Green Earth Volunteers (Yang 2005). The action strategies that such organizations have taken generally include conflict aversion, cooperation seeking, building relationships, and media support (Yang and Calhoun 2007). However, elite organizations with rich social resources and official support are undeniably only a small part of the thousands of environmental organizations in China. A large majority of environmental organizations are still seeking official collaborations and trying to obtain social resources by adopting various actions and strategies.

In contrast to studies that focus on widely reported environmental campaigns such as anti-dam movements (Lin 2007) or environmental organizations with rich resources, in this chapter we extend studies of Chinese environmental organizations from national campaigns and policy consultation to the everyday activities of a local organization. By examining the daily environmental protection activities carried out by Green Hunan – a small to medium-sized local environmental organization in Hunan Province – we have found that, by using two major strategies of "pushback" (倒逼 *Daobi*) and negotiation (协商 *Xieshang*), the environmental organization has carried out a form of soft confrontation to protect the environmental public interest within a restrained political space and with limited resources. Green Hunan uses the media as a platform and pushback as a strategy to attract government attention and thus forms an inter-dependable relationship between itself and the government. During the process of using soft strategies such as reporting and negotiating with the government, Green Hunan also continues with the strategy of pushback in order to maintain its power of being confrontational, thus achieving a balance of dependency and autonomy.

The completion of this chapter is a collaboration between the two authors, and the theoretical framework of soft confrontation was debated and developed by both authors. Xinhong Wang wrote the theoretical framework, literature review, and sociological analysis and Yuanni Wang conducted semi-structured qualitative interviews with workers and volunteers of Green Hunan, including interviews with four NGO workers and 17 volunteers, in addition to participation observation and informal talks. In July 2014, Yuanni Wang started volunteering as a river guardian at Green Hunan. Between July 2015 and February 2017, while continuing to volunteer, she also acted as staff worker responsible for the organization's culture construction. The research focused on organizational strategies for collective action and their overall purposes and effects. All interviews, talks, and participatory observation were recorded in extensive research notes, on file with the authors.

Nine dragons: The dilemma of reporting environmental pollution

Green Hunan is a local environmental public interest organization that was officially registered in 2011 in Hunan Province, China. Consisting of volunteers from various cities and towns in Hunan Province, the organization aims to promote ecological protection in the province through continuously and effectively encouraging local government to rectify environmental problems. One of the major environmental actions carried out by the organization is River Watchers, a project where volunteers of the organization are trained to monitor the four major rivers in Hunan by spotting sewage pollution, using simple water quality inspection packets, citizen photography, and information dissemination. When finding abnormal emission problems in the river, the volunteers call government hotlines, take samples for testing, use online social media to disseminate information, and also request the government to disclose relevant information.

Pollution reporting is one important channel for citizens to contribute to environmental governance in China. However, volunteers have found that the effect of using the reporting channel is very limited. As one interviewee explained:

> It was in 2012. I went fishing with my friend and found that the river nearby was running different colours and polluted. Then I started to make phone calls to report it. But it was not really useful, so I wrote to the provincial Governor. After writing the letter, it had some effect. Some local government officials contacted me and agreed that we could visit the sewage spot together. When we went there, we did not find any pollution problem. However a few days later, I went there again and noticed the pollution again. I also called the reporting hotline, but still nobody responded to tackle the issue.

Generally, the routine reporting method rarely leads to effective results. This is due not only to the collusion of local government and enterprises (Zhang 2006; Long and Hu 2014), but also to the complexity of environmental problems and the division of government departmental responsibilities. As another participant remarked:

> I often call 12369 or 12345 to report pollution issues, but reporting has little effect. Sometimes when we find pollution emission, people on the other end of the phone say that it was not the responsibility of the Environmental Protection Bureau, but of the Water Department. When we called the Water Department, they would say that it was not their work, and we should call other government offices. It is so difficult to report environmental problems. Then, even if you feel that your report went through, it is a different issue whether it will have an effect or not.

Chinese people use the term "Nine dragons controlling water" (九龙治水 *Jiulong zhishui*) to describe their current chaotic water management system. That is, with multiple government agencies being responsible for managing the water quality and usage, there is no consistent and well-coordinated water management system. This has also contributed to the failure of using official reporting channels. Facing these problems, volunteers have to seek other strategies to find effective solutions to environmental problems.

"Making bigger" and "pushing back"

According to Xie and Dang (2015), due to the unsatisfactory government responsibility system, the public has to utilize both government and social resources to create external public opinion and cause internal pressure to push local governments to fulfill their responsibility. "Making bigger" (闹大 *Naoda*) – to arouse public opinion and put pressure upon government – is usually the method volunteers take when they find that official routine channels do not work. In October 2011, for example, during their routine monitoring, volunteers found that a sewage exit in Xiang River was emitting a large amount of polluted water. They called the government reporting hotlines and also took photos and samples as evidence. However, the local government did not respond or take any other corresponding action as required by law. Volunteers came back to the pollution location several times and found the problem was still there. They were worried because the river was upstream of a drinking water source for millions of residents. To push for government reaction, they started to make the issue bigger and louder. First, they initiated a Nightingale Action to attract media attention and arouse public concern. As one interviewee explained: "A nightingale is a bird that sings at night. We monitor Xiang River at night and use new media to 'shout loud' its environmental problem, just like the nightingale sings at night. Thus we name our actions – environmental monitoring, attracting public concern and creating public opinion to make government take actions – 'Nightingale Action.'"

Volunteers made their plans to hype up the issue online and offline, while emphasizing that all actions must conform to their principle of "standing opposite the government, but not against it." In other words, their target is the environmental problem but not the government. Additionally, volunteers also agreed to maintain objectivity and avoid using radical and critical words that might offend the government. Generally, environmental pollution victims focus more on individual and group damages compensations, thus they are likely to point directly to the polluting enterprises and local governments, and disclose their accomplices to appeal for public attention and empathy. In contrast, civil environmental organizations aim to push the local government to solve environmental problems and safeguard public environmental interests. Therefore, environmental organizations act differently from individuals who fight for their interests by any means. In China, in order for an organization to persist and work toward its causes, it is crucial to avoid any type of opposition against the government.

Since enterprises do not discharge their polluted water at specific times, volunteers initiated a 24-hour continuous monitoring plan on 8 December to obtain the evidence on site and in time. They stayed at the pollution site and took samples every two hours to be tested in a professional lab. At around 8.30 p.m., after almost 20 hours of continuous monitoring, volunteers found that the sewage spot started to discharge dark and foul-smelling waste water. To show their respect to the local government, and also to comply with their principle, volunteers first called the local environmental protection bureau and hoped that they would send people to investigate. However, this did not work. Therefore, volunteers started to pin their hope on online "hyping up." They published photos and messages with the hashtag *Nightingale Action* on Weibo, one of the most popular Chinese online social media platforms, to disseminate the polluting situation. At the same time, they also used the theme *Our Mother River Cannot Bear It* to launch the campaign on various other social forums. By doing this, they aimed to arouse public environmental consciousness and create common resonance and thus make the issue a public concern. To maintain the issue as a hot topic online and create sufficient public opinion in the online public space, volunteers continuously posted, commented, and forwarded messages on various social media.

After volunteers widely disseminated their concerns on the Internet, many people started to join the campaign. On the first day after the Weibo post, more than 100 online users forwarded the original post of the emission pollution to express their support. Some comments reflected people's anger toward enterprises and government. Some online users also relayed the information to relevant media or provincial government officials. In print media, several local newspapers, including *Hunan Daily* and *Sanxiang Metropolitan Daily*, reported on the environmental pollution issue after noticing that it had caused public attention. The involvement of traditional media made the campaign more authoritative. On one hand, this further fermented public opinion, and on the other, it attracted government attention. Under the pressure of public opinion created by both new and traditional media, on 10 December the Provincial Environmental Department and the local Environmental Protection Bureau formed an investigation team. That very night, the local Environmental Protection Bureau published their investigation result and its polluter liability decision. Most important of all, local government officials also began their communications with volunteers. The government expressed that they would respond immediately if volunteers reported similar issues in the future.

Through rational "making bigger," volunteers not only gained public support and trust, but also social capital to interact with local government. This has become a cutting point for environmental volunteers to have an equal footing to confront the local government.

Negotiation rather than cooperation

The actions of the environmental volunteers have also received official acknowledgment. In 2013, the organization received several awards: CCTV (China Central Television) rule of law model, Hunan Province Learning from Leifeng Excellent Prize for Volunteer Service, and the *Morning News Weekly* City Dream Award. These awards have granted the organization the status of Xiang River Protector, and, more importantly, provided it more space and resources for its survival and development. Furthermore, this made it possible for the organization and volunteers to initiate negotiation with the government. "Since we won the award from the central government, more and more people started to know us," explained one participant. "Our contact with the provincial government has become more frequent. The provincial government also started to give us awards and established official Green Guardians, aiming to integrate our action network." In 2013, in order to promote wider public participation in Xiang River protection, the provincial government recruited Green Guardians along the river. Some volunteers of Green Hunan also joined the Green Guardians and thus built a vertical relationship among themselves and the provincial government. This has also granted them official status. Under the influence of volunteers' work, the provincial government strengthened the environmental governance along the Xiang River. In September 2013, Hunan provincial government made the Xiang River pollution treatment their top priority and allocated responsibilities to city- and town-level governments.

Nevertheless, in China the cooperative relationship between civil society and government is unequal and against the background of "Strong State, Weak Society," meaning civil organizations have to sacrifice their own autonomy to cooperate with the government. Thus, it is of vital importance that civil organizations use strategies to maintain autonomy for their survival as well as development (Yao 2013). While gaining the opportunity to initiate an equal dialogue with the government, Green Hunan has also maintained two principles: first, they have expressed their attitude of standing on the opposite side to the government but never opposing the government; second, their persistent aim is to improve local environmental protection. Therefore, if the local government's aim is consistent with theirs, the organization will commit all its effort to support the government; however, if the local government acts to the contrary, the organization will use its capacity to rectify the government's (in) actions. In either way, what the organization does is within a politically tolerable scope: it is not opposing the government. As one civil society volunteer explained:

> Our cooperation with governmental departments is based on our own aim of action; if the local governmental department is making environmental protection its aim, then we will be their assistant; however if they are working against the aim, then we will insist on our aim and use our own resources and methods to solve the problems. It is negotiation rather than cooperation.

Regarding environmental pollution reports submitted by volunteers, the government generally takes measures to solve the problem on time; if it is unable to do it immediately, it will also provide feedback accordingly. The local government also established an internal reporting channel for volunteers, such as giving environmental enforcement officials' contact numbers to volunteers and using internal Wechat groups to communicate directly with the volunteers. Generally, when volunteers find problems, they will first use the internal reporting system. Reporting to the government first has effectively made the local government the vanguard for tackling environmental problems. This makes it possible for the government to take credit and thus safeguard its public image and performance achievement.

Nevertheless, soft strategy does not always work. Under such circumstances, Green Hunan has to adopt both soft strategy and hard strategy to achieve its aim. In 2016, local residents complained to the government that ZBG Company emitted below standard waste water, but did not receive any response. Residents then informed volunteers of Green Hunan. The volunteers felt a bit surprised when they also did not hear any response from the local government. For example, one participant explained how, "Generally, once we see any environmental problem, and post it in our group, or make a phone call, the Environmental Protection Bureau will respond very soon. The waste water pollution was related to an important model project of heavy metal production, why did the Environmental Protection Bureau not take any action this time?" Feeling disappointed, volunteers went to the pollution site that very night and confirmed the pollution situation. They called the local environmental protection bureau's 24-hour-hotline but to no avail. Then they called the director of the local Environmental Protection Bureau (EPB) and reported the situation of the pollution together with the non-responsive government hotline. Later, although both local EPB officials and the company came to the site, both parties only explained that they were not responsible for it and wished the matter to be left as it was.

The volunteers did not give up. The following day, they published the pollution situation online. Due to the company status as a model project, the online post attracted attention from the central government. On the following day, both the Emergency Center of the Ministry of Environmental Protection and the

Provincial Environmental Protection Department sent officials to the pollution site. The local government had to take corresponding actions to solve the problem. Inevitably, noticing that the local government had taken concrete actions, and in order to safeguard their negotiation relationship with the government and show their respect to the local government, volunteers immediately posted another online article to praise the quick and effective response of the local government: "Of course, we need to give consideration of the local government since the establishment of our collaborative relationship. Thus, once they start to take action, I will write an article to praise their effective action," explained one environmental volunteer.

Depending on the situation, volunteers have adopted a strategy of integrating negotiation and confrontation. When they found that negotiation does not work toward the aim of environmental protection, they started making the issue bigger to create public pressure as well as to attract attention from higher governmental institutions to exert official pressure upon local governments. Hence a confrontation occurred.

Discussion

When environmental issues become the focal point of public attention, more and more Chinese citizens start to initiate voluntary environmental protection activities. Volunteers differ from stakeholders in local NIMBY ("not in my backyard") campaigns (local protests against new or existing industrial facilities are often dismissed – or politically accepted – because they are framed as only related to local, personal interests); generally, they do not have direct personal interests pertaining to the environmental problems. Compared to pollution victims' environmental struggle for damages and compensation, volunteers of Green Hunan aim to protect the environment per se. This has, on the one hand, effectively helped them to gain public support and strengthened their social and political legitimacy; on the other hand, it has also offered them resources and platforms to communicate more forcefully and effectively with the local government.

At present, influenced by the political system, and against the background that resources and power relationships are in a greatly imbalanced situation where enterprises and governments have been playing a dominant role, citizens face great obstacles in using the official channels to achieve their aims. "Making bigger" has thus become the core logic for many stakeholders to push for solutions to social problems (Han 2012). At the same time, along with the changes in social structure and increasing citizen rights consciousness, many social groups have taken all kinds of methods to impose pressure upon policy makers (Wang 2006), as is demonstrated in our case study of Green Hunan. The organization has adopted both soft strategy and hard strategy of negotiation and "pushing back" – creating public opinion and attracting upper-level government attention to impose pressure upon local government. This "pushing back" is a confrontational strategy of the environmental organization to gain social resources when the official channels, such as calling the government hotline, had no result.

One co-founder of Green Hunan explained: "Many … think there is no way for Chinese people to protest, but I want to say that this is changing. We are protesting and the government is listening" (De 2016). Using the strategy of "pushing back" to create public pressure, Green Hunan volunteers have become able to negotiate with the local government. Negotiation has thus effectively formed the base from which Green Hunan can develop within the limited political space where Chinese government imposes various controls upon social organizations. Regarding civil organizations, particularly those with little potential to challenge the government, the government generally holds an attitude of non-interference; however, regarding organizations that express clear politically opposing opinions, the government maintains a strict policy of banning and cracking down (Kang and Han 2005). This has clearly affected how environmental organizations choose to take action. On the one hand, they have to adapt to the current political environment, thus forming an embedded activism; on the other hand, they also need to be acknowledged and supported by the public. The latter requires the organizations to maintain their autonomy.

Autonomy refers to the process in which civil organization can make its own decision on actions and programs to carry out (Fan 2010; Yao 2013). Autonomy is the basis for local environmental organizations to gain social trust and public support. It also provides the condition for the organization to attract attention from various levels of government and safeguards its capacity to negotiate with the local government. By adopting the strategies of "pushing back" and negotiation, and emphasizing its non-oppositional attitude, Green Hunan has achieved official legitimacy while at the same time also maintaining its autonomy and activism.

As discussed by Ren (2013), several factors have contributed to public participation in China's political system: the difference between the central and local government regarding environmental governance, the division of state and cities in various interests, the power relationship among various departments of the government, the state *Xinfang* (letter and visit) system for citizens to submit complaints, and the commercialization of social media. The achievement of Green Human also benefits from China's administrative system. In China, the administrative system requires the lower-level administrations to be responsible to the higher-level administrations (Xie and Dang 2015). Being carriers of the central policies, local governments bear the responsibility of taking measures to achieve concrete results for central government discourses, laws, and policies (Ran 2015, 63).

China's environmental governance is essentially a closed, internal, self-monitoring system, and there is no effective monitoring system to check whether local governments have fully carried out the policies (Ran 2015, 129). Very often, local governments put economic development as their first priority, and thus neglect environmental policies, leading to environmental degradation. The monitoring and dissemination of environmental problems via social media by volunteers of Green Hunan has helped to create a new channel for the higher-level government to obtain information and carry out supervision in relation to the local environmental situation. This, in a way, helps the central government respond to local problems through ad hoc solutions and make it an integral part of the regime's dynamic stability (Froissant 2007, 119). As long as the actions taken by the environmental organization do not interfere or oppose the political power, a volunteer organization can take advantage of their being in an alliance with the central government to strengthen its own capacity and to gain bargaining power against the local government (Lin 2007).

Technically, using the media as a platform has provided local organizations the opportunity to interact directly and effectively with both the government and the general public. Before establishing their cooperative negotiation relationship with the local government, Green Hunan had to use "pushing back" to lay the basis for the government to respond. Through the Internet, civil organizations have initiated information dissemination, which leads to public reaction and wider public participation. This has further made the issues more influential and created pressure upon the government to take action. More importantly, the strategy of "pushing back" has not only made the local issues public, but also pushed the environmental organization to center stage. This has greatly strengthened its social recognition and political legitimacy, making it deeply and effectively rooted in the public space. While the local organization has gained more and more social influence, its political influence has also increased. Inevitably, the local government does not wish the organization to be more influential than the government itself; it also does not want the organization to escalate environmental issues to higher-level governments. Therefore, to maintain its controlling power, limit the influence of social organization, and avoid being inconsistent with central government policy, local government has to respond by initiating communications with the environmental organization. Negotiation with the government has thus been established.

In contrast to the local government, environmental organizations do not have the power to solve environmental problems, even though they are capable of monitoring them; therefore, they must rely on the government to resolve environmental issues. Under this situation, the local organization must maintain a sophisticated balance in its interactions with the government. On the one hand, volunteers have to adopt hard methods such as "pushing back" to impose pressure upon the local government through making issues bigger and louder; on the other hand, they need to restrain their actions to as not to anger all levels of government. It is rather a soft confrontation: actions taken by Green Hunan are neither completely compromising nor confrontational, but an integrated approach of being both confrontational and cooperative. It can be represented by the Chinese word Ren (韧) that refers to an indomitable and persistent spirit that is soft but resilient, and unlikely to break.

Conclusion

Chinese civil organizations are not the opposite of the party of the state, nor do they represent completely independent social groups. In order to continuously push for solutions to environmental problems, they have to maintain an embedded activism within the political institutions while letting the government play the dominant role. This nevertheless does not mean that civil organizations are only collaborating with the government, though, inevitably, they are not confronting the government either.

By sticking to the principle of "to stand opposite the government, but not against it," Green Hunan has played an effective role in environmental governance in China, a country with limited space for public participation. By negotiation and pushback, the organization has maintained both a collaborative organization and a bargaining power against the local government. When it spots an environmental problem, the organization first raises it in a rational way via official channels. This is cooperation. When facing inaction or negligence by the government or enterprise, members make efforts to mobilize both online and offline media to attract both public and higher-level government attention, and initiate a pushback effect upon the local government in the pursuit of the public interest. This is where the confrontation happens. However, when the government takes measures to solve the problem under public pressure, they choose not to take credit but praise the government for resolving the issue. This effectively reduces their initial confrontation, and shifts into soft confrontation. When encountering government or enterprises cosying up, they choose to collaborate and let them be the frontline soldiers. These specific actions have clearly strengthened Green Hunan's capacity and legitimacy, and maintained its autonomy in the fight for environmental protection.

By making environmental claims based on evidential factors, as opposed to environmental post-truths, Green Hunan has helped to provide knowledge to counterbalance the nature of expertise in China, where mainstream official discourse is generally considered the only truth, and voices of citizens are largely neglected or even repressed (Chen 2017).

Born locally, with a focus on local issues, engaging both the society and the government, and using an integrated strategy of pushback and negotiation in a form of soft confrontation, Green Hunan has created its own opportunities in its interactions with the government against the limited space for civil society in China. "Soft confrontation" perhaps sounds oxymoronic, yet under the current political system in China, it has provided the opportunity for the local organization to play an effective role in pushing forward its aim of environmental protection. Inevitably, Green Hunan is not the only one that has adopted this strategy. Many other organizations have been "confronting" the government as well, though focusing on different issues and varying in specific methods and actions. However, to what extent this strategy will continue to work depends largely on the government. If the Chinese government needs to further depend upon environmental organizations in tackling its existing rampant environmental problems, and thus offers more levers to the organizations, it is possible that organizations could be able to adopt more confrontational actions to further strengthen their capacity to interact with the government. Yet with the Chinese government gradually increasing its control over civic organizations, the question of whether future soft confrontations will continue to be acceptable is impossible to answer.

References

Chakib, A. 2014. Civil society organizations' roles in land-use planning and community land-rights issues in Kapuas Hulu Regency, West Kalimantan, Indonesia. Centre for International Forestry Research, Working Paper 147.

Chen, Z. 2017. Hou zhenxiang dao xin zhixu: bieyang gonggongxing jiqi gonggong zhili (Post-truth to new order: Different commonness and public governance). *Tansuo yu zhengming* (Exploration and Free Views), 4, 29–32.

Du, J. 2016. With network of river watchers, Green Hunan opens second front in China's war on pollution. *NewSecurityBeat*, December 26. Available at https://www.new securitybeat.org/2016/12/network-river-watchers-green-hunan-opens-front-chinas-war-pollution/ (last accessed February 6, 2020).

Fan, M. L. 2010. Feizhengfu zuzhi yu zhengfu de hudong guanxi: jiyu fatuan zhuyi he shimin shehui shijiao de bijiao gean yanjiu (Interactions between government and different types of NGOs: A comparative case study from perspectives of corporatism and civil society theory). *Shehuixue yanjiu* (Sociological Studies), 3, 159–176.

Froissart, C. 2007. Book review of *Rightful Resistance in Rural China*. *China Perspectives*, 4, 117–120.

Han, Z. M. 2012. Liyi biaoda, ziyuan dongyuan yu yicheng shezhi – duiyu "naoda" xianxiang de miaoshuxing fenxi (Interest expression, resource mobilization and agenda setting: An descriptive analysis on the Nao-da phenomenon). *Gonggong guanli xuebao* (Journal of Public Management), 9(2), 52–66.

Hildebrandt, T. 2011. The political economy of social organization registration in China. *China Quarterly*, 208, 970–989. DOI: 10.1017/S0305741011001093.

Ho, P. 2001. Greening without conflict? Environmentalism, NGOs and civil society in China. *Development and Change*, 32, 893–921. DOI: 10.1111/1467-7660.00231.

Ho, P. 2007. Embedded activism and political change in a semiauthoritarian context. *China Information*, 21, 187–209.

Kang, X. G. and Han, H. 2005. Fenlei kongzhi, dangqian dalu guojia yu shehui guanxi yanjiu (Differentiated control: Current state and society relationship research in mainland China). *Shehuixue yanjiu* (Sociological Studies), 1(6), 73–89.

Lin, T. C. 2007. Environmental NGOs and the anti-dam movements in China: A social movement with Chinese characteristics. *Issues & Studies*, 43(4). 149–184.

Long, S. and Hu, J. 2014. Zhengqi hemou shijiaoxia de huanjing wuran: lilun yu shizheng yanjiu (On environmental pollution from the perspective of government-enterprise collusion: Theoretical and empirical analysis). *Journal of Finance and Economics*, 40(10), 131–144.

Ran, R. 2015. *Zhongguo difang huanjing zhengzhi: zhengce yu zhixing zhijian de juli* (*China's Local Environmental Politics: Differences between Policy and Implementation*). Beijing: Zhongyang bianyi chubanshe (Central Compilation and Translation Press).

Ren, B. Q. 2013. Wangluo, "ruozuzhi" shequ yu huanjing kangzheng (Internet, weak organization community and environmental struggle). *Henan shifan daxue xuebao* (zhexue shehui kexue ban) (Journal of Henan Normal University (Philosophy and Social Sciences Edition), 3, 43–47.

Stern, R. E. 2013. *Environmental Litigation in China: A Study in Political Ambivalence*. Cambridge: Cambridge University Press.

Stern, R. E. and O'Brien, K. J. 2012. Politics at the boundary: Mixed signals and the Chinese state. *Modern China*, 38(2), 174–198.

Wang, S. G. 2006. Zhongguo gonggong zhengce yicheng shezhi de moshi (Public policy agenda-setting patterns in China). *Zhongguo shehui kexue* (Social Sciences in China), 3, 86–99.

Xie, Y. and Dang, D. S. 2015. Caogen dongyuan: guojia zhili moshi de xin tansuo (Grassroots mobilization: A new exploration of state governance mode). *Shehuixue yanjiu* (Sociological Studies), 3, 1–22.

Yang, G. 2005. Environmental NGOs and institutional dynamics in China. *China Quarterly*, 181, 46–66. DOI: 10.1017/S0305741005000032.

Yang, G. and Calhoun, C. 2007. Media, civil society, and the rise of a green public sphere in China. *China Information*, 21(2), 211–236.

Yao, H. 2013. NGO yu zhengfu hezuo zhong de zizhuxing heyi keneng – yi Shanghai YMCA wei gean (The possibility of NGO autonomy during its cooperation with government: A case study of Shanghai YMCA). *Shehuixue yanjiu* (Sociological Studies), 1, 21–42.

Zhang, Y. I. 2006. Zhengjing yitihua kaifa jizhi yu zhongguo nongcun de huanjing chongtu – yi Zhejiang de sanqi "quntixing shijian" wei zhongxin (The integrated system of politics and economy and China's rural environmental conflicts – A study of three "mass incidents" in Zhejiang Province). *Tansuo yu Zhengming* (Exploration and Free Views), 5, 26–28.

Part IV

Expanding citizen science

Introduction to Part IV

Thom Davies

Data is discard: in an uneven world of cloud-sourced devices, we are rendered data factories, spilling our information in real time to anyone who might be listening. Everything we tweet, "like," or Google has become a marketized product to be salvaged, mined, and rendered capital. Never before has the volume and velocity of data been so *available* and so open to manipulation. Some have argued that data has replaced oil as the world's most valuable commodity (The Economist 2017): a resource that can pollute politics and link power and big business in unforeseen ways. While it might be wrong to imagine "a prelapsarian past in which truth legitimately preceded and guided politics" (Jasanoff and Simmet 2017, 753), today, the rise of "big data" has opened up new avenues for "post-truth" to thrive, with potential environmental consequences. The success of populist movements such as Trump and Brexit, as well as political campaigns in Kenya and Nigeria, have all been linked to the data analytics of political consulting firms such as Cambridge Analytica (Persily 2017); future elections, it seems, may be won and lost by the crunch of code.

If data is the new oil, when it comes to *actual* pollution, data also plays a vital role. The pollution data produced by multinational companies and environmental regulators is often at odds with the lived experience of frontline communities. In response, environmental justice activists have often attempted to record their own data about toxic hazards using a gamut of citizen science techniques. This is especially important considering that the burden of proof of environmental damage often falls on affected communities, as opposed to the polluters themselves (Mah 2017). In an age of post-truth and alternative facts, questions of data, proof, and even citizenship have become especially acute. How can people who live with toxic injustice create their own facts about pollution? How can non-scientists make their alternative data *count* in environmental disputes? Can *citizen* science be expanded to include people whose citizenship is disputed? Can the practices of citizen science ever create environmental justice, if injustice is built on a bedrock of political inequality? These are some of the questions explored by the authors in the final section of *Toxic Truths*.

Citizen science refers to research that is performed *by*, and in the interests *of*, citizens. In the context of environmental justice, citizen science means adopting technoscientific practices by the public themselves to measure, assess, and sometimes protest their concerns about the environment. Though citizen science may sometimes ape formal science – ventriloquizing its symbolic capital – it also offers a form of public fact-making that is unencumbered by the burden of official training. It allows frontline communities to tell their own non-hegemonic "guerilla narratives" (Armiero et al. 2019) about the toxicants that they live and breathe with. Often it involves simple, low-cost, open-source devices, sensors, and strategies that enable ordinary people to make sense of toxic pollution, and advocate for a healthier environment. As we discussed in the introduction to this book, citizen science covers a wide range of practices and techniques which involve varying levels of participation by non-professionals. Though scholarship on citizen science took hold from the end of the last century (Irwin 1995; Bonney 1996), it built upon the legacies of amateur naturalists in the nineteenth century and radical scientists in the 1960s (Strasser et al. 2019). Today, this amateur and radical legacy pulls citizen science in different directions, as evidenced in the wide range of citizen science performed today. It can include the relatively passive crowdsourcing of information from the public – where citizens become little more than data points or "sensing nodes" (Gabrys 2014, 32) – to deeply participatory research, where community members themselves lead the planning, production, and analysis of environmental research (see Allen, this volume). Citizen science has particular relevance as we navigate an era of post-truth, which "emphasizes the weakness of factual, science-based explanations in the face of strong narratives or a compelling story" (Berling and Bueger 2017, 332). Citizen science challenges this supposed dichotomy between fact and narrative, allowing local communities to tell their own stories about pollution using publicly generated science.

Noise, ozone, oil, chemical, nuclear, water, and air pollution have all been monitored through citizen science campaigns, with cheap particle sensors, DIY devices, and open-source hardware allowing volunteers to provide new nar-

ratives about environmental injustice, using their own data. Famous examples of citizen science include the Louisiana Bucket Brigade, who used simple
"bucket samples" of polluted air as part of grassroots environmental justice
campaigns against the toxic racism of petrochemical companies (see Ottinger
2010). Citizen science has also been deployed in the wake of disasters such as
the 2010 BP oil spill in the Gulf of Mexico – the largest maritime industrial acci-
dent the world has ever seen – where Public Lab deployed kite-flown cameras
to witness the extent of crude oil pollution on the vulnerable wetlands of the
Gulf coast (Breen et al. 2015); or the 2011 nuclear disaster in Fukushima, Japan,
where Safecast provided cheap Geiger counters, and self-assembly monitors, to
help concerned Japanese citizens measure the levels of harmful radiation in and
around their homes, creating reliable crowdsourced radiation maps (Brown et
al. 2016).

The link between citizen science and environmental justice is not always a
smooth process, however. Some scholarship has started to question whether
public participation and citizen science necessarily leads to environmental justice at all (Topçu 2013). Some citizen science schemes have been actively reluctant to take sides in environmental controversies, and have instead adopted for
an outwardly neutral "'pro data' policy" (see Brown et al. 2016, 93). In some
cases, citizen science can produce cases of "conflictual collaboration" (Polleri
2019, 214) where publicly generated data becomes co-opted by state actors to
reinforce hegemonic governance of toxic risks. In the USA, for example, several
US departments, including the Environmental Protection Agency, have adopted
the language of citizen science, promoting an "Air Sensor Toolbox" as means to
tackle air pollution (Bonney et al. 2016).

There is a danger of citizen science being uncritical of wider political structures, where a frictionless pathway is imagined between citizen science data and
environmental justice: according to this fiction, the "right facts" will create the
right political ecology. In this sense, citizen science not only emulates some of
the practices of formal science, but also some of its ontological shortcomings.
To put it another way, in order for citizen science to produce environmental
justice, it "will require joining the epistemological with the political" (Strasser et
al. 2019, 53). As Shapiro and Kirksey (2017, 488) observe, "the epistemological
affordances of sensors risk reinforcing the dominance of science in society and
promoting the modernist dream of the imminent calculability and knowabil-
ity of the material world." And here lies the problem: not even the strongest
sensor with the highest-resolution open-source real-time data will be enough to
magically manifest environmental justice, especially if that injustice is built on
a firm foundation of inequality and oppression. No amount of public participation, however "data rich," will overturn toxic decisions if the participants do not

"*count*" (Davies 2019). Put differently, the *agency* of citizen science – with its offer of a low-fi technological fix – comes into conflict with the *structure* of environmental injustice – with its entrenched political inequalities. Data, in other words, will only ever be part of the struggle.

Though citizen science may not be the panacea it is sometimes cracked up to be, it nevertheless opens up important debates about the creation of toxic truths. It pulls in fresh perspectives on pollution, enlivens new narratives about injustice, and questions the salience of normative expertise. The authors in this last section of *Toxic Truths* offer distinct case studies that critically unravel questions about the fundamental nature of citizen science itself. For example, Elizabeth Hoover asks what happens to the notion of citizen science if the very idea of citizenship is contested. By exploring how citizen science and environmental injustice have interacted with an indigenous Mohawk community that spans the US–Canadian border, Hoover shines light on the fact that, for many communities, "citizenship" is not a simple category, especially in settler colonial contexts. João Porto de Albuquerque and André Albino de Almeida also unsettle the lopsided relationship between experts and citizens, and ask if pedagogical perspectives might help produce counter-hegemonic understandings of pollution. Building on this, Anneleen Kenis examines the political *work* that is needed to translate techno-scientific "fact" into a political reality, by exploring how air pollution data from citizen science programs in Belgium and the UK have produced differing political ecologies. In the last chapter of *Toxic Truths*, Nick Shapiro, Nasser Zakariya, and Jody Roberts reflect on the limits of creating citizen science data, when data alone will not be enough to deter toxins or produce political change. By pulling apart the taken-for-granted notions of science and citizenship, expert and citizen, data and narrative, these chapters allow deeper reflection on the place of citizen science within environmental justice campaigns. In a post-truth age where all kinds of expertise are regularly being questioned, expanding citizen science might also mean acknowledging its limitations.

References

Armiero, M., Andritsos, T., Barca, S., Brás, R., Ruiz Cauyela, S., Dedeoğlu, Ç., Di Pierri, M., Fernandes, L. D. O., Gravagno, F., Greco, L., and Greyl, L. 2019. Toxic bios: Toxic autobiographies – a public environmental humanities project. *Environmental Justice*, 12(1), 7–11.

Berling, T. V. and Bueger, C. 2017. Expertise in the age of post-factual politics: An outline of reflexive strategies. *Geoforum*, 84, 332–341.

Bonney R. 1996. Citizen science: A lab tradition. *Living Bird*, 15, 7–15.

Bonney, R., Phillips, T. B., Ballard, H. L. and Enck, J. W. 2016. Can citizen science enhance public understanding of science? *Public Understanding of Science*, 25(1), 2–16.

Breen, J., Dosemagen, S., Warren, J., and Lippincott, M. 2015. Mapping grassroots: Geodata and the structure of community-led open environmental science. *ACME: An International E-Journal for Critical Geographies*, 14(3).

Brown, A., Franken, P., Bonner, S., Dolezal, N., and Moross, J. 2016. Safecast: Successful citizen-science for radiation measurement and communication after Fukushima. *Journal of Radiological Protection*, 36(2), S82.

Davies, T. 2019. Slow violence and toxic geographies: "Out of sight" to whom? *Environment and Planning C: Politics and Space*, 1–19.

Gabrys, J. 2014. Programming environments: Environmentality and citizen sensing in the smart city. *Environment and Planning D: Society and Space*, 32(1), 30–48.

Irwin, A. 1995. *Citizen Science: A Study of People, Expertise, and Sustainable Development*. London: Routledge.

Jasanoff, S. and Simmet, H. R. 2017. No funeral bells: Public reason in a "post-truth" age. *Social Studies of Science*, 47(5), 751–770.

Mah, A. 2017. Environmental justice in the age of Big Data: Challenging toxic blind spots of voice, speed, and expertise. *Environmental Sociology*, 3(2), 122–133.

Ottinger, G. 2010. Buckets of resistance: Standards and the effectiveness of citizen science. *Science, Technology, & Human Values*, 35(2), 244–270.

Persily, N. 2017. The 2016 US election: Can democracy survive the internet? *Journal of Democracy*, 28(2), 63–76.

Polleri, M. 2019. Conflictual collaboration: Citizen science and the governance of radioactive contamination after the Fukushima nuclear disaster. *American Ethnologist*, 46(2), 214–226.

Shapiro, N. and Kirksey, E. 2017. Chemo-ethnography: An introduction. *Cultural Anthropology*, 32(4), 481–493.

Strasser, B. J., Baudry, J., Mahr, D., Sanchez, G., and Tancoigne, E. 2019. "Citizen science"? Rethinking science and public participation. *Science & Technology Studies*, 32(2), 52–76.

The Economist 2017. The world's most valuable resource is no longer oil, but data. *The Economist*, available at https://www.economist.com/leaders/2017/05/06/the-worlds-most-valuable-resource-is-no-longer-oil-but-data (last accessed February 6, 2020).

Topçu S. 2013. Chernobyl empowerment? Exporting "participatory governance" to contaminated territories. In S. Boudia and N. Jas (eds), *Toxicants, Health and Regulation since 1945*. London: Pickering & Chatto.

11

Whose citizenship in "citizen science"? Tribal identity, civic dislocation, and environmental health research

Elizabeth Hoover

Introduction: Citizen science

After decades of traditional health and environmental studies which left many communities – especially low-income and communities of color – feeling disempowered, community involvement in the production of science is being heralded as necessary for the achievement of environmental justice (Shepard 2002; Cohen and Ottinger 2011; Wylie et al. 2014). Citizen science (CS) is broadly defined as partnerships between scientists and laypeople (non-scientists) in which data is collected, analyzed, and shared (Irwin 1995; Jordan et al. 2012).

Under the broader umbrella of citizen science, there are varying levels of public involvement in the initiation of the research project, research design, data collection and analysis, and dissemination of results. In science-education-based CS projects, the public is invited to play a contributory role, taking part in the data collection for environmental or ecologically focused projects commonly based out of a university setting (Bonney et al. 2009; Havens and Henderson 2013). By involving the public directly in the production of scientific knowledge, this type of CS is intended to help enhance the public understanding of scientific processes – including knowledge gained from the study outcomes as well as data collection and other practical skills utilized by scientists that will help participants become better citizens, better contributing members of society (Jordan et al. 2012; Riesch et al. 2013).

At the other end of the spectrum, "street science" (Corburn 2005) and "popular epidemiology" (Brown 1992) are approaches utilized in community-driven projects in which laypeople utilize scientific methods to answer questions about, or draw attention to, issues in their communities, often working independent of research institutions. These approaches reverse the order of the traditional contributory CS model and resemble more of a co-created CS project, entailing "community initiation of investigations, gathering of scientific knowledge, and if necessary, recruiting of scientific professionals" (Ramirez-Andreotta et al. 2014, 655).

Communities sometimes use street science to initiate more formal research partnerships in CBPR (community-based participatory research) projects, or what Woolley et al. (2016) have called "extreme citizen science." These projects are co-created between community members and professional scientists, a process in which power should be shared between both parties in all aspects of the research process, and study outcomes benefit the community via interventions and policy change (Brown et al. 2011; Ramirez-Andreotta et al. 2014). CBPR "begins with a research topic of importance to the community with the aim of combining knowledge and action for social change to improve community health and eliminate health disparities" (Minkler and Wallerstein 2008, 7). In recent years, community/academic partnerships using a CBPR approach have played an important role in bringing attention to, and addressing situations of, environmental injustice (Shepard 2002).

Unlike the broad-scale nature of many education-based CS projects, CBPR projects are often rooted in a localized issue. In the Native American community of Akwesasne, which I will describe below, participatory research that stipulated the collection of scientific data by tribal members was utilized to determine the health impacts of environmental contamination. The series of environmental health research projects conducted in this community faced a number of challenges as a result of the need for collaboration between parties with very different backgrounds and knowledge experiences, but also benefited both the scientists and the community members who took part.

But who constitutes the "citizen" in citizen science has generally not been considered critically. "Citizens" have been conflated with volunteers, amateurs, or "members of the general public."[1] Ostensibly, this is anyone who is not a scientist. The noble intention behind many citizen science projects is to create a nation with a more educated citizenry, which will then in turn support scientific principles and projects.

In writing about how the citizen in CS can be theorized, Leach and Scoones (2005, 16) note that we need to "embrace a more fluid, decentered and experience-based notion of both citizenship and expertise, but without losing sight of the historical, political and institutional structures that shape often highly contrasting forms of engagement." They cite differing perspectives from which the role of the citizen can be defined, starting with the "liberal perspective," which sees the state as the benevolent protector of individuals, protecting them against major risks, utilizing science to guarantee their safety through food safety regulations and pollution risk management. "Liberal understandings of citizenship thus hold faith in the modern state's expertise, and science has become its core currency in the technology arena" (Leach and Scoones 2005, 22). But as we will see below in the case of the Mohawk community of Akwesasne, the state – as exemplified by New York state and US federal entities – bases standards and enforcement on what is economically beneficial for industry, rather than the protection of Indigenous people, thus not guaranteeing their safety. Participatory development attempted within this framing usually entails individuals choosing among an array of options and services, without playing a major role in setting policy agendas. The "communitarian perspective" centers on the notion of the socially embedded citizen and membership of a community, in which individual identity is subsumed to that of the group, and the common good is prioritized over individual interests, with the state appearing more distantly if at all. Communities are often seen as bounded and homogeneous with people acting toward a common goal (Leach and Scoones 20005, 23). And the "civic republican perspective" bridges the liberal and communitarian perspectives, situating individuals as part of collectives that press for claims in the political realm. Leach and Scoones (2005, 24) note that people will factionalize based on interests, and so citizenship is thus related to a common civic identity based on common public culture, and individual obligations to participate in communal affairs. "Civic republican thought generally assumes that nation-states provide the organizing frameworks for political dialogues, and by implication the epistemological basis for such interactions" (Leach and Scoones 2005, 25). In the case of the collaborative research at Akwesasne, the organizing framework of the dominant nation-state occasionally came up against that of the tribal government, as well as that set by the community organization Akwesasne Task Force on the Environment (ATFE), as tribal citizens often took diametrically opposing views to clean-up solutions from those of their non-Native neighbors.

But as political scientist Sarah Marie Wiebe (2016, 60) notes, "Western liberal notions of citizenship that separate land from life and that blame individual citizens for their health and well-being" diverge from Indigenous values and beliefs. Notions of citizenship have always marked the threshold between inside and outside of political life. Wiebe calls for an intersectional interpretation of citizenship, that moves beyond binaries and rethinks citizenship as inherently ecological, based on reciprocal relationships between human and more-than-human worlds. Along these lines, she describes ecological citizenship as illuminating the inherent deep-seated interconnection between human and more-than-human life. In her work with the Anishinaabe of Aamjiwnaang, an Indigenous community faced with an abundance of petrochemical pollution, Wiebe (2016, 121) explains that an Indigenous approach to "ecological citizenship" can be understood through the words, actions, and practices of citizens trying to maintain their Indigenous way of life. For Native people, she notes, "citizenship is corporeal, territorial, and practiced. It cannot be separated from consideration of land, treaties and the environment" (Wiebe 2016, 124).

Each of these theories conceptualizes "citizen" as a category of participation. But what does it mean to be a "citizen," as distinct from a professional scientist, and what about when Indigenous citizen scientists do not necessarily feel they share nationhood and citizenship with the scientists with whom they are working? The case study of Akwesasne explored below gives us the opportunity to consider how environmental justice differs for tribal communities as opposed to other ethnic or racial minority communities, and what "citizen science" means for citizens of a tribal nation, where participants are contending with citizenship identities across tribal, state, and federal governments.

Environmental justice and research in Indian country

In the United States, Native communities live in close proximity to approximately 600 Superfund sites, and environmental mitigation for these communities lags significantly behind that for non-tribal communities (United States Environmental Protection Agency 2004). Sites ranging from industrial plants to mines to military bases – as well as places affected by the release of pesticides and other agricultural by-products – have negative effects not only on their surrounding environments but also on the health and cultures of the Indigenous communities they border (LaDuke 2005). But although Indigenous people have made important contributions to the environmental justice (EJ) movement, when the study of EJ is applied to a tribal context, environmental issues cannot be contemplated apart from a recognition of American Indian tribes' unique cultural, historical, political, and legal circumstances (Ranco et al. 2011). As Potawatomi philosopher Kyle Whyte (2017) notes, settler colonialism actively works to disrupt Indigenous abilities to maintain relationships with other-than-human communities, destroys Indigenous food systems, and overall denies Indigenous communities the ability to maintain an adaptive capacity in their homelands. On a legal and political level, geographer Ryan Holifield notes,

"Environmental justice in Indian country is intimately bound up in the complex matter of tribal sovereignty," which differentiates EJ cases in these communities from those in other racial or ethnic communities (Holifield 2012).

Mohawk midwife Katsi Cook highlighted this important difference between American Indians and other EJ groups in a keynote speech she delivered to environmental health researchers in 2015:

> It's important to understand that North American Indigenous are not a racial or ethnic minority, but are one of three sovereignties in the United States. These are the federal, state and tribal levels of government. And so our traditional cultural property is protected by whole body of case law and Supreme Court decisions, treaty rights, and has significance for the work that's being done to recover our community from this historic moment of the post-WWII economic boom and the development of the St Lawrence Seaway. (Cook 2015)

Any consideration of environmental issues in Indian country needs to take into account the unique colonial history of Native Americans and the relationship that tribes have with the United States. A tribe is not simply another ethnic minority group; tribes are also sovereign nations, with their own governments, courts, laws, healthcare systems, and citizenship rules. In many Native communities, tribal police enforce tribal laws and patrol borders. Healthcare for tribal nations is generally delivered through tribal clinics, primarily funded by the Indian Health Service, or by traditional healers. Tribal enrollment offices keep citizenship records, determining eligibility based on each individual tribe's stipulations that may include a specific blood quantum, lineal descent from a particular tribal register, and/or clan membership, or any combination of the above. Tribal institutional review boards determine whether or not research can be conducted in some Native communities. Recognizing that CBPR cannot be conducted in exactly the same way in tribal communities as in other communities, researchers in the fields of cancer research, public health, psychology, and environmental health have laid out key principles for conducting CBPR in Native communities (Schell and Tarbell 1998; Fisher and Ball 2003; Burhansstipanov et al. 2005; LaVeaux and Christopher 2009). Researchers must also consider these communities' particular contexts and histories.

For a number of racial and ethnic minority groups in the United States, mistrust of research is rooted in a general mistrust of mainstream society, where exploitative or unethical treatment remains a serious problem (Lex and Norris 1999; Epstein 2007). Historically, research conducted on Indigenous peoples has served to advance "the politics of colonial control," which is often obsessed with classifying and labeling Indigenous peoples in an attempt to "manage" them (Cochran et al. 2008). Research studies conducted on Native Americans have often been exploitative and have not contributed to community empowerment. In many cases, researchers have entered with pre-developed projects, failed to ask for community input, pressured people into taking part, treated Native people as subjects or informants and not as colleagues, sensationalized problems in the communities in their publications, and used Native people's blood samples for unauthorized projects (Schnarch 2004). Among the negative views that community members have expressed are that researchers receive career advancement from their studies of tribal communities, while the communities themselves get poorer; that researchers are disrespectful of cultural practices; that research studies are actually designed to harm Indians; that participation in disease studies may cause the disease to manifest in one's family or the community; and that the benefits of studies rarely reach tribal members. Many complain that results are not shared with the tribal community, or, if they are, they are presented in a way that is too technical to understand (Morton et al. 2013; Burhansstipanov et al. 2005). Overcoming this legacy of past research projects is one of the difficulties that researchers now face when they embark on studies to explore and address community problems. It is for this reason that CBPR research specifically, which actively engages tribal community members, is the only type of research that some communities will allow.

Akwesasne

Akwesasne is a Mohawk community of about 15,000 people that shares a border with New York, Ontario, and Quebec. Because of the myriad borders that crisscross Akwesasne, residents must contend with two federal, three state/provincial, and three tribal governments, along with all of their accompanying agencies. If they step off either end of the reservation, they are also dealing with two different New York counties, Franklin County and Saint Lawrence County. Children in Akwesasne have the option of attending public schools on either side of the international border (or the community-based Akwesasne Freedom School), and many have dual US and Canadian citizenship in addition to their tribal citizenship.

The southern portion of the community is governed by the St Regis Mohawk Tribe (SRMT), the elected tribal government recognized by the US federal government. The Mohawk Council of Akwesasne (MCA), the elected tribal government recognized by the Canadian government, governs the northern half of the community. A third governing body, the traditional clan-based government empowered by the Haudenosaunee Confederacy, the Mohawk Nation Council of Chiefs, considers the entire territory of Akwesasne as its jurisdiction, although it is not recognized by either the US or the Canadian federal governments. Each of these tribal governments maintains separate tribal registers, and their affiliated citizens carry membership identity cards. Most Native American communities are jurisdictionally challenging, but Akwesasne is exceptionally so.

The community is bisected by the St Lawrence River, which was developed into the St Lawrence Seaway in 1954. The project included the construction of hydroelectric dams, which brought industry to the area – General Motors (GM), Alcoa, and Reynolds[2] – all of which are just upstream of Akwesasne. While it is the responsibility of state and federal agencies, as well as the industries themselves, to monitor these industrial plants to ensure they are not harming the local environment, this was often not the case. Over the years since the GM foundry was established directly adjacent to the Raquette Point portion of Akwesasne, Mohawk people attempted to report issues related to the plant to the New York State Department of Environmental Conservation (NYSDEC). But rather than holding GM responsible, the state often wrongly blamed Mohawks for the problems. In the early 1970s, when the open dumps at the GM site spontaneously combusted, state agencies blamed Akwesasro:non (people of Akwesasne) for setting the fires. In 1972, a nurse at Akwesasne's medical clinic reported to regional environmental officers that open dumping and burning were taking place at the GM site, within 450 feet (137 meters) of Mohawk homes. The district health department director's comment was that "Indians did all the burning at the dumpsite," which angered community members that Mohawks were being blamed for the reactions of chemicals dumped by GM (Cook and Nelson 1986, 6). The slowness of response from state agencies led someone to call the US Environmental Protection Agency (EPA), which acknowledged GM's illegal dumping (Cook and Nelson 1986). Even as NYSDEC acknowledged that GM was operating a landfill in violation of New York law, the director of the state's Division of Solid and Hazardous Waste conceded that it was only one of 300 illegal landfills in New York at the time (Andrews 1989). The GM landfill remained open, without a permit, for another six years after NYSDEC discovered the problem, and continued to contaminate the environment.

Until they were banned in 1978, GM utilized PCB-laced hydraulic fluids that were periodically flushed from the plant and disposed of in reclamation lagoons, which were periodically drained and the sludge buried onsite in the unlined landfill. The use of the lagoons was intended to prevent the direct contamination of the rivers, but the waste overflowed into the St Lawrence at least seven times between January and September 1982 alone, contaminating the beds of the St Lawrence River, the Raquette River, and Turtle Creek (Grinde et al. 1995). GM also had an outfall that discharged into the St Lawrence River that led to sediment contamination, especially in Turtle Creek ("Superfund" 12).

In addition to the lagoons, in December 1981, NYSDEC found the ground-water on the GM property to be contaminated with PCBs (polychlorinated biphenyls), heavy metals, chromium, mercury, and cadmium. A month later, tests found PCBs in the 220-foot-deep private well of Raquette Point residents Tony and Ella Cole. Rather than hearing directly from regulators, Mohawks found out about these tests through articles in the local newspaper. NYSDEC blamed the breakdown in communication on the fact that although the GM plant is adjacent to Akwesasne, the plant is in Saint Lawrence County, which is in NYSDEC Region 6, while Akwesasne is in Franklin County, in NYSDEC Region 5. This failure of both industry and regulatory agencies to communicate with the community, coupled with a general distrust of many of the institutions that were tasked with ensuring the environmental health and safety of people in the region, led to the development of the community organization Mohawks Agree on Safe Health (MASH), which was founded in an attempt to ensure that health-related information was reaching residents and that their needs were properly represented.

The 270-acre General Motors site was nominated to the National Priorities List as a Superfund site in the fall of 1983 and was placed on the list in early 1984. That same year, a Mohawk midwife from Akwesasne, Katsi Cook, invited NYSDEC wildlife epidemiologist Ward Stone to Akwesasne to test fish and wildlife in the vicinity of the GM plant. In 1985, he began announcing his results, revealing levels above what was safe to consume:[3] 190 ppm (parts per million) PCBs in a duck, 11 ppm in a sturgeon, and 3,067 ppm in a male snapping turtle (Andrews 1989).

Cook then began to set the stage for scientific studies to demonstrate whether the PCB contamination found in their food source was impacting the health of mothers and their infants. While Cook acknowledges she did not have the credentials of most researchers, she recognized the importance of her position in the community for bringing women's issues to the fore: "I don't have an engineering, environmental engineering degree, I don't have anything like that, but what I do have as a midwife and as a Mohawk woman moving through the small world webs of the community, I would hear this one had a miscarriage, that one over here is sick with this" (Cook 2008). Because of this "situated knowledge" (Haraway 1988), Cook ultimately proved to be one of the "champions" who emerged "to design innovative public participation processes" (Gallagher 2009, 914). One of Cook's main concerns was whether she should be encouraging mothers to breastfeed their babies, as milk concentrates lipophilic pollutants. Mothers had contacted her asking, "'Gee, Katsi, these scientists are coming to my home taking samples of everything but me. Is it safe to breastfeed?' And I said, 'You know what? I don't really know. I wish I did'" (Cook 2005).

To answer some of these questions, Cook contacted a chemist at the New York State Department of Health (NYSDOH) about conducting a breast milk study. In 1985 Cook embarked on what she terms "barefoot epidemiology," personally collecting samples of milk from 10 nursing Mohawk mothers, and sending them to a private lab in Wisconsin, in addition to the NSYDOH lab, because she did not initially trust the state to give her accurate results.[4] The samples contained PCBs, Mirex, and hexachlorobenzene at levels that the NYSDOH did not think were dangerously high, but that warranted further investigation. This initial "street science" study led to a health risk assessment (Fitzgerald et al. 1992), and then two Superfund Basic Research Program (SBRP) grants[5] that supported several research studies designed and carried out in collaboration between the State University of New York (SUNY) Albany and the grassroots organization Akwesasne Task Force on the Environment (ATFE), the first such community-based participatory research project of its kind with an Indigenous community.

As opposed to traditional health studies in which the study is designed entirely by outside scientists, and professional researchers or graduate students collect samples, the Mohawk community insisted from the beginning of this research that they be included as equal partners, and that SUNY Albany hire and train local residents for the project. As Cook described, "At the very outset, I demanded that the only way we're going to work with Mohawk women in the precious intimacy of Mohawk mothers' milk is to ensure the mothers that they are co-investigators in this study … we're not going to be guinea pigs" (Cook 2005). Cook began the First Environment Research Project (FERP) as a means of organizing Mohawk women fieldworkers, and coordinating the data for the health studies. FERP employees collected blood and breast milk samples, and for some studies conducted cognitive assessments, body measurements, and nutritional surveys. The data was sent to Albany for analysis, and in time, a letter was sent back to the participant explaining their individual results (Schell et al. 2007). Periodically, the SUNY researchers would also host retreats at Akwesasne, where they would present the progress of the studies to the community.

In 1987 MASH merged with a new group, the Akwesasne Task Force on the Environment. The purpose of ATFE, which is still active today and has become well known as an Indigenous grassroots environmental organization, is to bring together representatives from all three tribal governments in the community of Akwesasne, as well as any community members who want to attend meetings and be involved. The New York state and US federal governments had procedures in place for working with the federally recognized St Regis Mohawk Tribe (SRMT), but in a politically complicated community like Akwesasne, this meant that a number of stakeholder voices were not being formally included.

ATFE was developed to reach across these different political lines to create a united front, a unified community voice, that would represent the best interests of all Akwesasro:non. Because ATFE is removed from the political process, it can both advocate for community-based solutions to environmental issues and ensure that researchers do not "take advantage of intra-tribal differences" (Akwesasne Task Force on the Environment 1996, 95).

ATFE also established a Research Advisory Committee and developed the Good Mind Research Protocol to ensure that any research conducted in Akwesasne is to the benefit of the residents there. The goal of the advisory committee is to help ensure that the proposed research will benefit the whole community, give the people of Akwesasne opportunities to be involved in decision-making processes during the research, and empower those involved through education, training, and/or authorship.

As detailed in the Good Mind Research Protocol, a research team must begin working with ATFE in the earliest stages of study planning, so that community members have sufficient time to thoroughly review and understand all aspects of the proposed research. The research team must submit a synopsis of the project that includes information about the methods that will be employed, how the project results will benefit or harm the community, how confidentiality will be protected, how data will be stored, and how study participants and the community at large will be fairly compensated through grant money and shared authorship.

While the community was coalescing to develop grassroots organizations that could operate outside the political system, the SRMT government was also working to improve its own capacity to deal with the environmental situation. The SRMT Environment Division grew out of a single position sponsored by the federal Indian Health Service, which then developed over the years into a large division with departments devoted to air quality, brownfields, solid waste management, water resources management, wetlands protection, Natural Resource Damages Assessment, hazardous materials, and Superfund oversight.

In 1980 and 1984, the EPA adopted official Indian policies that aimed to allocate more responsibility for the development of environmental standards to qualified tribes (Du Bey and Grijalva 1993–1994). These were then followed by amendments to federal legislation. In October 1986, the Superfund Amendments and Reauthorization Act added Section 126 to the Comprehensive Environmental Response, Compensation, and Liability Act (CERCLA), directing the EPA to treat qualifying tribal governments substantially the same as states for specified provisions of CERCLA. A qualifying tribal government is one that is federally recognized, has a governing body with authority to protect the health and welfare of tribal members and the environment, and has jurisdiction over the site where CERCLA actions are contemplated.[6] Under this law, the SRMT now had authority over the contamination that had left the GM site and flowed onto tribal land (Du Bey and Grijalva 1993–1994). In 1987, amendments to the Clean Water Act allowed the EPA to delegate programs for establishing water quality standards to tribes, and 1990 amendments to the Clean Air Act allowed similar reallocation for air quality standards (Du Bey and Grijalva 1993–1994). Because of this series of amendments, when it comes to cleaning up Superfund contamination on tribal lands, tribal "applicable or relevant and appropriate requirements" (ARARs) are treated consistently with state requirements – meaning that if a tribe adopts standards that are stricter than those put in place by the federal government, the portion of clean-up that affects reservation land must meet the stricter standards.[7] In 1989, the SRMT developed ARARs for PCBs of 1 ppm for soil and 0.01 ppm for sediment, numbers far lower than the state and federal standards that were applied on land outside the Tribe's juris-diction (1 ppm for sediment and 10 ppm for soil).[8] In reflecting on the process through which the Tribe chose the standard, Jim Ransom stated: "When we set the Tribal ARAR for PCBs, we recognized that it had to be scientifically and technically achievable. Our preference would have been zero. However, our lawyers advised that this would not meet technological requirements."[9] Because of the SRMT's status as a federally recognized tribe, and thereby a sovereign entity, the EPA was bound by law to follow the stricter standards for clean-up on Mohawk land.[10]

That the Mohawks were pushing for stricter standards than those applied to the general public was a recognition of the differences between the aver-age American and the Mohawk tribal citizen. As members of the ATFE note, Akwesasne's cries for environmental justice were brushed aside by government agencies who stated that Akwesasne was not being treated any differently than any other community, ignoring that Mohawk people and culture are "unique." They write:

> Akwesasne, like many other Native communities, needs additional consideration and more stringent remediation. Standards and regulations have been tailored to meet the needs of industrialized society, not subsistence cultures and endangered peoples. These standards are often minimalist in nature and do not begin to address special tribal rights. Conventional risk assessments which drive remediation are severely limited in their application to Native peoples because they fail to adequately value cultural, social and religious factors as well as sovereignty, treaty rights and issues of self determination. (ATFE 1997, 272)

For this reason, the SRMT Environment Division worked to enforce stricter clean-up standards than the EPA would ordinarily impose.

Residents of the neighboring town of Massena and the Tribe had diametrically opposed positions on this clean-up. The tribe called for the landfill to be excavated to prevent any further exposure of Mohawk people in the future, and Massena residents called for it to be capped, concerned that too great a financial hardship would cause GM to lay off more workers. During a Public Meeting held in Massena on April 25, 1990, several Massena residents bristled at statements made by Akwesasro:non, and the descriptions given by EPA staff, arguing that their town should not be described as "an industrial wasteland," "a chemical wasteland," or "an environmental wasteland" ("Public Meeting," 1990, 38, 84). Instead, Frank Alguire, Director of the Massena Economic Development Council, called for a "factual, scientific and objective approach to the issues. We need to, if we can, separate emotion and politics from our task at hand," which he saw as remediating the site in the least economically detrimental way possible ("Public Meeting," 1990, 84). Since their culture and livelihood had not been disrupted to the same extent as their Mohawk neighbors downstream, but rather relied on the presence of employing industries in the area, Massena residents downplayed, and took offense at, the characterizations of environmental contamination, and thus advocated for very different clean-up strategies and results.

But for Akwesasne Mohawk people, there was no separating emotion and politics from the task of pursuing environmental remediation. At another public meeting a year later, Jim Ransom, who at the time was on the staff of the Tribe's environment division, and a member of the Akwesasne Task Force on the Environment, beseeched the EPA and GM staff to think of the land as a human relative suffering from cancer, describing the waste dumps as cancerous lumps in our earth mother's breasts that needed to be removed.[11] Mother Earth and her other-than-human children that Jim describes were not included in the agency's health risk assessment – most conventional risk assessment processes do not consider this extended system of non-human relatives. For this reason, the Akwesasne Task Force on the Environment (ATFE) has been critical of these processes, expressing that "all peoples, including plants, animals and the earth herself must be included in defining environmental justice" (ATFE 1997, 268; Tarbell and Arquette 2000, 95). Conventional risk assessments are severely limited in their application to Native peoples "because they fail to adequately value cultural, social, subsistence, economic, and spiritual factors" (Tarbell and Arquette 2000, 102). As Whyte's (2013) work in Indigenous communities highlights, this includes the way in which the relational responsibilities between these communities are not valued or taken into consideration when conducting these conventional assessments. This is the type of "ecological citizenship" described by Wiebe (2016) that is rooted in place and extends to other-than-human elements.

Studies conducted at Akwesasne through the first Superfund Basic Research Project grant connected levels of PCBs in participants' breast milk and blood to fish consumption, which decreased as community members began heeding fish advisories published by the tribal government. This decrease in fish consumption proved a complex trade-off, as community members and scientists would later cite how the substitution of affordable foods for fish has contributed to other health problems. SUNY Albany and Akwesasne acquired a second SBRP grant (1996–2000), which enabled them to conduct studies that began to document health impacts in community members with higher PCB body burdens. These impacts include abnormal thyroid functioning in adolescents; earlier menarche in adolescent girls; a greater propensity for diabetes; higher levels of total serum lipids, which contribute to heart disease; affected cognitive function in older adults; and reduced testosterone levels in men, as well as adolescent boys. While data collection ended a decade ago, data analysis has been ongoing, and papers continue to be published. (For full citations of all of the studies connected to each of these results, see chapter 2 in Hoover 2017a.)

Methods

As part of a broader project on environmental health research in Akwesasne (see Hoover 2017a), in March of 2008, I traveled to SUNY Albany and the NYSDOH to interview seven scientists who had worked directly with the community while conducting health studies at Akwesasne from 1986 to 2003. I spoke with each of them about their experiences in organizing the study, in working directly with Akwesasne community members, and their ideas about how the studies could have been conducted. From June to November 2008, I interviewed 64 Akwesasne community members, 32 of whom had been involved in environmental health studies in some capacity. Five of these interviewees worked as FERP fieldworkers, six consulted with SUNY as members of the Akwesasne Task Force on the Environment (ATFE), and the remainder were study participants. The interviews lasted between 45 and 120 minutes, and pertained to the health studies, perceptions of change in the health and environment of the community, and participants' suggestions for how to improve future environmental health studies. Interviews with scientists and Akwesasne community members were transcribed and then uploaded to two separate NVivo8 files, and coded for themes. Below I have included the names of interviewees who allowed me to do so, and designated those who wished to remain confidential with a number. This research culminated in a book (Hoover 2017a) and several articles (Hoover 2013, 2016, 2017b; Hoover et al. 2012, 2015). While these other publications go into greater detail regarding the results of this research, this chapter details some of the challenges that came out of the environmental health citizen science research because tribal subjects and fieldworkers recognized that they held different cultural and citizenship affiliations from university and government researchers, as well as regulators.

Benefits and challenges

Akwesasne community members and scientists came to take part in these studies with slightly different motivations: members of the ATFE and FERP wanted to gather the necessary data to determine the health impacts of neighboring industries, force the industries to clean up, and acquire financial compensation for damages. Researchers at SUNY Albany took part in these studies to not only further their own professional careers, but also help the Mohawk people and other communities affected by PCB contamination better understand the potential health impacts of exposure. The outcome was 47 peer-reviewed publications (which have collectively been cited 863 times as of May 2014)[12] that contributed to the broader scientific understanding of the impact of PCBs on human health.

There were a number of benefits accrued by scientist researchers, community partners, and Mohawk fieldworkers (see Hoover 2016). For community members, this included information gained through the research, the education and job skills gained by the FERP fieldworkers, and the grant money spent in the community. Several participants were happy to receive their individual results and to find that their blood did not contain levels of contaminants that were as high as they thought they would be. Fieldworkers benefited from full-time employment and the classes they received on research methods and testing measurements, which resulted in some of the fieldworkers finding employment after the studies ended. The scientists benefited from being included in a project that allowed them access to a community that will no longer allow research to be conducted without their input. A greater number of participants were also likely included in the studies because of the role of Mohawk fieldworkers. Scientists also stated that they received an education about Indigenous communities as a result of being part of this study. At the conclusion of the SUNY SBRP studies, scientists have gone on to conduct research with Indigenous communities in Alaska (Miller et al. 2013), and continue to do research with Akwesasne Mohawk people (Gallo et al. 2016).

In addition to contributing to the capacity development of the scientists and community members who worked together on these health studies, environmental health research at Akwesasne also served to benefit the development of science more broadly at a time when CBPR was just beginning to become a standard of community research. Science and technology studies scholars Cohen and Ottinger (2011) offer a theory of how science and engineering can change through "ruptures" in the routines of scientific practice. Because they are often viewed as static, scientific knowledge, institutions, and experts are sometimes excluded from accounts of the transformative nature of environmental justice work, but "environmental injustice is an important source of ruptures in technical practice, and thus a powerful force for the transformation of science" (Cohen and Ottinger 2011, 4). Creating a more dynamic research environment and relationship in which community members shape study design as well as data collection and analysis and continue to provide feedback and ask questions allows for "transformations" that "grow out of routine ruptures in everyday technical practices, where scientists and engineers have room to make new choices about how to do their work" (Cohen and Ottinger 2011, 4). By having members of the affected community contribute directly to study design and data collection, the Akwesasne SBRP studies altered the status quo of environmental health research. By refusing to remain on one side of the researcher/subject divide, Akwesasro:non brought environmental health research into discussions about tribal sovereignty, forever changing how this type of work will be done in this and other tribal communities.

However, there were also distinct challenges faced by community and scientific partners as a result of working together in this study, including over what data would be collected, by whom, and what could then be done with that data. Although understood as necessary, it was difficult, and contrary to their training, for the scientists to give equal control over the data to the community, to "citizens." The anthropologist/epidemiologist I spoke with described how field staff would go and collect all of the data: "It was very unlike anthropology, having someone else do your data collection. Would you have someone do your interviews? ... We had to do that ... It's a kind of letting go. You can't be a control freak. You have to really channel that control."

Even beyond relinquishing control of the data collection, the Good Mind Research Protocol states that if the community feels that harmful data is being collected, they reserve the right to retrieve it and bring it back to the community. This happened to some of the surveys, a Cultural Affiliation Scale, that one of the research projects collected. Although the scale was used without issue in an earlier study, when other community members found out about its use for another SUNY study, they became uncomfortable with the scale, demanded that its use cease, and that all data collected with this scale be returned to the community. One woman (26C) remembers it as eight questions, and from these "they could determine how Indian you were, and we didn't like that at all [sarcastic laugh]. We made them return them all, and I think they were destroyed … We didn't think it was their place to determine peoples' heritage. And that kind of thing could be used against you. It just didn't serve a good purpose."

This distrust about the possible misuse of results extended to blood as well. Two of the SUNY scientists I spoke with described how, when they began to develop a continuation plan for the Superfund project renewal grant, the Mohawks refused to allow for genetic study of any kind. Because the focus of many funding agencies had turned to genetic testing, and their renewal grant did not contain a genetic component, the SUNY team believes that this is why their grant was not renewed. The scientists respected that these were the wishes of the community, but never fully understood why the Mohawks were so opposed to genetic testing. When I interviewed the FERP employees, I asked them why they thought the community was so resistant to this form of study, especially after being party to so many other types of research. The answers were similar to the resistance to the Cultural Affiliation Scale: the government could and would distort and use any information gained from these measures to "prove" somehow that Akwesasne Mohawks are no longer Indians. Regardless of the citizenship rules applied by the tribal governments in Akwesasne, the concern was that outside government entities would work to discredit these affiliations – not because the community felt that this was true, or had any doubts about their own "Indianness," but because past experiences, especially with the state government, have supported a concern that outsiders would use any tools at their disposal to disenfranchise the community.

One of the fieldworkers, Loralee, described the scenario in terms of government programs that non-Native people thought they no longer deserved on the basis of being a distinct population: "The big concern among the staff is that there's always been this big push to prove that Mohawks aren't Indian any more … because the big thing that people would say is 'oh, you're not anything special. You've been mixed up with all these other races for so long that there's no such thing as a Mohawk anymore.'" She pointed out that it would be difficult to do any kind of genetic analysis on the data they collected anyway, because some of the people who took part in the study were not Mohawk by blood. Some couples included a non-Native, but if they had been living in the community for more than 20 years they were included, since they had been just as exposed as anyone else. "We figured they are just as exposed as everybody else here. They're eating the same food, drinking the same water so we let them take part too." Throughout the study, there was the concern that New York state would misappropriate the blood samples in some way.

As described above, Cook initially sent the first blood samples to an outside laboratory, because she did not trust that the NYSDOH lab would give her accurate results. After the SBRP project began, the first batch of blood samples that were sent down to Albany to the Wadsworth Lab were stored for an extended period of time but not analyzed, which made the community nervous. A FERP fieldworker named Alice described the concern in the community: "They weren't letting us have the blood samples, and there was a fear at the time that NY State, the Department of Health, Wadsworth Center is going to use those blood samples for genetic testing. At the time, the Human Genome Project was a big thing and they really wanted Native blood to look at." Because Wadsworth had been storing the samples without analyzing them, the community became anxious and increasingly distrustful. FERP decided that the best thing to do would be to bring the samples back to Akwesasne. The office had a -8 degree freezer to keep the samples preserved until a course of action around analysis could be set. Over 200 samples were stored there until an epic ice storm struck, during which they lost power, but Alice managed to secure a generator to keep the freezer operating. She was eight and a half months pregnant at the time, but she and another worker, Agnes, took turns going down to the office three or four times a day to make sure the generator had enough gasoline and oil. It was imperative to preserve these samples, because if they tried to go back and re-collect them, the samples would not match the interview data, and an incredible amount of time would be lost. They kept the generator going for five days before making an arrangement with SUNY researchers to meet them at a halfway point, where they handed over the samples and the chains of custody. Shortly after, the lab was able to begin processing the samples.

Since the serum was the only part of the blood analyzed, once the samples began running, the Mohawks insisted anything left over be destroyed. The reason, Loralee explained, was "so somebody couldn't come in and say 'oh, well, you're not using these red blood cells, I'll just take them for my study,'" thereby conducting research with Mohawk blood that Mohawks might not approve of and that could prove detrimental to them.[13]

The Mohawk tribe's fear of having their blood misappropriated for unauthorized testing is not unfounded: the Havasupi tribe in Arizona took part in a study focused on diabetes, only to learn their blood samples had been used in research on schizophrenia and consanguinity, as well as migration theories. The community felt deeply betrayed that they had allowed their blood to be collected for a project that was supposed to help them, and the samples were then used without their permission to conduct a study they did not agree with. Rather than punishing the scientists who had participated in this betrayal, the system rewarded them. The geneticist who was the key person responsible for the misuse of the blood samples was awarded the Presidential Award for Excellence in Science, Mathematics, and Engineer Mentoring, followed by a million-dollar NIEHS grant (LaDuke 2005; TallBear 2013). A similar betrayal happened to the Nuu-chah-nulth tribe, who agreed to a study on rheumatoid arthritis, but whose samples were then sent around the world, contributing to hundreds of academic papers on controversial topics such as the spread of lymphotrophic viruses by intravenous drug use, and research on human migrations (TallBear 2013).

To some scientists, especially those convinced of their own ethics and good intentions, these fears may seem paranoid. Akwesasne is clearly a Native American community, culturally, ethnically, linguistically, politically, and – as their citizenship records with blood quantum requirements would show – "racially." But Akwesasne has a long-standing, well-founded distrust of New York state and the neighboring industrial plants. Episodes of direct conflict between Akwesasne Mohawks and the state government are still recent in the community memory, and so the possibility of being maltreated at the genetic level as well does not seem farfetched.

Civic dislocation

Throughout the clean-up process, their interactions with the state and federal agencies reaffirmed for members of the Akwesasne community their impression that these entities were not working in their best interest. In many instances, Mohawks experienced what Sheila Jasanoff calls "civic dislocation," which she defines as

> a mismatch between what governmental institutions were supposed to do for the public, and what they did in reality. In the dislocated state, trust in government vanished and people looked to other institutions ... for information and advice to restore their security. It was as if the gears of democracy had spun loose, causing citizens, at least temporarily, to disengage from the state. (Jasanoff 1997)

The dislocated state is characterized by a breakdown in communication between the government and its citizens, and doubt that the government is playing the role it should of protecting the public "against the complex uncertainties of the modern condition" (Jasanoff 1997, 223). Without the ability to assure the public of this protection, public institutions lose legitimacy, and other entities sometimes step in, or are created, to ensure safety. Akwesasro:non have had a contentious relationship with New York state and the US federal government for more than two centuries, and this was further compounded by the lack of support they felt they were receiving for the clean-up. Of the Akwesasne community members I interviewed, several articulated a general distrust of the state

and federal governments, and others took the view a step further with the belief
that these entities were actively working to undermine Akwesasne.

Like other communities fighting for environmental justice, Akwesasne suffered through mitigation politics, fighting against a powerful corporation whose
main goal was to protect its bottom line, and working both against and alongside state and federal agencies – agencies that were in many cases underfunded,
understaffed, and mired in bureaucracy, and whose interests were sometimes
influenced by industry. What made Akwesasne different from other communities fighting similar corporate powers was that, as a tribal nation, the Saint Regis
Mohawk Tribe had federally ensured rights and powers to dictate clean-up
levels on tribal land, and to have a seat at the table negotiating the site clean-up.
Given the previous two and a half centuries of history in which Mohawks clashed
with settler colonial powers regarding jurisdiction over and governance of the
Akwesasne Mohawk community, that they were able to develop and assert their
own environmental governance, and then collaborate with entities in New York
state, is indeed impressive and important.

Conclusion

What does it mean to be a "citizen," as distinct from a professional scientist, and
what about when citizen scientists do not necessarily feel they share nationhood
and citizenship with the scientists with whom they are working? As described
above, citizenship at Akwesasne is complicated. Many of these citizen scientists
are tribal citizens first. The Akwesasne Task Force on the Environment worked
to bring together people from all of the various political entities in the community
to form one grassroots organization that would govern research at Akwesasne.
The Mohawks who founded this organization, which includes both professional
scientists and amateur scientists, sought to work toward the broader goal of a
healthier community and a cleaner environment. They fought against the distinctions of "citizen" and "scientist" – as noted above, Katsi insisted that women did
not need to have degrees to be trained in data collection, and "there's not going
to be any one of you researchers that stand taller than the Mohawk mothers."
The binaries between citizen and scientist, between subject and researcher, were
blurred through this research process (as Katsi insisted, "We're not going to be
guinea pigs"). This is just one more way in which Akwesasne as a case study in
CBPR and citizen science leads us to intentionally consider the social, cultural,
and political processes that structure research in an Indigenous community.

Political scientist Kevin Bruyneel (2007) refers to this resistance to existing solely inside or outside the system as a "third space of sovereignty." Similar

to Indigenous nations that have for centuries demanded rights and resources from the settler state while also challenging its impositions on them, Mohawks resisted the binary of researcher/subject, citizen/scientist, to create a third space of sovereignty in the context of research, in which they refused the subjugated role to which communities under study are commonly relegated. Through the creation of the ATFE Research Advisory Committee (RAC), Akwesasne community members took a position of authority in the research process. They did not reject the institutions of science altogether, recognizing the need for this type of knowledge. But neither did they agree to a conventional research study. Instead, they created the ATFE RAC, a new community governance body, and developed a hybrid research model that has in recent years been emulated in increasing numbers of community-based research projects. Within this third space, Mohawks and SUNY researchers navigated the challenges of different identities, loyalties, and affiliations, and created room for a new research culture at the beginning of the CBPR movement.

But at the same time that Mohawks were fighting for this blurring of the lines between citizen and scientists, as well as for a recognition of the different experiences they held as citizens of a tribal nation, they were also fighting for a recognition of ecological citizenship, for a recognition that maintaining a Mohawk way of life requires reciprocal relationships with other-than-human elements to whom citizenship rights need to be extended as well. As ATFE members describe, "Conventional risk assessments are severely limited in their application to Native peoples because they fail to adequately value cultural, social, subsistence, economic, and spiritual factors" (Tarbell and Arquette 2000, 102). Mohawk philosophy espouses a precautionary approach, a paradigm of holistic, risk-based decision making, which is more protective of a wider range of "citizens" under an ecological citizenship mode.

Notes

1   OED Online, s.v. "citizen." www.oed.com (accessed February 21, 2017).
2   Alcoa acquired Reynolds in 2000, renaming the site Alcoa East.
3   Chicken containing more than 3 ppm of PCBs is considered unfit for human consumption, and over 50 ppm qualifies as toxic waste.
4   The two labs returned similar results, and future samples were processed in Albany.
5   The National Institute of Environmental Health Sciences (NIEHS) Superfund Research Program (SRP) (prior to a name change in 2009, the program was called Superfund Basic Research Program), funds university-based multidisciplinary teams to conduct research on human health and environmental issues related to hazardous substances (National Institute of Environmental Health Sciences (NIEHS), n.d.).

6   H.R. 2005 Superfund Amendments and Reauthorization Act of 1986, https://www.congress.gov/bill/99th-congress/house-bill/2005. See also Du Bey and Grijalva (1993–1994).
7   US Environmental Protection Agency, "Applicable or Relevant and Appropriate Requirements (ARARs)," https://www.epa.gov/superfund.
8   Saint Regis Mohawk Tribal Council, Resolution No. 89-19, "A Resolution of the Saint Regis Mohawk Tribal Council Adopting Ambient Standards for PCBs on the Saint Regis Mohawk Reservation," 1989, cited in Lewis and DelVecchio (2007). As a side note, all of the land contaminated by GM is Mohawk territory and considered within the land claims territory. However, for legal purposes, the Tribe's standards for PCB clean-up could be applied only to land technically within the current boundaries of the reservation.
9   Jim Ransom, e-mail communication with author, June 9, 2015.
10   George Pavlou, associate director for New York programs for the EPA, stated at a public meeting held April 25, 1990, regarding the GM Central Foundry Division Superfund site in Massena: "Please bear in mind that EPA Regulations recognize that the Tribe is a sovereign state and require that we apply their standards for any cleanups that we undertake on Akwesasne lands. The law is very specific in requiring EPA to apply the more stringent requirements be it State or Federal for Superfund cleanups." See "Public Meeting" (1990, 6).
11   For full quote, see Hoover (2017b, 9).
12   Citations were found in Web of Science.
13   Saliva samples collected for the most recent study on reproductive health were returned to the tribal health center in 2014 for their disposal (Schell 2015).

References

Akwesasne Task Force on the Environment 1996. Akwesasne Good Mind Research Protocol. First published in *Akwesasne Notes*, available at https://reo.mcmaster.ca/download/akwesasne.pdf (last accessed February 6, 2020).
Akwesasne Task Force on the Environment 1997. Superfund clean-up at Akwesasne: A case study in environmental justice. *International Journal of Contemporary Sociology*, 34(2), 267–290.
Andrews, R. 1989. Ruin on the reservation. *Post Standard*, pp. 4–6.
Bonney, R., Cooper, C. B., Dickinson, J., Kelling, S., Phillips, T., Rosenberg, K. V., and Shirk, J. 2009. Citizen science: A developing tool for expanding science knowledge and scientific literacy. *BioScience*, 59(11), 977–984. DOI: 10.1525/bio.2009.59.11.9.
Brown, P. 1992. Popular epidemiology and toxicwaste contamination: Lay and professionalways of knowing. *Journal of Health and Social Behavior*, 33(3), 267. DOI: 10.2307/2137356.
Brown, P., Brody, J. G., Morello-Frosch, R., Tovar, J., Zota, A. R., and Rudel, R. A. 2011. Measuring the success of community science: The Northern California Household

Exposure Study. *Environmental Health Perspectives*, 120(3), 326–331. DOI: 10.1289/ehp.1103734.

Bruyneel, K. 2007. *The Third Space of Sovereignty: The Postcolonial Politics of U.S.–Indigenous Relations*. Minneapolis: University of Minnesota Press.

Burhansstipanov L., Christopher, S., and Schumacher, A. 2005. Lessons learned from community-based participatory research in Indian country. *Cancer Control*, 12(S2), 70–76.

Cochran, P. A. L., Marshall, C. A., Garcia-Downing, C., Kendall, E., Cook, D., McCubbin, L., and Gover, R. M. S. 2008. Indigenous ways of knowing: Implications for participatory research and community. *American Journal of Public Health*, 98(1), 22–27.

Cohen, B. and Ottinger, G. 2011. Introduction: Environmental justice and the transformation of science and engineering. In G. Ottinger and B. R. Cohen (eds), *Technoscience and Environmental Justice*. Cambridge, MA: MIT Press, pp. 1–18. DOI: 10.7551/mitpress/9780262015790.003.0001.

Cook, K. 2005. Interview with Katsi Cook, conducted by Janet Follett. http://www.smith.edu/library/libs/ssc/vof/transcripts/Cook.pdf.

Cook, K. 2008. Interview with Katsi Cook, conducted by Elizabeth Hoover. Syracuse, NY.

Cook, K. 2015. Critical contexts: Research to support community environmental reproductive health. Keynote speech delivered at the Social Science Environmental Health Research Institute conference, Northeastern University, Boston, May 21, 2015.

Cook, K. and Nelson, L. 1986. Mohawk women resist industrial pollution. *Indian Time*, January 9, p. 6.

Corburn, J. 2005. *Street Science? Community Knowledge and Environmental Health Justice*. Cambridge, MA: MIT Press.

Du Bey, R. and Grijalva, J. 1993–1994. Closing the circle: Tribal implementation of the Superfund Program in the reservation environment. *Journal of Natural Resources and Environmental Law*, 9, 279–296.

Epstein, S. 2007. *Inclusion: The Politics of Difference in Medical Research*. Chicago: University of Chicago Press.

Fisher, P. A., and Ball, T. J. 2003. Tribal participatory research: Mechanisms of a collaborative model. *American Journal of Community Psychology*, 32, 207–216.

Fitzgerald, E. F., Hwang, S.-A., Brix, K. A., B., B., J., Q., and Cook, K. 1992. *Chemical Contaminants in the Milk of Mohawk Women from Akwesasne*. Report for the Health Risk Assessment of the General Motors Central Foundry Division Superfund Waste. Albany: New York State Department of Health.

Gallagher, D. R. 2009. Advocates for environmental justice: The role of the champion in public participation implementation. *Local Environment*, 14(10), 905–916. DOI: 10.1080/13549830903244417.

Gallo, M. V., Ravenscroft, J., Carpenter, D. O., Frye, C., Cook, B., and Schell, L M. 2016. Endocrine disrupting chemicals and ovulation: Is there a relationship? *Environmental Research*, 17(151), 410–418. DOI: 10.1016/j.envres.2016.08.007.

Grinde, D. A., Johansen, B. E., and Zinn, H. 1995. *Ecocide of Native America: Environmental Destruction of Indian Lands and Peoples*. Santa Fe, NM: Clear Light Publishers.

Haraway, D. 1988. Situated knowledges: The science question in feminism and the privilege of partial perspective. *Feminist Studies*, 14(3), 575. DOI: 10.2307/3178066.

Havens, K. and Henderson, S. 2013. Citizen science takes root. *American Scientist*, 101(5), 378. DOI: 10.1511/2013.104.378.

Holifield, R. 2012. Environmental justice as recognition and participation in risk assessment: Negotiating and translating health risk at a Superfund Site in Indian country. *Annals of the Association of American Geographers*, 102(3), 591–613.

Hoover, E. 2013. Cultural and health implications of fish advisories in a Native American community. *Ecological Processes*, 2(4). DOI: 10.1186/2192-1709-2-4. Available at http://www.ecologicalprocesses.com/content/2/1/4/abstract (last accessed February 6, 2020).

Hoover, E. 2016. "We're not going to be guinea pigs": Citizen science and environmental health in a Native American community" *Journal of Science Communication*, 15(1). Available at http://jcom.sissa.it/archive/15/01/JCOM_1501_2016_A05 (last accessed February 6, 2020).

Hoover, E. 2017a. *The River Is in Us; Fighting Toxics in a Mohawk Community*. Minneapolis: University of Minnesota Press.

Hoover, E. 2017b. Environmental reproductive justice: Intersections in an American Indian community impacted by environmental contamination. *Environmental Sociology*. DOI: 10.1080/23251042.2017.1381898.

Hoover, E., Brown, P., Edelstein, M., and Renauld, M. 2015. Social science collaboration with environmental health. *Environmental Health Perspectives*. DOI:10.1289 http://ehp.niehs.nih.gov/1409283/.

Hoover, E., Cook, K., Plain, R., Sanchez, K., Waghiyi, V., Miller, P., Dufault, R., Sislin, C., and Carpenter, D. O. 2012. Indigenous peoples of North America: Environmental exposures and reproductive justice. *Environmental Health Perspectives*, 120, 1645–1649.

Irwin, A. 1995. *Citizen Science: A Study of People, Expertise and Sustainable Development*. Hove: Psychology Press.

Jasanoff, S. 1997. Civilization and madness: The great BSE scare of 1996." *Public Understanding of Science*, 6(3), 221–232.

Jordan, R. C., Ballard, H. L., and Phillips, T. B. 2012. Key issues and new approaches for evaluating citizen-science learning outcomes. *Frontiers in Ecology and the Environment*, 10(6), 307–309. DOI: 10.1890/110280.

LaDuke, W. 2005. *Recovering the Sacred: The Power of Naming and Claiming*. Saint Paul, MN: South End Press.

LaVeaux, D. and Christopher, S. 2009. Contextualizing CBPR: Key principles of CBPR Meet the Indigenous Research Context. *Pimatisiwin*, 7(1), 1–25.

Leach, M. and Scoones, I. 2005. Science and citizenship in a global context. In B. Wynne, I. Scoones, and M. Leach (eds), *Science and Citizens: Globalization and the Challenge of Engagement*. London: Zed Books, pp. 15–38.

Lewis, C. and DelVecchio, R. 2007. *Data Report: PCBs in Garden Soils of Akwesasne*. Report prepared for the Environment Division, Saint Regis Mohawk Tribe, April 17, 2007. http://www.srmtenv.org/web_docs.

Lex, B. W. and Norris, J. R. 1999. Health status of American Indian and Alaska Native women. In A. C. Mastroianni, R. Faden, and D. Federman (eds), *Women and Health Research: Ethical and Legal Issues of Including Women in Clinical Studies*, vol. 2. Washington, DC: National Academies Press, pp. 192–215.

Miller, P. K., Waghiyi, V., Welfinger-Smith, G., Byrne, S. C., Kava, J., Gologergen, J., Eckstein, L., Scrudato, R., Chiarenzelli, J., Carpenter, D. O., and Seguinot-Medina, S. 2013. Community-based participatory research projects and policy engagement to protect environmental health on St. Lawrence Island, Alaska. *International Journal of Circumpolar Health*, 72. DOI: 10.3402/ijch.v72i0.21656.

Minkler, M. and Wallerstein, N. (eds) 2008. *Community-Based Participatory Research for Health: From Process to Outcomes* (2nd edn). San Francisco, CA: Jossey-Bass.

Morton, D. J., Proudfit, J., Calac, D., Portillo, M., Lofton-Fitzsimmons, G., Molina, T., Flores, R., LawsonRisso, B., and Majel-McCauley, R. 2013. Creating research capacity through a tribally based institutional review board. *American Journal of Public Health*, 103(12), 2160–2164.

National Institute of Environmental Health Sciences (NIEHS), n.d. NIEHS Superfund Research Program. Available at https://www.niehs.nih.gov/research/supported/centers/srp/index.cfm (last accessed February 14, 2020).

"Public Meeting General Motors Corporation Central Foundry Division Superfund Site" 1990. Transcript. Massena, New York, April 25, 1990.

Ramirez-Andreotta, M. D., Brusseau, M. L., Artiola, J. F., Maier, R. M., and Gandolfi, A. J. 2014) Environmental research translation: Enhancing interactions with communities at contaminated sites. *The Science of the Total Environment*, 497-498, 651–664. DOI: 10.1016/j.scitotenv.2014.08.021.

Ranco, D. J., O'Neill, C. A., Donatuto, J., and Harper, B. L. 2011. Environmental Justice, American Indians, and the cultural dilemma: developing environmental management for tribal health and well-being. *Environmental Justice*, 4(4), 221–230.

Riesch, H., Potter, C., and Davies, L. 2013. Combining citizen science and public engagement: The Open AirLaboratories Programme. *JCOM*, 12(3), 1–19. Available at http://jcom.sissa.it/archive/12/3-4/JCOM1203%282013%29A03 (last accessed February 6, 2020).

Schell, L. 2015. Personal communication, October 12.

Schell, L. M., Ravenscroft, J., Gallo, M., and Denham, M. 2007. Advancing biocultural models by working with communities: A partnership approach. *American Journal of Human Biology: The Official Journal of the Human Biology Council*, 19(4), 511–524. DOI: 10.1002/ajhb.20611.

Schell, L. M. and Tarbell, A. M. 1998. A partnership study of PCBs and the health of Mohawk youth: lessons from our past and guidelines for our future. *Environmental Health Perspectives*, 106(suppl. 3), 833–840.

Schnarch, B. 2004. Ownership, control, access, and possession (OCAP) or self-determination applied to research: A critical analysis of contemporary First Nations research and some options for First Nations communities. *Journal of Aboriginal Health*, 1(1), 80–95.

Shepard, P. M. 2002. Advancing environmental justice through community-based participatory research. *Environmental Health Perspectives*, 110 (suppl. 2), 139.

"Superfund Proposed Plan General Motors Corporation Central Foundry Division" 1991. Hogansburg, NY, June 26, 1991, 12, transcript provided by the EPA Office of Public Affairs.

TallBear, K. 2013. *Native American DNA: Tribal Belonging and the False Promise of Genetic Science*. Minneapolis: University of Minnesota Press.

Tarbell, A. and Arquette, M. 2000. Akwesasne: A Native American community's resistance to cultural and environmental damage. In R. Hofrichter (ed.), *Reclaiming the Environmental Debate: The Politics of Health in a Toxic Culture*. Cambridge, MA: MIT Press, pp. 93–111.

United States Environmental Protection Agency. 2004. *Tribal Superfund Program Needs Clear Direction and Actions to Improve Effectiveness*. Evaluation Report No. 2004-P-00035. US Fish and Wildlife Service, Natural Resource.

Whyte, K. P. 2013. Justice forward: Tribes, climate adaptation and responsibility. *Climatic Change*, 120, 517–530.

Whyte, K. P. 2017. Indigenous food sovereignty, renewal, and US settler colonialism. In M. Rawlinson and C. Ward (eds), *The Routledge Handbook of Food Ethics*. Abingdon: Routledge, pp. 354–365.

Wiebe, S. M. 2016. *Everyday Exposure*. Vancouver: UBC Press.

Woolley, J. P., McGowan, M. L., Teare, H. J. A., Coathup, V., Fishman, J. R., Settersten Jr., R. A., Sterckx, S., Kaye, J., and Juengst, E. T. 2016. Citizen science or scientific citizenship? Disentangling the uses of public engagement rhetoric in national research initiatives. *BMC Medical Ethics*, 17(33). DOI: 10.1186/s12910-016-0117-1.

Wylie, S. A., Jalbert, K., Dosemagen, S., and Ratto, M. 2014. Institutions for civic technoscience: How critical making is transforming environmental research. *The Information Society*, 30(2), 116–126. DOI: 10.1080/01972243.2014.875783.

12

Modes of engagement: Reframing "sensing" and data generation in citizen science for empowering relationships

João Porto de Albuquerque and André Albino de Almeida

Introduction

The dissemination of digital technologies has provoked a renewed interest in initiatives that seek to involve citizens and communities in the generation of data and in "citizen science." The aim of these initiatives is often to widen participation by including citizens in processes hitherto not very accessible to them, such as the collaborative mapping of human settlements (de Albuquerque et al. 2016), data collection for scientific research (Haklay 2013a), or the data gathering in Citizen Observatories (Degrossi et al. 2014), which can be used to support claims for environmental justice (Mah 2017). In the age of "big data" and "data-driven" decision making, the availability of mobile phones, often equipped with GPS receivers, gives rise to the alluring vision of 6 billion "citizens as sensors" – according to the influential term coined by Goodchild (2007) – who are able to generate "volunteered geographic information" with a level of precision that was only possible before with the aid of highly specialized instruments and by means of specific scientific practices (e.g., those of cartographers and surveyors).

The potential for democratization and empowerment through digital participation and citizen-generated data has not only been acknowledged by grassroots organizations and activist groups but is also being increasingly advocated by a wide range of mainstream actors such as governmental agencies involved in disaster risk management (Wehn et al. 2015), smart city initiatives (Townsend 2013), and humanitarian organizations working on crisis management (Givoni 2016), as well as international organizations involved in sustainable urban development such as the United Nations Programme for Human Settlements (UN-Habitat 2016). However, alongside this acknowledgment of the potential benefits of citizen-generated data, there is a growing body of literature that offers more critical perspectives. For instance, a number of researchers have pointed to structural barriers in society that may prevent some social groups from producing or interpreting big data (Mah 2017). This could create a "delusion of democratization" (Haklay 2013b) by only extending participation to a relatively homogeneous group of citizens, and is thus unable to effectively overcome the problem of marginalization (Dourish 2016). Furthermore, the designed technologies may involve externally defined "programmes of participation" (Gabrys 2016), that carry out predefined practices of data production which do not necessarily allow contestation or empowerment (Perkins 2014).

In summary, recent research studies have made clear that citizen sensing projects are ridden with an ambivalent character. From one perspective, the production of data by citizens is associated with *empowerment*: digital technologies can enable citizens to produce data that reflects alternative and counter-hegemonic views of the world, and thus lead to the opening up of more inclusive and polyvocal information spaces. From another perspective, the digital technologies and data collection processes may entail *instrumentality*: citizens are invited to act as mere "data providers," as kinds of ersatz sensors – that is, their role is confined to capturing environmental signals, which are then used in ways that are frequently opaque and outside their control and accountability. In our view, these contradictory perspectives can be attributed to the intrinsic ambivalence of citizen sensing. This ambivalence is embedded in the connotations of the very terms used to describe this activity: the sensor metaphor when applied to citizens can mean either a *heightened* capacity to perceive phenomena and articulate an alternative worldview (and thus results in *empowerment*); or it can connote a *reduction* in citizens' capabilities that are constrained to mimic a technical sensorial device and capture (mostly predefined) environmental signals (and thus implies *instrumentality*).

In this chapter, we argue that this ambivalence can only be properly understood by reframing the way we think about citizen science and citizen sensing so that it includes considerations about the *process* and *mode* in which citizens are engaged, particularly in data generation. This is a topical issue since it has been suggested that we live in a "post-truth" era, which implies that the most common justification for data gathering – based on the grounds that data constitutes the epistemological basis of scientific "truth" – can no longer be taken for granted by everyone as being self-evident.

By resorting to the critical pedagogy developed by the Brazilian educator Paulo Freire (Freire 1987, 2000, 2001; Freire and Faundez 1985), we seek here to provide a fresh perspective on the role of "sensing" and data generation within citizen science. This perspective will be able to account for the ambivalences outlined above by shedding light on the critical importance of the way citizens take part in these processes, particularly when they involve marginalized and disadvantaged groups of people. Furthermore, the purpose of our critical pedagogical approach is to contribute to citizen science theory and practice by proposing an additional set of ethical-methodological criteria that are aimed at establishing empowering relationships.

In the remainder of the chapter, we begin by putting forward our new perspective on citizen sensing by entering into a dialogue with Freire's critical pedagogy. Following this, we discuss particular insights that this perspective can bring to citizen sensing through three groups of concepts based on Freire's work. Finally, we suggest conclusions from our arguments.

Citizen sensing from a critical pedagogical perspective

We believe a change is needed in the conceptual approach to citizen sensing if we are to properly understand the nature of the ambivalence discussed in the previous section. The generation of data by citizens is usually viewed through an *epistemological lens*: digital technologies enable the generation of new data, which acquire the epistemic function of information by providing access to a "reality" which was previously unknown or inaccessible. This is frequently referred to as the citizen's "local knowledge." However, we believe that this epistemological lens is insufficient for understanding and designing citizen sensing initiatives for two key reasons.

First, there is a need to understand "sensing" as being embedded in a wider set of "sense making" practices. The practice of sensing the environment using digital tools involves a specific "framing" (Callon 1998; Lury 2004) of the complex relationships established in citizen sensing initiatives, which include objects, citizens, technologies, coding schemes, researchers, and so forth. This epistemological framing is generally used to explain and foster citizen sensing projects and highlights the practices that render the sensed objects knowable (through data generation) at the same time as constituting citizens as knowing/knowledgeable subjects. However, a number of other relationships established in citizen sensing initiatives necessarily fall outside the epistemological framing, in particular those that include the relationships established between citizens and the researchers who designed/deployed them (understood here as the leading agents of the citizen sensing initiative, who could be scientists, government policy makers, or grassroots leaders). In other words, this framing acts as an epistemological lens that magnifies some specific aspects of the citizen sensing practices related to the sensed objects, data, and citizens; however, it devotes much less attention to other aspects, such as those related to the role of researchers and their relationship with citizens.

Second, we seek to investigate here the *process* by which these relationships between citizens, digital technologies, and researchers are established, thus going beyond epistemological concerns. For it is only through a careful analysis of this process – that is, of the *modes of engagement* between citizens and researchers mediated by digital technology – that we will be able to gain a proper understanding of the ambivalent perspectives regarding citizen sensing discussed earlier.

In light of this, we propose here a *pedagogical lens* to citizen sensing. This means departing from the traditional view of citizen sensing as synonymous with "data gathering" of the epistemological framing. In contrast, we think that citizen sensing should be embedded in a process of knowledge co-production, only one component of which is the generation of data, albeit an important one. However, it should be noted that "pedagogy" for us means more than a mere transfer of knowledge from teacher to learner; we seek to understand the active role and particular circumstances of citizens, as well as to recognize their value as co-producers of knowledge. To achieve this, we resort here to the critical pedagogy of the Brazilian educator Paulo Freire.

Freire developed his critical pedagogical approach, which is introduced in his seminal book *Pedagogy of the Oppressed*, in the 1960s and 1970s, when he worked on adult literacy programs for the poor communities of Brazil and other countries in South America. One of the key features of this approach is a radical opposition to what Freire calls the "banking model of education": a pedagogical conception in which the teacher acts as the sole custodian of knowledge and makes "deposits" into the empty minds of learners. Although the critique of conceptions of education as "knowledge transfer" are not confined to Freire, his concern with the particular circumstances of the "oppressed" and the way he structures his critical arguments are of great value to rethinking about sensing and data generation in citizen science, especially when marginalized groups of people are involved.

In the following sections, we explore three groups of selected conceptual contributions made by Freire's critical pedagogy which are particularly valuable in providing innovative perspectives on citizen sensing.

Toward a pedagogy of questions

Freire described his approach as a "pedagogy of questions" (Freire and Faundez 1985), which he contrasts with the traditional "pedagogy of answers" of the banking model of education, that is, a process of inducing the learners to provide answers in ways and at times that are determined by the teachers. An analogy can be made here with the instrumental modes of engagement in citizen sensing in which citizens are expected to provide answers – that is, input specific data – in response to a set of predefined questions that are prompted by the interfaces of the digital technologies employed. Thus, it will be useful to describe in some detail the terms in which Freire defines his approach.

In Freire's view, a kind of education that prepares individuals to give answers to predetermined questions is basically grounded on a *dehumanizing antagonism* between the educator and learners. On the one hand, the educator is the person who knows, thinks, speaks, and acts. On the other, the learners are considered absolutely ignorant, as they are thought (instead of thinking), hear (instead of speaking), and have the illusion of acting by means of the actions of the educators. As Freire argues:

> [T]here is an undeniable relationship between wonderment and asking questions, taking risks and existence. At root, human existence involves wonderment, questioning and risk. And, because of all this, it involves action and transformation. Bureaucratisation, however, means adaptation with a minimum of risk, with no wonderment and without asking questions. And so we have a pedagogy of answers, which is a pedagogy of adaptation, not a pedagogy of creativity. It does not encourage people to take the risk of inventing and reinventing. For me, to refuse to take risks is the best way there is of denying the human existence itself. (Freire and Faundez 1985, 51, own translation, compared with Freire and Faundez 1989, 40)

The state of passivity imposed on learners by a "pedagogy of answers" thus degrades them into "adaptive beings." By being confined to receiving "deposits," and then storing them and filing them, the learners "tend to adapt to the world, to the partial aspects of reality contained in the received deposits" (2005 [1970], 68). In this kind of relationship, the learners are only expected to memorize but not reflect, and thus their role is confined to giving answers to questions made by others, who are the only ones able to assess if they are correct. Learners are thus deprived of a capacity to ask questions and hence to wonder and marvel about their environment. From Freire's standpoint, these are the necessary conditions for the creativity and risk-taking that characterize not only a true pedagogical process but human existence itself. This is why the antagonistic relationship established by the "pedagogy of the answer" *dehumanizes* not only the learners (oppressed), but also the teachers (oppressors).

Freire's critical arguments and sharp distinctions in his pedagogical concepts are useful to our analysis of citizen sensing. In this context, when pedagogical issues are raised, they tend to center on critiques of expectations put on citizens to receive "training" so that they can act as competent "smart citizens" (Gabrys 2016, 2010). This is connected to the frequent concerns with the quality of data resulting from citizen sensing (Degrossi et al. 2018), in response to which some initiatives include the training of citizens in the ability to carry out high-quality data collection (Bordogna et al. 2014). However, the task of decision making about which data to collect and defining the criteria for assessing the quality of the data are often assumed to be the sole remit of researchers, as pointed out by Haklay (2013a). This is analogous to Freire's critical comments on the "pedagogy of the answer," and the resulting expectations from citizens bear a passive, instrumental character similar to those of sensor devices that must be calibrated to provide appropriate measurements of environmental variables.

However, it should be stressed here that we do not believe that this kind of passive/instrumental relationship with citizens only takes place when citizen participation is focused on data collection (even if it is perhaps most visible in these cases). A number of hierarchical typologies of tasks in citizen science were proposed in previous research – for example, by Haklay (2013a) and Cardullo and Kitchin (2017) – which commonly assume that effective participation can only be achieved when they are involved in "higher" types of tasks, such as research design.

In contrast, from our pedagogic perspective, the instrumental character of sensing is caused by a specific framing of the relations of citizens and digital technologies, which can also take place when they are expected to participate in other (and perhaps more complex or elaborate) tasks, including, for instance, the analysis of the data or the definition of environmental variables. Following Freire, we believe that the determining factor is not the particular task undertaken by citizens – in opposition to the typologies of participation defined by Haklay (2013a) and Cardullo and Kitchin (2017) – but the *mode of engagement* established and whether this enables citizens to wonder about and reflect upon their environment, and thus be prepared to take the risk of being creative and posing questions while engaging in citizen sensing. With a view to examining this mode of engagement in further detail, we now turn our attention to a different aspect of the role of citizens in the next section.

Asymmetry, directedness, and cultural invasion

Another important set of concepts that will be of value, when rethinking citizen sensing, comes from an important distinction. Although Freire's dialogical approach is fundamentally based on a critique of antagonistic relations between educators and learners and a reframing of their roles, these two roles are never fused into a single category. The distinctive roles in the pedagogical process (between educator and learner), as well as in citizen sensing (between citizen and scientist) are asymmetrical. This asymmetry should be considered carefully, as it is particularly important with regard to the contributions made by the participants in citizen sensing.

According to Freire, the raison d'etre of the pedagogical act means that educators must play a differential role which is distinctively marked by a *directive* character:

> A non-directive form of education does not exist because the very nature of education is based on directedness. However, even though the educators are not neutral and must direct, in their role of educators, this does not mean that they should manipulate the learner in the name of knowledge that they already know *a priori*, that is, *a priori* from the standpoint of the learner. (Freire 1987, 41, own translation)

The educator and the learner should educate each other in a dialogical process. This is indispensable to what Freire considers to be an existential human condition: that of mankind comprising "unfinished beings" or the "ontological vocation of human beings to be more" (Freire 1997, 14). Although they share the same existential condition, the roles of educator and learner do not coincide completely but retain an asymmetric character within the dialogical process (the word "dialogue" etymologically rests upon the distinction of two in the Greek prefix *dia*). By analogy, an asymmetrical relationship cannot be ignored in citizen sensing, as scientists and citizens do not play the same role.

Nevertheless, it should be noted that Freire is not suggesting that the asymmetry between educator/learner involves either a hierarchy or antagonism. A fierce critic of the antagonistic system of traditional education (examined in the previous section), the author even suggests using the binomial terms "educator-learner" and "leaner-educator" to make clear that both roles educate as well as learn from each other (Freire 2000). However, the use of a different order in the binomial for each role makes clear that they do not completely overlap. Freire points this out clearly and argues that if one assumes there is an overlap of educators and learners, it would simply change the error of authoritarianism, made in traditional conceptions of education, with an error of "spontaneism," in which "with the aim of not imposing a truth, we end up having nothing to propose and if we simply refuse to do this, nothing else is left to be truthfully done in the educative practice" (Freire and Faundez 1985, 41).

Freire argues that there is another consequence of denying the asymmetric condition of educators and learners, which is of particular relevance to our reflections on citizen sensing. If the two roles are assumed to be identical or antagonistic (in the sense explored in the previous section), it becomes impossible to take into consideration the cultural background of the learner, and as a result the "culture" of the educator is often the only one acknowledged in this relationship. Freire criticizes this position as resulting in a "cultural invasion":

> In cultural invasion (as in all the modalities of antidialogical action) the invaders are the authors of and actors in, the process; those they invade are the objects. The invaders choose; those they invade follow that choice – or are expected to follow it. The invaders act; those they invade have only the illusion of acting, through the action of the invaders. (Freire 2000, 152)

The culturally invasive character of an anti-dialogical pedagogical process is thus largely caused by a static concept of culture as accumulated knowledge (in the educator) which has to be transferred to those that are empty of culture/knowledge (the learners). This results in a process in which "with the goal of preserving culture and knowledge, there is no truthful knowledge nor culture" (Freire 2005 [1970], 79).

These arguments are of great significance when thinking about citizen sensing initiatives. Following Freire, the instrumentality of some initiatives in citizen sensing discussed earlier can be attributed to a "culturally invasive" mode of engagement. This is caused by paying insufficient attention to the specific cultural background and worldviews of the citizens and communities involved. Paying attention here means being sensitive to the "otherness" of the epistemic and cultural practices of citizens/communities, to what Jasanoff (2007) calls "civic epistemologies." In addition, it means acknowledging that the definitions of the environmental objects that have to be sensed, and their potential properties/attributes, are a part of "ontological politics" (Mol 1999), that is, the assumptions about the basic elements that constitute the world reflect particular worldviews and therefore carry political implications. It should be emphasized that these ontological assumptions are often unquestioned and regarded as universal and neutral frames of reference associated with "Nature," as argued by Latour (1993) and others.

However, as da Costa Marques (2014) sharply points out, frames of reference of better-off social groups, "colonizers" usually stemming from the West/the global North, often clash with the perspectives and knowledge practices of the marginalized, or "colonized," who are often (but not entirely) located in the global South. As previous research in development studies has shown, digital technologies can embed assumptions and categories that are derived from the worldviews of the designers ("colonizers"), but these often do not coincide (or are not aligned) with the practices and perceptions of citizens from marginalized ("colonized") communities (de Albuquerque et al. 2013). Against this backdrop, it can be seen that Freire's critique of a culturally invasive pedagogy has an important bearing on the field of citizen sensing (particularly when it involves marginalized groups). The common assumption that scientific perspectives on the environment are neutral, and can thus form the basis for the design of digital sensing technologies, may, at the same time, lead to a devaluation of Indigenous/non-Western(ized) ways of knowing, living, and relating to the environment.

This resonates with the critical arguments made by Perkins (2014) when analyzing collaborative mapping platforms such as OpenStreetMap. Although these platforms enable individual and social mapping practices to be carried out with a degree of flexibility (e.g., "tagging" an object with freely defined labels), the mapping is in fact constrained by fixed structures based on underlying assumptions that are much harder to change (e.g., particular types of mapping that are scripted by the interface). A similar tension between flexibility/openness (of contributions) and rigidity/closeness (of structures) has also been found in crowdsourcing platforms such as Wikipedia (Tkacz 2014) and in the use of diagrams to model work practices (de Albuquerque and Christ 2015). In contrast, looking at this question from Freire's pedagogical perspective leads to a shift in perspective toward the relationships that are established between scientists, citizens, and the kind of structural/closed features of the digital technologies that are employed for citizen sensing. If there is an antagonism between scientists and citizens where the culture of the latter is not acknowledged or else is undervalued, the assumptions embedded in sensing technologies will indeed act as a culturally invasive instrument. Although citizens are given the opportunity to generate data and thus "speak," they do so by following the possibilities foreseen in extraneously designed digital technologies, which in turn rest on a set of non-problematized (and potentially problematic) ontological assumptions and interests. Citizens are apparently given a voice while in fact they are more likely acting as a ventriloquist's dummy for those who shape the sensing technologies and frame what is "sensed' and how.

However, Freire's thinking not only enables us to have a clear picture of the perils of establishing culturally invasive relationships in citizen sensing but, most importantly, it opens up pathways to forging more emancipatory and empowering relationships – a point we will explore further in the next section.

The "risk of openness" as a constitutive tension

Freire's approach to overcoming antagonistic and potentially invasive educational methods involves establishing what he calls a dialogical and "problematizing" type of relationship, which, in our view, is particularly useful as a foundation for a new approach to citizen science and sensing. As pointed out earlier, Freire's aim is not to obliterate the differences between learner and teacher. Rather, an asymmetry between learner and teacher is essential to his approach, since it is this asymmetry that can configure the two required elements in the dialogue. By analogy, we argue here that the asymmetry between citizens and scientists should not be blurred in citizen sensing, but reconfigured based on Freire's pedagogy; in other words, the distinction between these two roles should be leveraged so that they can reconfigure not only their reciprocal relationships but also their relationship with knowledge.

Freire firmly opposes a view of knowledge that assumes a type of objectivity which is independent and precedes the educational process. Objectivity acquires, for Freire, the status of a "problem," a challenge that must be addressed by teacher and learner working together: "to live in openness toward others and to have an open-ended curiosity toward life and its challenges is essential to educational practice" (Freire 2001, 120). This practice requires a pedagogical process which is open-ended and risky, or even more, that entails what Freire calls the risk of being open (or available) to reality: "It is in openness to the world that I construct the inner security that is indispensable for that openness. It is impossible to live this openness to the world without inner security, just as it is impossible to have that security without taking the risk of being open" (Freire 2001, 120). Openness to the world (which in Freire's original words in Portuguese would be literally translated as "availability to reality") also means being available for or willing to have encounters with other human beings and things in a way that recognizes "Otherness" and respects differences. It is only through this openness to the Other and openness to take risks that confidence (and thus objectivity) can be dialectically established. A pedagogical process becomes culturally invasive if there is a denial of the risk that comes from being open to a relationship with the Other and with the world.

Being willing to take the "risk of openness" is thus a mandatory requirement for establishing emancipatory relationships in a pedagogical process. Drawing an analogy, we argue that accepting risks and being "available" to the Other and to Otherness is a mandatory requirement for undertaking truly participatory and emancipatory citizen sensing projects. The process of citizen sensing can only be an effective and inclusive mode of knowledge production by means of a truly dialogical process, rather than culturally invasive practices that instrumentalize and silence individuals and communities behind a facade of participation.

Freire's dialogical perspective reveals an intrinsic asymmetry (between the roles of scientist and citizen) and requires dealing with this asymmetry through openness and willingness to take the "risk of openness." Together, the intrinsic asymmetry and risks amount to a *constitutive tension* that must be acknowledged and embraced in citizen sensing practices that are inspired by a critical pedagogy. In our opinion, it is only by accepting this constitutive tension as an essential feature, and making it productive, that we will be able to carry out citizen science initiatives which lead to truly dialogical, emancipatory, and empowering forms of knowledge production.

Conclusion

We have sought to provide a new perspective on "sensing' in citizen science which departs from a widespread view that is focused on epistemological concerns, by entering into a dialogue with the pedagogical works of Paulo Freire. Initiatives that are based on citizen-generated data start with an encounter between two roles: the scientist (or leaders of the digital sensing project) and citizens (or the people who will generate the data). We established an analogy between these two roles and the roles of the pedagogical process: educator and learner. This analogy allows us to draw on concepts from Freire's critical pedagogy to reframe citizen sensing and, as a result, reveal an underlying "constitutive tension": the asymmetric condition between scientists and citizens requires an openness and willingness to face the risk of Otherness so as to be truly inclusive. Understanding the participative production of data, from Freire's perspective, entails paying attention to the form and means with which the *relationship* between scientist and citizen is established as a dialogical process – to the *modes of engagement* between citizens, scientists, and digital technologies.

By focusing on the modes of engagement engendered in citizen sensing, a new perspective is opened up on the ambivalent effects of citizen sensing between empowerment and instrumentality. Some of the previous critical studies of this question seem to suggest that this ambivalence can be explained by means of a differentiation between "good" and "bad" citizen sensing projects: if a project is designed to involve the "right" groups of people, taking part in the "appropriate" tasks of the process (data collection, analysis, or design), it entails empowerment; otherwise, instrumentality. However, Freire's dialogical perspective allows us to challenge this view by arguing that the ambivalence between empowerment and instrumentality reflects a *constitutive* tension that underlies *all* initiatives based on citizen-generated data – even if this tension has not been explicitly articulated nor theorized. The tension originates from the asymmetric roles of scientists and citizens and from the differences in their cultural and epistemic practices. Following Freire, it is only by acknowledging this constitutive tension and being open/"available" to face the risk of Otherness that citizen sensing will be able to promote a critical and inclusive knowledge production process that is truly empowering and capable of giving people a voice.

The exploration of citizen sensing through dialogue, on the basis of Freire's critical pedagogy, can elucidate areas in citizen sensing that bear some similarity to current critical studies of participation in citizen science and of recent "citizen-centric" smart city projects (Cardullo and Kitchin 2017; Gabrys 2016; Haklay 2013b). However, these studies represent an orthogonal line of argument to the points we made earlier, since the former focus their criticism on the lack of representation of certain social groups and on the types of tasks carried out by citizens. In contrast, the reframing of citizen science and sensing advocated here encompasses a critical appreciation of the extent to which current initiatives are establishing empowering relationships by taking account of the modes of engagement of citizens.

Clearly, the prevailing citizen science projects vary considerably in this regard: they range from projects based on environmental data gathering with digital technologies that are designed to supply scientific or government projects in largely instrumental ways – for example, in the Citizen Observatories reviewed by Wehn et al. (2015) – to environmental justice movements, where citizens play a leading role in community-based participatory research (see Brown; Allen; this volume). However, upon a closer look, the modes of engagement of the different people involved may vary even within a strongly participatory, citizen-led project. More often than not, a small group of people (often, white and male) is much more actively engaged in shaping the project and making its most critical decisions, which then form the basis on which the contributions of a much larger number of participants are made (see, for instance, the discussion of this issue in Wikipedia, in Tkacz 2014). Our Freirean perspective is thus not only aimed at highlighting the perils of disregarding the different types of asymmetries and inequality in citizen science projects (e.g., with regard to education, gender, economic power, and worldviews), but also proposing a dialogical approach as a means of dealing with them in a productive way. This approach can enable a "data pedagogy," with ways of carrying out citizen science projects that are able to leverage the realities, worldviews, and epistemologies of marginalized and disadvantaged people, which is likely to be particularly important in the "global South."

Furthermore, we hope that our critical pedagogical approach will pave the way to establishing new methodologies and ethical-methodological criteria for participatory research and practices in citizen-generated data and citizen science. These should not replace the existing concerns/framings about validity (e.g., on the quality of the generated data and its ability to serve as scientific evidence) but, rather, supplement them. In doing so, they should make it possible to take account of the modes of engagement of citizens and of the extent to which the research is "available to the risk" of the Other and sensitive to asymmetries and inequalities – as was initially attempted in the research study by de Albuquerque et al. (2019). In doing so, it is hoped that this approach can contribute to the establishment of empowering and "humanized" dialogical relationships, and thus enable us to regain the confidence needed to collectively undertake truth-building processes for the co-production of knowledge.

Acknowledgements

We would like to express our thanks to the following for partially funding this research project: the Economic and Social Sciences Research Council, in coordination with Belmont Forum and Norface within the "Transformations to Sustainability" program (project "T2S Waterproofing Data," grant ES/S006982/1). The authors are also grateful to the members of the Centre for Interdisciplinary Methodologies, University of Warwick, for their valuable suggestions based on an oral presentation of this material, as well as Celia Lury, Thom Davies, Alice Mah, and Joanne Garde-Hansen for their generous and very helpful comments on the first drafts of the text.

References

Bordogna, G., Carrara, P., Criscuolo, L., Pepe, M., and Rampini, A. 2014. On predicting and improving the quality of Volunteer Geographic Information projects. *International Journal of Digital Earth*, 1–22. DOI: 10.1080/17538947.2014.976774.

Callon, M. 1998. An essay on framing and overflowing: economic externalities revisited by sociology. *The Sociological Review*, 46(1_suppl), 244–269. DOI: 10.1111/j.1467-954X.1998.tb03477.x.

Cardullo, P. and Kitchin, R. 2017. Being a "citizen" in the smart city: Up and down the scaffold of smart citizen participation. NIRSA, National University of Ireland Maynooth, County Kildare, Ireland, PP. 1–24.

da Costa Marques, I. 2014. Ontological politics and Latin American local knowledges. In E. Medina, I. da Costa Marques, and C. Holmes (eds), *Beyond Imported Magic: Essays on Science, Technology, and Society in Latin America*. Cambridge, MA: MIT Press, pp. 85–110.

de Albuquerque, J. P. and Christ, M. 2015. The tension between business process modelling and flexibility: Revealing multiple dimensions with a sociomaterial approach. *Journal of Strategic Information Systems*, 24(3), 189–202. DOI: 10.1016/j.jsis.2015.08.003.

de Albuquerque, J. P., Cukierman, H. L., da Costa Marques, I., and Feitosa, P. H. F. 2013. *Challenging the Ontology of Technoscientific Artefacts: Actor-Network Theory in Developing Countries*. Manchester. http://hummedia.manchester.ac.uk/institutes/cdi/resources/cdi_ant4d/ANT4DWorkingPaper7AlbuquerqueEtAl.pdf (last accessed March 16, 2020).

de Albuquerque, J. P., Herfort, B., and Eckle, M. 2016. The tasks of the crowd: A typology of tasks in geographic information crowdsourcing and a case study in humanitarian mapping. *Remote Sensing*, 8(859), 1–22. DOI: 10.3390/rs8100859.

de Albuquerque, J. P., Yeboah, G., Pitidis, V., and Ulbrich, P. 2019. Towards a participatory methodology for community data generation to analyse urban health inequalities: A multi-country case study. In *Proceedings of the 52nd Hawaii International Conference on System Sciences* (3926–3925). DOI: 10.24251/HICSS.2019.476.

Degrossi, L. C., de Albuquerque, J. P., Fava, M. C., and Mendiondo, E. M. 2014. Flood Citizen Observatory: A crowdsourcing-based approach for flood risk management in Brazil. In *Proceedings of SEKE 2014 – 26th International Conference on Software Engineering and Knowledge Engineering, Vancouver, Canada*. Skokie, IL: Knowledge Systems Institute Graduate School, 570–575.

Degrossi, L. C., de Albuquerque, J. P., Santos Rocha, R. dos, and Zipf, A. 2018. A taxonomy of quality assessment methods for volunteered and crowdsourced geographic information. *Transactions in GIS*, 22(2), 542–560. DOI: 10.1111/tgis.12329.

Dourish, P. 2016. The internet of urban things. In R. Kitchin and S.-Y. Perng (eds), *Code and the City*. London: Routledge, pp. 27–48.

Freire, P. 1987. Sobre educação popular: entrevista com Paulo Freire (On popular education: interview with Paulo Freire). In *Educação Popular: um encontro com Paulo Freire (Popular Education: An Encounter with Paulo Freire)*. São Paulo: Edições Loyola.

Freire, P. 1997. Papel da Educação na Humanização (The role of education in the humanization). *Revista Da FAEEBA*, 7(Jan/Jun), 9–17.

Freire, P. 2000. *Pedagogy of the Oppressed*. New York and London: Bloomsbury Academic.

Freire, P. 2001. *Pedagogy of Freedom*. Lanham, MD: Rowman & Littlefield.

Freire, P. 2005 [1970]. *Pedagogia do Oprimido (Pedagogy of the Oppressed)* (9th edn). Rio de Janeiro: Paz e Terra.

Freire, P. and Faundez, A. 1985. *Por uma Pedagogia da Pergunta (For a Pedagogy of the Question)*, ed. R. M. Torres. Rio de Janeiro: Paz e Terra.

Freire, P. and Faundez, A. 1989. *Learning to Question: A Pedagogy of Liberation*, trans. T. Coates. Geneva: WCC Publications.

Gabrys, J. 2016. *Program Earth: Environmental Sensing Technology*. Minneapolis: University of Minnesota Press.

Givoni, M. 2016. Between micro mappers and missing maps: Digital humanitarianism and the politics of material participation in disaster response. *Environment and Planning D: Society and Space*, 34(6), 1025–1043. DOI: 10.1177/0263775816652899.

Goodchild, M. F. 2007. Citizens as sensors: The world of volunteered geography. *GeoJournal*, 69(4), 211–221. DOI: 10.1007/s10708-007-9111-y.

Haklay, M. 2013a. Citizen science and volunteered geographic information: Overview and typology of participation. In D. Sui, S. Elwood, and M. Goodchild (eds), *Crowdsourcing Geographic Knowledge*. Dordrecht: Springer, pp. 105–122.

Haklay, M. 2013b. Neogeography and the delusion of democratisation. *Environment and Planning A*, 45(1), 55–69. Retrieved from http://www.envplan.com/abstract.cgi?id=a45184.

Jasanoff, S. 2007. *Designs on Nature*. Princeton, NJ: Princeton University Press.

Latour, B. 1993. *We Have Never Been Modern*. Cambridge, MA: Harvard University Press.

Lury, C. 2004. *Brands: The Logos of the Global Economy*. London: Routledge.

Mah, A. 2017. Environmental justice in the age of big data: Challenging toxic blind spots of voice, speed, and expertise. *Environmental Sociology*, 3(2), 122–133. DOI: 10.1080/23251042.2016.1220849.

Mol, A. 1999. Ontological politics. A word and some questions. *The Sociological Review*, 47(1_suppl), 74–89.

Perkins, C. 2014. Plotting practices and politics: (Im)mutable narratives in OpenStreetMap. *Transactions of the Institute of British Geographers*, 39(2), 304–317. DOI: 10.1111/tran.12022.

Tkacz, N. 2014. *Wikipedia and the Politics of Openness*. Chicago: University of Chicago Press.

Townsend, A. M. 2013. *Smart Cities: Big Data, Civic Hackers, and the Quest for a New Utopia*. New York: W. W. Norton.

UN-Habitat. 2016. *Urbanization and Development: Emerging Futures. World Cities Report 2016*. Nairobi: United Nations.

Wehn, U., Rusca, M., Evers, J., and Lanfranchi, V. 2015. Participation in flood risk management and the potential of citizen observatories: A governance analysis. *Environmental Science & Policy*, 48, 225–236. DOI: 10.1016/j.envsci.2014.12.017.

13

Science, citizens, and air pollution: Constructing environmental (in)justice

Anneleen Kenis

Introduction

In their efforts to put air pollution on the public agenda, citizens cannot avoid engaging with science. Being a largely invisible socio-natural artifact, air has to be translated into a subject of contestation and debate for it to become politically salient. Which choices do citizen movements make during this process and what effect do these choices have on particular constructions of environmental (in)justice?

To formulate an answer to these questions, I engaged in a study on the politicization of air pollution in two major cities: Antwerp (Belgium) and London (UK). After decades of relative silence, air pollution figures high on the public agenda in these cities. This increase in awareness, contestation, and debate is not only reflected by the number of newspaper articles dealing with the topic (Kenis 2017), but also by the rise of citizen movements trying to tackle it. Importantly, these movements do not only struggle to get the topic on the agenda, but also engage in a debate on the terms in which the problem has to be understood and, consequently, what has to be done about it. Crucial is *how* the topic is framed and which discursive strategies are used to this aim.

In this chapter, I analyze the increasing attention paid to urban air pollution and investigate the discursive strategies used by citizen movements in this context. The main focus is on the way in which particular spatial interpretations, related to the focus on particular pollutants rather than others, lead to diverging claims about environmental (in)justice and to the advocacy of different types of action. The cities of Antwerp and London not only exhibit a number of similarities in this regard, but are also significantly different in terms of the way air is mobilized and made into a central topic of contestation and debate.

Being a largely invisible socio-natural artifact, putting air on the public agenda requires a complex exercise of translation. The air we inhale appears, commonsensically, to be "just air." Its composition, the pollutants that it contains, and its effect on human health remain largely invisible. As a result, not only the "embodiedness" and "embeddedness" of human beings (Mellor 1997), but also the "unequal power relations [which] are 'inscribed' in the air" can easily remain unheeded (Bryant 1998, 89). As a consequence, the politicization of air requires particular discursive manoeuvres.[1] To an (even) greater extent than other socio-ecological predicaments, the framing of air pollution as "a problem" requires (citizen) scientists who measure, model, and/or monitor it, and a whole range of actors who translate these scientific artifacts into politically salient issues. This translation exercise, and its interdependent relationship with science, makes the politicization of air both difficult and interesting. Crucially, it entails a process of discourse construction, whereby specific elements are included and excluded and particular discursive frameworks are used.

This chapter focuses on this translation exercise and studies the decisions, choices, and exclusions that take place during this process. It analyzes the discursive formations through which this increasingly salient issue is put on the political agenda. It argues that the framing of a political problem starts at the level of the construction of a scientific fact. This construction entails making choices about what to include and exclude. Choices that seem neutral at first sight, such as the location of measurement devices or monitoring stations, the chosen time frame, or the pollutant focused on, all affect the scientific observations made, and thereby the way the problem is (or is not) politicized and appears in the public domain. These scientific choices do not happen in a political vacuum. Which of the multitude of potential scientific observations gets seen or selected is influenced by a broader "political" interest or stake (Goeminne 2012).

It has to be noted that the notion of the political should be interpreted here in the broad meaning of the term. By "political" I do not refer to political institutions like parliament or elections, but to a logic of thinking and acting in which the constitutive character of power, plurality, conflict, and decision is recognized (Mouffe 2006; see also Kenis and Lievens 2014). It is in this sense that science is always intrinsically political, even if not all science is political in the same way (Lievens and Kenis 2018).

Staging air as a politically salient issue starts with the construction of a scientific "fact," but it does not stop there. A whole range of actors (citizens, medics, journalists, policy makers) then take up the issue (or do not), and participate in its further creation. Take for instance the problem of NO_2 (nitrogen dioxide) pollution related to diesel exhaust. Though this has only recently figured centrally on the public agenda, the problem has been known about in scientific circles for decades. The first newspaper articles on the issue were published as early as the 1970s. However, it is only recently that the problem started to engage the public and create a prominent debate. Such examples show that staging air pollution as an important political theme not only depends upon the construction of scientific facts, but also on whether this scientific fact is taken up and framed in a way that allows it to gain center stage. Finally, tension can arise between different ways of framing the problem and different ways of actually tackling it.

In what follows, I will first delve in more detail into what I will refer to as the three steps of translation, after which I will present two case studies: first, the city of Antwerp (Belgium) and, second, the city of London (UK). The focus will be on how the representation of air pollution as a spatially unevenly distributed phenomenon contributes to its (de)politicization. Therefore, I will focus on the spatial imaginaries underpinning processes of (de)politicization. In order to make empirical sense of these processes, I engaged in a document analysis of the air pollution debate during the last decade, did interviews with key actors, and participated in numerous lectures, workshops, and debates.[2] In total I spoke with more than 30 key actors (civil movement representatives, policy makers, scientists, entrepreneurs). This triangulation of data allowed me to take a broad view of the topic and to acquire an in-depth understanding of how discourses are articulated and constructed (Baxter and Eyles 1997; Esterberg 2002).

Visualizing air pollution

Spatializing "us" and "them"

As Chantal Mouffe (2002, 2006) famously argues, us–them distinctions are crucial for politics: conflict engenders political passions, mobilizes people, and gets them involved. Collective identification is crucial here: individuals have to transform themselves into a collective actor, a common interest has to be identified, a shared identity has to be constructed. In this process of construction, both conscious and unconscious choices are made, and a continuous negotiation between in- and exclusions takes place. A discourse is not static, not fixed forever, but always in motion. Different elements come together, are interwoven, and start to shape the narrative that symbolizes the movement (Howarth 2000; Howarth et al. 2000). This narrative is never entirely coherent (Gramsci 1971). It inevitably contains tensions, fissures, distortions. Significantly, it establishes boundaries around an "us," in relation to a "them." Every attempt to form a collective identity, to bring people together behind a common goal, requires the implicit or explicit definition of a "them," an opponent: someone or something that is opposed (Mouffe 2006).

With an intangible object such as air quality, citizen movements are confronted with an extra challenge: How to build an "us" and "them" around something that is as invisible as air (Loopmans et al. 2017)? How to represent the interests involved, the actors at play, the political fault lines at stake? In other words, how to make the invisible visible, and turn it into a topic of contestation and debate?

In this contribution, I argue that that putting air pollution on the public agenda requires a specific kind of discourse construction whereby the pollutants in the air are not only made visible, but made visible in a particular way. More specifically, it is my contention that in order to politicize air pollution, social differentiation – as in who is more or less exposed – has to be revealed, and I argue that the most straightforward way to do that is by representing air pollution in a spatially differentiated way. Indeed, there are good reasons to assume that space is the single most visible factor determining who is more or less exposed to air pollution, even if space is, in its turn, often a function of other factors like class, gender, or race. By pointing to spatial differentiations, potential injustices can be brought to the fore. This can then trigger indignation and other political passions. Furthermore, pointing to spatial differentiations can stimulate processes of collective identification. This creation of an "us" and "them," the exposure of underlying conflict, is crucial in every process of politicization.

Put differently, articulating spatial patterns can help to make a largely invisible socio-ecological artefact like air pollution into a distinctive issue: "we are *not* all in this together." Indeed, as Erik Swyngedouw (2007, 2010) famously argues, the framing of contemporary social-ecological issues into an "all together" discourse is precisely what makes them so liable for depoliticization. As he argues, the construction of the struggle against climate change in terms of "all together against CO_2," is exactly what circumvents conflict amongst "the people" and thereby the mobilization of a privileged subject of change. Pointing to spatial differentiations, and thus injustices, in the distribution of air goes against this logic, and allows the emergence of specific actors of change. Perhaps, more than any other approach to air pollution, focusing on spatial characteristics brings differentiations to the fore and makes them visible. In other words, the imagination or representation of air pollution as a spatially differentiated issue is key to processes of (de)politicization.

Importantly, however, there is *not just one way* of spatializing, and thus politicizing, air. As Mustafa Dikeç (2012, 670) argues: "space is a mode of political thinking, and different spatial imaginaries inform different understandings of politics." Furthermore, not "all spatial metaphors are good or unproblematic" (Dikeç 2012, 670). As he contends: "[c]ertain spatial metaphors may … fail to account for the complexity and multiplicity of the world, and limit, rather than expand, political imagination."

From another perspective, Gordon Walker (2011, 40) argues that it is important to "explore how different spatialities are being tied in congruent and supportive ways to produce … resilient multidimensional justice discourses." In other words, there is *not one just way* to politicize air. The question is therefore not only which spatial representations citizen movements mobilize and whether they support, rather than undermine, just imaginaries, but also which view on justice they defend this way. As Mouffe (2006) argues, a democratic society is a society that shares a common symbolic framework centered around key principles such as equality and freedom, though at the same time allows for conflict about the specific meaning these terms can get. Consequently, democracy is about letting different interpretations of justice come to the fore and engage in discussion, struggle, and dialogue. Therefore, there can be no conclusive answer to the question of what a just spatial imaginary entails.

The construction of a fact, the framing of a problem

Visualizing air in spatial terms is only possible with the help of science. Indeed, for air pollution to be made visible we need (citizen) scientists who measure, monitor, and/or model it. At the same time, this first step in the process of discourse construction does not happen in a political vacuum. It only happens if air pollution is already seen as a matter of concern. (Citizen) scientists' attention will only be drawn to air pollution if there are reasons to assume "something can be found in the air." In what follows, I will discuss in more detail the three levels of discourse construction delineated above as: (1) The construction of a scientific "fact," (2) the framing of a political "problem," and (3) the establishment of political agonisms and fault lines around diverging responses to the problem. Importantly, I make this distinction only for analytical reasons. As a matter of fact is necessarily always a matter of concern (Latour 2004), these three cannot be viewed as consecutive steps in a sequence; rather they should be understood as interactive elements in an iterative process.

The first "step" in the translation of air pollution into a politically relevant issue relates to the choices made by scientists or other actors involved in measuring, monitoring, and modeling air pollution. During this first stage, forms of in- and exclusion are already at play (Demeritt 2001; Wynne 2010; Goeminne 2012). Even the spatial location of monitoring stations has an effect on how we understand air quality and its distribution (Buzzelli 2008). Political maneuvers and struggles about whether and how to monitor air pollution in the UK show that this is far from a neutral issue (Leake 2014). But also, the decision to focus on particular pollutants, to adopt a particular timing or time frame (hourly, daily, yearly measurements), to use a particular type of monitoring device, or to choose measuring or modeling all affect the way air pollution is constructed as a scientific "fact."[3] Different choices on all these levels lead to different "realities." As Gordon Walker (2012, 107) observes: "The choices that are made in putting together and carrying out a study inevitably shape the scope and form of the evidence claims that can be made and the knowledge that is generated – and, it follows, what knowledge is *not* generated." Importantly, a map is always a representation of a particular moment and construction of reality, but this is seldom fully recognized. To paraphrase the words of the famous surrealist artist René Magritte: "*ceci n'est pas la pollution.*" While this is generally acknowledged with regard to air pollution maps based on modeling, it is also true for maps based solely on measuring methodologies, such as the maps made from a mass of single measurements often produced by citizen science projects.[4] In this sense, the recurrent call for more monitoring stations, to enable us to arrive at more accurate maps, should be nuanced. The resulting maps also inevitably depend on the choices that are made at the measuring stage: the exact location of the measuring devices, the focus on particular pollutants, the subdivision of particular pollution levels into categories, or the precision of the devices used. The point is not to start a discussion about what is most accurate – modeling on the basis of professional monitoring stations or measuring on a much larger scale with less precise devices, as often used in citizen science projects – but to acknowledge that scientific facts, like those that appear on air pollution maps, are always and by definition, at least to a certain extent, constructions and should be interpreted as such.

That it is not easy to find a good balance between searching for "the truth" (and making political claims on that basis) and recognizing the intrinsically constructed nature of every scientific "fact" was shown in the CurieuzeNeuzen citizen science project in Antwerp in 2017. This project contested existing maps of air pollution by showing that these maps, which were based on modeling, had significantly underestimated the pollution in particular streets (Brussel and Huyse 2017). For instance, the models did not account for street canyon effects

– the phenomenon whereby pollution gets "trapped" in streets with high buildings on both sides of the road – thereby increasing the pollution levels in these streets. Similarly, a number of citizen science projects in London, such as those carried out by London Sustainability Exchange and Mapping for Change, pointed to pollution hotspots in the city which had not been fully recognized as such before and demanded action to be taken straightaway. A number of scientists, in turn, expressed concerns that the measuring devices used by these citizen science projects were not accurate enough and therefore not only their findings but also their policy suggestions should be viewed in that light. They questioned whether a multitude of single measurements – produced by cheaply manufactured measurement devices – would by definition be better than models based on a more limited number of professional monitoring stations. Interestingly, while citizens plead for more financial resources for measuring and monitoring, a number of scientists question this need, arguing that we might not win much with extra investments on this terrain.

While the process of discourse construction starts with the construction of a scientific fact, it does not stop there. As Olga Kuchinskaya (2014, 2) argues: "Our experience of imperceptible hazards is always necessarily mediated by measuring equipment, maps, and other ways to visualise it, but also with narratives." Indeed, the second step is the translation of these "scientific facts" into specific narratives or discourses which frame "the problem" of air pollution. (Citizen) scientists can play a role on this level, for instance in the way they represent the issue in their communication to the scientific community, policy makers, or the broader public. But the choices and decisions made by citizen groups, politicians, policy makers, or business representatives in their efforts to put air quality on (or off) the public agenda are at least as important. From observing particular levels of "air pollution" to a "public health emergency," from "high" to "illegal levels" of air pollution, from the number of "deaths" to the number of "costs, from 'people's health' to "children's health," from "the loss of 1 year of life expectancy/person" to "40,000 premature deaths a year": whether concerns about air pollution are framed in terms of health problems, health inequality, real estate prices, or the potential for further city development – the chosen angle makes a huge difference. This observation is ambivalent: on the one hand, we need to underline that the adoption of a particular way of framing an issue is an inevitable aspect of every form of science communication, while on the other hand, it can appear that all framings distort "the truth" equally. Take the last example, the framing of mortality. The European Environmental Agency (EEA 2016) focuses in its communication on the loss of 8 months of life expectancy for every European citizen. Evidently, this is a scientific arti-fact. In reality, some people lose 20 years of their lives, while others are not affected at all. Importantly, these deviations in translation should not be understood as mere wrongs which have to be addressed, as if it was possible to achieve a flawless translation. Every choice in constructing a discourse inevitably produces blind spots and forms of exclusion (Howarth 2000; Howarth et al. 2000). It is not the exclusions or the blind spots as such that are the problem, as these are unavoidable, but the fact that the political processes at stake are often rendered invisible. Paradoxically, when air is visualized, the act of doing so often remains hidden. The crucial question is *which* choices are made and what the effects are. Indeed, observing that exclusions are inevitable should not lead us to suppose that all choices are therefore equal, or that the processes of making these choices are of no significance.

In a third step, political antagonisms and fault lines emerge around diverging responses to what was framed as "the problem." Specific political agendas and priorities are put forward, actions are proposed, culprits are pointed at. Crucial questions are: which measures are proposed, by whom, on what basis? How do these proposals relate to the way the issue is framed? How are they justified by making reference to particular scientific claims? What is the analysis of the root causes of the problem, and which visions on alternatives and strategies for change are put forward as a result? Proposals like electric cars, road charging, and pedestrianization are each based on entirely different analyses of the root causes of air pollution and divergent visions on strategies toward change. In turn, these more openly political divergences also inform other choices to be made: the ways in which the issue is framed and the particular scientific observations which are emphasized. As already stated, the three levels cannot be entirely separated, as they are intrinsically interwoven. Choices made at one level inevitably influence those made at other levels in an iterative, interactive process. As the next section of this chapter will show, even seemingly neutral choices like the focus on a particular pollutant (PM or NO_2) can lead to different policies or measures being advocated. Or is it rather that a preference for specific policy measures leads to a focus on other pollutants?

The case of the city of Antwerp: PM is bad

Air pollution has acquired a central place on the public agenda in Antwerp during the last decade (Loopmans 2014; Loopmans et al. 2017). The trigger was the plan to extend the Antwerp ring road, which is actually not a complete ring road as it crosses the city. Moreover, it is only three-quarters of a ring, which is considered one of the reasons why the city is confronted with huge traffic jams. In May 2000, the Flemish government decided therefore to expand the Antwerp ring road by developing a third crossing over the river Scheldt: the so-called Oosterweel connection. A newly established public corporation, the BAM (Beheersmaatschappij Antwerpen Mobiel), of which the Flemish government is the single main shareholder, was made responsible for the development of the project. In February 2005, when the plans were made public, it became clear that this new connection would be constructed close to a major urban redevelopment area, the "Islet" (*het eilandje*), including a huge bridge (*De Lange Wapper*) over this area, followed by a tunnel under the river Scheldt.

Calling for alternative locations for road infrastructure and/or alternative forms of mobility, citizen movements actively contested the plans. Popularizing scientific knowledge and disseminating it among the wider public has been a main strategy in this endeavor. Through awareness-raising campaigns the movements succeeded in creating a well-informed citizenry and raising the level of debate considerably. In a short space of time, the planned Oosterweel connection became a well-known and key political issue, actively involving not only tens of thousands of citizens, but also important businesses and political parties in a contentious debate about mobility, urban development, and health. While the movements contesting the project objected in the first instance to the construction of "a new highway through the city," after a while, they widened their aims, advocating other visions of mobility and city development, green space, and, importantly, air pollution. Indeed, one of the most important merits of this citizen mobilization is that it has put air pollution high on the political agenda, not only on a local, but also on a regional and national level. Interestingly, the plans to build new road infrastructure stimulated several actors to also question already existing sources of air pollution. Politicians, policy makers, and entrepreneurs were forced to recognize and respect the crucial role played by citizen movements like stRatenGeneraal and Ademloos in this regard. As a policy maker stated in an interview: "Actually, according to us, as an agency, the trigger has been Ademloos and stRageneraal who have made Antwerp aware of air quality and health. We were already conscious of the problem, but the public apparently not. Now, in Antwerp, they are.'

Alongside other groups, the citizen movement Ademloos ("Breathless") made air pollution a topic of general public knowledge and debate by organizing a public referendum and actively campaigning in the run-up to the vote. Under the slogan "Particulate matter is bad" ("Fijn stof is slecht") the movement organized hundreds of citizens who went from door to door to inform people about the effect the Oosterweel connection would have on their health and to collect signatures for the referendum. The key argument was that the proposed building of the Oosterweel connection would drastically increase the particulate matter (PM) levels in Antwerp and would thereby contribute to further worsening the air-related health situation faced by the Antwerp citizenry.

In these campaigns, reference was made to the finding that the average European citizen loses 8,1 months of her life due to long-term exposure to PM2,5, while this would be 13,2 months for the average Belgian citizen and more than 3 years for the average Antwerp citizen, a situation which was considered by the movement as socially unjust (Amann et al. 2005; EEA 2013). In other words, Ademloos politicized air pollution by framing air pollution as a geographically differentiated health risk. Whereas the European framing of 467,000 premature deaths per year or the loss of 8,1 months of life expectancy for every European citizen (EEA 2016) homogenizes the effects within the population, and thus conceals actually existing spatial differentiations, citizen movements in Antwerp succeeded in pointing to these differentiations and thereby mobilized a significant part of the citizenry around a call for environmental justice. Or, to put it in political terms, whereas the European Environmental Agency (EEA) has framed the problem in a way that risks leading to a situation in which no group feels particularly addressed or affected (and, therefore, motivated to take action), citizen movements in Antwerp have politicized the issue by pointing to spatial differentiations between different cities and between cities and the countryside. These spatial differentiations are triggers of indignation, and of contestation, conflict, struggle, and debate, and this helped to move the topic to the top of the public agenda.

However, while slogans like "Living in Antwerp is unhealthy" ("Leven in Antwerpen is ongezond!") increased awareness of the spatial specificity of Antwerp in contrast to other places, internal differentiations (differences "within" the city) remained hidden, or at least underemphasized. While the movements' communication focused to a certain extent on the idea that people living near the ring road (or near other major roads) are especially exposed to air pollution,[5] this idea did not constitute the nodal point of the movements' discourse (Howarth 2000; Howarth et al. 2000). The main narrative is that of all Antwerp citizens together, united against the ring road, an us–them distinction that differentiates between residents of Antwerp and people living elsewhere, and unifies Antwerp's citizens as a common agent against the BAM. There are evidently good reasons to opt for such a discourse and the related fault lines, but critical reflections should also be made. In the context of this chapter, it is especially important to notice that knowledge about the spatiality of air pollution is used in a selective way. Particular injustices are emphasized while others come less to the fore. The reasons for doing so are obviously strategic, even if this is not always done in an explicit or conscious way: pointing to the Antwerp citizenry as a comment agent, an "us" which is constructed against a common "them," helps to mobilize as large a group as possible without the group losing its particular aim. For this reason, the size of the group should be limited: it cannot be so big that it makes the injustice intangible or invisible. But it should not be too small either: otherwise no political movement or potentially winning strategy is possible anymore. Focusing on the citizenry of Antwerp as an actor of change helped the movements to find a temporary equilibrium which enabled them to win the referendum. However, at the same time this balance remained unstable and hid particular privileges and vulnerabilitie, as became clear afterwards: the intersectionality of air pollution was partly put aside to enable and sustain unity among the Antwerp citizenry (Kenis and Loopmans 2016).[6] As stated above, the fact that there are blind spots and exclusions is not a problem in itself, as they are inevitable. Every form of discourse construction will always include particular elements and exclude others. The point is not to refute this, but to investigate which decisions are made in this process, whether they are made visible and contestable and what the consequences are. Indeed, Mouffe's (2002, 2006) political theory is not about refuting the exclusions it generates, but about unmasking the ways in which a discourse conceals its own contingency, its own instability, and the conflicts it engages in (see also Kenis 2018).

Interestingly, a particular use of scientific information has been crucial in constructing Antwerp's citizens movements' discourse. Specifically, the decision to focus on PM as the pollutant of concern has largely shaped the movement's outlook and aims. Most importantly, this choice contributed to the concealment of intra-urban variations in health risks. When mapping PM, almost the whole city of Antwerp gets the same color. Overall, the picture is one of too high concentrations. Even the highly contested Antwerp ring road is barely visible on the map, and probably the Oosterweel connection would not be all too visible either. Because of its chemical and physical characteristics, PM is not a good indicator of traffic-related air pollution, even if road transport is an important cause. Maps based on black carbon or nitrogen dioxide (NO_2) show an entirely different picture. The ring road and other main roads are highly visible, while the further one goes from the ring and other main roads, the more red changes to orange, to yellow, and to green. Because of its chemical and physical characteristics, mapping NO_2 gives a much more differentiated picture of traffic-related air pollution.

It is a paradoxical observation. The movement's focus is on traffic-related air pollution, but the main nodal point around which its discourse is woven, PM, does not reflect this. As a representative of the movement claimed: "[t]here is no city in the world where they know more about PM than Antwerp." But PM is probably not the main, or at least not the most differentiating, health risk that arises in the context of the movement's main focus, the ring road.

As mentioned earlier, this focus also has an effect on the process of politicization. Interestingly, different measurements not only underpin different narratives, but also inform varying us–them distinctions and thus varying levels and kinds of politicization. While citizen movements in Antwerp have been astute in pointing to the spatial differentiations between Antwerp and other places, they pay much less attention to intra-urban variations and the related intersectionalities and social differentiations. This not only has a significant effect on the kind of environmental discourse that the movements construct to further their aims, but also influences the kind of measurements that are promoted as a result. In this way, the decision to focus on a particular pollutant reaches beyond mapping and framing into policy answers and solutions in an interwoven and intangible way. Interestingly, targeting PM means focusing on the general quantity of traffic: too many vehicles on too many roads. Citizen movements in Antwerp therefore demand the cessation of the construction of the Oosterweel connection. To the problem of too many cars, the logical answer is: no more roads.

The case of the city of London: NO_2 is bad

London is another city where air pollution features high on the public agenda. Here too, citizen movements played a crucial role in focusing public attention on air pollution during the last decade. However, interestingly, quite different choices have been made in the efforts to make air pollution visible. To start with, instead of framing the health risks of air pollution in terms of loss of life expectancy, the predominant discourse has focused on the absolute number of premature deaths every year. Highlighting the fact that 9,500 people die prematurely due to air pollution in London every year has been crucial in framing air pollution as a "public health crisis" that urgently needs to be addressed.[7] Another important, and differentiating, choice that has been made relates to the use of European legislation as a discursive framework. Concentrating on the extent to which air pollution exceeds the limits set by the European Commission (EC) made it possible to call existing levels of air pollution "illegal" and to demand action on that basis. Interestingly, the levels of air pollution are just as illegal in Antwerp. However, the citizen movements there did not make that claim, or at least did not use it as a nodal point around which the mobilizing discourse of their movement was woven. This illustrates that there is a contingency to the particular choices that are made – choices that determine the way that air pollution is staged in different contexts. The central role of ClientEarth, an environmental law organization that tries to force action on air pollution by taking the government to court, is crucial here. One of the main aims of the organization is to assist citizens in fighting environmental destruction in a legal way. Using European environmental law as an anchor point, the focus is on those pollutants for which legal limits are exceeded. As a result of political compromises at the European level, the limits set for NO_2 are much closer to World Health Organization guidelines and therefore much more stringent than those for PM.[8] As a result, NO_2 limit values are a lot more severe and exceedances take place much more frequently. Summarized, the construction of air pollution levels as "illegal" was only made possible by focusing on another pollutant, namely NO_2.

However, the focus on NO_2 was not just a result of the adoption of a legal perspective; it also stemmed from the fact that most citizen movements that deal with air pollution in London originated in specific streets, boroughs, or neighborhoods, rather than being city-wide initiatives from the outset. Since their initial concern was the extent to which their particular borough, street, or neighborhood was particularly badly affected by air pollution, their focus quickly turned to NO_2.

This focus on NO_2 strongly affects the way air pollution is represented or imagined in spatial terms. Whereas the case of Antwerp exemplifies how concentrating on PM leads to general differentiations between cities or between cities and the countryside being highlighted, the emphasis on NO_2 in London yields a much more refined pattern of spatial and thus, potentially, political differentiation. Interestingly, the London strategy does not only draw attention to the center of the city as a place of high levels of pollution and to the need for action to mitigate this – it also engenders and facilitates a politicization along lines of ethnicity and social deprivation.

However, this focus on a different pollutant is mirrored not only in a different type of environmental justice claim – focusing on differences "within" the city – but also in more environmental justice claims as such. A short media search immediately shows that terms like "justice" and "equality" are much more frequently linked to air pollution in London than in the Antwerp case. Furthermore, there is far more research dealing with the relation between air pollution and ethnicity or social deprivation. The special importance that is given to this issue was highlighted when a political scandal broke out in 2016 over a report linking exposure to air pollution to social deprivation which the then Mayor, Boris Johnson, was accused of burying (Vaughan 2016a). The report, titled *Analysing Air Pollution Exposure in London* (King and Healy 2013), was commissioned by the Greater London Authority in 2013, but never published. It revealed that 433 of the 1,777 primary schools in London are located in areas that exceed European limit values for NO_2 – and that 83% of those schools are in deprived areas.

In the London context, analyses in terms of class or race are also more generally seen as common and acceptable ways of understanding the issue (Kenis

2017). Most notable in this regard was the action of the citizen movement "Black Lives Matter" in September 2016, when activists blocked London City Airport. They used the slogan "Black people are the *first* to die, not the *first* to *fly*" and declared that air pollution is therefore a racist crisis. In the weeks after, the claims of the movement were backed by studies showing that black communities in London are indeed disproportionately exposed to air pollution (King and Brook 2016; Vaughan 2016b). Environmental racism was considered a fact. In Antwerp, on the other hand, citizen movements felt that bringing in a similar argument or terminology would harm their movements (Kenis and Loopmans 2016). They did not consider it as the right way to frame the problem, even though the relations between social deprivation, ethnicity, and air pollution are similar to those in the London case (Loopmans et al. 2017).

In other words, there is an observable difference between the two case studies in terms of both the types and levels of politicization that are created through the construction of a particular scientific "fact." The decision to focus on a specific pollutant, respectively PM or NO_2, played a crucial role as a vehicle for and justification of the movements' claims. Furthermore, these choices also brought different kinds of policy measures to the fore. In the London case, because of the focus on small-scale spatial varieties and patterns, there seems to be more of a call for small-scale actions to mitigate local effects. The risk is that this results in small-scale policies which only focus on particular neighborhoods or even streets, or, more problematically, in policies which "level out" pollution. Air pollution is mitigated in one area by simply shifting it to another area. The European limits are no longer exceeded, but neither does air quality improve as a whole. Examples are the transferring of polluting buses to routes where air pollution levels are lower (Cecil and Sleigh 2017) or experiments with anti-pollution bus stops and other – often expensive – techno-fixes which only deal with air pollution in a superficial and very local way (Fleming 2017).

Moreover, the focus on NO_2 has yet another effect in terms of policy measures that come to the fore. As NO_2 is above all a by-product of diesel combustion, proposals like the extension of the low emission zone and the diesel scrappage scheme figure high on the public agenda. These proposals are underscored by slogans like "Ban diesel" or "Doctors against diesel." The result is a further differentiation: the focus is less on reducing the amount of traffic as a whole, but mainly on cutting down the number of cars that contribute to a particular kind of pollution, in this case NO_2.

What is of special relevance in the context of this chapter, however, is to elucidate the interplay between the focus on a particular kind of pollutant and particular political narratives. The choice of a particular pollutant (respectively PM or NO2) is not just related to another scientific "truth" about the spatialities

of air pollution, and thereby to particular political focuses and actions. Public
reports and statements also tend to use those maps which favor their case.
The process of discourse construction should thus be considered as circular. It
moves from the construction of a scientific fact to the development of political
discourses and back again, in an iterative process which weaves scientific (and)
political elements into a more or less coherent – though always contentious
– narrative.

Conclusion

As I stated at the beginning of this chapter, uneven distributions of air pollution
do not acquire a place on the public agenda all by themselves. Scientists, policy
makers, citizens, and a whole range of other actors are needed to translate air
from a largely invisible social-natural artifact into a political issue. This process
of translation entails making choices and this inevitably results in inclusions and
exclusions that inform particular forms of politicization and preclude others.
The staging of particular "us–them" distinctions is crucial here, as they define
which environmental injustices are brought to the fore. Though making choices
is unavoidable, the choices that are made are never neutral. Different ways of
staging the problem appeal to different actors, generate different fault lines, trigger different political passions, and help explain the (lack of) activity of citizens
and other actors.

Starting from David Harvey's (1996) claim that justice and geography matter
together, Gordon Walker (2011, 39) argues that "how space is conceived will
open up certain avenues for claiming environmental injustice, and close down
others." Furthermore, he argues that this also works the other way around:
"how environmental justice is conceived will bring forward certain understandings of space and hide others" (Walker 2011, 39). This is what we have seen
happening in the cases of Antwerp and London in relation to particular choices
of scientific "facts" and how they are interpreted. I have shown how in the case of
Antwerp a kind of environmental justice discourse was mobilized, based around
the claim that it is not fair that the citizens of Antwerp are more exposed to air
pollution than people living in other cities or in the countryside. At the same
time, this discourse failed to politicize other distinctions and fault lines, such as
those based on ethnicity of social deprivation. This depoliticization was linked
to a particular representation of space: more spatially refined patterns of air pollution, differentiating between levels of air pollution within the city, were not
revealed. This shows how spatial and environmental justice are both intrinsically
interlinked and at the same time inevitably plural. There is not just one space,

not just one environmental justice that can be claimed, but rather a continuous negotiation about where to draw the fault lines, about which "us" and "them" is created or rendered (in)visible, about how to color in the maps. These negotiations do not only happen between actors but also in the (collective) minds of individuals and movements. In this interplay of elements, "different forms and scales of space" can become "a strategic resource" for movements (Walker 2011, 40). As Walker argues: "[j]ust as 'different groups will resort to different conceptions of justice to bolster their position' (Harvey, 1996, p. 398), so will different groups work with different understandings of the spatiality of the issues at hand" (Walker 2011, 40).

Fundamentally, there is no right or final answer to these disputes. There is an unavoidable tension in terms of where fault lines should be located, and every decision involves a risk: adopting a large-scale perspective may make relevant spatial differentiations invisible, while focusing on the smaller scale may lead to such a high degree of fractioning that no movement can be built on such divided foundations. The challenge is thus not to overcome these disputes. Indeed, what is important is that these disputes should be recognized for what they are, and not concealed under a veil of so-called neutral and objective scientific facts. Maybe paradoxically at first sight, they should not lead to the conclusion that everything is political or ideological and therefore one should not search for the facts anymore. As Bruno Latour (2004, 231) famously argues in his response to the reproach that his theory of deconstructionism would have played in the hands of post-truth ideologues: "The question was never to get *away* from facts but *closer* to them."[9]

Notes

1 This largely invisible character of air pollution could explain why air, in contrast to more tangible socio-ecological predicaments like food, water, or parks, remains a blind spot within the field of urban political ecology which typically deals with such issues (Véron 2006; Buzzelli 2008; Heynen 2013).

2 All these activities took place in the period 2014–2017.

3 With regard to the use of diverging measuring devices, the question is not only how accurate they are but also which impression of accuracy they give. By giving precise, decimal numbers, several devices which are on the market these days give a false impression of a level of accuracy which they cannot deliver.

4 Gary Fuller (2018, 124) refers to an old adage in air pollution science in this context: "No one believes the results from predictive computer models other than the modellers who make them, and everyone believes the measurements apart from the people who run the instruments."

5   For instance, reference is made to the Amsterdam norm which states that facilities for
    vulnerable populations like schools or nurseries cannot be built within a given distance
    of major roads.
6   As shown in Loopmans et al. (2017), the extent to which Antwerp citizenry is exposed
    to air pollution varies to a significant degree, depending on where they live. These dif-
    ferences in place correspond with differences in income and ethnicity-related variables.
7   In May 2016, a cross-party committee of Members of Parliament stated that air pollu-
    tion is a "public health emergency" and called for immediate action to be taken on these
    grounds (Carrington 2016).
8   This information comes from interviews with scientists and policy makers.
9   Bruno Latour wrote this text in 2004, in other words before the term "post-truth" was
    widespread as an analytical tool. However, as Latour argues in that very same text, the
    challenge for intellectuals is to put themselves ahead of developments taking place in the
    world (or at least not to be always two decades behind) and that is what he famously did
    in his text. Though already significant at that time, Latour could not have known how
    relevant and salient this observation would be a few years later.

References

Amann, M., Bertok, I., Cabala, R., Cofala, J., Heyes, C., Gyarfas, F., and Wagner, F.
    2005. *A final set of scenarios for the Clean Air For Europe (CAFE) programme.* Available
    at https://ec.europa.eu/environment/archives/cafe/activities/pdf/cafe_scenario_
    report_6.pdf (last accessed February 10, 2020).
Baxter, J. and Eyles, J. 1997. Evaluating qualitative research in social geography: Establishing
    "rigour" in interview analysis. *Transactions of the Institute of British Geographers*, 22(4),
    505–525.
Brussel, S. V. and Huyse, H. 2017. *How a large-scale citizen science project managed to combine
    scientific rigour, policy influence and deep citizen engagement by measuring ambient air qual-
    ity in Antwerp.* Paper presented at the Annual RGS-IBG Conference, London, August
    29–September 1.
Bryant, R. L. 1998. Power, knowledge and political ecology in the third world: A review.
    Progress in Physical Geography, 22(1), 79–94.
Buzzelli, M. 2008. A political ecology of scale in urban air pollution monitoring. *Transactions
    of the Institute of British Geographers*, 33(4), 502–517.
Carrington, D. 2016. MPs: UK air pollution is a "pulic health emergency." *The Guardian*,
    April 27. Available at https://www.theguardian.com/environment/2016/apr/27/
    uk-air-pollution-public-health-emergency-crisis-diesel-cars (last accessed February 10,
    2020).
Cecil, N. and Sleigh, S. 2017. Dirtier diesel buses removed from Putney High Street
    put onto new route near pupils. *Evening Standard*, March 29. Available at https://
    www.standard.co.uk/news/london/dirtier-diesel-buses-removed-from-putney-

high-street-put-onto-new-route-near-pupils-a3501901.html (last accessed February 10, 2020).

Demeritt, D. 2001. The construction of global warming and the politics of science. *Annals of the Association of American Geographers*, 91(2), 307–337.

Dikeç, M. 2012. Space as a mode of political thinking. *Geoforum*, 43, 669–676.

EEA 2013. *Air Implementation Pilot: Lessons Learnt from the Implementation of Air Quality Legislation at Urban Level*. EEA Report no. 7/2013. Available at https://www.eea.europa.eu/publications/air-implementation-pilot-2013 (last accessed February 10, 2020).

EEA 2016. *Air Quality in Europe – 2016 report*. EEA Report no. 28/2016. Available at https://www.eea.europa.eu/publications/air-quality-in-europe-2016 (last accessed February 10, 2020).

Esterberg, K. G. 2002. *Qualitative Methods in Social Research*. London: McGraw-Hill.

Fleming, A. 2017. 10 ways to beat air pollution: How effective are they? *The Guardian*, February 15. Available at https://www.theguardian.com/cities/2017/feb/15/10-ways-to-beat-air-pollution-how-effective-are-they (last accessed February 10, 2020).

Fuller, G. 2018. *The Invisible Killer. The Rising Global Threat of Air pollution and How We Can Fight Back*. London: Melville House UK.

Goeminne, G. 2012. Lost in translation: Climate denial and the return of the political. *Global Environmental Politics*, 12(2), 1–8.

Gramsci, A. 1971. *Selections from the Prison Notebooks*. Londen: Lawrence & Wishart.

Harvey, D. 1996. *Justice, Nature and the Geography of Difference*. Oxford: Blackwell.

Heynen, N. 2013. Urban political ecology I: The urban century. *Progress in Human Geography*, 38(4), 598–604.

Howarth, D. 2000. *Discourse*. Buckingham: Open University Press.

Howarth, D., Norval, A. J., and Stavrakakis, Y. 2000. *Discourse Theory and Political Analysis: Identities, Hegemonies and Social Change*. Manchester: Manchester University Press.

Kenis, A. 2017. The politics of science and the media: The controversy on record air pollution in Oxford Street and other debates on bad air in London. Paper presented at the RGS–IBG Annual International Conference, London.

Kenis, A. 2018. Post-politics contested: Why multiple voices on climate change do not equal politicisation. *Environment and Planning C. Politics and Space*. DOI: 10.1177/0263774X18807209.

Kenis, A. and Lievens, M. 2014. Searching for "the political" in environmental politics. *Environmental Politics*, 23(4), 531–548. DOI: 10.1080/09644016.2013.870067.

Kenis, A. and Loopmans, M. 2016. Politicising spatial injustice: The struggle against urban air pollution in Antwerp (Belgium). Paper presented at the Historical Materialism conference, London.

King, K. and Brook, R. 2016. *Updated Analysis of Air Pollution Exposure in London – Interim Report*. Available at https://www.london.gov.uk/sites/default/files/aether_updated_london_pollution_exposure_interim_report.pdf (last accessed February 10, 2020).

King, K. and Healy, S. 2013. *Analysing Air Pollution Exposure in London*. Retrieved from https://www.london.gov.uk/sites/default/files/analysing_air_pollution_exposure_in_london_-_technical_report_-_2013.pdf (last accessed February 10, 2020).

Kuchinskaya, O. 2014. *The Politics of Invisibility: Public Knowledge about Radiation Health after Chernobyl*. Cambridge, MA: MIT Press.

Latour, B. 2004. Why has critique run out of steam? From matters of fact to matters of concern. *Critical Inquiry*, 30, 225–248.

Leake, J. 2014. Toxic air monitors may be scrapped. *Sunday Times*, December 28, 9.

Lievens, M. and Kenis, A. 2018. Social constructivism and beyond: On the double bind between politics and science. *Ethics, Policy & Environment*, 21(1), 81–95.

Loopmans, M. 2014. David tegen Lange Wapper. *Agora*, 30(3), 16–19.

Loopmans, M., Marrécau, F., and Kenis, A. 2017. Louter lucht? Lucht, ongelijkheid en sociaal protest. *Agora*, 2, 18–21.

Mellor, M. 1997. *Feminism and Ecology*. Cambridge: Polity.

Mouffe, C. 2002. *Politics and Passions: The Stakes of Democracy*. London: CSD Perspectives.

Mouffe, C. 2006. *On the Political*. London: Routledge.

Swyngedouw, E. 2007. Impossible "sustainability" and the postpolitical condition. In R. Krueger and D. Gibbs (eds), *The Sustainable Development Paradox*. London: Guilford Press.

Swyngedouw, E. 2010. Apocalypse forever? *Theory, Culture & Society*, 27(2–3), 213–232.

Vaughan, A. 2016a. Boris Johnson accused of burying study linking pollution and deprived schools. *The Guardian*, May 16. Available at https://www.theguardian.com/environment/2016/may/16/boris-johnson-accused-of-burying-study-linking-pollution-and-deprived-schools (last accessed February 10, 2020).

Vaughan, A. 2016b. London's black communities disproportionately exposed to air pollution – study. *The Guardian*, October 10. Available at https://www.theguardian.com/environment/2016/oct/10/londons-black-communities-disproportionately-exposed-to-air-pollution-study (last accessed February 10, 2020).

Véron, R. 2006. Remaking urban environments: The political ecology of air pollution in Delhi. *Environment and Planning A*, 38(11), 2093–2109.

Walker, G. 2011. Beyond distribution and proximity: Exploring the multiple spatialities of environmental justice. In R. Holifield, M. Porter, and G. Walker (eds), *Spaces of Environmental Justice*. Chichester: Wiley-Blackwell.

Walker, G. 2012. *Environmental Justice: Concepts, Evidence and Politics*. London: Routledge.

Wynne, B. 2010. Strange weather, again: Climate science as political art. *Theory, Culture & Society*, 27, 289–305.

14

Beyond the data treadmill: Environmental enumeration, justice, and apprehension

Nicholas Shapiro, Nasser Zakariya, and Jody A. Roberts

Introduction

The eerie, lumbering chords of the Call of Duty soundtrack, looping on the TV, suffused the air with an added texture of unease. I (Nick) leaned over to the window, rolling the colorimetric tube back and forth between my fingers, trying to discern the length of discoloration in the formaldehyde detection tube. The material in the tube changes from yellow to pink as it encounters formaldehyde, producing a length-of-stain reading like a pastel thermometer (Figure 14.1).

"Hopefully the results are not worrisome," said Joe in a controlled yet expectant manner, one that wavered on the last word and pivoted his statement into a tentative question. Reading and then temperature correcting the tube, I responded slowly, "It is not too bad … but they are not … ya know … incredible. They are about 20 parts per billion. Which is …"

"What's the danger zone?" Joe, an increasingly red-faced 24-year-old trailer resident whose indoor air quality was under scrutiny, interjected, "can you put it into perspective for me?"

"Yeah, of course," I reassured before joking, "It's 20! There you go. Bye," and feigned walking out the door, satirizing the extractive data collection practices that community science aims to overcome. We both laughed nervously, but for different reasons. I began to tie lines of relation between his home and his

14.1 Holding the formaldehyde tube in Joe's home. Photo by Mariel Carr.

reading to readings in other homes: "This level is five times better than this same model of trailer four years ago, but it is double a "normal" home … It is more than double the non-cancer federal guaranteed safe level for a year of inhalation, but that doesn't mean they found levels at 9 or 10 ppb (parts per billion) to be harmful, the state applied precautionary factors … [and on and on]." As we spoke it became increasingly clear that Joe's home atmosphere occupied a scientific no-man's-land. All of these relational perspectives cast from governmental guidelines, from monitoring homes, from modeling cancer risk, all fell short of solidifying the meaning of this number that had been plucked from his air. His level bore some proximity to "average" domestic air quality, but still maintained a distance from the safety-in-numbers comfort of a "normal" exposure. Twenty parts per billion is more than double the federal minimum response level and the EPA (Environmental Protection Agency) 1 in 10,000 cancer risk level, levels below which mitigation is generally understood as unnecessary, but much lower than the levels I normally found in the homes of people with acute effects from formaldehyde, of which he felt none.[1]

As we charted the fractured landscape of toxicological, epidemiological, and regulatory guidelines, Joe came to recognize that adverse health effects were possible, but not exceedingly probable.[2] As we talked, he became more and more comfortable inhabiting a grey zone of chemical exposure – as his levels were not alarming even if they were not unequivocally "safe." But while Joe became more comfortable, I was becoming increasingly uncomfortable with what I was reproducing. My initial joke, distancing myself from conventional scientific practice, was giving way to the suspicion that my research was not as distinct from the knowledge-power orthodoxy as I would like to think, even if the research instruments and study design were intended to challenge that culture: highly inexpensive, openly licensed instruments in pursuit of a research agenda driven explicitly by concerns of the disproportionately exposed rural poor. While I was troubling how to ask a question, I was also thereby reassuring myself it was indeed the right question to be asking.

Pull back from the close-up of the formaldehyde tube and the anticipation of whether or not its results are worrisome and you will see that Joe's home is one of 120,000 former emergency housing units that FEMA (the US Federal Emergency Management Agency) had built for those displaced by Hurricanes Katrina and Rita in 2005. These bare-bones homes became internationally infamous for harboring elevated indoor formaldehyde concentrations. Zoom out further still and you will see that his trailer is one of thousands of identical units that wound their way through quasi-legal economies and landed on the Bakken shale field in rural North Dakota. Pan over to the oil and gas well pads a half-mile from Joe's trailer to find the extraction of methane, from which formaldehyde is derived. Oilmen had streamed into rural boomtowns to land hydrocarbon extraction jobs, sending rents skyrocketing. Rural towns experienced rents higher than those of Manhattan. What was supposed to be a summer job for Joe in the hospitality industry – where oil profits inflated wages – turned into a multi-year stint after a DUI ("driving under the influence") saddled him with a sizable debt. Cutting down debt or building up a nest egg were the only two justifications I heard for subjecting oneself to the Bakken.

If we do resist the stock dramas of science and technology, the promises of empowerment and of making the invisible visible as data points, we can see beyond the individual toxicity or lack thereof to understand the widespread patterns, cultural forms, building practices, and commodity pathways that purvey harms well beyond the molecular register. In this light, we can see micro-toxicities as indexical of their macro-toxicities: Joe's home can be seen as the crystallization of the legacies of epochal disasters, extractive economies, promises of fortune that yield debt, multiple shades of the housing crisis, and the molecular trajectories of formaldehyde that returned to a site of its geological extraction (formaldehyde is derived from methane – part of the hydrocarbon brew extracted on oil fields like the Bakken). All of these intricately entangled infrastructures and phenomena reveal multiple hows and whys of exposure, yet are eclipsed by the questions raised by the analytical chemistry and whether or not the measurement by the detection tube, the enumeration, was within a "danger zone."[3]

A discrete formaldehyde concentration routed both Joe and me into a search for the perpetually out-of-reach threshold of tolerability – a boundary at which his home atmosphere transforms from bearable to dangerous. Even if this threshold could be numerically pinpointed, what is Joe to do, armed with that number, as he looks out at the unflinchingly flat horizon punctuated only by oil wells and trailers? As he checks his bank account on his phone? As he looks at other comparable places to live that cost a thousand dollars more per month? Joe's quandary is ultimately not just the individualist dilemma of how to navigate uncertainty. The very pursuit of finding buoyancy and meaning among indeterminate data resists bigger/ ancillary/other questions becoming askable. Even if Joe were to feel his atmosphere intolerable and found someplace else to live, his trailer would be reoccupied in a matter of hours. Just 100 feet away (30 meters), five men share an identical 150 sqare foot FEMA trailer and collectively pay $1,200 more per month than Joe, who lives on his own. How much of what is shared in their situations is addressed by the enumerations measurements provide, and how much is bracketed? Beyond routing us toward unanswerable questions, quantifying and contextualizing a potential toxicity also works to direct us toward straightforward, but potentially superficial, solutions.

How can the gravity of human molecular harm serve as an opportunity to make sense of the infrastructures, logics of capitalism, regimes of perception, and industrial practices that manifest and maintain the possibility of formaldehyde toxicity in all of our lives and thus better render a way out? These questions do not abandon Joe and his concerns but evince how removing him from the trailer (the putative outcome of a definitive assessment of toxicity) would mitigate one exposure while maintaining other shared exposures – exposures of the market, debt, brutal winters, fugitive endocrine disrupters from nearby wellheads,[4] and so on. Stepping out of the frame of risk distillation as an enumerative practice provides a better picture of what the impossible prize of the certitude of absolute monitoring could not accomplish and calls attention to the fact that prevention of such exposures requires interventions beyond the mere engineering of the home.

The reflections that grew into this chapter began with a conversation between the authors a couple months prior to being in Joe's trailer in which one of us (Jody) wondered out loud whether those who practice citizen science in relation to toxic environmental exposures are the people that potentially have the most to lose when the transformative promises of science do not pan out. Not only does enumerating the environment tend to maintain a certain hegemony about which questions are available for the asking, but it can lead to a situation in which those with the fewest resources and the highest exposure have the greatest investment in sciences that are relatively ineffective, or "powerless" (Boudia and Jas 2014), on their own to rectify the problems that they seek to elucidate. These questions took further root as one of us (Nasser) situated these concerns within a longer historical trajectory, substantiating and questioning the scientization of society and its concomitant effects on democracy in practice.[5]

In uniting our own research trajectories and agendas, we came to focus on four interconnected reasons for caution in deploying enumerative practices in pursuit of environmental and health justice: (1) projects engaged in the use of science for justice claims cannot fully escape reproducing hierarchies of knowledge-power, type, and knower; (2) the pursuit of science in these instances has the potential to foreclose imaginative horizons of "how" and "why" in favor of "how much"; (3) the pursuit of more data sets the stage for adversarial epistemological encounters that can lead to entrenchment rather than resolution; and (4) these practices have the resultant effect of defining and confining (democratic) participation to one in which data becomes an essential gateway to having a voice. These are not unique insights to the three of us, but rather the collective resulting work of our and other communities' probing analysis of the place of science in their societies. While some of these specific issues are taken up more specifically in what follows, our goal in this chapter is to build from these insights so that we can begin to articulate an approach toward a more expansive toolkit of interventionist practices.

While Nick's practice – as indicative of a larger rise in "civic technoscientific" practice within STS (science and technology studies) (Wylie et al. 2014) – may move to expand those invited to sit at the table of science and what tools can be wielded in the name of technocratic reform, we also must pay close attention to the ceilings in capacity, community building, imagination, and efficacy when tendering and transacting in scientific data. By foregrounding what we call the "politics of enumeration," we situate community science here not just within the emancipatory rhetoric of democratization, creative commons, and the blurring of the bulwarks of expertise, but also within a potentially constrictive instrumentalist scientific idiom. Many of the civic environmental monitoring projects that have been most successful by their own standards have been those not leveraging numerical data but curating and testifying in images of oil-soaked marshlands, effluent discharge in urban waterways, dead flora from an aerial perspective as evidence of subterranean toxicant perfusion, or gas rig workers not wearing required protections. The aforementioned four reasons for seeking alternatives to enumerating ecological threats certainly hang more loosely on these extra-numerical evidentiary projects, perhaps precisely because they exceed the scope of data sciences.

This introduction is not a mea culpa on Nick's behalf that seeks to cast a sinister light upon the work pursued by practitioners of community science. The self-reflexive critique of the first half of this chapter is an introduction to the more affirmative philosophy of this paper, which attempts to say "yes, and" (or

perhaps more specifically, "yes, but first") to civic science, and point to efforts
that may make our publicly engaged work better able to give rise to possibilities
of living otherwise, or at least to orientations toward more capacious other-
wises. In the second half of this chapter, we both theorize and take preliminary
steps toward empirically substantiating an approach that we call "inviting apprehension." These reflections on method are offered as outlines for further elabo-
ration and not a prescription for how work must be done. Our intention is to
shift the conversation and leave it open, not to critique it and treat it as settled.

  We work from the observation that "toxicity" often functions as a proxy for
a range of cultural, economic, or infrastructural instabilities that are, indeed,
something "toxic" but are far more complicated and difficult to identify. Perhaps
more consequentially, focus on discrete "toxic" elements of a material or system
reifies the fantasy that we can escape from specific materials to achieve a salu-
togenic world rather than pointing to the necessary deeper engagement that is
required to reinvent the materials of our everyday life (Roberts 2010). So, a
core question to us seems to be: How do we sustain a more trenchant examination not only of the thick constructions of and surrounding toxicity, but also of
what specific deployments of "toxic" can work to silence?

  To summarize, our inquiry here is two-part. How, we wonder, do enumerative engagements with the environment delimit how we conceive of the chemical ecologies that we are immersed within and perpetuate? Following that, what
are the approaches to apprehending the environment that might not so easily
boil down to binaries of benevolence or harm, or to renderings of uncertainty
confined to the specifications of statistical confidence intervals, that in turn jus-
tify further scientific inquiry? To find a route around these shortcomings that
reduce the capacity for substantive reflection and/or intervention, we look to
patterns of work already at play, approaches "inviting apprehension," beckoning
multiple strata of apprehending the environment to provoke public, often (but
not only, or necessarily) participatory, inquiry and intervention into the questions that undergird what we assume are the problems of today and the avenues
through which we must engage them.

Science for justice, and critiques

Enumerative projects bear unimaginably diverse manifestations, from technological standardization and innovation and measurements of labor time and
productivity, to state surveying, mapping, and concomitant planning, and population demographics, health, and governance.[6] Even in a cursory view, such calculative initiatives present a thicket of precedents that inform current practices

of environmental monitoring, whether couched in terms of citizen science, community science, civic science, or state science. In short, enumerative practices have been so culturally pervasive and extensive as to threaten to make any historical analysis of them an exercise in the assessment of modernity.

Long before a ubiquitous social trust in numbers, their broad use elucidated and made visible social values and accountability. In Mary Poovey's (1998) telling of the transfer and evolution of practices of accounting in early modern Europe, enumerative technologies (not numbers alone) neatly fold the physical, social, and political worlds into a single calculative practice. Numeric outcomes become the obligatory terrain upon which knowledge of and about a people or place must be contested. These practices of trade and commerce quickly found themselves applied to transfers of land and peoples as well as goods, becoming a key tool in the production and maintenance of sovereign and colonial power. These histories suggest the need to examine the degree to which the use and exercise of the tools of technoscience can be extracted from their dual role in the maintenance of power as inextricable from the maintenance of life (Foucault 2003, 2009).

Past critically minded theorists – whether natural or social scientists, philosophers, novelists, or artists – have wrestled with the impact of scientific enumerative practices on their own critical perspectives and assessments. The abundance of these reflections underscores the fact that the drive to "democratize" science in order to empower the citizen(ry) can surrender a critical perspective on the state, economy, and science to the rubrics by which they know and substantiate themselves. Even so, it remains difficult to imagine a future that must wrestle with the possible impermanence, impotence, or harmfulness of either official governance or formalized sciences. As is the case with civic science, the spaces we are left with for critical reflection tend to constrain intellectual endeavor to deliberating over the relationship between science and governance, rather than questioning the institutions themselves.[7]

Already by the mid-nineteenth century, mathematician and astronomer John Herschel averred that science – and "no other quarter" – would satisfy the pressing material demands of human life. A century later, social scientists such as Otto Neurath in Austria and natural scientists such as J. D. Bernal in England continued to insist that scientific knowledge and its universalization is the key to solving social problems. In looking to science to address social inequity, which Bernal saw as the core obstacle to more general improvements, he declared the need for a citizenry that knows and understands modern science "possibly better than the scientists themselves" (Bernal 1945, 476). Bernal's dream citizen takes the form of scientific auditor, keeping science on its rails, through critiques internal to its logic. This rendering of civic engagement is uncannily similar to a dominant imagined role of citizen science today, yet the present-day citizen scientist is tasked with keeping not just science on an even keel but also government and industry. This model of active citizenship, which holds the enumerative powers of science as the key to collective betterment, precedes the rise of self-conscious neoliberal policy and the oft-cited free-labor justification for and critique of citizen science (see Kinchy et al. 2014).

Data treadmill

Critiques of scientific enumerations of social worlds could be found broadcast in the "untimely" meditations of Nietzsche or in Dostoyevksy's *Notes from Underground*, each in their way challenging the promises that contemporary scientific theory held for the possibility of human flourishing. Likewise, the continued wariness of enumeration (understood both narrowly as discourse tending to numeric scientific verdicts, and as a figure for naturalizing scientific determination more generally) played a role in debates thereafter on the question of scientific instrumentalism.[8]

Despite the diversity and voracity of these critiques, socially or politically engaged enumerative processes have continued largely unabated. Indeed, one might argue that we are ever more self-consciously enmeshed in a scientized world and an enumerated environment. Data defines, and repeatedly and multiply redefines, our landscapes, communities, and bodies. Our regulations, laws, critiques, and conversations depend upon that data. And yet, as Boudia and Jas (2014) provocatively question: are we placing all of our hopes – for justice, for sustainability, for flourishing – on a "powerless science?" Infrastructure invested in these regulatory and research activities only grows more extensive in scope and sophistication. And yet, for all of this effort, toxicants and their effects on environments and landscapes can never be enumerated enough – eternally requiring further verification and precluding more expansive lines of inquiry.[9] In this way, the restrictive modes of problem-setting in environmental enumeration are entwined with a shortcoming of feasibility, of delivering on its own terms. Such a combination yields confined dreams that are impossible to attain. From plastics (Liboiron 2013; Vogel 2013) to pesticides (Saxton 2015), from flame retardants (Cordner 2016) to formaldehyde (Shapiro 2014), the landscape of toxicant-related science is strewn with examples of intensive data production in a preset direction and an intrinsically unreachable destination, a phenomenon we might call the "data treadmill," as a way of framing our hesitancy, or wariness, about projects of enumeration (Gould et al. 1996). This situation is most visible in the communities where science, exposure, and injustice are most immediately felt. In her work documenting the evolving relationships between the residents of New Sarpy in southern Louisiana and their industrial next-door neighbors, Gwen Ottinger (2013) explores the conflicts that arise when the production, management, and application of data underpin arguments for environmental justice. The community was experiencing a multitude of health and local environmental challenges due to the daily dosings associated with life in close proximity to a petrochemical facility. Residents sought a radical solution to their predicament: they wanted the company that operated the facility to relocate the entire population of their small town, yet the community lacked sufficient public or political power to leverage their neighbor to the negotiating table. Enter the Louisiana Bucket Brigade (LBB), a non-profit situated within the chemical corridor of Louisiana that specializes in the deployment of low-cost, community-operated air monitoring devices. Their eponymous tool, the air sampling bucket,[10] was lent to the community so that they could create their own arsenal of data to be mobilized in dealings with their industrial neighbors. The implicit assumption of both the LBB and New Sarpy residents was that the data would give the community a voice.

The mobilization of data led to an epistemological stalemate as adversarial positions were redrawn to include questions of standards, methods, and significant digits. The community-generated data lacked standing in legal settings that would have mobilized (already difficult to mobilize) state forces. The generation and presentation of data did succeed in mobilizing one previously silent group – the industrial engineers employed by the refinery. Where the LBB and community residents hoped to show systemic harm associated with life along a fenceline, engineers saw structural inefficiencies – leaking pipes, renegade emissions, faulty valves and gauges. The claimed fugitive emissions were likely real, but were due to aberrations fixable at their most proximate source and not a foundational hazard. The engineers appreciated the data. They wanted this data. They would use this data to fix the problem. And, after all, the engineers were the only ones expert enough to translate this data into action – to decide what numbers indicated real versus imagined problems. In this uptake, the data generated by the community simultaneously reconfigured the nature of the problem, the possible solutions, and those with the authority to manage this process.

Following the advice of its engineers, the company did eventually make an offer of assistance to the community. It offered to clean up its structural problems, to pursue more aggressive monitoring (with the help of the community), and to provide financial assistance to community members looking to improve their own homes in the community. That is, these efforts did not result in a clean separation or a complex troubling of the sustainability of cohabiting with refining, but rather a deepening of the connections between the two neighbors.

Those still involved with the community from the LBB advised community members to hold out, to hold their ground, to wait for the relocation. But the residents of New Sarpy had seemingly always known that this fight was far more complicated than any outsiders could know – that the production of data gave the residents a voice, but simultaneously at the cost of reducing their plight to discrete measurable quantities that could never represent the questions of home, life, and family that were always at stake. This use of civic science made the multiply corrosive state of things more bearable rather than substantially questioning the state of things (Fortun and Fortun 2005).

Such historical and contemporary cases and critiques lead us to both wariness and alliance. It is not only those who emphasize the power of technoscientific knowledge who provide reminders of how much social welfare may depend on scientifically minded intervention. Even those who condemn privileging calculative thought themselves concede its importance as one component of a response to the material conditions of living, as part of the work of survival.[11] We turn now from what provokes hesitation to proposing inroads into a wary alliance between STS and enumerative environmental practices that may help us to better apprehend and differently imagine our world.

Inviting apprehension

Drawing from our own individual and collective experiences of STS-in-practice, and those of others who have experimented with and reflected on their own practices, we suggest an approach, or an orientation toward multiple approaches, that we call "inviting apprehension." By this we mean any efforts seeking to articulate "the question before the question," refering to the questions often many steps before the burning questions that charge and delimit toxicant-related community science and other contentious environments where science is being brought to bear. Such a retreat of sorts, one that is in hope of destabilizing the attritional epistemological struggles that enumerative environmental engagements route into, is not an unfamiliar maneuver. However, the point here is less to emphasize what makes a current situation knowable or possible, or what historical contingency allowed a given situation to arise, than to find in those prior conditions the possibility of new terms of engagement in the present.

We use the word "apprehension" because of its multiple valences in the context of protracted and invisible exposures that, as environmental writer Rob Nixon has pointed out, draw "together the domains of perception, emotion, and action" (Nixon 2011, 14). Our invitation to apprehension is an attempt to more self-consciously take stock of, connect, and endorse current methodologies and sets of practices that themselves build on and draw together multiple registers of public collective inquiry and humanistic-troubling of seemingly well-established terrain. Inviting modes of thinking through the world that exceed enumerative data will no doubt also induce some unease in scientists and data-driven policy makers, and indeed one of the connotations of inviting apprehension is encouraging a comfort with the discomfort of operating outside of the security of enumerative empiricism and the questions it makes possible and restricts. Nixon locates the writer-activist as his hopeful figure of toxic apprehension:

> Writer-activists can help us apprehend threats imaginatively that remain imperceptible to the senses, either because they are geographically remote, too vast or too minute in scale, or are played out across a time span that exceeds the instance of observation or even the physiological life of the human observer. (Nixon 2011, 15)

What Nixon describes as apprehension is the receiving end of charismatic literary representations. Such an understanding of apprehension assumes knowledge of environmental exposure that "exceeds the instance of observation or even physiological life of the human observer" and "requires rendering them apprehensible to the senses through the work of scientific and imaginative testimony" (ibid., 14). We use apprehension, then, to include Nixon's sense of apprehending, holding on at the same time to its standard sense of anxiety. While in agreement with the need for inventive reimagining of environmental conflict, we disagree on where that intervention is best implemented. In our view, it is not that we need better communication, as the power of apprehending exposure is not exclusive to charismatic activists, trailblazing scientists, or clever writers[12] but rather is (or ought to be) a precursor to the idea of what needs to be communicated.

To invite apprehension is not to provide counter or alternative facts to established questions, but to reimagine what the appropriate questions (and therefore facts) might be in the first place. At first glance, the move resembles the dramatic analytical U-turn Latour (2004) executed more than a decade ago when he proposed, like a mathematician, that he had been subtracting reality from matters of fact when he should have been adding reality to matters of concern. His analytical apparatus still works, he contends, it was just running backwards. Assemble around our concerns, he urged, rather than unpack the contingencies of facts. Whether we should be subtracting, adding, or multiplying reality, his repentant revisions leave the other variables of his formula, and its axis of creation and destruction, untouched.

Whether endorsed, dismissed, or ignored, the history the Latourian reversal frames much of our discipline and the worlds we investigate. It leaves us asking: What if our goals bridged the investigative with the instigative – seeking to explore the construction of the present moment with methods and tools that help us (and larger publics) to imagine alternative narratives, materialities, and more-than-human relations? What if, instead, the paradigmatic practice of the STS scholar/practitioner included the creation of spaces in which a multiplicity of actors are invited to gather themselves to think through and experiment with the ancillary questions, sensory practices, infrastructures, assumptions of risk, and so on that are bundled up in matters of fact or concern, which are never really that far from each other? To be clear, the move here would not be sorting concerns from facts and choosing to move with one over the other, but collectively leveraging diverse empiricisms to raise, interrogate, and be put into motion by the question(s) before the fact(s) and the question(s) before the concern(s).

This practice is akin to what Noortje Marres has, in the context of the artist collective Hehe's interventions in energy production and urban toxic concerns, called a "deliberate occasion," a forum that "enables all at once research on, the amplification of, and intervention in environments and their attendant issues." Such a happening "seduces actors to stage environmental controversies, rendering them recordable and documentable in a public way" (Marres 2013, 13). The role of the STS practitioner, then, is to create this space where the concerns, rationales, values, and assumptions that lead into an environmental conflict are laid bare, and, through their display, reorganize what futures are possible, desired, causes of suspicion, or already present.[13]

To illustrate invitations to apprehend, we turn to practices that often slide into the broad category of the arts, although the work of community organizing and informal education at times already align with what we are envisioning. Our recourse to creative social practice is likely both active and passive, as the arts are afforded room to act non-instrumentally and "art" often is a residual category applied to public practices that resist easy categorization. Take for example the work of Jenny Price, a PhD historian who practices public environmental humanities work in Los Angeles. Through this work, she came to be known as an "artist," though with no such claim for herself. In a 2014 interview, Price, a co-founder of the LA Urban Rangers, briefly summarizes their practice:

I've written op-eds shaking my fists and being polemical to say this is the problem with privatization of public space. As LA Urban Rangers, we don't do that. We take people down to the Malibu beaches and we perform the ranger character, which is all about public space, we basically perform the beaches as public and we create activities [through which] people can experience the beaches as public. (Carruth and Price 2014)

In their collective practice they do not enact enemies against whom to claim victories for the creation of public space but rather perform elements of their desired future in the present, which then provokes stakeholders to ask histori-cal, technical, legal, and sociological questions that were previously hidden in plain sight.

An alternative set of practices is at play in the improvisational realist film *WINDJARRAMERU, THE STEALING C*NTS* by the Karrabing Film Collective in Darwin, Australia. The film enacts a form of collective storytelling without scripts that is simultaneously not strictly true and a crystallization of constantly occurring mundane phenomena that hang heavy in the lives of the Aboriginal community that wrote, filmed, and starred in *WINDJARRAMERU*. The collective concisely summarizes the practice as "faking it with the truth." As Karrabing member Elizabeth Povinelli writes, "Perhaps the central purpose of Karrabing's films is to discover what we never knew we knew by hearing what we say in moments of improvisation" (2015). In the film, Indigenous actors portray a fictionalized assemblage of all-too-real toxic encounters and end up hiding from the police in territory with known radioactivity produced by illegal mining activities. The hideaways reassure themselves of the protection their exposure provides them, "Don't worry, RJ. They won't come in here. We're safe, too much radiation here; we're safe." And in that moment the actors vocalized a paradox of Indigenous sovereignty that they had only tacitly known: that their self-determination was limited to land that settler-colonialists had rendered uninhabitable. In addition to improvising a better understanding of their own condition, the local health department read the film as a hyper-real truth, open-ing up a line of dialogue that had not been possible to stimulate by traditional means. While the Urban Rangers perform a desired present over its less desir-able actuality as a way of posing the questions of both why this dream did not become realized and how it can be realized, Karrabing performs their own immiseration as a means of reflexive inquiry that is made public through film and demands apprehension of the numerous material and immaterial infrastructures which maintain that condition.

In the work of both the LA Urban Rangers and the Karrabing Collective, we see the opportunities that performance creates for reframing current debates so as to blur distinctions between categories of health, policy, data, and jus-tice and reorganizing temporal elements of presents, futures, and pasts. In his work with the REACH Ambler project,[14] a collaboration between researchers at the Science History Institute and the University of Pennsylvania School of Medicine, Jody experimented with ways of theatrically recasting a community's entrenched understanding of the material and cultural legacies of industry in their small Pennsylvania town.

In Ambler, Pennsylvania, the word "asbestos" carries multiple meanings: the material and industry that built the town; an irrecoverable economy; the

14.2 Leslie Nevon Holden and Pat Lamborn in *The White Mountains*, performed at the ACT II Playhouse in Ambler, PA, April 2015. Photo by Conrad Erb.

"White Hills" that represented the second largest mound of asbestos material in the United States; the loss of a public space; a shifting health hazard; and an uncertain future. After the plant's closure in the 1970s, public conversation about asbestos was buried, only re-emerging long enough to sustain moments of renewed interest and reburial.[15] A 2005 proposal to build a 17-story building on the remaining, un-remediated site exhumed the manifold meanings of asbestos. Residents, new and old, were made to confront the material and cultural legacy of the town simultaneously. Controversy and contestation about the management of the new Superfund site pitted community members against the EPA and against one another.

Transcripts of oral histories with community members and other related historical ephemera became the basis of a newspaper insert, a portable exhibition about the history of the town, and ultimately a series of composed and performed one-act plays (collectively known as *The White Mountains*) (see Figure 14.2).[16] In having their perspectives narrated back to them, mediated by curation and interpretation, residents confronted the multiple histories coexisting alongside one another in the community that were shaping how they (individually and collectively) made sense of their present circumstances and imagined what the future of the community could or should be.

There were openings, as well, for unexpected participants to inflect seemingly old questions with new solemnity. The daughter, perhaps 10 years old, of a couple recently arrived in the community asked about asbestosis and mesothelioma, "Can these diseases be cured?" This simple question from a small voice transformed what are typically fact-laden, expert-driven conversations about risk and exposure and probability statistics, like those that Nick rehearsed at the beginning of this chapter, into a frank and compassionate discussion about the long-term effects of asbestos exposure. Even long-standing activists in the community found an opportunity to briefly be, or approach being, elective community members, part of an audience deliberating over multiple iterations of common experiences. As one attendee noted in a follow-up interview, "I think that the play actually allowed a lot of that surface tension to break … [W]e didn't wear our hats [and so] we could see [each other]." Watching the plays that night helped her to step outside the role she had been playing for the last decade and instead simply watch herself and her community with a sense of clarifying distance. EPA and ATSDR (Agency for Toxic Substances and Disease Registry) staff, too, were in the audience that night and began to rethink how their technical staff conceptualize and intervene in community toxics issues.[17]

This work evinces the two-way proxy status of toxicity, the community issues for which it can be a cipher and the communal valuations it appears to privilege, which can also encode dilemmas of material toxicity. Asbestos – and what to do about it – had become a proxy for discussions that had no other forum in the community: about community development and identity, access to greenspace and recreational space, race relations, and heritage in this demographically shifting town, as well as the health and safety of residents. The specter of toxicity thus motivates participation in public deliberative processes, like those sponsored by the EPA, to achieve extra-toxic goals and justifies non-participation by minority (largely black) community members that suspected toxicity to be another means of maintaining the racialization of space and capital. But the direct relations between the toxic and the social orders to which it relates are not exhausted by even the far-reaching concerns of individual communities.

In more recent work, Nick follows the proxy of toxicity in a direction that moves from the specific locations of human exposure, like Ambler or the one that opened this essay, to geographically larger processes and relations that inform and sustain a multitude of linked exposures. Scholarship traces many genealogies that help us understand why toxic atmospheres, for example, hang heavy when and where they do (industrialism, imperialism, capitalism, etc). Yet, naming contributions to problems does not easily translate to the genesis of crosscutting alternative configurations. In their work, Nick and collaborators experiment with building an alternative way of conceiving of energy, mobility, and human–environmental relations that does not proceed from problematization or ideological diagnoses. It also does not limit its scope of intervention to sociomaterial processes that one could cleanly identify as having proxy relations with the chemicals he studies. Instead of succumbing to the impasses of

14.3 Two Aerocene solar sculptures floating above Paradise Bay, Antarctica as a part of the Antarctic Biennale, March 2017. The albedo (reflectivity) of the snow keeps the aerostats afloat even with partial clouds. Photo by Nicholas Shapiro.

adversarial epistemological challenges that attempt to make "necessary evils" less evil, and often end up spinning out on the data treadmill, this process of cultivating alternative desires, dreamworlds, and infrastructures attempts to make toxic infrastructures unnecessary. The approach cultivates abandonment rather than direct dismantlement.

The project, led by artist Tomas Saraceno, is called the Aerocene. The Aerocene is an aspirational epoch that beckons a world in which human circulation is achieved through solar balloon flight, putting to imaginative use the only hydrocarbon-free means of aerospace travel.[18] A solar balloon is an envelope that is filled with ambient air, gains altitude with the heat of the sun, and moves with the wind (Figure 14.3). Conceiving of wind and solar rays as critical infrastructures for the ongoing present demands that our desires for energy and mobility be re-engineered through the planet's shared atmosphere. Working with collaborators at MIT's Department of Earth, Atmospheric and Planetary Sciences to create a float trajectory calculator, a platform that enables one to imagine how to navigate 30 kilometers of different winds at different

altitudes, the Aerocene team is not turning its back on science (float.aerocene.
org). Rather, the project yokes science to a dreamworld that begins by attuning to and moving with the elemental forces that animate our planet (see Choy
2011; Engelmann and McCormack 2018).[19] Advancing the Aerocene, the team
avers, bears the capacity to do subjectivity and concept work, cultivating a cal-
culated submission to the environment rather than engineering's current unend-
ing quest to interrupt, manipulate, overcome the environment. It requires a
deferent relation to geophysical forces, surrendering the all-too-human desire
for mastery to an outlook in line with what Boyer and Morton (2016) have just
begun calling "hypo-subjects," as one potential countervailing force against the
hyper-subjects that yield the hyper-objects of the Anthropocene.

The project does not engage with pollution in the terms on which capitalism, governance, and science typically know themselves. It is not chemical-
species specific, as a regulation would be. It does not ask for a specific aberrant
pollution source to be brought into line. It does not make a claim through a
process of adjudication that privileges quantified forms of knowledge. Instead,
the Aerocene swims upstream from toxicity, beyond its many proxies (corporations, infrastructures, political and economic regimes, etc.), and is an intervention into the very desires that yield a world with cheap fossil fuels, ubiquitous
hydrocarbon-derived exposures, and a destabilizing climate (Shapiro 2015b).
Like the LA Urban Rangers performing the beaches as public, the Aerocene
performs the air as necessary to apprehend and inhabit. It further performs a
multi-modal credo for detoxification: to reduce the atmosphere's toxicity we
must change our many relations with it, from phenomenological attunement to
global engineered systems.

The cases above should not be understood as exemplars of a new method.
They are indications from earlier and ongoing efforts informing and concurrent
with our search for more capacious modes of apprehension. In the breadth of
their concerns, and the different sensibilities with which they are enacted, they
already suggest how expansive such apprehending can be. We now find our-
selves reflecting on those events and engagements as a means of exploring the
possibilities and pitfalls of pursuing a different strategy and approach to contentious questions of health, bodies, infrastructures, energy, and environments.

Imaginative limits and plausibilities

These approaches have also had their share of pitfalls and obstacles – including,
as an example from the Ambler project, community members who felt removed
or excluded from the process and an almost ever-present risk of practitioners

being enrolled into the charged political factions of the communities where they work. Some approaches might also be viewed or read as illustrations of numbers, and so reinforce rather than transform the enumerative discourses on which they rely, but to which they need not be subordinate. These challenges are not unique to any of these projects, but we do not want to suggest that tumultuous political landscapes simply erode into greener pastures and hand holding if the instruments are left strictly in the lab. Conversely, there should be no need to intimate a self-evident fact, that the most open-sourced, inexpensive, accurate, and easy-to-build sensor will not amount to an environmental justice excalibur or a toxin-deterring shield.

Regardless of how successful these experiments were/are/will be, collectively they point to what Fredric Jameson might articulate as the potential utopian dimensions represented or suggested by such works. For Jameson, utopian works reveal the limits of what can be imagined; but, simultaneously, the decline of faith in utopias itself becomes a measure of political disenchantment or cynicism (Jameson 2010, 23). Artworks (understood in the broad terms used here) exercise this capacity in ways that may resist such cynicism. Performances can instantiate a space and a moment that stand askew of the spatiotemporal frames they directly thematize. Such an approach suggests that these exercises can stand for what they already are – one of any number of meaningful attempts to reflect creatively, to conceive and convene, free from the obligation to look for their justification in terms of incalculable future consequences or devaluing time frames. And they can at times perhaps rise to what Carrie Lambert-Beatty has referred to as the "art of the plausible," which "works to edge an imagined state of affairs from the merely possible to the brink, at least, of the probable" (Lambert-Beatty 2008, 321). Lambert-Beatty calls attention to the institutional support of practices and products conferred the status of art. The establishment endorsement of art enables and constrains both the plausibility of the political resolutions they enact and the imaginative spaces in which they operate.

In the light of some sweeping, catastrophic scientific prognostications, environmental crises of toxicity, which in our minds also include climate change, appear too dire to leave any possibility of hope for a generative, systemic reconfiguration. But if so, then the utopian impulses at work in attempting to construct different ways of relating to these crises can hardly make those catastrophic futures worse. Thus, we might concede with Jameson, in the context of the utopian dimensions of artistic responses to environmental dangers, that "[s]uch a revival of futurity and of the positing of alternate futures is not a political program or even a political practice"; we might also accept with him, however, that "it is hard to see how any durable or effective political action could come into being without it" (Jameson 2010, 43). Waiting for political action based on more enumerated evidence in the absence of imagined possible futures will remain an exercise in frustration and futility.

This chapter is not about advancing a shift toward art instead of, or in place of, enumeration. Rather, we are suggesting that the humanities and social sciences might play a more critical role in mediating, resituating, or reimagining engagement and discussion about societal challenges – even those that seem to pivot on a scientific or technological axis. Artistic methods provide a wide palette of options. But so too does history in the form of oral history, or folk history, as well as a growing repertoire of tools in the digital humanities, public history, and what has recently been termed "applied history" (Rose et al. 2012).

A wary alliance

Why a wary alliance between enumerative environmental practices and science studies? STS is a political science insofar as it does its best to embrace rather than contest the inherent political nature of its work, its activity, and indeed its very existence. This is not meant to imply a specific or monolithic political action or agenda; nor does it hew to a specific or unified mode or method. In this vein, the turn within the field towards participating through and with new scientific and technological apparatuses is both an obvious outcome and a potentially potent one. This reproducing and remaking of the more familiar scientific modes of interaction/intervention does not negate the decades of research that have sought to uncover, disentangle, and otherwise explain the potent political power science possesses in our society. Navigating this past and present of power politics in and with science must continue to be the burden of the engaged science studies practitioner. But in the cases of work with communities, the sites for most of these interventions, the most dangerous traps lie not in weaknesses of science, but in its power to so easily, so quickly, become the dominant discourse of a space/issue. In these communities, discourses with the mantle of science are granted great power, though not unchallenged, to quash discussion and debate on or with other (moral, social, political, etc.) topics. We've seen this dominance lead to reifying the intrinsic answerability of enumerable questions, and therefore the denial of the data treadmill, as well as a strict demarcation of what paths are unrealistic and what compromised worlds are inevitable.

The participation of science studies scholars in closing those other discursive avenues, even if unwittingly, could mean relegating some voices to the sideline while simultaneously reifying social structures of expertise that assume the apolitical nature of science, define how activism and participation must be manifested, and the form by which grievances can be aired. For these reasons we feel compelled, in the context of this thematic collection, to think through what modes of expertise, authority, and power can't be shaken loose within the practice of civic science.

Our point is not, of course, that community science should not be practiced, but rather to endorse a multiplicity of practices in the critique and use of science, whether by attempts to remake science through bottom-up civic action (as many within this collection are working towards) and/or by promoting, instigating, and eliciting apprehension without stipulating a formula for how that will happen. The social and political power of science is both the reason why we should, perhaps even must, employ science, but it is also why we must remain wary and perhaps even at times slow our recourse to civic science to allow for other forms of imagination and engagement to take root or even take the lead before the pursuit of scientific enumeration.

As Cedric Price joked in 1966, "Technology is the answer but what was the question?" The allure of technology often enacts the question to which it responds. So, our hope is to make room with ecologies of instruments (Wylie et al. 2014) for diverse practices that prime apprehension, beckon further thought, illuminate radical alterities, or articulate the histories (supply chains, infrastructures, consumer demands, etc.) that lead to concerns of toxicity, while still leaving multiple meanings to exist simultaneously.

The inherent inability of science, conventionally understood, to provide political solutions is something that exists at the macro and the micro levels, both global and local. We should be careful not to assume that providing new data will provide new political answers (or even the resolve to seek new political answers). To the extent that new questions, new data, and new instruments can participate within this ecology of practices of understanding and experiencing environments, helping to invite apprehension that avoids facile or even false solutions, we have an obligation to use, remake, and leverage the power of science for these purposes. If we were to return to Joe in his trailer, our hope by this point in the chapter is that the reader would want to suggest changing the terms of the conversation (even while including the measurement) and perhaps deciding together with Joe what might amount to the plausible, the imaginable, and the livable. We hope these provocations help to open up seemingly intractable issues and inevitable toxicities, inviting those with the highest stakes to help realize the unlikely but very possible futures that route us away from such morasses as those faced by Joe and others who may take his place. And in so doing, we, however minimally, work toward a form of participation in our democratic systems that does not require a data set for entry into the dialogue.

Acknowledgments

We would like to thank the anonymous reviewer, Daniel Lee Kleinman, and Katie Vann for their generous insights, in addition to those by Max Liboiron, Sara Wylie, Ana Rosen Vollmar, the Center for the Study of Science, Technology, Medicine and Society at University of California, Berkeley, fellows and staff in the Institute for Research at the Science History Institute, Christy Schneider, and several close reads by Wyatt Galusky. This material was previously published as Shapiro, Nicholas, Nasser Zakariya, and Jody Roberts, "A Wary Alliance: From Enumerating Environments to Inviting Apprehension," *Engaging STS* 3 (2017), 575–602.

Notes

1   Selections from these moments can be viewed online in a mini-documentary for Distillations Magazine and 2 Grist, *Where Have all the FEMA Trailers Gone?*, directed by Mariel Carr: https://vimeo.com/137439033.

2   This is in line with Brody et al.'s finding that reporting uncertain toxicant monitoring data back to the individuals whose exposures are being studied does not create excessive worry or anxiety. The authors did, however, note that the process is "intellectually challenging, time consuming, and [made researchers] concerned that it required skills beyond their expertise" (Brody et al. 2014, 6). See also Roberts (2014).

3   Despite being based on a peer-reviewed method, this technique was later found to be potentially overestimating formaldehyde levels due to cross-reactivity with other aldehydes and ketones (Gehrke and Shapiro 2015).

4   "You smell that sweet smell?" Joe asked Nick when they were standing outside waiting for the test to finish, "that's from a [oil] flare."

5   The starting point for our joint conversations was the Science History Institute Matters and Materials Research Group, convened by Jody.

6   Among wide-ranging histories of race, eugenics, and population controls to those of state formation and colonization, we might include Hacking (1990), Stocking (1994), Porter (1996), Scott (1998), Paul (1998), and Mitchell (2002).

7   Social theorist Max Horkheimer argued that positivist and logical empiricist agendas constricted political emancipatory possibilities, addressing social problems only in narrow and non-transformational terms. In his view, the "mere recording and prediction of facts" inspired resignation and impotence in relation to "vital issues" while also rarifying the capacity to intervene in such systems to an exclusive powerful few who arbitrate the facts that matter, working to sustain a status quo. The goal, to his mind, was a "higher spontaneity" wherein thought is not restricted to examining apparently unalterable circumstances by the lights of "feeble and abstract" calculative thought alone but instead can ultimately be

traced to their social and political supports – circumstances that might therefore be recon-
ceived and reimagined. As a "prerequisite" for the achievement of a better community an
individual must "learn to look behind the facts; that he distinguish the superficial from the
essential without minimizing the importance of either; that he formulate conceptions that
are not simple classifications of the given; and that he continually orient all his experiences
to definite goals without falsifying them …" (Horkheimer 1972, 181).

8   In its broadest terms, this wariness is evident in the ongoing political theoretical legacy
     of the Frankfurt School and the contemporary question of instrumentalism; in per-
     sistent concerns with technological determinisms; in critical theory in relation to the
     histories and modalities of scientific knowledge-power. More immediate examples of
     enumeration, in which numeric verdicts can be foregrounded, also appear in recur-
     rent popular presentations of correlations of intelligence quotients and race; in pos-
     sible fetishizations of statistical significance across a wide range of scientific studies;
     in the monetary valuations of the cost of human and environmental life; in genetic
     testing producing probabilities of hereditary lines and the onset of future disease; in
     the question of toxicity and occupational exposure limits; and so on, through to the
     present discussions of the applications of algorithms and "big data." Throughout, social
     enumeration is resisted and deployed by political aspirants and activists, of whichever
     social status, affiliation, or belief.

9   Take ongoing chemical controversies such as those over the plasticizer bisphenol-A
     or the pesticide Atrazine. Each has produced voluminous research documenting the
     apparent toxicological hazards of use and exposure. And yet in each case action has
     largely been limited to the call for more definitive studies. While instances such as
     these are framed as debates about scientific certainty, they rarely (if ever) afford the
     opportunity to question the premises that led to the studies in the first place. Why do
     we need Atrazine? What sorts of worlds does its use make possible, or inhibit (whether
     discussed, for example, as issues of food sourcing, farm practices, diet, transport and
     infrastructure, or geographies of production)?

10   The bucket is a 5 gallon plastic bucket fitted with a plastic bag liner for sampling, air
     inlets, and 11 outlets drilled into its lid, and a vacuum pump for quickly retrieving real-
     time air quality samplings. See http://www.labucketbrigade.org/content/bucket.

11   Bernal might be an example of the former, Horkheimer the latter.

12   At a phenomenological level, this capacity for environmental apprehension, for exam-
     ple, is latent in our very ability to be affected by our environment (Shapiro 2015a).

13   Like Holmes and Marcus's "para-ethnographic" method that is advanced by "deferring
     to, absorbing, and being altered by found reflexive subjects," those that invite appre-
     hension view extra-academic collaborators as "epistemic partners" (2008, 84).

14   Resources for Education and Action for Community Health (REACH) in Ambler is
     supported by the National Institutes of Health Science Education Partnership Award:
     Office of the Director, National Institutes of Health, award number R25OD010521-01.

15   A first waste site, known locally as "the White Hills," was added to the EPA's National
     Priorities List in 1986. The process for remediation involved "capping" the site with
     fresh soil and grass to keep the material in place.

16   The oral histories were conducted by Lee Berry, a curator in the Center for Oral History at the Science History Institute. The project had a partnership with the Act II Playhouse, located in Ambler, to provide a space for the public performance of the plays. Bill D'Agostino, the director of communications and education at Act II, facilitated the process of sharing excerpts of the interviews with roughly a dozen local playwrights in Philadelphia. From the one-act plays written, 10 were selected for inclusion in the project, and seven were performed at Act II for the local community. Zach Biro conducted follow-up interviews 12 months later. All of these materials are available for use and review at http://reachambler.chemheritage.org.

17   Following the performance and talk-back event, they initiated conversations with the research team to explore how these methods could be brought to other sites in Region 3 and beyond. They have also expressed interest in annual training for their onsite coordinators. "Those coordinators are there to assess and manage a technical problem. They're engineers," suggested one toxicologist who has worked on the site. "But invariably they encounter these same issues, and they have no idea how to handle them."

18   For an initial outline of a terrestrial aspirational era, see Natasha Myers on the "Planthropocene" (2016).

19   This example of the flight trajectory planner underlines the modes of alliance between enumeration and broader apprehension that we are attempting to gesture toward. It is not an attempt to make environmental monitoring data more charismatic or beautiful, even if it achieves that accidently, but puts an immensely large data set to work toward making an otherwise unimaginable future closer to fruition. While visualizing the harm of toxicants in the air may be another on-ramp to the data treadmill, visualizing an alternative life in the air fundamentally questions the status quo and ideas of what sorts of future merit real consideration. For robust work on toxicant visualizations, see the oeuvre of Nerea Calvillo (e.g., http://intheair.es and Calvillo 2018).

References

Bernal, J. D. 1945. Transformation in science. *The Scientific Monthly*, 61, 474–476.

Boudia, S. and Jas, N. 2014. *Powerless Science?: Science and Politics in a Toxic World*. New York: Berghahn Books.

Boyer, D. and Morton, T. 2016. Hyposubjects – cultural anthropology. *Cultural Anthropology*, January 21. Available at https://culanth.org/fieldsights/hyposubjects (last accessed February 14, 2020).

Brody, J., Dunagan, S. C., Morello-Frosch, R., Brown, P., Patton, S., and Rudel, R. A. 2014. Reporting individual results for biomonitoring and environmental exposures: Lessons learned from environmental communication case studies. *Environmental Health*, 13(1), 40.

Calvillo, N. 2018. Political airs: From monitoring to attuned sensing air pollution. *Social Studies of Science*, 48(3), 372–388.

Carruth, A. and Price, J. 2014. The power of play in urban environmentalism: Interview with Jenny Price. *Resilience: A Journal of the Environmental Humanities*, 1(1).

Choy, T. K. 2011. *Ecologies of Comparison: An Ethnography of Endangerment in Hong Kong*. Durham, NC: Duke University Press.

Cordner, A. 2016. *Toxic Safety: Flame Retardants, Chemical Controversies, and Environmental Health*. New York: Columbia University Press.

Engelmann, S. and McCormack, D. 2018. Elemental aesthetics: On artistic experiments with solar energy. *Annals of the American Association of Geographers*, 108(1), 241–259.

Fortun, K. and Fortun, M. 2005. Scientific imaginaries and ethical plateaus in contemporary U.S. toxicology. *American Anthropologist*, 107(1), 43–54.

Foucault, M. 2003. *"Society Must Be Defended": Lectures at the College de France, 1975–1976*. New York: Picador.

Foucault, M. 2009. *Security, Territory, Population: Lectures at the College de France 1977–1978*. New York: Picador.

Gehrke, G. and Shapiro, N. 2015. Formaldehyde measurement: Testing Public Lab's kit with DOH's equipment. Available at https://publiclab.org/notes/gretchengehrke/10-07-2015/formaldehyde-measurement-testing-public-lab-s-kit-with-doh-s-equipment (last accessed February 10, 2020).

Gould, K. A., Schnaiberg, A., and Weinberg, A. S. 1996. *Local Environmental Struggles: Citizen Activism in the Treadmill of Production*. Cambridge: Cambridge University Press.

Hacking, I. 1990. *The Taming of Chance*. Cambridge: Cambridge University Press.

Holmes, D. R. and Marcus, G. E. 2008. Para-ethnography. In L. M. Given (ed.), *The Sage Encyclopedia of Qualitative Research Methods*. Thousand Oaks, CA: Sage, pp. 595–597.

Horkheimer, M. 1972. The latest attack against metaphysics. In *Critical Theory: Selected Essays. Vol. 1*. London: A&C Black.

Jameson, F. 2010. Utopia as method, or the uses of the future. In M. D. Gordin, H. Tilley, and G. Prakash (eds), *Utopia/Dystopia: Conditions of Historical Possibility*. Princeton, NJ: Princeton University Press, pp. 21–44.

Kinchy, A., Jalbert, K., and Lyons, J. 2014. What is volunteer water monitoring good for? Fracking and the plural logics of participatory science. In S. Frickel and D. J. Hess (eds), *Fields of Knowledge: Science, Politics and Publics in the Neoliberal Age*. Bingley: Emerald Group, pp. 259–289.

Lambert Beatty, C. 2008. Twelve miles: Boundaries of the new art/activism. *Signs: Journal of Women in Culture and Society*, 33(2), 309–327.

Latour, B 2004. Why has critique run out of steam? From matters of fact to matters of concern. *Critical Inquiry*, 30(2), 225–248.

Liboiron, M. 2013. Plasticizers: A twenty-first century miasma. In M. Michael, G. Hawkins, and J. Gabrys (eds), *Accumulation: The Material Politics of Plastics*. London: Routledge, pp. 22–44.

Marres, N. 2013. Who is afraid of the green cloud? On the environmental rendering of controversy. CSISP Working Paper No. 2, Centre for the Study of Invention & Social Process.

Mitchell, T. 2002. *Rule of Experts: Egypt, Techno-Politics, Modernity*. Berkeley: University of California Press.

Myers, N. 2016. Photosynthesis. *Theorizing the Contemporary, Cultural Anthropology*, January 21. Available at https://culanth.org/fieldsights/photosynthesis (last accessed February 14, 2020).

Nixon, R. 2011. *Slow Violence and the Environmentalism of the Poor*. Cambridge, MA: Harvard University Press.

Ottinger, G. 2013. *Refining Expertise: How Responsible Engineers Subvert Environmental Justice Challenges*. New York: NYU Press.

Paul, D. B. 1998. *The Politics of Heredity: Essays on Eugenics, Biomedicine, and the Nature-Nurture Debate*. Albany: State University of New York Press.

Poovey, M. 1998. *A History of the Modern Fact: Problems of Knowledge in the Sciences of Wealth and Society*. Chicago: University of Chicago Press.

Porter, T. M. 1996. *Trust in Numbers*. Princeton, NJ: Princeton University Press.

Povinelli, E. A. 2015. Windjarrameru, The Stealing C*nts. *E-Flux*. Available at http://supercommunity.e-flux.com/texts/windjarrameru-the-stealing-c-nts/ (last accessed February 1, 2020).

Roberts, J. A. 2010. Reflections of an unrepentant plastiphobe: Plasticity and the STS life. *Science as Culture*, 19(1), 101–120.

Roberts, J. A. 2014. Unruly technologies and fractured oversight: Toward a model for chemical control for the twenty-first century. In S. Boudia and N. Jas (eds), *Powerless Science?: Science and Politics in a Toxic World*. New York: Berghahn Books.

Rose, D. B., van Dooren, T., Chrulew, M., Cooke, C., Kearnes, M., and O'Gorman, E. 2012. Thinking through the environment, unsettling the humanities. *Environmental Humanities*, 1(1), 1–5.

Saxton, D. I. 2015. Strawberry Fields as extreme environments: The ecobiopolitics of farmworker health. *Medical Anthropology*, 34(2). 166–183. DOI: 10.1080/014597 40.2014.959167.

Scott, J. C. 1998. *Seeing like a State: How Certain Schemes to Improve the Human Condition Have Failed*. New Haven, CT: Yale University Press.

Shapiro, N. 2014. Un-knowing exposure: Toxic emergency housing, strategic inconclusivity and governance in the US Gulf South. In E. Cloatre and M. Pickersgill (eds), *Knowledge, Technology and Law*. New York and London: Routledge, pp. 189–205.

Shapiro, N. 2015a. Attuning to the chemosphere: Domestic formaldehyde, bodily reasoning, and the chemical sublime. *Cultural Anthropology*, 30(3), 368–393.

Shapiro, N. 2015b. Alter-Engineered Worlds. Aerocene COP21 Catalog.

Stocking, G. W. 1994. The turn-of-the-century concept of race. *Modernism/Modernity*, 1(1), 4–16.

Vogel, S. A. 2013. *Is It Safe?: BPA and the Struggle to Define the Safety of Chemicals*. Oakland: University of California Press.

Wylie, S. A., Jalbert, K., Dosemagen, S., and Ratto, M. 2014. Institutions for civic technoscience: How critical making is transforming environmental research. *The Information Society*, 30(2), 116–126.

Index

CPSIA information can be obtained
at www.ICGtesting.com
Printed in the USA
LVHW060901270820
664145LV00036B/362